Black and Brown Leadership and the Promotion of Change in an Era of Social Unrest

Sonia Rodriguez
National University, USA

Kelly Brown
Lamar University, USA

A volume in the Advances in
Religious and Cultural Studies
(ARCS) Book Series

Published in the United States of America by
IGI Global
Information Science Reference (an imprint of IGI Global)
701 E. Chocolate Avenue
Hershey PA, USA 17033
Tel: 717-533-8845
Fax: 717-533-8661
E-mail: cust@igi-global.com
Web site: http://www.igi-global.com

Library of Congress Cataloging-in-Publication Data

Names: Rodriguez, Sonia, 1962- editor. | Brown, Kelly (Kelly A.), 1978-
  editor.
Title: Black and brown leadership and the promotion of change in an era of
  social unrest / Sonia Rodriguez, and Kelly Brown, editor.
Description: Hershey PA : Information Science Reference (an imprint of IGI
  Global), [2021] | Includes bibliographical references and index. |
  Summary: "This book seeks to amplify voices of leaders who identify as
  Black, LatinX, Indigenous, or people of color as they navigate
  leadership during a time of tumultuous change and social unrest and to
  give future leaders a blueprint in how to succeed as a leader of color,
  navigate hostile spaces, and ultimately create a change in mindsets and
  practices that will lead to justice"-- Provided by publisher.
Identifiers: LCCN 2021004137 (print) | LCCN 2021004138 (ebook) | ISBN
  9781799872351 (hardcover) | ISBN 9781799872368 (paperback) | ISBN
  9781799872375 (ebook)
Subjects: LCSH: Educational leadership--United States--Case studies. |
  Minority college administrators--United States--Case studies. | Minority
  school administrators--United States--Case studies. | Minorities in
  higher education--United States--Social conditions--Case studies. |
  Minority students--United States--Social conditions--Case studies. |
  Social justice and education--United States--Case studies. | Educational
  equalization--United States--Case studies.
Classification: LCC LB2806 .B53 2021 (print) | LCC LB2806 (ebook) | DDC
  371.2/011--dc23
LC record available at https://lccn.loc.gov/2021004137
LC ebook record available at https://lccn.loc.gov/2021004138

This book is published in the IGI Global book series Advances in Religious and Cultural Studies (ARCS) (ISSN: 2475-675X; eISSN: 2475-6768)

Advances in Religious and Cultural Studies (ARCS) Book Series

ISSN:2475-675X
EISSN:2475-6768

Editor-in-Chief: Nancy Erbe, California State University-Dominguez Hills, USA

MISSION

In the era of globalization, the diversity of the world and various cultures becomes apparent as cross-cultural interactions turn into a daily occurrence for individuals in all professions. Understanding these differences is necessary in order to promote effective partnerships and interactions between those from different religious and cultural backgrounds.

The **Advances in Religious and Cultural Studies (ARCS)** book series brings together a collection of scholarly publications on topics pertaining to religious beliefs, culture, population studies, and sociology. Books published within this series are ideal for professionals, theorists, researchers, and students seeking the latest research on collective human behavior in terms of religion, social structure, and cultural identity and practice.

COVERAGE

- Politics and Religion
- Stereotypes and Racism
- Group Behavior
- Impact of Religion on Society
- Social Stratification and Classes
- Cross-Cultural Interaction
- Cults and Religious Movements
- Sociology
- Gender
- Globalization and Culture

IGI Global is currently accepting manuscripts for publication within this series. To submit a proposal for a volume in this series, please contact our Acquisition Editors at Acquisitions@igi-global.com or visit: http://www.igi-global.com/publish/.

Titles in this Series

For a list of additional titles in this series, please visit:
http://www.igi-global.com/book-series/advances-religious-cultural-studies/84269.

Overcoming Challenges and Barriers for Women in Business and Education Socioeconomic Issues and Strategies for the Future
Alice S. Etim (Winston-Salem State University, USA) and James Etim (Winston-Salem State University, USA)
Information Science Reference • © 2021 • 268pp • H/C (ISBN: 9781799838142) • US $195.00

Preservation and Restoration Techniques for Ancient Egyptian Textiles
Harby E. Ahmed (Cairo University, Egypt) and Abdulnaser Abdulrahman Al-Zahrani (King Saud University, Saudi Arabia)
Information Science Reference • © 2021 • 315pp • H/C (ISBN: 9781799848110) • US $195.00

Handbook of Research on Promoting Social Justice for Immigrants and Refugees Through Active Citizenship and Intercultural Education
Isabel María Gómez Barreto (Universidad de Castilla-La Mancha, Spain)
Information Science Reference • © 2021 • 468pp • H/C (ISBN: 9781799872832) • US $265.00

Handbook of Research on the Impact of COVID-19 on Marginalized Populations and Support for the Future
Haris Abd Wahab (University of Malaya, Malaysia) jahid siraz chowdhury (University of Malaya, Malaysia) Siti Hajar Binti Abu Bakar Ah (University of Malaya, Malaysia) and Mohd Rashid Mohd Saad (University of Malaya, Malaysia)
Information Science Reference • © 2021 • 450pp • H/C (ISBN: 9781799874805) • US $265.00

Understanding Ubuntu for Enhancing Intercultural Communications
Joseph Mukuni (Virginia Tech, USA) and Josiah Tlou (Virginia Tech, USA)
Information Science Reference • © 2021 • 299pp • H/C (ISBN: 9781799879473) • US $195.00

For an entire list of titles in this series, please visit:
http://www.igi-global.com/book-series/advances-religious-cultural-studies/84269.

701 East Chocolate Avenue, Hershey, PA 17033, USA
Tel: 717-533-8845 x100 • Fax: 717-533-8661
E-Mail: cust@igi-global.com • www.igi-global.com

There are two ways of exerting one's strength: one is pushing down, the other is pulling up. ~Booker T. Washington

This book is dedicated to all those leaders, named and unnamed, that continue to put in the work to pull up those that are underserved, underappreciated and underwater in systems that are inadequate.

Thank you for your perseverance to the cause of social justice. May the readers of this book learn and grow so every child can realize the freedom of opportunities that an education from caring and invested educators can provide.

This book is dedicated to all our children in systems affected by policies and practices that do not support your success. We are working and fighting for you. This is your world and we will make it not just a safer place, but a better place.

In solidarity,

Sonia and Kelly

Table of Contents

Detailed Table of Contents

The author uses testimonio as a way to situate the barriers and successes she has experienced as a Latina educational leader in Northern Colorado for 25 years. The setting is based in the backdrop of several worldwide issues in 2020 which created a dire need to address diversity, equity, and inclusion (DEI) and social justice within industries and organizations, including educational systems. 1) National political division, 2) disparate access to healthcare and the disproportionate numbers of deaths to COVID-19, and 3) murders of Black Americans by law enforcement have re-affirmed the dehumanization of Black and Brown Americans. Solutions and recommendations are shared based on her shared experiences in moving a DEI educational agenda forward.

The narratives in this chapter provide the reader with the perspectives of seven Black and Brown leaders who have experienced oppression in the workplace. Their stories highlight the depth of institutionalized oppression that exists in P-12 settings and the effect it has on health, family, and work performance. Nonetheless, these leaders have learned to navigate oppressive environments and engage in transformative practices. The purpose of the research was to gain an understanding of how Black and Brown leaders work through the daily challenges stemming from systemic oppression. Reading the authentic lived experiences of the participants can inspire others to be empowered and find hope.

Chapter 3

In this chapter, the authors report on their experiences as higher education faculty women of color through three narratives. They present the narratives from their perspectives as three full professors in educational leadership. In the first narrative, an African-American scholar reports on her experiences in academia. In the second narrative, a Latina scholar reports on former Latina students who are currently in school leadership positions enacting social justice leadership. In the third narrative, an Asian-American scholar reports on her current project about networking as a strategy for women of color.

There continue to be many issues women of color face as they pursue both an advanced education and leadership positions in education. There appears to be an increase in the number of women of color seeking advanced degrees and pursuing educational leadership positions, but the numbers are still small overall. While some educational stakeholders have worked to increase the number of women of color in educational leadership positions, it has been minimal. A central question that is often asked is, How does a school ensure that the educational leaders are capable of moving forward, with meeting the needs of a diverse student body? Many advocates say promoting a more diverse group of educational leaders, especially women of color, will only help increase student success. Increasing the number of women of color in educational leadership positions can help have a positive effect on the issues of racism, poverty, aggression, oppression, hostility, or even privilege.

Chapter 5

Alyncia M. Bowen, Franklin University, USA
Shaquanah Robinson, University of Phoenix, USA
Jim Lane, University of Phoenix, USA

The pandemic has operated within a cultural movement opposing systemic racism. Redux of Black Lives Matter was spurred by the killings of George Floyd, Ahmad Aubrey, Rashard Brooks, Breonna Taylor, and others, and resulted in prolonged protests throughout the country. This caustic backdrop has created unique challenges for female Black educational leaders. Thus, they are compelled to navigate their already challenging duties among the intersections of leadership, race, gender, power, and social justice. Black female education leaders are challenged to courageously lead during an unprecedented era of disruption.

Chapter 6

Portia Newman, Virginia Commonwealth University, USA

Societal perceptions of Black women are challenged by Black women's ability to survive in spaces that have historically been uninviting. Black women's leadership practice has developed in response to their racialized and gendered lived experiences. Through analyzing studies of Black women leaders, research suggests Black women have a strategic set of skills and practices that can be used to advance their leadership positionality. This chapter will describe the ways Black women operate at the intersection of resistance and leadership. Their leadership has become a skill, a practice, and a tool that creates space for themselves.

Chapter 7

Monique Willis, California State University, Dominguez Hills, USA
Jotika Jagasia, Lamar University, USA
Ada Robinson-Perez, Binghamton University, USA

The COVID-19 pandemic, racial injustice, and civil unrest of 2020 disproportionately impacted Black and Brown communities jolting "progressive" academic systems and exposing inherent inequities. Such inequality warrants authentic activism to promote social awareness and facilitate a culture of collaboration, respect, and inclusivity. This chapter centers on three early-career Black and Brown women leaders associated with counseling programs who voice their positionality statements, experiences, and views to align with relevant theoretical concepts. Black feminism, postcolonial feminism, and critical race theory pedagogies serve as the authors' foundation, highlighting race, culture, gender, and intersectionality to unmask cultural oppression in higher education. Committed to their lives' work as academics, researchers, and mental health practitioners, the authors assume substantial professional responsibilities and engage in emotional labor adopting a sense of family and mothering to support students. Finally, the authors provide suggestions to undo injustices during turbulent times.

Chapter 8

John J. S. Harrichand, The University of Texas at San Antonio, USA
S. Anandavalli, Southern Oregon University, USA
Cirecie A. West-Olatunji, Xavier University of Louisiana, USA

Black and Brown leaders in the counseling profession continue to be minoritized as they navigate a White dominant profession. It is important that the counseling profession take steps to empower Black and Brown counseling leaders with the tools needed to effectively and confidently lead. The authors examine the socially just and culturally responsive counseling leadership model (SJCRCLM), the inclusive leadership model (ILM), and culture-centered leadership models (CCLM) using personal narratives. Black and Brown counseling leaders at different levels of leadership (i.e., beginner, intermediate, advanced) are provided with recommendations for navigating life in the US and specifically a profession that is dominated by Whiteness.

Chapter 9

Tamara C. Cheshire, Folsom Lake College, USA
Crystal D. Martinez-Alire, Folsom Lake College, USA
Vanessa Esquivido, California State University, Chico, USA
Molly Springer, California State University, San Bernardino, USA

As Native women professors, counselors, and administrators within higher education, the four authors will focus on transformational change within oppressive environments, addressing institutionalized racism stemming from a colonial history of education. The authors will discuss identified barriers including operating in an oppressive work environment which can sometimes render us invisible and silent for self-preservation, threats to our positions from taking a stand against racial or cultural inequity, and resisting assimilation strategies created by structural racism. It is important to share experiences with working in systematically oppressive environments and the covert ways in which Black, Indigenous, People of Color (BIPOC) are transformational change agents, leaders against racial and cultural oppression.

Chapter 10

For decades, the voice of Black Americans has been systematically silenced: from the beginning, when African ancestors were ripped away from their home shores of Senegambia and West-Central Africa, through the civil rights movement of the '50s and '60s, to current civil unrest after America witnessed the murder of George Floyd. The Black Lives Matter movement's rise is a direct result of Black people who are sick and tired of being silenced. The purpose of this chapter is to describe four personalities—mediator, advocate, agitator, and activator—, the situations in which each would be appropriate, and the lessons learned through these experiences. This chapter will cover a brief personal narrative of the author growing up and taught to be seen and not heard and how the sheer notion of silence is golden is no longer appropriate in times of social unrest and when lives are at risk. The author highlights the cognitive dissonance felt as a school board member amid the new social justice movement of the late 2000s.

Chapter 11

Muslim American high school seniors navigate their educational spaces at a time when the 2016 Election has unleashed a rhetoric that is riddled with Islamophobia. The experiences of four female participants engages us in their counter-narratives, debunking stereotypes and assumptions that exist about their demographic. The formal and informal experiences of the educational journeys of these participants help us explore the role of family, faith-based education, mosque, and community in the lives of these students. The social and academic learning opportunities for these participants showcased instances of inclusion and marginalization, where there were times when the students underwent a double consciousness. Transitioning from faith-based schools to the public education system became easier when positioned in a climate of diversity. Muslim American students experience a dichotomous pull between religious values and American culture and remain cognizant of these differences. Muslim educational leadership will find the study insightful.

Chapter 12

This chapter is a critical autoethnographic analysis of a Black male school leader enacting racial and social justice in his school improvement efforts. A reflexive dialogue between dissertation research findings and related leadership experiences seek to extricate the colonial structure of public education and the colonizing intent of schooling as experienced by a Black principal and the communities of color from which his students and caregivers derive. Three dynamics are identified as oppressive: white moves towards Black domination, white privilege, and intersecting oppressions. Three decolonizing acts are highlighted: centering of racial justice, catalyzing critical community consciousness and agency, and dismantling intersecting oppressions through counter narration.

Preface

During the onset of this book, Americans dealt with a blow that included a pandemic, economic crisis, and racial unrest, which initiated an energized charge for social justice advocacy. The nation is currently facing an unprecedented challenge in ensuring that all citizens live in a fair, inclusive, and opportunity-rich society. These issues have heightened questions about racial justice that have been placated but can no longer be ignored. Marginalized communities cannot thrive if they continue to be oppressed, neglected, disinvested, and isolated from economic opportunity. The culture of allyship needs to be enacted thoughtfully and not performatively to create sustainable change through a critical mass of engaged advocates and activists. Many organizations enable the status quo by not confronting issues around race, gender and equity. Leaders of color want a seat at the table as highly valued contributors for the transformation of a just and equitable America. By listening to the voices of Black and Brown leaders the promoting change in this era of social unrest should finally occur.

This book amplifies the voices of leaders who identify as Black, LatinX, Indigenous, or people of color as they navigate leadership during a time of tumultuous change and social unrest. In turn, how are the current leaders making space, so the movement continues inside and outside mainstream spaces in order to sustain forward momentum. The authors highlighted a critical discourse surrounding the issues, dilemmas, struggles, and successes that persons of color experience. More specifically, the text portrays dilemmas that marginalized communities encounter while advocating for justice and social change within Whitestream organizational systems. The book delves into the definitions, perceptions, and lived experiences of Americanism, identity, otherness, and racism as it relates to leadership.

The purpose of this text is to give future leaders a blueprint on how to succeed as a leader of color, navigate hostile spaces, and ultimately generate change in mindsets and practices that will lead to sustainable justice for all. This text shares stories of Black and Brown leaders highlights their perseverance for seeking social reform and will inspire and empower others to continue the fight for justice by just doing it and taking a leap of faith.

CHALLENGES FOR BLACK AND BROWN LEADERS

Leadership is a continually evolving process, and the economic and political integration of Black and Brown influences can shape a just and equitable society. However, for the social justice leader, ethical dilemmas can arise when confronting systems that have historically oppressed, marginalized, and excluded certain groups from having a voice at the table. Critical race research has highlighted the biases related to race and exposed perceptions that have restricted contexts of leadership for Black and Brown leaders. Historically, the United States has oppressed minority groups and Whiteness is the dominant discourse (Bersh, 2009). Therefore, those who are not White, encounter cultural norms that have been predetermined, thus they may feel at odds with organizational systems. White mainstreamed organizational leadership embeds and perpetuates the power and privilege of the dominant culture. The conception of power aligns with the construction of social norms which has placed limited access to leadership roles for others (Rodriguez, 2019). The notion of "politics of fit" defines the environments that persons of color lead. The customary perception of right fit which is commonly used in leadership is one dimensional measure of fit and places limitations on individuals from diverse backgrounds (Tooms, Lugg, & Bogotch, 2010).

CULTURAL INFLUENCES AND EMBRACING CULTURAL CONFLICT

Black and Brown leaders tend to have to undertake the White discourse approach in leadership when working in most organizations. Thus, these experiences produce cultural clashes and incongruences. For Black and Brown advocacy, it is important to understand the cultural influences that persons of color encounter and how they struggle to find their own identity within different contexts of leadership and ethical decision making.

Culture is learned and the social environment cultivates one's culture and shapes their identity. Hofstede (2010) defines culture as the "collective programming of the mind that distinguishes the members of one group or category of people from others" (p. 7). Hofstede presents dimensions of culture, collectivism versus individualism.

The majority of the world's people live in collectivist societies; however, the United States has been categorized as an individualistic society, yet persons of color are cultivated in a traditionally collectivist society. Hofstede (20010) describes collectivism and individualism as opposites. In a collectivist society "the interest of the group prevails over the interest of the individual" (p. 91). In individualist societies "everyone is expected to look after him or herself" and ties among individuals are "loose" (p. 519). When decisions by others contradict their value of collectivism it creates moral dilemmas for the Black and Brown leader.

Currently, 53% of public-school students in the nation are non-White (IES, 2021). Specific groups of students have long experienced discriminatory practices (Samora & Simon, 1977). For example, second language learners have experienced persistent language suppression and cultural segregation (Valencia, 1991). The institutional practice of restricting the use of Spanish as a curricular vehicle was "intended to ensure the dominance of the English language and Anglo culture" (Valencia, 199,1p. 6). The traditional form of schooling is like a "filtering machine." The objective is to filter out the Non-White part and create a "White" script for those who were not "White" (Rodriguez, 2019).

Conversations about race and gender are difficult and uncomfortable for some people, but until these conversations begin, the status quo will remain the same and those "others'' will continue to face challenges when confronting exclusive decision making

TRANSFORMING POWER

A critical starting point to reevaluating the power dynamics of White mainstream organizations is gaining awareness of the dominant discourse and offering alternative multicultural paradigms that will lead to a more equitable and just community. Critically examining cultural identities, similarities, and differences is a necessary continuous exercise for just leadership in an increasingly diverse America. Deconstructing whiteness as the dominant discourse is crucial for challenging social injustice by reflecting on the social and cultural dynamics of power and inequality within systems (Applebaum, 2005).

Transformational leadership is the ability to empower others. By listening to the voices of Black and Brown leaders' organizations will have the capacity to shape and enhance just practices and nourish a common goal and vision in furthering the collective mission of the organization. This power is about enhancing those less powerful with collective problem-solving abilities among organizational members to influence others when advocating for social justice. One can give voice to the voiceless, by transferring one's power for good, those with power can continue to mentor and sponsor women's advocacy.

SEEKING SUSTAINABLE CHANGE

Covid-19 and the subsequent events that changed America during 2020 and 2021, highlighted the need for substantive and sustainable changes in those systems that perpetuate inequality. Leaders are reconciling how to effectively lead in this new post-covid era. While doing so, the forefront of change leadership should be those who have a vision for an America that lives up to its promises of inclusivity, engagement and freedom for all. This book while seeking sustainable solutions is full of accounts from social justice leaders working to ensure the change in our world is one for the betterment of all.

As leaders who are focused on justice move towards solutions, Black and Brown leaders are uniquely poised to meet the challenges ahead. As a framework, standpoint theory aptly describes the power to pursue change in this tumultuous time. Standpoint theory dismantles the notion that 'truth' is only objectively measured when it fits the normative ideas of the white, male, heterosexual, monolingual and able-bodied (Paradies, 2018; Haraway, 1988; Harding, 1991). This notion of truth is what has guided school systems for decades to the detriment of learners who did not fit the mold. Evidence of the opportunity and achievement gaps that have plagued our educational system can be found in local, state and national data sets (National Center for Education Statistics, 2019). However, those leaders who have the benefit of being bicultural innately understand that the traditional and dominant American culture is not experienced the same by all. As a result, the ability to be bicultural is an advantage in changing a system that can then address the needs of those that have been marginalized by the systems in which they live and work. "Although developed with concern for the oppressed, some scholars contend that 'standpoint theory is a theory for justice' which is 'inherently inclusive', being 'as much about equitable resources and opportunities for all people, as it is about recognizing… societal power'" (Braun 2016, pp. 81-82; Paradies, 2018).

Learning to be better leaders, activists, and advocates is merely the first level of creating change in our current culture. Social justice leaders have to be in this work for the long haul. Meaning, gaining the knowledge to effectively change their personal mindset, does not create a change in others. In addition, as the move to sustainability, one must instill that change in others. Specifically, the social justice mindset teachers working with children, the community that surrounds the schools, and policy makers that will write policy for everyone to follow.

"Specifically, what if we focused on everyone in our schools at the individual level taking the time to surface not just their knowledge of content, pedagogy, or leadership, but their biases, stereotypes, and belief systems? Are we as educators willing to consider that perhaps we have had this school reform concept all wrong? It has been argued that organizations do not change, the individuals in the organizations change (Fullan, 1993). If that is truly the case, then school transformation towards equity is in fact individual transformation towards equity" (Williams & Brown, 2019). Therefore, changing mindsets as a solution is not an easy road to take. The long-term game is the only game that will lead to sustainable solutions because leaders are not just addressing the frame but ensuring the builder and the tools are also in alignment. In doing so, change is always met with resistance. Unfortunately, leaders must proactively find ways to fight resistance to change. Since schools are not a closed system, resistance can come from various directions like the "demands of the principalship, the momentum of the status quo, obstructive staff attitudes and beliefs, and insular and privileged parental expectations (Theoharis, 2007, p.238). While all of this may frustrate leaders or stall progress, the goal of restoring dignity and human agency for those pushed to the margins must be the vision that keeps us moving forward.

So, as we all seek solutions for a more just society, remembering the fight is not yours alone. Instead, it should be the collective efforts of all of us focused on pushing a nation that is comfortable in the status quo, to become a home for everyone. As we all continue the work, consider all things, to center the children and look at the world from their standpoint. That will be the beginning of finding solutions to make their story one that leads to success for a nation.

ORGANIZATION OF THE CHAPTERS

Chapter 1 shares the author's testimonio that names the unrest that exists in dominant white communities where she lives and works. This chapter provides insight to specific issues, dilemmas, and struggles faced by the author while seeking fairness, equity, and justice for marginalized communities in a PK-12 school district.

Chapter 2 seeks to answer the question of how leaders of color navigate the racial and cultural oppression in their workspaces. The chapter addresses inequities in their organization and offers suggestions on how to enact transformative change.

Chapter 3 presents narratives from the perspective of three Professors in Educational Leadership from one African American, one Latina, and one Asian-American professor.

Chapter 4 discusses the need for promoting women of color in educational leadership positions and presents the positive effects they have on issues of racism, poverty, aggression, oppression, hostility and/or privilege.

Chapter 5 is a collaborative critical autoethnography that attempts to offer deep understanding into the lived experiences of female Black school leaders. The chapter analyzes overarching themes in autoethnographic narratives from seven Black female education leaders.

Chapter 6 describes the ways Black women operate at the intersection of resistance and leadership. The authors challenge the societal perceptions of Black women and highlight their ability to survive in spaces that have historically been uninviting.

Chapter 7 highlights the early career leadership experiences of Black and Brown women in counseling programs. The authors explore how gender, race, and culture intersectionality are integral to understanding transitional leadership during these tumultuous times.

Chapter 8 focuses on equipping and empowering Black and Brown counseling leaders with the tools needed to lead in their spheres of influence effectively and confidently without falling victim to being questioned for how American they are and /or being further minoritized/ 'Othered' for the (non-white) identities they embody.

Chapter 9 the four authors in this chapter focus on transformational change within oppressive environments, as Native women professors, counselors, and administrators within higher education. The authors present strategies for resisting assimilation which are historically driven to crush creativity and halt transformational change.

Chapter 10 highlights the cognitive dissonance felt as a school board member amid the new social justice movement of the late 2000s. It is a brief personal narrative about how silence is no longer appropriate in times of social unrest and when lives are at risk.

Chapter 11 covers a brief personal narrative of the author's lived experience of being taught to be seen and not heard. The author shares the experiences of Muslim's in a society where they are consistently judged for not being American enough if the label of religion is tagged to them.

Chapter 12 uses a critical autoethnographic analysis of a Black male school leader enacting racial and social justice in school improvement efforts and interrogates questions of race, power, justice, and leadership in public schools.

REFERENCES

Applebaum, B. (2005). In the name of morality: Moral responsibility, Whiteness, and social justice education. *Journal of Moral Education, 34*(3), 277–290. doi:10.1080/03057240500206089

Bersh, L. C. (2009). Deconstructing Whiteness: Uncovering Prospective Teachers' Understandings of Their Culture–A Latina Professor's Perspective. *Multicultural Perspectives, 11*(2), 107–112. doi:10.1080/15210960903028792

Bersh, L. C. (2009). Deconstructing Whiteness: Uncovering Prospective Teachers' Understandings of Their Culture–A Latina Professor's Perspective. *Multicultural Perspectives, 11*(2), 107–112. doi:10.1080/15210960903028792

Braun, V. (2016). Standpoint Theory in professional development: Examining former refugee education in Canada. *Education*, *22*(2), 72–86.

Fullan, M. (1993). *Change forces: Probing the depths of educational reform*. The Falmer Press.

Haraway, D. (1988). Situated knowledges: The science question in feminism and the privilege of partial perspective. *Feminist Studies*, *14*(3), 575–599. doi:10.2307/3178066

Harding, S. (1991). *Whose Science? Whose Knowledge? Thinking from Women's Lives*. Cornell University Press., doi:10.7591/9781501712951

Hofstede, G. (2001). *Cultural consequences: Comparing values, behaviors, institutions, and organizations across nations*. Sage Publications.

Hofstede, G., Hofstede, G. J., & Minkov, M. (2010). *Cultures and organizations: Intercultural cooperation and its importance for survival*. McGraw Hill.

Institute of Education Sciences. (2021, May). *COE - Racial/Ethnic Enrollment in Public Schools*. https://nces.ed.gov/programs/coe/indicator/cge

National Center for Educational Statistics. (2019). The Nation's Report Card: Highlights from the 2017 Results. National Center for Education Statistics, Institute of Education Sciences, U.S. Department of Education.

Paradies, Y. (2018). Whither Standpoint Theory in a Post-Truth World? *Cosmopolitan Civil Societies: An Interdisciplinary Journal*, *10*(2), 119–129. doi:10.5130/ccs. v10i2.5980

Rodriguez, S. (January, 2019). Latina Efficacy: Advocate, inspire, and take charge. In P. Keough (Ed.), *Ethical Problem Solving and Decision Making for Positive and Conclusive Outcomes*. IGI Publishing. doi:10.4018/978-1-5225-7582-5.ch009

Samora, J., & Simon, P. (1977). *A history of the Mexican-American people*. University of Notre Dame Press.

Theoharis, G. (2007). Social Justice Educational Leaders and Resistance: Toward a Theory of Social Justice Leadership. *Educational Administration Quarterly*, *43*(2), 221–258. doi:10.1177/0013161X06293717

Tooms, A. K., Lugg, C. A., & Bogotch, I. (2010). Rethinking the politics of fit and educational leadership. *Educational Administration Quarterly*, *46*(1), 9. doi:10.1177/1094670509353044

Valenzuela, A. (2002). High-stakes testing and U.S.-Mexican youth in Texas: The case for multiple compensatory criteria in assessment. *Harvard Journal of Hispanic Policy*, *14*, 97–116.

Williams, D., & Brown, K. (2019). Equity: Buzzword or Bold Commitment to School Transformation. Instructional Leader. *Texas Elementary Principals and Supervisors Association (TEPSA) Instructional Leader, 32*(1), 1-3.

Acknowledgment

We wish to express our appreciation to all the Black and Brown leaders and authors of this book for sharing their words of wisdom during the production of this book. We are eager to share this timely text with others as the author's contributions improved the book significantly and will inspire others to continue this much-needed work for social reform. The collective voices from these esteemed professionals will have a significant impact on social justice reform. We are also immensely grateful to our families, colleagues, and friends for their continued support of our social justice work. Without their support, our efforts would be tarnished and silenced by those who fear change.

Chapter 1
¿Cuándo Podemos Descansar?
When Can We Rest?
A Latina Leader's Testimonio

María L. Gabriel
Independent Researcher, USA

ABSTRACT

The author uses testimonio as a way to situate the barriers and successes she has experienced as a Latina educational leader in Northern Colorado for 25 years. The setting is based in the backdrop of several worldwide issues in 2020 which created a dire need to address diversity, equity, and inclusion (DEI) and social justice within industries and organizations, including educational systems. 1) National political division, 2) disparate access to healthcare and the disproportionate numbers of deaths to COVID-19, and 3) murders of Black Americans by law enforcement have re-affirmed the dehumanization of Black and Brown Americans. Solutions and recommendations are shared based on her shared experiences in moving a DEI educational agenda forward.

INTRODUCTION

"Because of her existence as a CLD [Culturally and Linguistically Diverse] individual, she knows what it is like to live on the margins, often as an outsider, to be excluded, and to have her voice silenced" (Gabriel, 2017, p. 100).

The author has been a public-school educator for twenty-five years in the Rocky Mountain Region of the United States of America (USA). Twenty of those years

DOI: 10.4018/978-1-7998-7235-1.ch001

have included school-based and district-level leadership, including a focus on Diversity, Equity, and Inclusion (DEI). While the author considers leadership to span across roles, age groups, and experience levels, this chapter focuses on the formal leadership and expectations held by educational systems for the positions she has held. Serving as a *Latina*—a woman of Latin American heritage—educational leader within the preschool-twelfth grade (PK-12) systems has had its challenges, consequences, and rewards.

As this important book description explains, "Many organizations enable the status quo by not confronting issues around race, gender, and equity." A Critical Race Theory (CRT) scholar clarifies the necessity of naming and situating race. "Race as a concept has no biological foundation. However, it would be a critical mistake to deny the lived realities of racism in daily life" (Stovall, 2006, p. 247). Therefore, naming the racial and ethnic background of the author is critical for the clear focus of this text, and in particular, this chapter as the author offers important opportunities for readers to engage in listening to the voices of Black Indigenous and People of Color (BIPOC) leaders. Understand that listening is a first step if we desire a positive promotion of change, particularly in an era of social injustice and uprising as experienced in 2020.

In this chapter, through the author's personal *testimonio*, the reader is invited to learn from "dilemmas that marginalized communities encounter while advocating for justice and social change within whitestream organizational systems" as articulated in the book description. Through the use of traditional chapter headings and content: background, main focus, naming of issues and problems, solutions and recommendations, and conclusion, this chapter will offer insider perspectives on the daily life and leadership experiences of one woman of Latin American heritage—a Latina School District Administrator in the USA set in multiple complexities of the sociopolitical context of the year 2020.

BACKGROUND

The author's experiences as a Latina educational leader for more than two decades have magnified and clarified the ways that institutions are committed to maintaining the status quo in educational systems. The status quo has included predictable educational and behavioral outcomes for students including high school graduation rates, wage gaps between male and female employees, consequences for supporting Diversity, Equity, and Inclusion (DEI), and dehumanizing working environments for BIPOC. Of the disparate impacts that exist for these valuable employees is "racial battle fatigue" (Smith, Yosso, & Solórzano, 2006, p. 301). This term references BIPOC being on the front lines of battle in predominantly white spaces such as work and school, and the stress it causes (Gorski, 2019; Smith, Allen, & Danley, 2007; Smith, et al., 2006). "The accumulative stress from racial microaggressions produces racial battle fatigue. The stress of unavoidable front-line racial battles in historically white spaces leads to people of color feeling mentally, emotionally, and physically drained" (Smith, et al., 2006, p. 301).

Other scholars refer to this term as experienced by social justice advocates of Color as 'burnout' (Gorski & Erakat, 2019). As a military veteran, Antoinette Lee Toscano removed the traditional battleground reference and highlights the disparate impacts across culture naming the experience as "cultural disparity fatigue" (personal communication, 2020). Due to the ethnic and racial background of the author and the centering of race in this text and chapter, the author refers to the stress and toll on one's emotional and physical being as racial fatigue. Racial fatigue experienced by BIPOC leaders is real, and it reached a new level of intensity across the United States and the world in the Summer of 2020 and the school year that followed. However, as you will read, while some of this author's story is set in 2020, racial fatigue has been an ongoing experience for her as an educational leader for most of her career.

In the course of the author's lengthy educational leadership career, not a single institution had been willing to address issues, concerns, and matters related to race. The dominant and patriarchal systems were maintained immaculately, just as they were designed—to prepare the various racial groups and genders for pre-assigned roles within society. For example, White men are more often prepared for leadership and advancement, women for work inside the home or at middle-management and service jobs, BIPOC to enter the prison industrial complex, the military, or low paying service jobs. In addition, students in the Lesbian, Gay, Bisexual, Transgender, Queer (LGBTQ+) community are more likely to be bullied, harassed, and skip school. In fact, "[LGBTQ+ students] are more than four times as likely to report attempting suicide in the past year as compared to straight/cisgender peers" (The Trevor Project, 2020, p. 1). Any one of these factors that marginalize students and adults have been exacerbated by multiple issues, including the underlying sociopolitical context within the US at the time of this publication. The next section of this chapter will clarify and examine the distinct sociopolitical context and its importance given the undergirding beliefs of systems within the context that create and maintain regulations, policies, conditions, laws, practices, traditions, and events.

MAIN FOCUS OF CHAPTER

The focus of this chapter is based in the backdrop of several worldwide issues in the summer of 2020 which created a dire need to address DEI and social justice within industries and organizations, including educational systems. Most notably were 1) the political divisiveness across the nation created by xenophobic, racist, and homophobic attitudes promoted through social media and television; 2) disparate access to health care and the disproportionate numbers of deaths from COVID-19 heightened the world's awareness of inequitable access and outcomes; and 3) overt racism and the continual murders of Black Americans by law enforcement being recorded and going viral throughout the world. The result of the combination of these issues has re-affirmed the dehumanization of Black and Brown Americans, and resulted in renewed calls for justice, equity, and inclusion. Describing the sociopolitical context of this time period is important, and it will be remembered by those who lived through this unpredictable and unbelievable time of social injustice in US history. The majoritarian narrative has named the uprising of social justice advocates as social unrest, but for BIPOC and their White allies, it is more accurately described as social uprising, protest, and advocacy for social justice.

Firstly, derogatory and exclusionary public comments and decisions at the national level incited further marginalization and discrimination of diverse communities throughout the US (Costello, 2106). US political campaigning beginning in 2015 through the end of 2020 included Muslims being banned from entering the US; video and audio evidence of misogyny and disrespect of women and their bodies; retracting of LGBTQ+ student supports (U.S. Department of Justice and U.S. Department of Education, 2017); removal of funding for Special Education services for students with identified disabilities; and border closures and family separations at the USA and Mexico border.

To further motivate social justice advocates, during a presidential debate in 2020, the Republican party's candidate openly incited the mobilization of White supremacists when he made a direct call to the Proud Boys, a White Supremacist group in the US, to "stand back and stand by" (Nix, 2020, para.3). The compound effects of these ongoing public displays of bigotry caused many women, members of the LGBTQ+ community, and BIPOC to feel cultural disparity fatigue. The incidents and attitudes impacted schools and the broader communities, in the same way as described as previous impacts in Costello's (2016) report: "More than two-thirds of the teachers reported that students—mainly immigrants, children of immigrants, and Muslims—have expressed concerns or fears about what might happen to them or their families after the election" (p. 4). Inflammatory and exclusionary comments and practices by political leaders created a divisiveness across the USA.

Secondly, amidst the backdrop of marginalizing the BIPOC community over several generations--400 years including the period of slavery--beginning in March 2020, the world began to see the early impacts of the COVID-19 pandemic, which led to a heightened understanding of inequities and disparities in family incomes, health issues, education as previously discussed by DuBose & Gorski (2019) and access to health care as People of Color died at a disproportionate rate compared to their White peers (Centers for Disease Control and Prevention, 2020). Additionally, the US President referred to COVID-19 as "the China virus", inciting discrimination and violence against Asian Americans. Among disparate outcomes uncovered, this included some BIPOC student's low-level of access to education. For example, virtual images of students accessing wi-fi in parking lots to complete online schooling went viral through social media and news coverage, and schools had to reckon with low attendance for students who were taking care of siblings or working to support their family with a surgency of job loss.

The impacts of closures and isolation were also impacting the mental health, well-being, and education of youth and adults. Where the author lives, there was an uptick in students reporting they did not feel safe and did not have adults to turn to, and local law enforcement was reporting an increase in incidents of sexual assault, hate crimes, and human trafficking. Black scholars such as Dr. Dena Simmons, Dr. Bettina Love, Dr. Gloria Ladson-Billings, and many others were prominent in offering educational webinars to bring about awareness of topics such as racial trauma, Transformative Social Emotional Learning (SEL), abolitionist teaching, culturally responsive and sustaining instruction in response to the dual pandemic of racism and COVID-19 (Discovery Education, 2020; Facing History and Ourselves, 2020; PBS Education, 2020; PBS Learning Media, 2020). Educators were urging the consideration of additional ways to support students and educational leaders as the US found itself in the middle of what Dr. Gloria Ladson-Billings named a "dual pandemic, if you will, of COVID-19 or the novel coronavirus AND the pandemic of racism which we have lived with for 401 years" (PBS Education, 2020). Simmons (2019) sums up some of this critical learning.

We can no longer avoid discussing topics that make us uncomfortable. Our students, incessantly inundated with divisive rhetoric and reports of premeditated acts of violence (or even themselves targets of violence), don't have that luxury...We owe our students an education that centers on their lives and explicitly addresses the sociopolitical context (para. 8).

Thirdly, as spring turned into summer in 2020, blatant and deadly acts of racism added to the stress and uncertainties for many People of Color living in this time. The Black Lives Matter (BLM) movement was revived. Author Dr. Bettina Love defines BLM as: people say Black Lives Matter because they want to emphasize that Black life is not disposable (PBS, 2020). BLM was a response to the deaths of multiple Black Americans including but not limited to Breonna Taylor, Ahmaud Arbery, and George Floyd who were all killed by law enforcement. BLM received international attention through protests and calls to action all around the world.

The summer also brought to light implicit bias; the hidden fear that White people hold of People of Color. Many people enacted their internal bias through their public use of "racialized police communication" (McNamarah, 2019, p. 342) by contacting law enforcement. A past example of the legacy of this phenomenon took place in 1987. In Hall v. Oches, the court considered the events that unfolded after a Black father, Bancroft Hall, entered the predominantly White suburb of Milton, Massachusetts to pick up his daughter Sandra from a friend's home. When Hall arrived, she was still not ready to go, and he returned to the car to read his newspaper.

While waiting, a neighbor, believing Hall to be "out of place," called the Milton police to "report a suspicious man parked in an old car in the Sullivan's driveway." The police dispatcher sent out a call that "suspicious car at 167 Dudley Lane with a [B]lack male behind the wheel and a possible breaking and entering in progress" (McNamarah, 2019, p. 342).

The belief that one can leverage support for their complaints against members of the BIPOC community by contacting law enforcement was revived by the racial tensions across the USA. An example includes the now-infamous phone call by Amy Cooper in Central Park, New York City, USA (NBC New York, 2020). This is among a long list of phone calls to law enforcement termed "white caller crime" by Michael Harriot (McNamarah, 2019, p. 335), which was seemingly reignited through racial tensions. Amy Cooper's video recorded phone call was one example of the wielding of racial superiority by her calling on law enforcement when faced with the discomfort of diversity, specifically of a Black male. The incessant racism, harassment, discrimination, legalized racial profiling, and stop-and-frisk without suspicion of a crime that have happened to BIPOC recently have been recorded and gone viral bringing an international spotlight on the insensitivity and erasure of humanity in the USA for People of Color. The sociocultural and sociopolitical context of this chapter is based on the lived realities of BIPOC in the time of two widely spreading pandemics: 1) racism, and 2) COVID-19, which created continued and heightened awareness of the dehumanization of BIPOC.

Many BIPOC leaders have known that microaggressions, bias, prejudice, and discrimination have existed over time in communities, schools, and organizations. They have felt the impacts of individual and institutional racism and have tried desperately to survive, lead, and thrive. Pertinent to the author's story, in the USA several studies have highlighted the experiences of Latina educational leaders (Méndez-Morse, Murakami, Byrne-Jiménez, & Hernandez, 2015; Murakami, Hernandez, Méndez-Morse, & Byrne-Jimenez, 2016; Murakami, Hernandez, Valle, & Almager 2018; Tayloe, 2016, 2017). Authors have discussed the influence of racial and ethnic identity on the leadership practice of Latina administrators, an additional term for leaders within PK-12 settings. For example, Tayloe (2017) found that practicing Latina administrators were recipients of "deficit thinking, micro-aggressions, institutional racism, and marginalization" (p. 1). Yet, what is taking place in the sociocultural context of educational leadership in the fall of 2020 is a remarkable and historic moment. It comes during a time full of unimaginable uncertainty and ambiguity as instructional models shifted multiple times between March through the end of 2020 due to COVID-19 health and safety guidelines such as the need to socially distance.

The stress was compounded by fear for many BIPOC leaders based on the experiences of Black Americans, Latinx/Hispanic and other immigrants, Muslims, members of the LGBTQ+ community, women, and Asians as discussed earlier. As a result of the issues and concerns raised, the author feared that important, yet marginalized, voices had been silenced. The narrative within these pages has been written in hopes it would create an opening for readers to reflect on the documented stories of one BIPOC leader; this chapter is an offering an opportunity to engage in learning about silenced voices of BIPOC leaders who are trying to promote change from within a fractured system. The author offers an opportunity to move forward even if the reader experiences discomfort, as described by DiAngelo (2018). It is with great hope that the majoritarian narrative will be rejected through reading and reflecting on the counter-story offered in this chapter. Additionally, a positive change in this era is possible, particularly in creating a more affirming and safe educational leadership environment.

Issues, Controversies, and Problems

Storytelling is a vital way of keeping history alive. "Voices are often found in storytelling" (Gabriel, 2011, p. 92). Storytelling is one way the author has practiced her commitment to DEI efforts: through truth-telling. "The use of voice or 'naming your reality' is a way that CRT links form and substance in scholarship" (Ladson-Billings, 1998, p. 23). Often, the majoritarian narrative about BIPOC communities in the USA is not told by BIPOC themselves. Majoritarian Storytelling is a method of recounting the experiences and perspectives of those with racial, cultural, and social privilege. "Counter-storytelling is a means of exposing and critiquing normalized dialogues that perpetuate racial stereotypes. The use of counter-stories allows for challenging privilege discourses, the discourses of the majority, therefore serving as a means for giving voice to marginalized groups" (DeCuir & Dixson, 2004, p. 27).

Counter-storytelling adds missing voices since dominant racial, cultural, and social groups typically control public discourse because they hold the power (Howard, 2006). Because of this continued practice, CRT scholars encourage the use of counter-story (Solórzano & Yosso, 2009) to make room for marginalized voices (Ladson-Billings,

1998) and to support a wider discussion of race in the U.S. educational systems that can lead to change. Therefore, the issues, controversies, and problems presented in this section of the chapter are offered as counter-storytelling and are built on two of the important tenets of CRT: 1) a 'unique voice of color' (Delgado & Stefancic, 2001); and 2) 'intersectionality' (Crenshaw, 1991).

First, the author demonstrates personal experiences with oppression that "Black, Indian, Asian, and Latino/a writers and thinkers may be able to communicate to their White counterparts" (Delgado & Stefancic, 2001, p. 9) that may be otherwise unknown. Second, "Because of their intersectional identity as both women *and* of color within discourses that are shaped to respond to one *or* the other, women of color are marginalized within both" (Crenshaw, 1991, p. 1244). Thus, the intersectionality of the author's marginalized identities including race, ethnicity, gender, language, and experience as a Brown, Latina, female educational leader, is critical to developing a comprehensive understanding of the issues faced by the writer. The context of ethnicity, race, and language are connected to Latina/o Critical Race Theory (LatCrit) scholarship which engaged a Chicana/o--Latina/o consciousness to CRT by examining racialized layers of subordination based on distinct identity markers unique to the Latina/o experience, such as immigration status, gender, sexuality, culture, language, phenotype, accent, and surname (Pérez Huber, 2010; Solórzano & Delgado Bernal, 2001; Villalpando, 2004).

Testimonio, a methodological storytelling approach with history around the world has close ties to LatCrit as *testimonio* has been used to frame unique experiences that include political, social, and cultural aspects of an individual's story (Burciaga & Erbstein, 2012; Delgado Bernal, 1998; Guzmán, 2012; Latina Feminist Group, 2001; Pérez Huber, 2010; Ramírez & González, 2012; Urrieta & Villenas, 2013) with a connection to a shared group of common roots in marginalization, oppression, or resistance (Delgado Bernal, 2018). "*Testimonio* and LatCrit both validate and center the experiential knowledge of People of Color, recognize the power of collective memory and knowledge, and are guided by the larger goals of transformation and empowerment of Communities of Color" (Pérez Huber, 2010, p. 83). Therefore, it is through a LatCrit lens that the author shares this *testimonio* as a Latina—a Brown female educational leader in this era of social injustice, tension, and uprising.

The *Testimonio*

The author's *testimonio* is set in the 2020 sociocultural and sociopolitical context shared at the beginning of the chapter, including a nation surviving in discontent and uncertainty due to 1) the political division of the US; 2) the many uncertainties due to COVID-19 and the many racial disparities as highlighted; and 3) racial trauma due to the loss of BIOPC human life projected on media.

As an Equity Director during the workday and a Latina around the clock, the author experienced all three of these issues first-hand. She was an Assistant Principal when the 2016 presidential campaigning was in full swing and greeted her students when they exited the school bus each morning and on the playground during recesses each day. She witnessed multiple incidents of students of color crying on the playground or when they arrived at school after a school bus ride. The students shared stories of their fears of being deported after hearing the news on the television and in fear-riddled conversations within their families. They were also being harassed by other students who told them that they would be deported when then candidate Donald Trump won the election. As the author moved back into district-level administration before the 2020 presidential election, she watched the community divide over mask-wearing, political candidacy support, and split leadership support for DEI at the city and county level. In small towns, local demonstrations for peace incited violence by supporters of the then president Donald Trump. Additionally, she attended peaceful demonstrations where Trump supporters antagonized protesters and heckled people wearing masks.

Beyond the mask-wearing, social distancing, and COVID-19 fatigue, there were ongoing shifts in instructional models to address the fierce and dangerous nature of COVID-19 transmission. Starting in March 2020, schools across the nation closed (Education Week, 2020). The author's school system closed also and subsequently her children's schools. She, alongside thousands of community members, learned what it was to be a 'home school' parent while simultaneously making systems-level decisions and supporting leaders and staff who were enduring rapidly evolving changes through the remainder of that calendar year.

Due to the author's professional career related to equity, she has utilized personal perspectives and experiences that her predominately white colleagues do not understand or respect. When she shared these perspectives with colleagues, she was judged, excluded, and reprimanded for it. First, she endured non-verbal microaggressions found in attitudes, 'the look', and symbology. The symbols she saw where she worked and lived sent strong messages of hate as evidenced through hanging confederate flags, flags supporting the divisive President Trump, a pop-up President Trump flag and apparel store, and 'a thin blue line flags'—in support of law enforcement—waving from cars, trucks, windows, and in the front yards of homes.

These symbols were stress-, anxiety-, and fear-inducing for the author as a Woman of Color, an immigrant, and a Spanish speaker given the sociopolitical context described earlier in the chapter. Yet, when she shared these feelings with colleagues in her communities, including work, home, and religious contexts, she was dismissed and silenced through verbal and non-verbal means. She was told that the flags and symbols are not documented symbols of hate, even though meanings of hate are well understood within the BIPOC community, as evidenced by the use of these very symbols at the rally for White supremacy in Charlottesville, Virginia in 2017, where Nazis and White Supremacists, such as the Proud Boys, rallied to 'Unite the Right', a White supremacist goal (Reeve, 2020). These non-verbal symbols of hate hanging around the community were not the only microaggressions the author endured.

While many teachers were determining how to address the race-based issues arising on social media, there was a compounding fear about how to do so without 'getting into trouble'. American politician and civil rights leader John Lewis had previously made a call for all Americans to get into 'good trouble' by actively supporting DEI, and his call to action was highlighted in his passing in the summer of 2020. Yet, there was a contradictory message in systems of power, such as education, in which many educational leaders who were standing up for DEI were being silenced by their leadership through lack of support or being disciplined (Dernbach, 2021; Kingkade, 2020; Teaching While White Staff, 2020; Westside News, 2020). "There's a pattern, in other words, designed to gird the status quo and dismiss those pushing for racial justice" (Teaching While White Staff, 2020, para. 13). The author's *testimonio* related to this issue as an equity educator promoting DEI highlights the connection between power and the fight for fairness, equity, and justice for marginalized communities in her PK-12 school district and surrounding communities.

In August 2020, the author was asked by her supervisor to develop asynchronous professional development for a system of 2,100 employees. The decision to create online teaching modules fell on four district leaders in a short amount of time. All training related to culturally relevant teaching and equity were delegated to her alone—the district's Equity Director. Considerations of a large amount of content, the readiness of educators in the system for the content, and the ways to create engaging asynchronous learning were flooding her mind. She was simultaneously building online content and learning technology tools such as Screencastify, WeVideo, and Google Classroom to create the lesson delivery. This was a sentiment many teachers expressed throughout the school closures and in the months that followed requiring online teaching. It was daunting. The author's professional learning modules were vetted by her immediate work colleagues and by her supervisor. Images that were used to engage the online learners included photographs from the community in which the school district resided and screenshots of headlines and images from the local newspaper and social media. The images created an opportunity to reflect on the sociocultural and sociopolitical context of the community of learning and to encourage educators to prepare safe and inclusive learning environments for their incoming students. Days after one of the four asynchronous modules went live in the school system, some district leaders began receiving negative feedback from community members related to the content. Those leaders did not reach out to the author. Some of them talked amongst themselves, but they did not contact the content creator—a District Leader herself—until community concerns reached the superintendent and the Board of Education. Then, she received a phone call on a weekend evening.

Several community members made public calls through individual or community social media platforms for others to contact top leadership to complain. Facebook community group sites and personal profile pages were discovered to have held damning content about the author and the district's decision to teach teachers about issues related to social justice and diversity, such as sexual orientation and gender identity. There was also disagreement about the author's use of images throughout the slide presentation including that of a gender spectrum continuum, a local newspaper article heading related to a young Black male being held at gunpoint while working within the school district community (West, 2020), and newspaper headline and a picture of "F---BLM" graffitied on a wall in the center of town (Julig, 2020). The author narrated the training and commented on the sociopolitical context of learning as important to understanding the social emotional learning needs of students. It was requested that educators acknowledge the different feelings of students, staff, and families. The intention was to model the usefulness of critical consciousness (Ladson-Billings, 1995), a questioning mindset about inequities and social justice, as related to the district's professional development model grounded in culturally relevant teaching. Building a sociocultural context and empathy for diverse students, staff, and families in schools is a first step for teachers to build relationships and connect with their students. The District demographics mirror that of most school districts across the US wherein a cultural mismatch exists suggesting "the classroom culture or the teacher's culture is at odds with the culture of the ethnic minority students" (Gregory, Skiba, & Noguera, 2010, p. 63) of whom they serve. This cultural gap in knowledge extends to race, ethnicity, home language, family income, sexual orientation, and gender identity. Nevertheless, the pushback was fierce.

One community member accessed one of the online 45-minute Professional Development (PD) teacher training modules, spliced sections of the content, and narrowed it down to a seven-minute video. Then, the creator of the shortened video posted it on their social media with mean-spirited comments and a call for others to contact the Superintendent and Board of Education to complain. The author's name, face, and email were on all of those training modules. When it began to go viral, she had an instant fear for her personal safety and that of her children. The author's name and face had been in the news and on televised board meetings over the previous year for high-profile equity work she led in her professional capacity, within the same communities. In August 2020, her name and picture returned in the underground world of social media where people villainized her and her work, saying things such as, 'she thinks because she has a Ph.D., she knows everything', that she was 'indoctrinating students', and 'sharing her personal beliefs'. Among others, a previous neighbor, a sibling of a couple the author grew up with, a couple she had never met, and a local police officer posted destructive and insulting messages on social media. Then, as social media allows, others joined in, commenting on the thread and lifting the shortened training video to place on their own social media. That is not where it ended. Much like "racialized police communication" (McNamarah, 2019, p. 1), the offended individuals employed a racialized Board of Education communication to leverage their implicit bias.

The disgruntled calls reached the Superintendent of Schools, the City Manager, and the local police department. The author was seen as has having engaged in misbehavior. The 'trouble' the author had unknowingly ensued was not seen as 'good.' The power of the majoritarian narrative about what can be taught in schools led to a personal communication (2020) she received from her employer stating that "The District received numerous emails and phone calls from concerned citizens and staff that these images were political in nature, and potentially damaging to relationships between the district and law enforcement" (p. 1). The reprimand was followed with clear expectations and requirements for the author to address, which included 'use good judgment', uphold high professional, ethical and moral standards, and ensure compliance and support of board policies and regulations. She was verbally instructed to follow the district policy, explicitly, "to avoid misbehavior or the appearance of misbehavior" (p. 2).

In the Summer of 2020, where racist ideology and behavior abounded, the author was distraught. She did not fight; she did not flee. She froze. The fear and stress ran through her body and mind. She knew she was stuck in a professional world that would require her to maintain the status quo, to not interrupt or disrupt the inequities that educational leaders continually discussed. She was silenced. She was put in her place. Good trouble was to be avoided. Three months later, she encountered a different experience as she was engaging in a personal activity which she refers to as 'running while Brown.'

In November 2020, the author called her best friend to go out running. They decided to meet at a half-way point between their homes, less than 10 miles from her own. They had run at the same location previously due to the open space and dirt roads which are kinder to a runner's feet and knees. Also, smaller running trails and parks were overrun with people, often those not wearing their masks. The author arrived first and parked, then when the other arrived they walked, ran, and talked. They were happy to share space and time together which had been limited during isolation and quarantining during the COVID-19 pandemic.

When they returned to the cars to leave there was a county sheriff's marked car parked and a female officer standing outside their cars. When the author and her friend approached the officer, they were detained and questioned. The officer radioed in the two license plate numbers. She told them that someone called the police station stating that there were suspicious people outside, and this implored her to find out who was suspicious out on the county road. She stated that she was not familiar with the area on the north edge of the city. Questions ensued such as "Are these your cars?," "Why are you out here?," and "Can I see your driver's licenses?" All too familiar fears and stresses caught up with the author again. Images of Ahmaud Arbery and his killers went through the author's mind like a slideshow. The stress-response kicked in and she froze. It took several days for the author to recover from this racial trauma. Days of work were lost as her mind froze. She was torn between working through the emotions brought on by this racial trauma and moving forward with her daily responsibilities of keeping her own children safe and leading equity work.

As the author processed the experience and the interaction with law enforcement for a second time within four months, she concluded that she was living in fear. Fear of a lack of safety. Fear of a lack of support. Internalized oppression had gotten to her. How do BIPOC leaders recover when they receive non-verbal and verbal messages that communicate that they are invisible yet hyper-visible; when they are unwanted, unvalued, and ultimately, do not belong? That day, the author was stopped by law enforcement, detained, questioned, and made to feel like a criminal because of the color of her skin. This is an experience of many of our BIPOC leaders. They are marginalized and silenced in the systems and communities in which they advocate for DEI. "Experiencing racial discrimination as a stressful life event can reduce one's personal sense of control and elicit feelings of loss, ambiguity, strain, frustration, and injustice" (Smith, et. al, 2006, p. 301). The stress ignites the brain's auto-piloted system of stress-response. When a Person of Color is consistently the recipient of racial microaggressions, the stress-response is consistently ignited.

Microaggressions can be both verbal and kinetic.

"These are subtle, innocuous, preconscious, or unconscious degradations, and putdowns, often kinetic but capable of being verbal and/or kinetic. In and of itself a microaggression may seem harmless, but the cumulative burden of a lifetime of microaggressions can theoretically contribute to diminished mortality, augmented morbidity, and flattened confidence. (Pierce, 1995, p. 281)

The accumulation of this type of stress is what has developed into racial fatigue for the author. She is grateful to put words to the experience, and she is clear it is not a healthy place to live. She has suffered emotional and physical impacts due to racial fatigue from an early age as described.

I was born in South America and raised in Colorado in a conservative White community where I attended all-White schools. By the time I reached junior high, I'd experienced racial microaggressions and outright bias, prejudice, and discrimination. These experiences continued throughout high school and into college where I was consistently asked to represent "the Latino perspective." (Gabriel, 2019, p. xvii)

It is lonely and painful to be sitting and struggling in the space where racial fatigue lives and thrives, particularly when well-meaning white colleagues in her workplace are unable to hear or listen to the experiences that have led to that pain. The prevalence of 'white fragility'- the inability to discuss racism without becoming angry and/or defensive (DiAngelo, 2018)- becomes a burden for BIPOC leaders. Additionally, as this author has navigated microaggressions, racial fatigue, and dehumanization in her personal and professional lives, she continues to pursue her passion of creating more socially just learning environments for students. She has re-committed to collective self-care and being conscious of when fear sets in, to focus on love. Based in her self-determination, she offers solutions and recommendations in the next section of this chapter.

SOLUTIONS AND RECOMMENDATIONS

For BIPOC educational leaders to address DEI work within their workplace in hopes of addressing change and bringing equity and social justice to fruition, there are several recommended steps to bring about solutions that will promote social justice: 1) Be an equity leader first and expect the same from your employees; 2) Acknowledge the sociocultural and sociopolitical context of your diverse employees; and 3) Implement evidence-based strategies to support BIPOC employees.

First, when considering DEI work, center equity and social justice to focus on equitable goals and outcomes. Specifically, when many organizations have created DEI efforts as a response to the problems noted earlier in the chapter, a better approach is to address EDI: Equity, Diversity, and Inclusion; in other words, to situate equitable outcomes for students and staff as the primary goal (Courageous Conversation, 2020). If not, systems put the goal of hiring diverse individuals first without the understanding of equity goals that can move toward transformational change of systems. When an educational system is focused on equity, the whole system will contribute to shared measurable outcomes for their marginalized and impacted youth, staff, and families. This also includes allies in positions of power who will not just be learners of racial equity, but who will speak up for racial equity as organizations strive to meet stated goals.

Leadership for equity also requires leaders to take a personal stand and commit to equitable practices. Some specific recommended steps include: 1) Equity leaders review disaggregated data each and every time they discuss EDI; 2) Equity leaders ask poignant questions about policies and practices that are contributing to the disparate outcomes found in data; 3) Equity leaders require their teams to write and make progress toward individual equity goals as part of their annual professional goal-making and review process, which is regularly monitored; 4) Equity leaders make equity a outcomes a part of their own work, as well. Some top-level leaders are comfortable assigning equity work to their subordinates, but movement is created when the focus on equitable outcomes exists at all levels in the system. Each stakeholder must be knowledgeable about equitable outcomes and must daily address the needs that have been identified in the data. The unified focus at all levels to address equity in specific student outcomes has the potential to center students and race at the front of creating, planning, and decision-making in organizations.

Second, equity leaders cannot fear retaliation when they dare to address the sociopolitical context of teaching and learning. In 2020, when school closures began and the media coverage of the deaths of Black Americans became an ongoing public conversation, many leaders across systems published statements of support. Many universities, companies, and organizations added a clear statement of support for Black Lives Matter on their webpages, on social media, and in print. Yet, other leaders stood back, afraid to further divide an already fraught community. Some leaders recoiled when parts of their divided community scorned them for having made a statement. The author reached out individually to each person she knew who was committed to social justice to ask how they were feeling. She checked on Black friends and colleagues acknowledging the racial uprising that was taking place and asked how they were feeling. It may seem trivial, but leaders who ignore the racial trauma that their employees are enduring are asking them to leave part of who they are at the door. Their silence is agreement. Asking them to ignore the suffering of their colleagues in favor of focusing on work tasks de-centers equity. Neutrality supports the oppressor.

Third, there must be intentional focus on funding to increase the capacity of the current system to support the diversity of the employees and the diversity in the community they serve. This can include a two-prong approach: 1) Employers must be committed to supporting diversity; and 2) Employers must be committed to inclusion. When institutions commit to EDI, there must be continued focus on supporting and affirming diversity and expecting and monitoring progress of inclusive behaviors from their employees. Employers and their leaders can support their BIPOC leaders. As discussed throughout the chapter, efforts must be made to create safe spaces in which BIPOC can safely share experiences with others from their same ethnic and racial background.

This chapter engages the reader in an experience of counter-story known as *testimonio*. The author practiced honesty and vulnerability as she believes that "sharing can begin a process of empowerment" (Latina Feminist Group, 2001, p.

1). Systems can be created in such a way that people in leadership positions can engage in this *testimonio* safely in the context of their current work environment. The author is beginning to find success in her school district, which had begun to offer safe space for truth-telling through the implementation of a strategy entitled 'affinity groups' (Education Trust, 2019) in which employees of a shared marginalized identity gather in an informal setting to openly share how their work and sense of belonging is impacted by their identity. Members of BIPOC communities are students of the life lessons they learn through on-going exposure to marginalizing images, verbalizations, and experiences. Everyone who identifies as BIPOC needs and deserves safe spaces for openly sharing their experiences of racial microaggressions, racial trauma, exclusionary practices, and discrimination. These spaces need to exist without fear of reprisal, silencing, or dismissal. In doing so, BIPOC can offer their perspectives and promote necessary actions to address social justice and equity, but must be protected in the process. This can be a first step toward successful implementation of EDI efforts.

A second recommended solution for implementing EDI efforts at an organizational level is the hiring of BIPOC communities and training of staff to honor diversity and to engage in inclusive practices. One example of a training goal is to include understanding the value of BIPOC voices, seeking BIPOC perspectives in decision making, and committing to believing the stories that are heard. One example of this perspective is shared by "Stovall, who is Black. You may have never owned slaves, you may have never uttered a racial epithet, but you live in a world that assumes my criminality over my humanity, and that I think is the toughest thing for people to grapple with" (Kingkade, 2020, para. 30). When leaders begin to acknowledge that the humanity of Black and Brown leaders has been questioned and/or eliminated, they will recognize there is EDI work to do. In response, leaders must require training across systems to ensure each member of the community has the internal capacity to stop themselves before they maintain the status quo, which is perpetrated in responding to the "white caller," or in fact, that they are not hiring a "white caller," (McNamarah, 2019, p. 335) Training can lead employees to examine existing policies and protocols and can highlight the expectations for all employees to 1) Be an equity leader first; 2) Acknowledge the sociocultural and sociopolitical context within which employees are working; and 3) Utilize evidence-based strategies to support fellow BIPOC employees.

FUTURE RESEARCH DIRECTIONS

This chapter focused on the experiences that many BIPOC endure in their leadership positions as illustrated through the author's personal *testimonio*. The need to address the residue that is left from past traumas and to validate and heal from the current traumatic racial stress is critical to equity leadership. While the author does not wish to pathologize People of Color, recognizing and honoring the history of traumatic and stressful encounters endured by many BIPOC leaders is a critical step to surviving, thriving, and leading in a context that is too often the setting for these disturbing encounters. To this end, school leaders may consider using strategies such as transformative Social-Emotional Learning (SEL) and Critical post-traumatic growth with students and staff, both of which are described in more detail in the following paragraphs.

Dominant cultures and communities rely on mindfulness and SEL that traditionally has not addressed racial trauma and has often led BIPOC to feel they are a problem that needs to be fixed. For example, the original SEL model left BIPOC needing to learn to regulate their emotions without explicitly addressing the sociopolitical context of teaching, learning, and living. Students and the adults in educational systems were left isolated and without the support to address their sociopolitical context. Dr. Dena Simmons asked important questions about these unaddressed needs. "What's the point of teaching children about conflict resolution skills if we're not talking about the conflicts that exist because of racism or white supremacy?" Without that nuance, SEL is "white supremacy with a hug" (Madda, 2019, para. 11) A new formation of this work is known as Transformative SEL, and it is seen as a lever to address equity in educational systems. (Jagers, Rivas-Drake, & Borowski, 2018; Jagers, Rivas-Drake, & Williams, 2019). "Consistent with the pursuit of educational equity, we recently offered the concept of transformative SEL to reflect our interest in making explicit issues such as power, privilege, prejudice, discrimination, social justice, empowerment, and self-determination in the field of SEL" (Jagers, Rivas-Drake, & Borowski, 2018, p. 3). This new tool may support the systems approach to SEL in schools, and the strategies can be useful for educational leaders, as well.

A second possible model for support of BIPOC in an organization is based in Critical post-traumatic growth (CPTG). CPTG was developed out of the intersections of CRT and Post Traumatic Growth (RAGE Project, 2019). Led by Stacey Chimimba Ault, her work is intent on building on previous dominant culture frameworks to explicitly address the impacts of oppression on BIPOC. "CPTG forces us to acknowledge that oppression is traumatic and offers us a framework of resistance and growth while current trauma-informed frameworks often rob us of agency and power" (RAGE Project, 2019, para. 4). These targeted and focused efforts to address oppression in its many forms will move systems toward achieving equity.

The author posits that with more study, this consideration of the possibilities of transformative SEL and critical post-traumatic growth can support the creation of understanding, believing, and supporting BIPOC leaders.

CONCLUSION

"Counterstories seek to document the persistence of racism from the perspectives of those injured and victimized by its legacy...[to] bring attention to those who courageously resist racism and struggle toward a more socially and racially just society" (Yosso, 2006, p. 10). The counterstories here are offered as a *testimonio* of a few of the racialized experiences of one Latina educational leader within the 2020 sociopolitical context of the Rocky Mountain Region of the United States. The *testimonio* is offered to the readers as a unique way to consider issues, controversies, and problems endured by BIPOC educational leaders. Now, readers need to ask themselves if they feel inspired, in what ways they are motivated, or how they have been led to respond to the racialized experiences of their colleagues and subordinates. The author believes that reading, listening, hearing, and believing BIPOC leaders is a first step in moving toward EDI efforts to promote change for social justice. The next step is taking time to reflect and consider what one's individual role as an equity leader is. Solutions and recommendations were offered in this chapter, and each reader must consider their own level of comfort and agency in addressing the status quo in their institution, system, or workplace.

The racial status quo is comfortable for white people, and we will not move forward in race relations if we remain comfortable. The key to moving forward is what we do with our discomfort. We can use it as a door out—blame the messenger and disregard the message. Or we can use it as a door in by asking, Why does this unsettle me? What would it mean for me if this were true? How does this lens change my understanding of racial dynamics? (DiAngelo, 2018, p. 14).

As the author's experiences illustrate in this chapter, her message and experiences have typically been disregarded, she has been blamed, and she is not the only one.

As those living in the USA in the beginning of 2021 collectively strive to survive the complexities of a politically divided country, the ongoing effects of COVID-19 on health, economics, and education, and open racism and bigotry, none of this work gets easier. The author has considered methods and strategies needed to live and thrive through cultural disparity fatigue, racial fatigue, and to remain whole. Due to the author's trauma history, she understands that ongoing racial trauma in the workplace creates a brain pathway that needs to be re-wired. She has sought guidance from key authors to address her racial trauma. As a key researcher states "If you feel safe and loved, your brain becomes specialized in exploration, play, and cooperation.; if you are frightened and unwanted, it specializes in managing feelings of fear and abandonment" (van der kolk, 2014).

More specifically, through the use of *testimonio* offered in this chapter, this counter-storytelling method centered on race. It has highlighted the counter-story of a Brown female educational leader, thereby inviting the reader to engage in further examination into the possibilities of understanding the impacts of oppression and marginalization in leadership on BIPOC leaders. The hope is that empathy can be built and leaders will work with BIPOC leaders in their own context to ensure these leaders are experiencing support rather than trauma. Leaders may begin to move beyond just listening, to become co-conspirators in undoing the inequities and disparities and to address the reasons for the current social uprising, known as "social unrest." This will allow exhausted BIPOC leaders a moment to rest, then to shine and to show their excellence. This will allow BIPOC leaders to be humanized in their roles as leaders and to realize their own true potential.

REFERENCES

Adams, B. (2016, December 5). *Microaggression and battle fatigue.* Salt Lake City, UT: The University of Utah. https://attheu.utah.edu/facultystaff/microaggression-and-racial-battle-fatigue/

Burciaga, R., & Erbstein, N. (2012). Latina/o dropouts: Generating community cultural wealth. *Association of Mexican-American Educators (AMAE) Journal*, 6(1), 24–33.

Calhoun, L. G., Cann, A., & Tedeschi, R. G. (2010). The posttraumatic growth model: Sociocultural considerations. In T. Weiss & R. Berger (Eds.), *Posttraumatic growth and culturally competent practice: Lessons learned from around the globe* (pp. 1–14). John Wiley & Sons Inc.

CASEL. (2021). *Transformative SEL as a Lever for Equity & Social Justice.* https://casel.org/research/transformative-sel/

Centers for Disease Control and Prevention. (2020). *Health Equity Considerations and Racial and Ethnic Minority Groups* https://www.cdc.gov/coronavirus/2019-ncov/community/health-equity/race-ethnicity.html

Costello, M. B. (2016). *The Trump Effect The impact of the presidential campaign on our nation's schools.* Southern Poverty Law Center. https://www.splcenter.org/sites/default/files/splc_the_trump_effect.pdf

Courageous Conversation. (2020, December 22). *Marcus Moore: Moving from DEI to EDI.* https://courageousconversation.com/

DeCuir, J. T., & Dixson, A. D. (2004, June/July). "So when it comes out, they aren't that surprised that it is there": Using critical race theory as a tool of analysis of race and racism in education. *Educational Researcher, 33*(26), 26–31. doi:10.3102/0013189X033005026

Delgado, R., & Stefancic, J. (2001). *Critical race theory: An introduction.* New York University Press.

Delgado Bernal, D. (1998). Using a Chicana feminist epistemology in educational research. *Harvard Educational Review, 68*(4), 555–582. doi:10.17763/haer.68.4.5wv1034973g22q48

Delgado Bernal, D. (2018). A testimonio of critical race feminista parenting: Snapshots from my childhood and my parenting. *International Journal of Qualitative Studies in Education: QSE, 31*(1), 25–35. doi:10.1080/09518398.2017.1379623

Dernbach, B. Z. (2021, May 12). Showdown at school board meeting: Elk River alumi of color say the 'never felt safe,' parents decry 'woke mob'. *Sahan Journal.* https://sahanjournal.com/education/elk-river-school-board-equity/

DiAngelo, R. (2018). *White fragility: Why it's so hard for white people to talk about race.* Beacon Press.

Discovery Education. (2020, May 14). *Educating the whole child in a time of loss.* Author.

DuBose, M., & Gorski, P. C. (2019). *Equity literacy during the COVID19 crisis.* Equity Literacy Institute. https://08a3a74adec5426e8385bdc09490d921.filesusr.com/ugd/38199c_c355c89c7634495584ead8f230c0d25b.pdf

Education Week. (2020, March 2). *Map: Coronavirus and school closures.* https://www.edweek.org/leadership/map-coronavirus-and-school-closures-in-2019-2020/2020/03

Facing History and Ourselves. (2020, July 21). *Abolitionist teaching and the pursuit of educational freedom: A conversation with Dr. Bettina Love.* New York, NY. https://www.facinghistory.org/

Gabriel, M. L. (2011). *Voices of Hispanic and Latina/o secondary students in Northern Colorado: Poetic counterstories.* http://hdl.handle.net/10217/70439

Gabriel, M. L. (2017). Building bridges or isolating families: When school policies conflict with cultural beliefs, values, and ways of knowing. In A. Esmail, A. Pitre, & A. Aragon (Eds.) (2017), Perspectives on Diversity, Equity, and Social Justice in Educational Leadership (pp. 99-114). Lanham, MD: Rowman & Littlefield.

Gabriel, M. L. (2019). Foreword. In M. C. Whitaker & K. M. Valtierra (Eds.), *Schooling multicultural teachers: A guide for program assessment and professional development* (pp. xvii–xix). Emerald Publishing.

Gabriel, M. L. (2021). Latina leading: Un testimonio toward self-love. In Latinas leading schools: A volume in Hispanics in education and administration (pp. 17-32). Charlotte, NC: Information Age Publishing.

Gorski, P. C. (2019). Racial battle fatigue and activist burnout in racial justice activists of color at predominantly White colleges and universities. *Race, Ethnicity and Education, 22*(1), 1–20. doi:10.1080/13613324.2018.1497966

Gorski, P. C., & Erakat, N. (2019). Racism, whiteness, and burnout in antiracism movements: How white racial justice activists elevate burnout in racial justice activists of color in the United States. *Ethnicities, 19*(5), 784–808. doi:10.1177/1468796819833871

Gregory, A., Skiba, R. J., & Noguera, P. A. (2010). The achievement gap and the discipline gap: Two sides of the same coin? *Educational Researcher, 39*(59), 59–68. http:// doi:10.3102/0013189X09357621

Guzmán, B. (2012). Cultivating a guerrera spirit in Latinas: The praxis of mothering. *Association of Mexican-American Educators (AAME) Journal, 6*(1), 45–51. https://amaejournal.utsa.edu/index.php/AMAE/article/view/101

Howard, G. R. (2006). *We can't teach what we don't know: White teachers, multiracial schools* (2nd ed.). Teachers College Press, Columbia University.

Jagers, R. J., Rivas-Drake, D., & Borowski, T. (2018, November). *Equity and social emotional learning: A cultural analysis.* https://measuringsel.casel.org/wp-content/uploads/2018/11/Frameworks-Equity.pdf

Jagers, R. J., Rivas-Drake, D., & Williams, B. (2019). Transformative Social and Emotional Learning (SEL): Toward SEL in Service of Educational Equity and Excellence. *Educational Psychologist, 54*(3), 162–184. doi:10.1080/00461520.2019.1623032

Julig, C. (2020, July 9). *Loveland community kitchen vandalized with anti BLM graffiti.* https://www.reporterherald.com/2020/07/09/loveland-community-kitchen-vandalized-with-anti-blm-graffiti/

Kingkade, T. (2020). *How one teacher's Black lives matter lesson divided a small Wisconsin town.* https://www.nbcnews.com/news/us-news/how-one-teacher-s-black-lives-matter-lesson-divided-small-n1244566

Ladson-Billings, G. (1995). But that's just good teaching: The case for culturally responsive teaching. *Theory into Practice, 34*(3), 159–165. doi:10.1080/00405849509543675

Ladson-Billings, G. (1998). Just what is critical race theory and what's it doing in a nice field like education? *International Journal of Qualitative Studies in Education: QSE, 11*(1), 7–24. doi:10.1080/095183998236863

Ladson-Billings, G. (2006). Foreword. In A. D. Dixson & C. K. Rousseau (Eds.), *Critical race theory in education: All God's children got a song* (pp. v–xiii). Routledge Taylor & Francis Group.

Latina Feminist Group. (2001). *Living to tell: Latina feminist testimonios.* Duke University Press.

Madda, M. J. (2019, May 15). *Dena Simmons: Without context, social emotional learning can backfire.* https://www.edsurge.com/news/2019-05-15-dena-simmons-without-context-social-emotional-learning-can-backfire

McNamarah, C. T. (2019). White caller crime: Racialized police communication and existing while Black. *Michigan Journal of Race & Law, 24,* 335–415. https://repository.law.umich.edu/mjrl/vol24/iss2/5

Méndez-Morse, S., Murakami, E. T., Byrne-Jiménez, M., & Hernandez, F. (2015). Mujeres in the principal's office: Latina school leaders. *Journal of Latinos and Education, 14*(3), 171–187. doi:10.1080/15348431.2014.973566

Murakami, E. T., Hernandez, F., Méndez-Morse, S., & Byrne-Jimenez, M. (2016). Latina/o school principals: Identity, leadership and advocacy. *International Journal of Leadership in Education, 19*(3), 280–299. doi:10.1080/13603124.2015.1025854

Murakami, E. T., Hernandez, F., Valle, F., & Almager, I. (2018). Latina/o school administrators and the intersectionality of professional identity and race. *SAGE Open, 8*(2), 1–16. doi:10.1177/2158244018776045

New York, N. B. C. (2020, July 6). *Amy Cooper, woman who called police on Black man in Central Park, charged.* https://www.youtube.com/watch?v=ilG3NpUn4IU

Nix, N. (2020). *Trump tells violent far-right group: Stand back and stand by.* https://www.bloomberg.com/news/articles/2020-09-30/trump-proud-boys-debate-stand-back-stand-by

PBS Wisconsin Education. (2020, June 30). *Building culturally relevant schools post-pandemic with Dr. Gloria Ladson-Billings.* https://www.youtube.com/watch?v=Rr2monteBbo

Pérez Huber, L. (2010). Using Latina/o critical race theory (LatCrit) and racist nativism to explore intersectionality in the educational experiences of undocumented Chicana college students. *Educational Foundations*, 77–96.

Pierce, C. M. (1995). Stress analogs of racism and sexism: Terrorism, torture, and disaster. In C. V. Willie, P. P. Ricker, B. M. Kramer, & B. S. Brown (Eds.), *Mental health, racism, and sexism* (pp. 277–293). University of Pittsburgh Press.

RAGE Project. (2019). https://www.rageproject.org/background

Ramírez, P., & González, G. (2012). Latina teacher agency in public schools: Love, tensions, and perseverance. *Association of Mexican-American Educators (AMAE) Journal*, 6(1), 34–44.

Reeve, E. (2020, November 25). *He's an ex-Proud Boy. Here's what he says happens within the group's ranks.* https://www.cnn.com/2020/11/25/us/ex-proud-boys-member/index.html

Simmons, D. (2019). Why we can't afford whitewashed social-emotional learning. *ASCD Education Update, 16*(4). http://www.ascd.org/publications/newsletters/education_update/apr19/vol61/num04/Why_We_Can't_Afford_Whitewashed_Social-Emotional_Learning.aspx

Smith, W. A., Allen, W. R., & Danley, L. L. (2007). 'Assume the position. . . You fit the description': Psychological experiences and racial battle fatigue among African American male college students. *The American Behavioral Scientist, 51*(4), 551–578. doi:10.1177/0002764207307742

Smith, W. A., Yosso, T. J., & Solórzano, D. G. (2006). Challenging racial battle fatigue on historically white campuses: a critical race examination of race-related stress. In C. A. Stanley (Ed.), *Faculty of Color: Teaching in predominantly White colleges and universities* (pp. 299–327). Anker Publishing.

Solórzano, D., & Delgado Bernal, D. (2001). Examining transformational resistance through a critical race and LatCrit theory framework: Chicana and Chicano students in an urban context. *Urban Education, 36*(3), 308–342. doi:10.1177/0042085901363002

Solórzano, D. G., & Yosso, T. J. (2009). Critical race methodology: Counter-storytelling as an analytic framework for educational research. In E. Taylor, D. Gillborn, & G. Ladson-Billings (Eds.), *Foundations of critical race theory in education* (pp. 131–147). Routledge.

Stovall, D. (2006). Forging community in race and class: Critical race theory and the quest for social justice in education. *Race, Ethnicity and Education, 9*(3), 243–259. doi:10.1080/13613320600807550

Tayloe, L. (2016). *A study of Latina K-12 public school administrators: Barriers and strategies to career advancement and the impact of race and gender on ascension and leadership.* http://ezproxy.flsouthern.edu:2048/login?url=https://ezproxy.flsouthern.edu:2297/docview/1870038156?accountid=27315

Tayloe, L. (2017). *Hablando de ellas: Experiences of Latina K-12 Public School Administrators with Race and Gender.* MujeresTalk.

Teaching While White Staff. (2020, December 16). *Resisting the pushback against the work for racial equity and justice.* https://www.teachingwhilewhite.org/blog/resisting-the-pushback-against-the-work-for-racial-equity-and-justicenbsp

The Trevor Project. (2020). *The Trevor project research brief: Latinx LGBTQ youth suicide risk.* https://www.thetrevorproject.org/wp-content/uploads/2020/09/Latinx-LGBTQ-Youth-Suicide-Risk-Sept-2020-Research-Brief.pdf

United States Department of Justice and United States Department of Education. (2017). *Dear Colleague Letter.* https://www2.ed.gov/about/offices/list/ocr/letters/colleague-201702-title-ix.pdf

Urrieta, L. J. Jr, & Villenas, S. A. (2013). The legacy of Derrick Bell and Latino/a education: A critical race testimonio. *Race, Ethnicity and Education, 16*(4), 514–535. doi:10.1080/13613324.2013.817771

Vestal, C. (2020). *Racism is a public health crisis, say cities and counties.* https://www.pewtrusts.org/en/research-and-analysis/blogs/stateline/2020/06/15/racism-is-a-public-health-crisis-say-cities-and-counties

Villalpando, O. (2004, Spring). Practical considerations of critical race theory and Latino critical theory for Latino college students. *New Directions for Student Services, 105*(105), 41–50. doi:10.1002s.115

West, J. (2020, June 13). *Colorado State football player held at gunpoint by man thinking he was with antifa.* https://www.si.com/college/2020/06/13/colorado-state-football-player-held-gunpoint-antifa

Westside News. (2020, September 13). *Spencerport administrator placed on leave following controversial social media video.* https://westsidenewsny.com/schools/2020-09-13/spencerport-administrator-placed-on-leave-following-controversial-social-media-video/

Will, M., & Schwartz, S. (2020, June 1). *Teachers cannot be silent: How educators are supporting black students after protests.* https://www.edweek.org/teaching-learning/teachers-cannot-be-silent-how-educators-are-supporting-black-students-after-protests/2020/06

Yosso, T. J. (2006). *Critical race counterstories along the Chicana/Chicano educational pipeline.* Taylor & Francis Group.

KEY TERMS AND DEFINITIONS

Black Indigenous and People of Color (BIPOC): Individuals who identify as members of various racial and ethnic backgrounds defined as Black, Indigenous, and other non-white communities.

Counter-Story/Counterstory: A story told by a person with a traditionally marginalized perspective to shed light and bring understanding to culturally, linguistically, or racially diverse experiences. Both of these spellings are found in the literature.

Diversity, Equity, and Inclusion (DEI): Efforts aimed at increasing the diverse representation of people within a system that include striving for equitable outcomes and engaging inclusive and affirming practices.

Majoritarian Narrative: The narrative held, maintained, and perpetuated by power brokers about people they may have no affiliation or relationship with.

Racial Microaggressions: Unconscious or conscious verbal slights or physical interactions that highlight the superiority over another person related to their perceived or actual racial background.

Sociopolitical Context: the undergirding beliefs of systems that create and support regulations, policies, conditions, laws, practices, traditions, and events within a named context.

White Caller Crime: Placing a phone call to leverage support from law enforcement when People of Color are reported for daily activities that are not criminal.

Chapter 2
Leading for Liberation:
How Black and Brown Leaders Navigate Oppression

Laurie D. Inman
California State University, Dominguez Hills, USA

Kitty M. Fortner
California State University, Dominguez Hills, USA

ABSTRACT

The narratives in this chapter provide the reader with the perspectives of seven Black and Brown leaders who have experienced oppression in the workplace. Their stories highlight the depth of institutionalized oppression that exists in P-12 settings and the effect it has on health, family, and work performance. Nonetheless, these leaders have learned to navigate oppressive environments and engage in transformative practices. The purpose of the research was to gain an understanding of how Black and Brown leaders work through the daily challenges stemming from systemic oppression. Reading the authentic lived experiences of the participants can inspire others to be empowered and find hope.

INTRODUCTION

Workplace challenges for Black and Brown people are complex situations that arise from varying forms of discriminatory practices. These practices are often systemic forms of oppression that affect health and work performance creating constraints to their ability to make efficacious changes. Oppression is present in many institutions of society–the legal system, the education system, hiring policies, public policies,

DOI: 10.4018/978-1-7998-7235-1.ch002

housing development, media images, and political power (Chinook Fund, 2015). Changing this paradigm requires active engagement, courage, and determination by leaders who challenge the status quo. In these unprecedented moments defined by the COVID-19 pandemic and racist aggressions, Black and Brown leadership is critical for dismantling inequities and challenging oppressive behaviors that impact the most marginalized groups in society.

To gather current and relevant information on this topic, the authors invited Black and Brown leaders who work in the field of education to narrate their lived experiences. These leaders understand first-hand the racial, cultural, and individual oppression in workspaces. Despite the microaggressions, biases, and racism, these leaders have found ways to navigate this space and address racial, cultural, and other types of oppression in their workplaces.

This chapter seeks to answer the question of how leaders of color navigate the racial and cultural oppression in their workspaces. Using related literature on the topics of oppression, transformative leadership, and leaders of color, this research will clarify and illuminate how Black and Brown leaders navigate oppression and result in recommendations relative to the transformation of workspaces to inclusive and safe spaces. While the contents of this chapter will focus on public education in the P-12 arena, it also offers ideas that will add to the conversation and identify behaviors that any entity actively seeking to address inequities in their organization can use to enact transformative change.

BACKGROUND

Every day, leaders of color have to navigate the racial and cultural oppression that is manifested in their workspaces. During the interviews of seven leaders, the authors posed several questions, including but not limited to how oppression is defined, what practices and policies perpetuate injustices, how oppression impacts their abilities to influence change in their organizations, and what dispositions they foster and embrace to guide and facilitate just and equitable change. The authors used five faces of oppression (Young, 2004) and transformative leadership (Shields, 2013, 2018, 2020) as theoretical frameworks to identify and name oppression, as well as to categorize the respondents' leadership as liberating. Critical race theory (CRT), as a lens for analyzing their narratives, describes the impact of race and racism on their daily lives.

Oppression

Leaders of color face a multitude of issues and problems in their daily work. With a keen focus on instruction, student achievement, faculty/staff morale, and family engagement, little time is left to attend to their own experience. Daily reflections focus on others, rather than self, and the issues that personally impact their well-being are not the priority. Through all of this, Black and Brown leaders navigate spaces that are inequitable, unjust, and oppressive.

Oppression by dictionary definition is "unjust or cruel exercise of authority; something that oppresses, especially in being an unjust or excessive exercise of power; a sense of being weighed down in body or mind" ("Oppression," n.d.). Furthermore, Hannah et al. (2000) described force and deprivation as two modalities of oppression. As actions of oppression, force and deprivation are detrimental physically, psychologically, and emotionally. To be imposed upon, forced, or coerced by those more powerful and/or privileged creates oppressive conditions similar to that of being deprived. Oppression can also be intentional and unintentional, done consciously or unconsciously, and, whether overt and blatant or subtle and covert, it is a manifestation of power and privilege.

Microaggressions and Bias as Oppression

Some of the most common oppressive behaviors come in the form of microaggressions, which, according to Sue et al. (2007), are intentional and unintentional insults towards individuals in marginalized groups that are derogatory, negative, and/or hostile messages enacted in their daily life. These verbal and nonverbal slights create oppressive environments that manifest inequities and injustices that invalidate the identity and reality of the marginalized group or "reflect the active manifestation of oppressive worldviews that create, foster, and enforce marginalization" (Sue, 2010, p.5). Microaggressions are often based on thoughts, belief, feelings, and attitudes also known as biases that are determinate of actions. Actions can either privilege or discriminate groups of people. Biases are said to be explicit, if they are consciously endorsed, or implicit, if they are rooted in the subconscious. A few types of biases that exist are towards race (Greenwald et al., 1998), body type (Buhlmann et al., 2011), gender (Eagly & Wood, 2012), and sexual orientation (Cullen & Barnes-Holmes, 2008).

Microaggressions can take shape in three different ways, as microinsults, microassaults, and microinvalidations (Sue et al., 2007). Regardless of the differences, these actions create a challenge in the environment that can affect mindset and trivialize existence of race and culture. Microassaults are the most intentional of microaggressions because they are based on conscious biased beliefs held by the individual expressing his/her values from a place of privilege and power. Statements to a marginalized person or group are directly and publicly made to devalue them unapologetically. In contrast, microinsults usually occur unintentionally through subtle slurs or snubs that are given as compliments, when they are effectually demeaning. The authors, as women of color, have been told that "we are a credit to our race" many times, as an illustration of this. Microinsults can also be found in daily environmental factors and conditions that send messages of inferiority to people of color. Similar to microinsults, microinvalidations are not always conscious or intentional acts; however, these are perhaps the most dangerous and disingenuous of all because they deny and devalue the entire existence of the targeted person or group. Consider the statement of someone saying they do not see color; their colorblindness denies the race, culture, and lived experiences of the individual receiving their biased thoughts.

Sue et al. (2007) cited Abelson et al.'s (1998) work demonstrating "empirical evidence exists showing that racial microaggressions become automatic because of cultural conditioning and that they may become connected neurologically with the processing of emotions that surround prejudice" (p. 277). Research also shows that microaggressions result in psychological harm that affects a person for his/her lifetime and creates disparities, inequities, and injustices. Microaggressions as acts of oppression can occur because of gender, sexual orientation, age, disability, and other –isms. However, this chapter will focus on race, ethnicity, and culture with the caveat that it is difficult to separate these factors due to the nature of intersectionality (Crenshaw, 2018). While Crenshaw's work centers on the intersection of race and sex, specifically for Black women, intersectionality is a concept that considers the multiple identities of individuals of whom many are oppressed.

Levels of Oppression

A conversation about oppression would be incomplete without discussing the levels of oppression–interpersonal, institutional, and internalized. David and Derthick (2018) suggested that "interpersonal oppression is driven by and expressed as *Biased CAB*, wherein C is cognition for stereotypes, A is affect for prejudice, and B is behavior for discrimination" (pp. 10-11). The most blatant, conscious, and intentional act against an African American is being called the "N" word by a White person; it is an oppression that is both historical and current.

Institutional oppression is seen in institutions and organizations through their policies, practices, guidelines, and regulations, whereby the entire system has made inequities relevant and, in some cases, legal. The educational system is a prime example of this type of oppression.

Internalized oppression can be just as detrimental to marginalized people because it is derived from the remnants of historical oppression endured by one's ancestors and people. This is not due to a direct act of oppression, but rather an experience of attributional ambiguity described by Sue et al. (2007). This leads to an oppressed person blaming himself/herself for the acts put upon them, believing that they are experiencing something that has not happened. This leads to anger and, in some cases, choosing to turn against their own social group, who are the oppressed. An example of this would be a common occurrence in schools, when a parent of a marginalized group presents as an angry, loud individual and an administrator of the same group vilifies the behavior.

Five Faces of Oppression

Iris Young (2004) articulated a model to describe different forms that oppression takes. She called her model the five faces of oppression; this model qualitatively describes how oppression operates. The fundamental idea that the first concept of exploitation conveys is the understanding that oppression occurs through the continual practice of transferring the results of the labor of one social group to benefit another. Exploitation enacts "social rules about what work is, who does what for whom, how work is compensated, and the social process by which the results of work are appropriated," (Young, 2004, p. 50) which, in turn, establishes unbalanced relationships of power and inequality. "Marginalization raises basic structural issues of justice, in particular concerning the appropriateness of a connection between participation in productive activities of social cooperation, on the one hand, and access to the means of consumption, on the other" (Young, 2004, p. 55). The next face of oppression, powerlessness, speaks to the lack of authority or power of a group when it comes to "making decisions that affect the conditions of their lives and actions" (Young, 2004, p. 56). The concept of cultural imperialism is the valuing and enforcement of the dominant group's culture, norms, and characteristics as the norm. Those experiencing cultural imperialism suffer as the dominant group reinforces its position by bringing the other groups under the measure of its dominant norms. "The dominant meanings of a society render the particular perspective of one's own group invisible at the same time as they stereotype one's group and mark it out as the Other" (Young, 2004, p. 56). The final concept of violence includes random unprovoked attacks (physical, sexual, and emotional) and the threat of violence. This may be found in the policies and structures that tolerate and condone violence against particular groups. Violence is systemic because it targets group members for no other reason than they belong to that group. Violence is a social practice whereby everyone knows it occurs repeatedly and is continually on the minds of both the dominant and nondominant groups (Young, 2004).

Critical Race Theory as a Lens to Examine Portraitures of Leadership

CRT is used as a lens to observe the influence of race, power, lived experiences, and structures (Collins, 2000; Young, 2004). CRT necessitates the understandings that: (1) Racism operates and has deep roots in both society and organizations whereby racism (and oppression) is normalized (Bell, 1995b; Bonilla-Silva, 2011); (2) the dominate culture and white supremacy is positioned to protect the ideals, rights, privileges, and preferences of those perceived by society as more valuable (Harris, 1995); (3) interest convergence hinders the social progress for people of color (Bell, 1995a); (4) intersectionality and antiessentialism are critical concepts to be addressed (Ladson-Billings, 2013); (5) counternarratives are necessary to disrupt the power dynamic (Brown & Jackson 2013; Delgado et al., 2017; Ladson-Billings, 2013; Zamudio et al., 2011). CRT critiques white supremacy and the power structures that support it (Crenshaw et al.,1995; Delgado, 1989; Lynn & Dixson, 2013; Zamudio et al., 2011). CRT centers race and racism in the analyses of oppression, understanding that the lived racialized experiences of Black and Brown leaders have been woven into the fabric of current society. CRT also prioritizes and validates the voices and narratives of groups experiencing oppression. Finally, CRT is dedicated to bringing forward socially just narratives and dismantling inequitable systems.

PORTRAITURES OF LEADERSHIP

CRT stresses the importance of narratives of people of color as a means to describe, understand, and challenge racial oppression (Crenshaw et.al., 1995; Delgado & Stefanic, 2001). In this study, the authors utilized narrative inquiry, a qualitative form of research that allows the participants to use authentic voice to speak about their lived experience as educational leaders. Using semistructured interviews to collect data in the form of rich descriptions of the participants' experiences, these three-dimensional narratives contain the following elements:

1. **Interaction:** The participants look inward to internal conditions, feelings, hopes, and dispositions and outward to existential conditions in their environment and the intentions, purposes, assumptions, and points of view of others.
2. **Continuity:** The participants recount their stories steeped in their understanding of the past, present, and future.
3. **Situation:** The participants share their view within the physical landscape, context, time, and place situated in a setting bound by characters, intentions, purposes, and different points of view (Creswell & Guetterman, 2019).

The participants were allowed to be as specific and clear as they needed to be to describe their lived experiences. Further prompting from the investigators ensured the questions were thoroughly addressed. Using CRT as the critical lens for analyzing the narratives of these participants and the five faces of oppression as the theoretical framework to situate their experiences, an examination of the leadership journey of seven Black and Brown leaders of color will show how multiple forms of oppression work in concert to form a unique set of experiences for people of color.

Andrew: They See Me as White

Andrew is a unique leader of color; he is a Caribbean born Generation X male who identifies as Latinx but is perceived by others as White. He is very aware of the privilege that he is sometimes granted because of this perception. However, this same act of privilege and his "righteous indignation" that has come about due to the abuses that he sees are the impetus for his actions, his inner anger, and how he uses it to fight for students of color.

Andrew's first position in a middle school was as a day-to-day substitute just to pay the bills. As an aspiring actor, without steady work, he felt he could use his skills to work with children. His first day proved to be the start of his career in education, with a couple of missteps in between. He has always worked in the same area of Los Angeles, in the secondary school environment, with students of color who are/were blatantly disrespected, disenfranchised, and disciplined without dignity.

Although Andrew presents as a white American male, he is a foreign-born, Spanish speaking, fifth-generation college graduate who comes from a life of privilege. Coming into his work environment, he realized that he previously viewed the world from his family's perspective that everyone was equal. He soon discovered that for students of color "who they are" has been prewritten by the dominant culture. This reality constitutes cultural imperialism that has been institutionalized in the U.S. education system. Students of color, particularly male African Americans, are stereotyped and placed where the dominant majority says they belong. This is also true for Latinx males, so, for Andrew, this does not sit well.

Andrew will state very clearly that he has not experienced oppression as a leader of color; however, he has felt the weight of oppression through the actions enacted upon the students he serves. During his years in one middle school, which he resigned from a total of three times, he saw the inequities that occurred as colleagues did little to provide quality education, support or guidance for the students. He watched how they were quick to call the police without any personal interaction with the students or a fair and impartial investigation.

It was at this point that Andrew decided to shift to counseling and earned a master's degree. He also adopted his first son, with his partner, and this is where Andrew has been oppressed in life. Again, Andrew presents as the average white American heterosexual male, yet he is gay. Andrew remembers a situation in which he clearly experienced all five faces of oppression with microassaults on his sexuality. During a meeting to discuss how to transition sixth grade students into the middle school setting, the group was contemplating student behaviors. The topic of students using the word "gay" with each other and the ensuing arguments/fights came up. Andrew felt it appropriate to share that he is gay, and this could be a topic of discussions to be held with students. One man told Andrew that he found that offensive and did not really care. He added that he found it offensive because Andrew was an adult and should just deal with it. A woman also inquired as to Andrew's feelings when he saw a beautiful woman. Fortunately, a courageous white female colleague supported him and expressed her disgust with the group's reaction. For Andrew, "that meeting dampened my voice for gay, lesbian, bisexual, and transgender children, and, for several years, I did not speak up, until I opened IHS."

Thus, he began his last leadership position as the cofounder and principal of a charter school focused on ensuring the success of students of color by providing more than just an academic site of learning. The school approaches each child as a whole individual with emotional, social, and psychological needs that must also be addressed and supported by a team of caring adults. He continued to use his "white privilege" to fight the district authorizer, the city, and whomever else continued to marginalize his community. Andrew has learned to align his interest with those of the elite white to ensure that students of color are not left behind or destined to fall into the school to prison pipeline. This alignment, called interest convergence, was first put forth by Derrick Bell in 1980, during his retrospective review of the Supreme Court's school desegregation decision (Brown & Jackson, 2013).

Over the years, Andrew's journey has been filled with so many detrimental acts of oppression upon the students he serves, rather than himself, as a leader of color. Andrew vividly recalls the day in 2012, when the stress became so great that he left campus in a wheelchair and vowed to leave education completely. Instead of leaving, he has retreated from site leadership and is currently working on converting his model of supporting the whole teen into a process that all high schools can use to ensure students of color are treated equitably and given every opportunity afforded their White peers. He lives by what his grandmother once told him, "whatever you have, you have a little more to give to those who have less." A completely nonoppressive perspective that allows him to be true to his Latinx heritage, while living in a White majority world.

Heidi: Building Community

Heidi is a Generation X Asian American female and has worked in the field of education for over 30 years. She is a wife, mommy to three children, and currently works as a principal in an elementary school in the Los Angeles area. Her experience in education ranges from elementary to middle school, and she holds a master's degree in post-secondary education, counseling, and student affairs. Her work experience includes research assistant, teacher in a Korean Dual Language program, English learner Specialist, Testing and Data Coordinator, Secondary Coordinator for English Learners, and assistant principal. She has worked as a school leader for the last 10 years. She believes that she has had to make many sacrifices to get to where she is and would like to help others on this journey to navigate their way.

The demographic of the school where Heidi works is very similar to the district's demographics. Her school serves a diverse population, which is approximately 60% Hispanic/Latinx students and 30% African American students. The remaining population is a mix of Asian and Caucasian students. She works hard to make sure that the students and adults at her school feel valued, comfortable, and recognized. She knows every child at her school by their first name from preschool to 6th grade and has intentional procedures that create a safe and accepting space at her school. She believes that this desire to help students feel a sense of belonging stems from her memories of coming to the U.S. at age 10 and being a newcomer speaking only Korean. She remembers the struggle that she had and how she felt trying to make friends in a space that did not acknowledge her culture. She wants to make sure that all children feel welcome and a part of the school.

For Heidi, oppression is "when you are speaking, but you're not heard...Or when you say something, and it's misconstrued... Or when you want to move up, but you can't." When she describes oppression in her own life, she feels it has manifested in microinsults and microinvalidations based on perceived assumptions about Asian people, as well as her age. Heidi describes herself as a petite Asian woman who looks much younger than her actual age. She feels that her leadership capacity and ability are hampered by the fact that others do not see or respect her authority as the leader of her school. She shared a story of attending a meeting with a male colleague under her supervision and throughout the conversation people would ask for his input as if he was the principal rather than her.

Heidi also acknowledges that she has had to work hard to overcome stereotypical ideas about Asian women and that, if she were a Caucasian man, she would not have had to prove herself in the ways that were required of her as an Asian woman. She stated that, in her district, if a Caucasian male were up for the same job as she was and they both had the same experience and the same work ethic, the job would go to the Caucasian male without a doubt. She feels that she must work twice as hard to show that she is the better candidate. She explained it in this way, "if there's like something, a book, that I want to buy, I'd have to pay twice as much money as a Caucasian person with the same experience. That person might pay $5. I have to pay $10".

Heidi works to reduce oppression at her school by creating a space that recognizes every student individually not because they achieve academic excellence, but because they deserve to be seen and valued as humans. This mindset aligns with Muhammad's (2020) work in her book *Cultivating Genius: An Equity Framework for Culturally and Historically Responsive Literacy*. Muhammad promotes the identity, skills, intellectualism, and criticality to build literacy. Heidi uses this same frame to develop connections for students, so that they can see their own value as well as the value of their classmates. She creates agency for her staff by using the tools of restorative practices to ground the adults in the moment of what is happening outside of the school site, so that they can address the consequences within the school site. One example of an action taken during the pandemics of 2020 (i.e., COVID 19, racism, economic– unemployment, climate catastrophe), specifically when George Floyd was murdered, was to dedicate time and a space for people to talk about what was not being said. She asked people to "talk about the elephant in the room," about what events taking place in the U.S. meant to each of them, for the students at their school, the communities they served and for the country. Additionally, she asked how they would, as a community of educators, address this with their students.

She believes that to combat the social emotional load that is prevalent in the current time, it is important to be available for teachers, parents, and students. Her disposition to address issues of equity and access stems from a heart to serve. She recognizes the struggles that she has had with others and uses her experiences to help others navigate difficult situations.

Katherine: Under a Microscope

Katherine is an African American Generation X female with district and charter school experience. She began her career in education as a long-term substitute teacher 22 years ago; yet, most of her experiences have been in leadership roles. When asked about her transition into her current leadership role, Katherine shared that it was almost seamless going from principal in a district school to her directorship at a South Los Angeles charter organization. Most of the organizations for which she has worked are/were led by leaders of color, which may account for the smooth transitions.

Although the demographic at the charter school is 51% Latinx, the school was previously known for the larger African American population of students, which was by design. Katherine has found that, as this shift in race/ethnicity has occurred, she feels that she is "under a microscope," now more than ever. She also feels that being an African American leader in this community is a double-edged sword–on one hand, she is frustrated with "her people," and on the other hand she is committed to fully supporting them with compassion for their situations. This commitment follows Tillman's (2004) findings about African American leaders' style due to same-race affiliation.

Over the years, Katherine has consistently felt the pressure to do everything by the book, because "you know that we have to shine above and beyond to be at the same level." This is a prime example of how exploitation plays out in leadership for leaders of color. There is an underlying notion that one must prove oneself worthy of holding a position of authority unlike the dominant White culture where it seems to be a given that the work will be done well. Additionally, it is a common practice to have a person of color handle additional work of another position, when it goes vacant, without compensation while still having the expectation to do it all well.

In Katherine's case, there is no longer a top executive doing the work; instead, two directors and an operations manager are overseeing all functions and operations of the organization. As the most senior leader in tenure, all Executive Director functions fall on Katherine, and she has identified the structural challenges that are inherent in her work. She has learned to reach out for support, as there is none available within the system. While she does feel accepted and respected, Katherine does note that, while collectively the organization is largely African American, there is not an uplifting of the culture, and this has been disheartening for her. "We (African Americans) feel like we can't stand out or we can't be unapologetic or we can't fight for ourselves." Whether it be societal norms or institutional practices, the marginalization still occurs in P-12 environments.

She has also felt that she has been held down and held back–she has not always been able to demonstrate what she is capable of doing - which has felt oppressive over time. However, Katherine shared that she feels it may be more that she is a woman than that she is African American. Crenshaw (1989) would argue that this is the epitome of intersectionality and how difficult it is to separate the essence of who we are. Crenshaw suggested that African American women will have experiences of oppression that are much like those experienced by White women. However, African American women also face double discrimination that is different from both White women and African American men. Katherine may indeed fall into the latter description.

Daniel: Be True to Yourself

Daniel, a first-generation refugee from Vietnam, who identifies as an Asian American male in the Generation X age range. He has worked in education for over 24 years holding a variety of positions in both PK-12 and higher education settings. He began his career in education as a Martial Arts teacher and is now an assistant principal at a middle school in the Los Angeles area. In his reflection of how his ethnicity impacts his work in the various organizations with which he has worked, he stated that it had never occurred to him how few Vietnamese Americans are doing the work he is doing. He believes that his upbringing in the heart of Los Angeles in his mom's nail shop, surrounded by strong Black women, has influenced his work in education and helped him to connect with students and teachers in a powerful way. Daniel's personal definition of oppression

would be when a person or group of persons or an organization is either knowingly or unknowingly projecting onto me an expectation that is either unrealistic confined to a specific ideal that's rooted in an experience that may not be my experience.

Before this interview, Daniel did not consider ethnic oppression in his organization, but, after reflection, it was clearer that oppression can be felt and seen in the organization's structure.

The organization where Daniel works serves predominately Brown students with a couple of Black, Asian, and Caucasian students. However, the organization's upper leadership is predominately Caucasian. The organization brought in an outside auditor to complete an equity audit and the report came back that the school is diverse, but the organization itself is "too White." He stated that the only culture celebrated at his school is for Brown students. There is nothing done to uplift other ethnicities in his organization. There are a few token mentions made about Black History Month or MLK Day, but nothing to let students who are not Brown know that they are valued members of the community. Daniel also noted that often he has suggested ideas for uplifting the other cultures on campus, including his own, and was met with silence. This form of oppression is called cultural imperialism.

Oppression in the form of cultural imperialism can be seen in the idea that the only culture worth celebrating is the culture that the leadership (dominate group) deems worthy. In the organizations where Daniel has worked, he has never had his culture celebrated or acknowledged. He finds that only when people assimilate to the culture of the top-level leadership are they able to promote in the organizations. He spoke about the emotional load that this has caused for him and the tiredness that accompanies this load.

Daniel says that he has felt the powerlessness of being oppressed when told by someone in leadership to withhold information in an attempt to deceive or to say something that deceives people. He also stated that he has been silenced when advocating for issues of equity where organizations are not ready to hear or make the necessary changes due to a conflict in their perception of the issue. The thought that ethnicity plays a part in his upward movement in the organization is something that Daniel says he does not want to believe. However, he feels that marginalization happens in his workplace when it comes to hiring practices and upward movement of people of color. Daniel has been told that upper management is not sure that he is ready and that they are not sure he connects to the community they way that they want him to. He often feels that his organization is resistant to including people of color at the top-level leadership. He likened their ideology as something similar to a savior complex. Only they know what is best for the community, even if they are different from the community that they serve in thought, beliefs, and ethnicity. Even so, Daniel continues to seek a leadership position with his organization.

Daniel has noticed that, as people of color vacated positions, they were replaced with people who are blonde, blue eyed, and mostly females. This past fall, like many organizations, Daniel's organization has provided a statement acknowledging that historically they had been a racist organization and that they are going to work to become an antiracist, proBlack educational organization. Daniel's fear is that, like many other organizations, the actions will not come with these words. He acknowledges that the organization is asking for more voices to participate. An example is that people of color are leading the diversity groups within the organization. However, often the organization takes a defensive approach to what the voices are saying, rather than looking inward to make necessary change. It is business as usual. This is a form of emotional violence that keeps people of color thinking they are making a difference when policies and procedures are staying the same and creating an emotional and psychological load that is at times unbearable. Additionally, he recalled an experience where he was hired into a position where he was not the first pick of the administrator in charge and the stress that it caused. There was no reason for the pressure he was feeling from the management except that they wanted a different person.

Daniel feels that the fact that he has not assimilated into the White culture in the organizations where he has worked creates a struggle and a freedom. He believes that Asian people who assimilate are better able to move in the systems and organizations where he has worked. Taking from Dickens and Chavez's (2017) work, this would be described as *identity shifting*, when one alters his/her actions, speech, and appearance to adjust to cultural norms within a given environment. While their research was conducted in the workspaces of Black women, this oppressive behavior holds true for many people of color. Daniel shared that, when an individual assimilates, he/she can lose himself/herself and his/her purpose. Thus, Daniel pushes against the status quo by working to help people's voice be heard. He believes that communication between management and workers create space for change and growth. For him, there is a need to not only hear the voices but listen to the voices and act upon what the voices are saying. He shared, "when there's a preponderance of voices saying that there's a problem, then there's a problem. Just because you do not want to admit it doesn't mean that there isn't a problem. There's a problem." Recognizing that a problem exists is the first step.

Jonathan: Credibility Is Not Automatic for Us

Jonathan has been in the field of education for 20 years, after a career as a chemical engineer. Holding a Master's in Education and an M.B.A. from Harvard, his dream had always been to bring corporate skills into the field of education. Jon, a Generation X male, is of Caribbean descent and identifies as Black by race and Latinx by ethnicity; yet, he is perceived as Latinx by his colleagues. He also shared that, with his heritage, he does not identify by his race, but rather his culture, and, in fact, he grew up with the term "mulatto," which, during that time, was not a derogatory term. He stated that he grew up "with a naïve perception of what the world is and how it functions," as a result of his developmental years in the Caribbean, New York, and Miami.

The communities in which Jon has worked span both the East and West Cost, as well as private, district, and public charter schools. His work in the private sector did not fulfill his goals of reaching the demographic that he wanted to reach and serve; thus, the change and moves. Jon soon found a pattern of being asked to turn-around and expand charters, which occurred in both Boston, Massachusetts, and in South Los Angeles. As his experiences evidenced, Jon has faced marginalization and cultural imperialism throughout his journey.

When Jon graduated from college at the top of his class and received offers as a chemical engineer, he thought it was based on his qualifications. He vividly remembers being told that he was hired under affirmative action, which immediately offended him, and he turned down that job. However, he quickly learned that, even in the employment of his choice, where he thought he was defining himself based on his achievement, it was the same–they just did not say it. "I was a victim of prejudice and racism and I just didn't even know it. You know I didn't have a clue at the forces that were coming at me."

In his current role of Executive Director of a charter school in Northern California, Jon is in a community that is more affluent than his previous location in Los Angeles. While the transition was seamless and despite his credentials, he did not get the "automatic" credibility and respect that he has consistently afforded his white colleagues. He shared that the concept of White fragility (DiAngelo, 2018) was demonstrated recently in his school, when an African American parent described her anger to a White teacher as being "f-ing pissed." Her irritation lied in the fact that her son was about to go to high school and, after receiving six years of speech services, his impediment had not improved. The white woman took so much offense that she cried to her teammates and demanded that the woman be dealt with by administration. She never took the time to recognize that not providing the child with the required articulation goal and Individual Education Plans minutes was the reason for the outrage; instead, she allowed her entitlement and privilege to guide her actions.

It is this attitude of indifference and invisible lack of acceptance that John identifies as oppression because the limits exist when "the inability to be yourself, having to prove yourself, and fight against the proactive closing of the path that you are on" is constantly present. He feels that oppression "demands that you realize that you are inferior or not good enough for the space and you must act white, so that in order to succeed, you learn the rules and play the game." Perhaps it is as Du Bois (1898) contemplated in his early work that Black Americans possess a "double consciousness" and must navigate their own racial identity as well as White norms.

Jon sees how the inequities are perpetrated in his work environment, which he joined less than six months ago. "I have a group of well-intentioned white ladies that have self-proclaimed themselves the Anti-racist Equity Committee." One of Jon's first actions was to disband the group, and he had to fight his Board of Directors (one African American, the remainder are White) to support him. The group was not needed to revise the curriculum, which would have been based on their beliefs about what is best for their children, as opposed to all children.

In addition, Jon sees the unjust behaviors towards two African Americans placed in critical positions at the school simply because they do not hold advanced degrees. In essence, the two White principals with degrees are held in higher regard than his two organizational leaders, which can be attributed to explicit and implicit biases. Jon says his greatest wish is to see his Black and Brown peers and students seen as a blessing. "Just because your color is different, because your culture is different... you still have a sacred purpose in this life."

Ari: Transforming Communities Using Physical and Mental Wellness

Ari is a Generation X male who identifies as a multiethnic. His ethnicities include White, Arabic, and African American. He says that most people see him as Middle Eastern. He has worked 12 years in the field of education at the community college, university, and now the P-12 level as a coprincipal at a high school. He has worked in both private and public education. The populations he has worked with include students who are Haitian, Hispanic, Black, and special needs. His career in P-12 has always been in charter schools and he has held a variety of leadership positions, such as Department Lead, Restorative Practices Lead Dean of Students, Assistant Principal, Principal, and now is a Coprincipal in charge of instruction. Ari works for generational education, educating a pathway that opens doors and understanding for everyone. Ari believes that to address the oppressive system of prejudice and racism, people need to constantly grow, evolve, and better equip themselves to transform U.S. schools, organizations, and communities.

When Ari talks about his ethnicity, he recalls being the one who always had to check the "other" box because he did not fit just one. As a child, most of his friends were African American, Hispanic, Lebanese, and Cambodian, which influences his identity as a multicultural man. The organization where he works now is also multicultural or multiethnic at all levels. Ari says, "this organization is completely different from any other organization I have worked at." He stated that from top leadership down there is a diverse group leading and working at the organization, even to the point that there are no White teachers on staff at this time. He stated that this is the first time in his life that he has worked for and with people of color. In contrast he described work at previous organizations as "run by White men, business backgrounds, not necessarily educational backgrounds, very White staffs at the home office making decisions for curriculum, for programs." Another contrast between the current organization and previous organizations is that the current organization has much retention and works to develop leadership from within the organization, while previous organizations preferred to hire for leadership positions from outside of the organization and predominately White.

Ari defines oppression as

a system that keeps a group of people from living their lives as they see fit. I think that oppression for me is racism, discrimination, and prejudice. ... It's systematizing those things. It's not just being racist or having prejudice, but it's systematizing and making sure that the structures and the functions of the structures are designed to keep people from actualizing.

Oppression in the form of marginalization can be seen in one of the stories that Ari tells. He recalled a story from high school where he definitely knew that his skin color mattered. He tells the story this way:

I can recall vividly my history teacher my freshman year of high school refusing to give any of the Black or Brown students above a "C." My mom eventually had to have a conference with this woman. It was interesting because when the woman saw my mom, she was just shocked. She was like, "You're his mom? How are you his mom? My grade immediately went up from there... immediately! But I can remember [it was] like the air in the classroom felt different. You felt like you did not belong. You felt like you were not part of the dominant culture. You were not part of what was considered appropriate.

Ari recalls another instance when he was working in an organization, taking on additional roles and putting in extra hours in hopes of moving into the leadership of the organization. He says that he did this for several years until he took a moment to look up, and what he felt was that there was a ceiling and class distinction where, if you were a teacher, then you remained a teacher and there was little chance for moving up into leadership. He talks about the unavailability of upward movement. He did not feel that the people making the decisions were necessarily racist, but that the system itself is racist. This form of oppression is a called exploitation. The oppressor sets the rules that support their needs to get what they want but relegates limits on other cultures that keeps them in a particular space or place.

Ari also remembered a time when oppression took on the face of powerlessness. He shared a story of a time as a special education teacher when he was in a meeting and he made suggestions and proposed ideas and it was if he was not even talking. Even though he was the expert in the room, it was as if he did not have the authority to give that expert advice. For him this was frustrating, and he felt that he had no voice in the process.

Ari stated that oppression has had a huge impact in his life, in negative ways. As he looks back over his life, oppression has had a direct impact on his life in areas such as his general health, eating habits, over stressed, taking on more responsibility and "having less time for myself and my wife," and not being able to find balance in my life. He has friends who have developed various health issues and diseases such as ulcers and diabetes. Since he has become aware of the way that stress affects him, he has become proactive about becoming a healthier person. Ari works to counter oppression in his life by being intentional about finding balance, having positive mindful conversations with family and friends, silencing voices that negate my ability and capacity. In the previous organizations, there were little to no support for the adults to assist them in working through issues of mental and physical wellness. However, in his current organization, there are supports in place for the adults in the organization. There are opportunities to engage in both physical health activities and mental health activities. The counseling the is available for students is also available for the adults on the campuses. He says that he believes that the example modeled by the executive directors about caring for themselves has been extremely beneficial for the organization.

Mae: Hidden Agendas

Mae, like Katherine, is a female African American Generation X female, whose experiences have been more diverse in positions and spaces, but with similar demographics. She has been a science teacher, a teacher of the gifted and talented, an instructional coach, an instructional specialist, and responsible for professional learning and talent management in the human resources department of a large district. For the last six years, she has been a site level principal. She has worked primarily in South Los Angeles with a brief period in a neighboring city. Mae also identifies with her Latinx and Native American heritage, which is important to who she is, especially when working with parents of color. She feels it is an advantage to helping them understand who she is, and she takes pride in mirroring the communities she serves.

Mae has experienced several instances when she lacked the "freedom, capacity, and autonomy" in the workplace. Much of this occurred in the various roles she held while employed in one of the nation's largest school district. Whether she was teaching, providing professional development or leading, the institutionalized oppression has been problematic for her. Imagine riding the elevator with fellow workers and receiving no response when saying good morning. A clear microinvalidation occurred when her department unveiled a new guide for which Mae was a significant contributor to the collaboration. During the well-attended event, Mae was forgotten when the team members were introduced and the guide did not include her name, thereby nullifying her contributions to the project. Intentional or unintentional, blatant, and covert interactions that diminish a person's worth create a space of marginalization and violence.

As a person of color, Mae takes great pride in her accomplishments, once of which was earning her doctoral degree. She has experienced both indifference and a lack of respect as a leader of color when White colleagues have either refused to call her Dr. Mae or intentionally called her Ms. Mae to exert power. Oppression does not truly exist without power and/or privilege and this is an example of how it is enacted. Even after 25 years, Mae feels as if she is not being trusted or respected for what she "brings to the table." She recognizes that it impacts her morale and spirit; yet, what is even more "tragic, it affects the growth and proclivity of that organization." In her opinion, oppression impacts the oppressed and everyone that experiences it, even when they do not know it.

In Mae's current organization, she had high hopes of finding a workspace that would allow her to contribute and serve. Being recommended by a colleague who works in the location, she thought she was going in with her eyes wide open. She quickly found that there was a hidden agenda, which she discovered from the "background noise" that was happening. Mae filled a position which had been previously held by an African American female, who was promoted to a position held by an African American female. The entire leadership of the school, which is predominantly Latinx, is held by African American females–a fact that does not sit well with the Latinx community who is not feeling well represented when decisions are made. Nonetheless, Mae sits in a precarious position because she did not come to fill a space to maintain the status quo in leadership, but to be an asset and contribute to the team.

Even though Mae is a member of the larger leadership structure, she and two others make up the immediate, instructional team. While she feels safe within the "triad" of principals, she does not feel the same with the executive level of leaders, including the colleague who recommended her. Even within an all-Black structure, Mae feels a level of exploitation by the power structure which demonstrates how even a social group that is consistently oppressed can become the oppressor (Hardiman et al., 2007).

After hearing the narratives of these leaders, a few themes emerged for the authors. Many of these leaders consider servantship to students as important to who they are and what they do. Some have experienced physical health issues, and all have felt some level of emotional violence in the form of microaggressions and bias. They all have felt their voices quieted both individually and institutionally. Despite the oppressiveness of their circumstances, it is apparent that each is very resilient. This resiliency has allowed them to extend their abilities and capacity to engage in the use of the tenets of transformative leadership to reconstruct their environments.

TRANSFORMATIVE LEADERSHIP

Transformative leadership (Shields, 2018) is a model of leadership which is focused on critically addressing issues of equity, justice, democracy, and oppression in diverse contexts by acknowledging the existence of the unequal playing field. This model has been applied specifically to school leadership, in which the chasm between socioeconomic levels steadily grows, requiring extraordinary efforts of leaders to dismantle inequities and build just and democratic spaces (Shields, 2018). The tenets of transformative leadership call leaders to make deep and equitable changes as they challenge existing knowledge, address the inequitable distribution of power, promote the collective good, and create agency for others to take action. Additionally, the tenets call leaders to take an activist approach through courageous engagement confronting inequities to address policies, structures, and practices to ensure hope and a more equitable future for all. This section looks at the recommendations from the Black and Brown leaders who participated in this project and their alignment with Shield's tenets of transformative leadership.

The Mandate to Effect Deep and Equitable Change

Andrew has spent his entire career as an educator challenging the status quo steeped in institutional oppression. He recalls a time early in his career when he was asked to remove his name from an opportunity that was based on seniority vs. capacity. Union rules were more important than the administrator's recommendation of the best qualified individual, which was Andrew, in this case. In many situations, he has challenged policies and structures that district leaders had set and that are inequitable and demeaning towards the students he serves. In most circumstances, he has fought against the assumptions, biases, and stereotypes that are omnipresent for is African American and Latinx students.

During the interview, the hurt was apparent in is voice and expressions as he shared story after story of situations when policies, structures, and instructional decisions created inequities for him and his students. He believes that his personal and professional mission is first and foremost to be the voice and advocate for his students, while investing in his faculty and staff. With a focus on improving lives through a holistic approach in the schools he leads, Andrew's commitment to equitable change at the systems level is resounding. "I view systemic issues as mental health issues, because it (mental health) is systemic. I don't care what the law is."

The Need to Deconstruct and Reconstruct Knowledge Frameworks That Perpetuate Inequity and Injustice

For Jon, who has experienced the private and public school systems as well as the corporate sector, inequities have been ever present. He acknowledges that he was a victim of prejudice and racism in many of these workspaces and stated very succinctly that "I don't ever want to have a victim mentality, because that has never been me. But I can also mot be so naive and blind to the fact that systemic racism has impacted me." This reality has affected the way in which he approaches leadership with a more focused and proactive stance at creating agency.

Leaders are finding that critical and difficult conversations are relevant and necessary for equity and change. In his new position, Jon has found that he must have these conversations with his Board, his administrators, faculty, and parents to ensure fair practices. Coming from an environment that is very focused on student's funds of knowledge and rich, cultural, and linguistic resources as a plus, Jon finds that this must be his primary goal in his new school, as they recruit students who do not fit the traditional norm. Providing professional development around equity and antiracism is just one step, but Jon feels it will take so much more. "I'd like to say (during these conversations), let's get real! They may be looking for ED number eight, but I am going to tell them the truth."

A Focus on Emancipation, Democracy, Equity, and Justice

Ari talks about his deep commitment to change the curriculum. He sees the curriculum as a huge part of the problem and is actively involved to ensure a racial justice and antiracist component exist in each lesson. He assists his math teachers to build curriculum that disrupts the racist and oppressive nature of the curriculum. Math teachers are pushed to teach financial literacy, the stock market, generational wealth, and how to accumulate it. He does not want to just educate. He wants to build activists who can carry on this work to change the system, promoting learning environments that are more socially just and equitable. Additionally, Ari talks about building partnerships with parents by "introducing antiracist materials and resources through parent workshops, town halls, and conversations informing parents about marginalization and oppression. Thus, allowing their voices to become a part of the work.

The Need to Address the Inequitable Distribution of Power

Perhaps most prevalent in Andrew's work as a leader of color has been his push against the power structures and, more importantly, how to use that same power to advantage his communities. As a Latinx male who is perceived by others as White, Andrew has been able to push back and challenge the majority voice in spaces that other leaders of color could not. His goal is always about evening the playing field to ensure that all students can benefit and help them understand how to also do this for themselves. Andrew leads with his heart and every action in which he engages demonstrates this clearly.

An Emphasis on Both Private and Public (Individual and Collective) Good

One change that Ari identifies is that schools need to consider the removal of standardized testing. It was one of the first things that was gone when the COVID-19 pandemic occurred. He states, "I understand that it is a part of the American educational system and that funding is tied to it, but it is inherently racist, and opportunities, privileges, and access is relegated to those who make the score." In conversations with the leadership of his organization, they work to eradicate this oppressive system to establish success and empower students to participate as world citizens. Efforts to get parents involved promotes community engagement in school and the school's engagement in the community.

An Emphasis on Interdependence, Interconnectedness, and Global Awareness

Heidi works in her school to help students and adults to build community by providing opportunities for them to share their stories and create a deeper awareness of themselves and others. Students are invited to share their stories during lunch with the principal, and the staff are invited to share at staff meetings. Heidi shared that these practices have created a caring environment within her school campus between students and staff alike. Heidi's determination to create interconnectedness and interdependence stems from her early years as a newcomer who did not have the language to make friends at school. She believes having a sense of community can dismantle inequities and build an understanding of and value for individuals.

The Necessity of Balancing Critique and Promise: Daniel

Although Daniel's understanding of how oppression had impacted his life was limited, he could see how it had impacted the students at the school where he worked. Schools are diverse spaces that have the potential to launch a student into a variety of successful pathways. The promise of success is met often by denial of access, inclusion, and opportunity. Understanding that people can be more critical of themselves and their work, Daniel strives for a position in his organization where his voice can shape policies, structures, and pedagogy that supports student success. Using his voice as a leader to dismantle inequities and to ensure students have access is how he will promote the promise of education.

The Call to Exhibit Moral Courage

Katherine shared the many challenges she faces that diminish opportunities to make significant and lasting changes. It has been difficult to present policies or changes in the organizational structure. However, she has found much success in creating agency in the African American community of learners and their parents. With the changing demographics, Katherine feels that the African American cultural traditions, experiences, and contributions of the children at the school are being forgotten or ignored. The school was originally founded for African American students to ensure they were provided an equitable education and access to what all students should receive. This is one of the reasons that Katherine wanted to work at this particular school to support her community; this is both a conviction and a passion. Shield (2013) referred to this as a leader's "true North." Katherine finds that disrupting marginalizing practices and enacting opportunities to uplift communities of color are nonnegotiables. In the end, Katherine shares, "I feel like collectively, we can be doing more."

RECOMMENDATIONS

The transformation of workspaces requires energy, collaboration, and intentionality at all levels of an organization. The goal of any organization, and in particular U.S. educational system, is to ensure there is no hegemony, oppression or danger to any human being. This means that practices, policies, and structures are challenged, dismantled, reimagined, and/or created. Doing the work requires a mindset of inclusiveness and building safe spaces for all. These seven leaders shared their recommendations for behaviors that any entity actively seeking to address inequities in their organization can utilize to enact transformative change.

Heidi's recommendation to improve working environments is to make connections. Connection at both the work level and the personal level is important, too. When people connect to each other, share with each other, and grow together, they have opportunities to build community and tear down barriers that separate. When she first started her position, Heidi shared her story, and each year after that she has had two teachers share their stories. These sharing opportunities have surfaced many barriers, such as abuse, racialized experiences, assumptions, and stereotyping, as well as constructs that unite, such as going to the same high school or university or enjoying the same vacation spot. She believes that, when people get to know each other connecting through community, lives are changed and oppression is reduced.

Daniel and Mae share the recommendation for improving work environment. They both agree that organizations must intentionally make opportunities to celebrate and promote differences. Organizations should acknowledge the value in each individual and the culture that they bring to the organization.

Communication was a common recommendation from the leaders, and Jon stated that it must be authentic. Communication must take place about common goals, team development, accountability, best practices, and problems of practice, so that everyone is informed and, even more importantly, every voice is not just heard, but included in the decision making.

Several of the leaders recommend that organizations create space and time to have meaningful conversations with the people of the organization, which differs from the communication the authors mentioned above. Daniel suggests that these conversations center around getting to know each other and what each person brings to the organization that can benefit the organization. Doing this will help entities to develop a caring environment, as people get to know each other and learn how to care for each other.

Andrew recommends taking the conversations much deeper into critical conversations about issues such as race and not being afraid to have the uncomfortable conversations. He calls it the "audacity of hope," and encourages organizations to embrace the changes that come with these courageous conversations. He reiterated that it is important to pay attention to "who is not in the room," any time that crucial conversations occur. Andrew, Mae, and Jon all emphatically recommend that safe spaces be purposefully created to make comfortable the ability to say "what needs to be said" without repercussions of losing one's job.

Daniel also recommends that people be themselves and allow others to see the greatness that they bring to organizations. He says that assimilation does make the journey easier, but it also takes much from the persons of color, and often they cannot get back what has been taken. Daniel's final two recommendations are for people to accept it not being perfect and for people to be able to let go: Letting go of the idea of being right, letting go of the idea that everyone needs to think and act the same way, letting go of the stereotypes that they hold about people of color, and accepting that it takes all kinds of people to build great organizations.

Ari's recommendation to organizations is to continually learn and grow, so that they can become antiracist in their foundation. Much work that needs to be done to combat oppression that is prevalent in the system. Organizations should interrogate their systems to find inequities and address them. Organizations need to survey the staff and teachers to find out how to include their voices into the governance of the organization. Organizations should create systems that empower and encourage people to use their voices to create positive change. Sustainable change can only happen when everyone works together. Ari also suggests that organizations look outward and not just inward at what works and try to implement those things into their organization to dismantle oppressive systems within the organization.

A final recommendation is to place more emphasis on mental and physical health. To navigate oppression, people of color need to be healthy in mind and body. This can look like a school organization offering nutrition programs and classes taught by the Physical Education teachers, Mental Health Day where counselors are brought in to support people in trauma or by organizing a weekly or monthly hike where colleagues come together to enjoy each other's company. Ari said:

We are talking about bending a system by asking Black and Brown people to go into positions that have been traditionally held by White people. The space must look different and feel different or it will continue to be an oppressive space. Mental and physical health is a huge part of being able to care for and love ourselves and others.

FUTURE RESEARCH DIRECTIONS

In light of the understandings the authors gathered from the portraitures of the Black and Brown leaders who participated in this research, it is imperative to continue to gather recommendations from the voices that are doing this work. More research should be completed with specific questions that address the actions behind the recommendations giving examples of how to accomplish this work. When thinking about oppression and how Black and Brown leaders navigate it, the understanding of the many facets of this work opens a gateway for other research projects that can support and assist organizations, as well as the people of color who are doing the work.

CONCLUSION

In conclusion, even in the 21st century, Black and Brown leaders face oppression in their work environments. The leaders that the authors portrayed in this study have faced a lack of credibility and disregard for their knowledge, experiences, and talents. Their voices have been ignored and quieted through power and privilege. Prejudice, discrimination, and racism have impacted them professionally and personally. Through it all, they work every day to navigate their environment with actions and behaviors that are challenging the status quo and focused on equitable change. They are transformative leaders.

REFERENCES

Abelson, R. P., Dasgupta, N., Park, J., & Banaji, M. R. (1998). Perceptions of the collective other. *Personality and Social Psychology Review*, 2(4), 243-250. https://doi-org.libproxy.csudh.edu/10.1207/s15327957pspr0204_2

Bell, D. A. (1995a). Brown v Board of Education and the interest convergence dilemma. In Critical race theory: The key writings that formed the movement (pp. 20-28). The New Press.

Bell, D. A. (1995b). Racial realism. In Critical race theory: The key writings that formed the movement (pp. 302-314). The New Press.

Bonilla-Silva, E., & Dietrich, D. (2011). The sweet enchantment of color-blind racism in Obamerica. *The Annals of the American Academy of Political and Social Science*, 634(1), 190–206. doi:10.1177/0002716210389702

Brown, K., & Jackson, D. (2013). The history and conceptual elements of critical race theory. In M. Lynn & A. D. Dixson (Eds.), *Handbook of critical race theory in education* (pp. 9–22). Routledge.

Buhlmann, U., Teachman, B. A., & Kathmann, N. (2011). Evaluating implicit attractiveness beliefs in body dysmorphic disorder using the Go/No-go Association Task. *Journal of Behavior Therapy and Experimental Psychiatry*, *42*(2), 192–197. doi:10.1016/j.jbtep.2010.10.003 PMID:21315881

Chinook Fund. (2015). *General terms and forms of oppression*. https://chinookfund. org/wp-content/uploads/2015/10/Supplemental-Information-for-Funding-Guidelines.pdf

Collins, P. H. (2000). *Black feminist thought knowledge, consciousness, and the politics of empowerment*. Routledge.

Crenshaw, K. (2018). Demarginalizing the intersection of race and sex: A Black feminist critique of antidiscrimination doctrine, feminist theory, and antiracist politics. *Feminist Legal Theory*, 57-80. doi:10.4324/9780429500480-5

Crenshaw, K., Gotanda, N., Peller, G., & Thomas, K. (Eds.). (1995). *Critical race theory: The key writings that formed the movement*. New Press.

Creswell, J. W., & Guetterman, T. C. (2019). *Educational research: Planning, conducting, and evaluating quantitative and qualitative research* (6th ed.). Pearson.

Cullen, C., & Barnes-Holmes, D. (2008). Implicit pride and prejudice: A heterosexual phenomenon. In M. A. Morrison & T. G. Morrison (Eds.), *The psychology of modern prejudice* (pp. 195–223). Nova Science Publishers.

David, E. J. R., & Derthick, A. O. (2018). *The psychology of oppression*. Springer.

Delgado, R. (1989). Storytelling for oppositionists and others: A plea for narrative. *Michigan Law Review*, *87*(8), 2411–2441. doi:10.2307/1289308

Delgado, R., Stefancic, J., & Harris, A. P. (2017). *Critical race theory: An introduction*. New York University Press.

DiAngelo, R. J. (2018). *White fragility: Why it's so hard for white people to talk about racism*. Beacon Press.

Dickens, D. D., & Chavez, E. L. (2017). Navigating the workplace: The costs and benefits of shifting identities at work among early career U.S. Black women. *Sex Roles, 78*, 760-774. doi:10.100711199-017-0844-x

Du Bois, W. E. B. (1898). The study of the Negro problems. *The Annals of the American Academy of Political and Social Science, 568*(1), 13–27. doi:10.1177/000271620056800103

Eagly, A. H., & Wood, W. (2012). Social role theory. In P. van Lange, A. Kruglanski, & E. T. Higgins (Eds.), *Handbook of theories in social psychology* (pp. 458–476). Sage Publications. doi:10.4135/9781446249222.n49

Greenwald, A. G., McGhee, D. E., & Schwartz, J. L. (1998). Measuring individual differences in implicit cognition: The implicit association test. *Journal of Personality and Social Psychology, 74*(6), 1464–1480. doi:10.1037/0022-3514.74.6.1464 PMID:9654756

Hanna, F. J., Talley, W. B., & Guindon, M. H. (2000). The power of perception: Toward a model of cultural oppression and liberation. *Journal of Counseling and Development, 78*(4), 430–466. doi:10.1002/j.1556-6676.2000.tb01926.x

Hardiman, R., Jackson, B., & Griffin, P. (2007). Conceptual foundations for social justice education. In M. Adams, L. A. Bell, & P. Griffin (Eds.), Teaching for diversity and social justice (pp. 35–66). Routledge/Taylor & Francis Group.

Harris, C. I. (1995). Racial realism. In K. Crenshaw, K. Thomas, G. Peller, & N. Gotanda (Eds.), *Critical race theory: the key writings that formed the movement* (pp. 276–291). The New Press.

Ladson-Billings, G. (2013). Critical race theory– What it is not! In M. Lynn & A. D. Dixson (Eds.), *Handbook of critical race theory in education* (pp. 34–47). Routledge.

Lynn, M., & Dixson, A. D. (2013). *Handbook of critical race theory in education*. Routledge. doi:10.4324/9780203155721

Muhammad, G. (2020). *Cultivating genius: An equity framework for culturally and historically responsive literacy*. Scholastic Inc.

Oppression. (n.d.). In *Merriam-Webster.com dictionary*. https://www.merriam-webster.com/dictionary/oppression

Shields, C. M. (2013). *Transformative leadership in education: Equitable change in an uncertain and complex world*. Routledge.

Shields, C. M. (2018). *Transformative leadership in education: Equitable change in an uncertain and complex world* (2nd ed.). Routledge.

Shields, C. M. (2020). *Becoming a transformative leader: A guide to creating equitable schools*. Routledge.

Sue, D. W. (2010). *Microaggressions and marginality: Manifestation, dynamics, and impact*. Wiley.

Sue, D. W., Capodilupo, C. M., Torino, G. L., Bucceri, J. M., Holder, A. M. B., Nadal, K. L., & Esquilin, M. (2007). Racial microaggressions in everyday life: Implications for clinical practice. *The American Psychologist*, *62*(4), 271–286. doi:10.1037/0003-066X.62.4.271 PMID:17516773

Tillman, L. C. (2004). African American principals and the legacy of Brown. *Review of Research in Education*, *28*(1), 101–146. doi:10.3102/0091732X028001101

Young, I. M. (2004). Five faces of oppression. In L. M. Heldke & P. O'Connor (Eds.), *Oppression, privilege, and resistance: Theoretical perspectives on racism, sexism, and heterosexism* (pp. 174–195). McGraw-Hill.

Zamudio, M., Russel, C., Rios, F., & Bridgeman, J. L. (2011). *Critical race theory matters: Education and ideology*. Routledge. doi:10.4324/9780203842713

ADDITIONAL READING

Ahmed, S. (2012). *On being included: Racism and diversity in institutional life*. Duke University Press. doi:10.1215/9780822395324

Delpit, L. (2019). *Teaching when the world is on fire*. The New Press.

Ishimaru, A. M. (2020). *Just schools: Building equitable collaborations with families and communities*. Teachers College Press.

Johnson, A. G. (2017). *Privilege, power, and difference*. McGraw-Hill.

Lourde, A. (1999) *There is no hierarchy in oppression*. http://www.pages.drexel.edu/~jc3962/COR/Hierarchy.pdf

Love, B. L. (2019). *We want to do more than survive: Abolitionist teaching and the pursuit of educational freedom*. Beacon Press.

Oluo, I. (2019). *So, you want to talk about race*. Seal Press.

Tatum, B. D. (2017). *Why are all the Black kids sitting together in the cafeteria?* Basic Books.

KEY TERMS AND DEFINITIONS

Collective Good: Items and resources that benefit everyone, and from which people cannot be excluded.

Cultural Oppression: Norms and patterns that perpetuate implicit and explicit values that guide or bind individuals and institutions; the cultural perspectives of dominant groups are imposed on individuals by institutions, and on institutions by individuals.

Democracy: A system of government by the whole population or all the eligible members of a state, typically through elected representatives.

Equity: The notion of being fair and impartial as an individual engages with an organization or system.

Institutional Oppression: The network of structures, policies, and practices that create advantages and benefits for some, and discrimination, oppression, and disadvantages for others.

Internalized Oppression: The results of a process by which members of an oppressed group come to believe and act as if the oppressors' belief system, values, and way of life were correct. External oppression becomes internalized, resulting in shame, the disowning of people's previous understandings of reality, and previously unseen levels of violence within communities. Internalized oppression means the oppressor does not have to exert as much pressure, because people now do it to themselves and each other.

Interpersonal Oppression: Interactions between people where individuals use oppressive behavior, insults, or violence.

Intersectionality: The interconnected nature of social categorizations such as race, class, and gender as they apply to a given individual or group, regarded as creating overlapping and interdependent systems of discrimination or disadvantage.

Oppression: When a person or group of people who have power use it in a way that is not fair, unjust, or cruel.

Transformative Leadership: A critical leadership theory that emphasizes inclusion equity excellence and social justice.

Chapter 3

The Resilient Women of Color Leaders:
Narratives of Black and Brown Leaders in P-16 Settings

Noni Mendoza-Reis
San Jose State University, USA

Angela Louque
California State University, San Bernardio, USA

Mei-Yan Lu
San Jose State University, USA

ABSTRACT

In this chapter, the authors report on their experiences as higher education faculty women of color through three narratives. They present the narratives from their perspectives as three full professors in educational leadership. In the first narrative, an African-American scholar reports on her experiences in academia. In the second narrative, a Latina scholar reports on former Latina students who are currently in school leadership positions enacting social justice leadership. In the third narrative, an Asian-American scholar reports on her current project about networking as a strategy for women of color.

DOI: 10.4018/978-1-7998-7235-1.ch003

INTRODUCTION

The impact of the novel coronavirus 2019 (COVID-19) has affected all aspects of our everyday lives globally. This pandemic devastated public health, cost lives, lost employment, fostered economic instability, and challenged the in-person model of schooling and higher education. It has created "undeniable chaos" (Douglas et al., 2020; Hargreaves & Fullan, 2020; Donthu & Gustafsson, 2020), shaking the very foundation of our lives. During the COVID-19 lockdowns world-wide, the traditional model of in-person education, from elementary to the post-secondary levels, collapsed, except for very few countries like Taiwan and Singapore where traditional in-person instruction continued but with strict health precautions and protections.

Faculty faced the challenge of work-family balance before COVID-19. With K-12 schools going online during the pandemic, faculty with school-age children had to support their children's online learning, while many faculty had to learn how to teach college courses online themselves. What does this mean to women of color in higher education? Studies report that the pandemic exacerbated gender inequality in academia (Kim & Patterson, 2020; Minello et al., 2021). The impact of working from home on female academics and the disproportionate burden they experienced, especially if they had young families or were caring for elderly parents, may take years to manifest (Fuchs-Schündeln, 2020; Viglione, 2020; Vincent-Lamarre et al., 2020).

These are troubling statements considering the already precarious status of women of color in higher education. In 2018, the National Center for Education Statistics (2020), citing the gender and ethnicity of full-time faculty in higher education, found that while "forty percent were White males and thirty-five percent were White females," only five percent of faculty were Asian/Pacific Islander females, three percent were African American females, three percent were Hispanic females, and one percent were American Indian/Alaska Native. As the data suggests, the percentages of African American, Hispanic, and Asian/Pacific Islander female professors in higher education remains extremely low.

This chapter illuminates the stories of so many female academics, stories that have gone unnoticed and unacknowledged. The authors relate their experiences as higher education faculty women of color through three interwoven narratives that address their experiences, barriers and challenges, and successes in navigating their professional lives in higher education. The narratives are presented from the perspectives of three full professors in educational leadership. In the first narrative, a Latina scholar reports on her role in preparing aspiring school leaders. The stories in this section are from former Latina students who are currently in school leadership positions, successfully enacting social justice leadership in P-12 schools. In the second narrative, an African American scholar reports on her experiences in academia. She focuses on her professional journey, one where too often she is the lone African American in the classroom, on the campus, and on committees while being the voice of women of color in educational leadership. In the third narrative, an Asian American scholar reports on her current project of networking as a strategy of resilience for women of color who have been marginalized in higher education. Recommendations for policy and research follow each of the narratives.

Critical Race Theory (CRT) is the framework used to examine these narratives about faculty women of color in higher education. Five elements have been identified in CRT in education: (1) the centrality of race and racism and their intersectionality with other forms of subjugation in education, (2) the challenge to dominant ideology around school failure, (3) the commitment to social justice in education, (4) the centrality of experiential knowledge, and (5) the transdisciplinary perspective (Solorzano, 1997, 1998; Solorzano & Delgado Bernal, 2001; Solorzano & Yosso, 2000). While all elements of CRT are represented in this chapter, the first-person narratives reflect element four, the centrality of experiential knowledge. In further explanation of CRT element four, Yosso (2005) emphasizes the importance of sharing the experiences of people of color through methods that include stories, narratives, and testimonios for the purpose of using the voices of people of color to deepen our understanding of the role of race in education.

In these narratives, the experiences of three women faculty of color are presented.

NARRATIVE ONE: PREPARING SOCIAL JUSTICE SCHOOL LEADERS

As a Latina professor of educational leadership, I prepare aspiring school administrators for social justice leadership. My role is that of an activist scholar with a moral imperative to prepare leadership students to improve schooling for all students, especially those students who have been marginalized through systemic inequities in education. This imperative is grounded in my background as the daughter of a farmworker family from the poverty class. (To this day, I can engage anyone in conversations about fieldwork, including the organization involved in harvesting crops, such as carrots or tomatoes.) My work is guided by Critical Race Theory. The fourth element identified in Critical Race Theory is "the centrality of experiential knowledge." Yosso (2005) describes this element as legitimizing the experiential knowledge of people of color as critical to understanding issues of race and power. Among the ways experiential knowledge can be gathered are through family histories, biographies, scenarios, testimonies, and narratives (Yosso, 2005). My experiential knowledge was gained through the lived experiences of my childhood that led to an understanding of the sociopolitical context in which leaders of schools with students of color operate. Growing up in a farmworker family provided me with community cultural wealth that supported my career in P-20 education as a bilingual teacher, administrator, principal coach, professor, department chair, and currently as a professor in an educational leadership doctoral program. This influence is manifested in the ways that I prepare social justice school leaders. I define social justice leaders as those who place marginalized students and families at the center, rather than the periphery, of their leadership (Dantley & Tillman, 2010).

The recent report, *How Principals Affect Students and Schools* (Grissom et al., 2021), supports the efficacy of preparing social justice leaders. One conclusion from this report is that school leaders need an *equity lens to meet the needs of growing numbers of marginalized students.* The authors note that equity-oriented leaders can make schools more inclusive and instruction more culturally responsive. They further recommend that pre-service leadership preparation programs focus on developing equity-oriented school leaders. Moreover, this report notes the link between principal demographics and better outcomes for students of color and encourages leadership preparation programs to foster diversity in order to better prepare our principal workforce.

The need for effective leadership in our schools is at a critical point. The COVID-19 pandemic forced schools into distance learning with little or no preparation. School leaders, whether novice or veteran, were tasked with developing and implementing an online delivery model of instruction. Inequities were soon evident as in unequal access to the necessary technology for some of our student populations. For those of us who prepare school leaders, now more than ever, we must intensify our efforts to prepare exceptionally well-prepared, flexible, and creative pre-service students to successfully lead these schools post-pandemic.

Barriers, Challenges, and Successes of Latina Social Justice School Leaders

This section includes stories of former Latina students who are now social justice school leaders, possessing the necessary skills, dispositions, and attitudes to effectively lead their schools post pandemic. Further, these are school administrators in schools with predominantly English Learners. Barriers and challenges are presented first to establish the context that Latina leaders face in schools. The successes follow and are presented in a conceptual framework which includes three areas of focus or lenses for leadership: (1) Institutional, (2) Pedagogical and (3) Personal (Mendoza-Reis & Flores, 2014).

The barriers and challenges experienced by these former students, now in positions of school leadership, are similar to barriers and challenges experienced by the women faculty of color in higher education whose stories compose the second and third narratives of this chapter. The literature on Latina leaders also reports on barriers and challenges, including racial challenges, implicit bias, and feelings of isolation and invisibility (Martinez et al., 2020; Murakami et al., 2016). Among the racial challenges experienced by the Latina leaders documented in this paper, one that was frequently mentioned involved White parents' reaction to meeting them. Several noted that White parents asked if they "were the school secretary" upon meeting them. When they learned that they were speaking to the principal who was a Latina, these White parents expressed disbelief, demanding "to speak to the real principal." Others shared feelings of invisibility and isolation. They recounted meetings of principals where each was competing to give his or her opinion. The loudest tended to be heard; however, when a leader of color spoke, he or she was not given the same level of attention as a White leader: "...the loudest voices are trying to get heard. They say what they are going to say and don't then listen to others."

Feelings of isolation were evident when they were outside of their schools, for example in the district office: "When I'm here [school], I know everyone, teachers, and children. But when I go to the district office, I see a way of thinking that I do not belong. I see a disconnect." Similar to previous studies on Latina leaders, these women do not let these incidents of stereotyping and discrimination deter them from their determination to provide equitable education for all students in their schools and in the larger district (Mendez-Morse et al., 2015).

Despite encountering a number of barriers and challenges, these Latina leaders persevere. The next section discusses the successes experienced by these Latina leaders. The stories are presented through the tri-level framework described previously.

Successes With a Social Justice Leadership Framework

Institutional Lens

The Institutional Lens requires leaders to examine and disrupt oppressive policies that perpetuate inequities in schools. The institutional lens requires leaders to hold an advocacy stance in leadership. These leaders recognize that centering discussions about systemic inequities due to race, class, and gender are critical to dismantling conventional approaches to leadership that have not resulted in academic gains for all students (Theoharis, 2007; Mendoza Reis & Smith, 2013). The COVID-19 pandemic has added more inequities that school leaders will need to address. Of the students who are falling behind in schools, the majority are students of color in schools with high rates of poverty (Schwartz et al., 2020).

Principal Gloria is the principal of such a school. Based on her previous actions, Principal Gloria will assume the advocacy stance required in the Institutional Lens through which to address the inequities from which students in her school suffer due to COVID-19. For example, when Principal Gloria became aware that her 5th graders were not successfully transitioning to middle school at high academic levels, she quickly advocated with her district for additional funds to implement an after-school literacy program. After initial resistance from the district and union, she was allocated the necessary funds. The program was so successful that the following year it was implemented district-wide (G. Puga, personal communication, February 7, 2021).

It is important to note that this scenario might have ended differently except that Principal Gloria also understood her stance as a social justice leader. In the article, "A Social Capital Framework for the Study of Institutional Agents and Their Role in the Empowerment of Low-Status Students and Youth," Stanton-Salazar (2011) defines an institutional agent as "an individual who occupies one or more hierarchical positions of relatively high-status and authority." Principal Gloria's actions reflect those of an institutional agent. She used her position of leadership to disrupt a system and negotiate additional opportunities to learn on behalf of English Learner students, not just in her school but district-wide.

Pedagogical Lens

Successful post-pandemic leadership will require a deep knowledge base concerning theories of teaching, learning, and leading in schools with students who are falling behind. The Pedagogical Lens is guided by sociocultural theoretical perspectives, culturally relevant pedagogy, and language acquisition and development. Principal Gloria, for example, understood the importance of first and second language development and advocated for a dual-immersion program at her school with its majority of English Learners. Additionally, her own educational trajectory was that of an immigrant who came to the United States as a child as a non-English speaker.

A pedagogical lens extends beyond the classroom. In another former student's story, Superintendent Galvan used Book Study to build pedagogical knowledge in her district. Book studies are often used by superintendents as a means of building pedagogical knowledge of school site leaders. Often the selected books are guided by mainstream trends in school leadership. In contrast, when a superintendent is a social justice leader, as is this Latina leader, book studies can be used to teach about social justice pedagogy. Superintendent Galvan is the superintendent of a small rural school with predominantly English Learners. In response to recent social unrest, she engaged not only leaders but other employees in a district-wide study of the book, *How to Be an Antiracist*, by Ibram X. Kendi. Team members met weekly to engage with deeper content about racism. As a result of the book study, the team members enacted organizational changes in the master schedule that added courses, such as robotics, engineering, and design experiences. These courses were made available to all students.

Superintendent Galvan is eloquent in her response about big takeaways from this book study:

Big takeaways included a deeper understanding of the student perspective and an empathy for the experiences that children of color endure as a result of colorism and racism. ... [T]hese changes were made to ensure diversity, equity, and inclusion in our battle against racism. If we don't focus on equity-driven, antiracist organizational systems and practices, no one else will. It is our moral and ethical responsibility. Our children are counting on us (Z. Galvan, personal communication, April 1, 2021).

Superintendent Galvan understood that her district employees required a deeper understanding of students of color in order to ensure equity for these students. To achieve this goal, she chose a pedagogical lens as the avenue to address this issue.

Personal Lens

Most important to the Personal Lens is development of ideological clarity that occurs by development of critical reflection or consciousness. The importance of critical reflection appears often in the literature on social justice leadership development frameworks (Furman, 2012; Capper et al., 2009; Khalifa & Gooden, 2016).

Ideological clarity refers to the process by which individuals struggle to identify and compare their own explanations for the existing socio-economic and political hierarchy with that of the dominant society (Bartolomé, 1994). In the tri-level framework, a personal lens requires leaders to have ideological clarity through continual critical reflection about deficit assumptions, beliefs, and attitudes regarding English Learners (Flores et al., 1991).

Principal Gloria and Superintendent Galvan, who share similar backgrounds to those of their students, exhibit critical consciousness. They view their school communities from a positive rather than a deficit lens. Their lived experiences provide a deep understanding and appreciation about the cultural wealth in communities of color (Yosso, 2005). Moreover, the leadership lesson they offer to those of us who prepare leaders is to teach our students to have the moral courage to lead.

NARRATIVE ONE: CONCLUDING REMARKS AND RECOMMENDATIONS

In this section, we have presented some of the barriers and challenges as well as the success stories faced by former Latina students practicing social justice leadership. These stories reflect the lived experiences of Latina leaders along with the skills, dispositions, and attitudes they possess as successful leaders of schools with English Learners. In closing this section, the following policy recommendations are proposed:

1. **Research on skills, dispositions, and qualities of leaders of color.** We support the recommendation from the Wallace Report (Grissom et al., 2021), calling for research on the skills, dispositions, and qualities of leaders of color in order to improve our leadership preparation programs for all students.
2. **Recruitment of students of color in educational leadership programs.** We encourage leadership preparation programs to strengthen recruitment efforts for students of color.

NARRATIVE TWO: INTERSECTIONALITY, ISOLATION, AND INFLUENCE

The impact that Black women have on equity and change is finally being recognized as these issues are pushed to the forefront of the national dialogue because of the 2020 election results. We have several examples of Black women in leadership positions at the state and national levels who continue to give credence to our presence and influence. For example, Kamala Harris is the first African Asian American Vice-President, the first woman of color to hold that office. Stacey Abrams of Georgia has been given much credit for the high levels of voter turnout in the state of Georgia, a state that for years had voted "red," but for this election voted "blue." No one can deny the obvious influence and role the founders of Black Lives Matter have played on the national and international stages over the past eight years, authoring a global movement. The impact these women have made on the social justice landscape have also reverberated across the nation, including educational institutions. The acknowledgement of their presence and influence to lead unapologetically while Black women, and to speak out against injustices with the intent to change previously predicted outcomes, are counter to the recurring reality of their invisibility. So many Black women in leadership positions in higher education encounter and experience inequities, racism, and downright disrespect, but we continue to have the fortitude to believe that social justice change is inevitable, and we strive to be a part of that change (BBC News, 2020; Thompson & Louque, 2005).

This section focuses on heightening the awareness of Black women in leadership positions and the value our perspective brings. Included are some personal reflections on being a scholar in the academy and lessons learned from almost 10 years of being a department chair of educational leadership. The second part of this section provides specific recommendations on how to support Black women professors and higher education and P-12 administrators.

For several generations, data and studies on racial inequality focused primarily on Blacks in general. Lately though, more thought has been given to focusing on the gender inequity which intersects with racial inequity for Black women. Kimberlé Crenshaw's (1989) work on the intersectionality of being Black and female can sometimes be viewed as a double-edged sword. This seems to occur because of the lack of acknowledging Black women's presence, knowledge, and influence.

Professor Crenshaw's (1989) work on intersectionality asserts that race and gender are not compounded identities, but intersections of political identities. The intersection of race and gender can be seen as positive or negative, but most definitely they both must be acknowledged. Clark-Louque and Sullivan (2020, p. 13) wrote:

Crenshaw, in her 1989 paper, "Demarginalizing the Intersection of Race and Sex: A Black Feminist Critique of Antidiscrimination Doctrine, Feminist Theory and Antiracist Politics," wrote about and coined the term "intersectionality" – the intersection of being Black and female. Later, in 1994, she explained that her objective was to "illustrate that many of the experiences Black women face are not subsumed within the traditional boundaries of race or gender discrimination as these boundaries are currently understood, and that the intersection of racism and sexism factors into Black women's lives in ways that cannot be captured wholly by looking at the women's race or gender dimensions of those experiences separately" (p. 94).

The intersectionality of being Black and female, Professor Crenshaw surmises, can mean the discrimination is about being Black (racial) or about being female (gender), and the double discourse is from the combination and mix of being both. Thus, overlapping systems of oppression catch us "coming and going."

McCollum (2005) notes a discussion in a study by Bell and Nkomo (2003) of barriers which Black women encounter in their career paths and career choices:

(a) stereotypes of incompetence due to race; (b) assimilation or loss of their "Blackness" for others to be comfortable with them; (c) limited access to informal and social networks within their organizations; and (d) a hollow commitment to the advancement of women and minorities within their organizations.

Isolation and Invisibility: Not Seen, but Always Watched

Before arriving at a public higher education state institution, I had been a faculty member at a private institution for several years. There I learned that I was definitely "one in a million" as I was the only Black faculty on the entire campus. Thus, being at a public state institution was a welcomed change because I would be one of four Black female faculty in the College of Education. However, this was four out of approximately ninety faculty when I was hired, and the other three Black women were in another department. I was the only Black faculty member in my department, so I still felt isolated most of the time. Further, being new to the university brought its own challenges as I had to learn about the culture of higher education and specifically the culture of my new university.

As a newly tenured and full professor four years after my arrival, I was elected by fellow faculty to serve as department chair. The Educational Leadership Department was primarily one of older, previously retired from K-12 administration, White men. I was the only woman of color among the department of 13 faculty: 8 White males (mostly former superintendents), 3 White females, and 1 Hispanic male. Serving as a department chair of a leadership program in a public state institution brought more than its share of attention to racism, inequity, and favoritism. Although I ran the formal department meetings, other faculty participated in regular, informal meetings on the golf course (Whitford, 2020).

At the end of my service as chair, the department was one of the most ethnically diverse on campus. I cannot take all the credit for it but will take some. Because of the commitment by the department and some organizational changes, the Educational Leadership Department at its most diverse had two African Americans (one male and the author), three Asian Americans, two Native Americans, two Latinas, two LGBQTIA, and five Whites.

Although many may believe a person is given preferential treatment when in a leadership position in higher education, this is definitely not so if you are a Black woman. I was noticed, of course, in the university-wide department chair meetings because I was the only Black, and the only Black woman in those meetings for many years. To clarify, I was the only Black woman, so I was noticed, but not noticed; heard, but not heard; seen, but unseen. Thus, being treated as if I were "invisible" was the common approach of my university colleagues and peers. Even when I had something to contribute, I soon realized that my voice and opinion mattered "not-at all" to any of my colleagues. After a while, I just showed up to the meetings as required and used the time to address my personal agenda, finishing my own tasks while "the others" in the room decided those of the university. This detachment mechanism became a useful defense for being ignored and invisible.

Emerging Successful Practices of Leaders

Being a professor of leadership, I have the opportunity to read, study, gain insights, and write about leadership and leaders. What I have discovered studying leadership is that many people who are in a leadership position know little about actually being a leader. They have not studied the theoretical aspects of leadership, how to obtain results, how to interact with others in a respectful manner, how to value and promote diversity, and how to work with Blacks. A person cannot fairly and equitably evaluate Black female faculty, assess their work, or consider them for promotion if that person has no understanding of the Black faculty experience of being isolated, ignored at times, and discriminated against. I assert that such leaders are ill-equipped to do so; and, that this is too often the case results in additional stress and alienation for Black female faculty.

Across the nation, incidences continue to occur that demonstrate inequitable treatment towards Black, Indigenous and people of color, and, in particular, Black females in higher education. It is not uncommon for Black female faculty to be reprimanded with little or no due process, little or no communication, or even having an opportunity to provide an explanation; instead, the rush to judgement proceeds without due diligence or a thorough, yet fair, investigation. Numerous Blacks report that unfair teaching evaluations, the denial of promotions, and being overlooked for leadership positions continue the marginalization practices that occur in the "ivory tower" (Thompson & Louque, 2005). The educational and systemic institutional changes that need to be made are specifically in the areas of diversity, equity, and inclusion, as well as support.

The issues of isolation and invisibility also have long been concerns of Black faculty. Not having significant numbers of Black faculty on campuses cause the racial climate to be unwelcoming and confirms the university's comfort with the status quo. Participants in a study for the book, *Exposing the "Culture of Arrogance" in the Academy* (Thompson & Louque, 2005), reported that to improve the racial climate, universities must focus their efforts on recruiting, hiring, and supporting Blacks. The onus should not be on Black faculty to "change" the institution; but, rather, that all the constituents and administrators of the university need to be trained to work with and support Black faculty, especially Black women; and training should be conducted by Black women in higher education. Feeling isolated and having no support system contribute to the dissatisfaction of Black faculty in higher education which leads to a failure of retention for which the fault lies with the university.

Thus, the recommendations that derive from both personal experience and that of other Black female academics focus on using anti-racist, equitable practices from culturally proficient leaders to establish and sustain systemic changes in policies and practices.

Recommendations

1. **Prepare the table before we (women of color) get there.** Start with diversity, equity, and inclusion training and professional development now before we are hired. Don't wait until we arrive to put something in place. In fact, go hard and go with anti-racist and abolitionist training.

2. **The anti-racist training** should be specific regarding the groups or persons your institution is trying to recruit. That is, if you are looking for Black women, then your institution needs to have training specifically and intentionally about Black women academics by Black women academics.

3. **Have conversations with women of color** who are already on your campus. Just because you believe everyone is happy and getting along, doesn't mean that women of color at your institution actually are. Remember, our perspective is different and doesn't always match the experiences of others on campus.

4. **Increase support for mentoring women of color.** This could be formally or informally done.

5. **Hire in pairs or triads in the same department of a college**. Some institutions swear they don't have the money, but they usually find it for the events and programs they want to sponsor. The university signals its commitment to hiring and retaining Black female and women of color faculty by pairing such hires with each other as to minimize and avoid isolation and marginalization.

NARRATIVE THREE: BUILDING PROFESSIONAL NETWORKS DURING THE PANDEMIC

"If you want to go fast, go alone. If you want to go far, go together." ~ African Proverb

While the impact of COVID-19 will take years to manifest (Fuchs-Schündeln, 2020; Viglione, 2020; Vincent-Lamarre, Sugimoto & Larivière, 2020), the pandemic challenges each and every one of us to do things differently, including networking. This section of our chapter discusses professional networking as a response to the barriers and challenges faced by women of color in higher education. This narrative will describe ways faculty women of color can initiate new ventures beyond the boundaries of the physical university walls of their universities.

Barriers, Challenges and Opportunities: Personal Story

As a full professor in the Department of Educational Leadership, I came from a humble background. I am an immigrant and a first-generation college student. English is my third language. Additionally, I have been dealing with a speech impediment all my life. I am a stutterer. I am also an Asian American; and every day, I must fight the marginalization and stereotyping of Asian Americans, including models of minorities in the media. This past year has seen a significant surge in racially motivated hate crimes against Asian Americans that involve physical violence, harm, and harassment (Gover et al., 2020; Ho, 2021; Lee & Hong, 2020). Asian Americans have traditionally been treated as "perpetual foreigners." According to a recent study by UC-Irvine (2021), "One in ten Asian Americans and Pacific Islanders reported hate crimes and hate incidents in 2021, ... [T]his rate which is higher than the national average is driven by a specific harmful stereotype [perpetual foreigner]." The pandemic exacerbated the harassment and attacks. For example, the famous NBA Basketball player, Jeremy Lin, was called "Coronavirus" on the court (NBC news, 2021).

Nevertheless, I see these barriers and challenges as opportunities, for example, my speech impediment -- stuttering. I have been pushing myself out of my comfort zone since middle school to participate in speech competitions. With the support of amazing teachers and excellent speech therapists, I have succeeded in minimizing my stutter. As of today, I have been given over 120 conference presentations and over 20 keynote speeches nationally and internationally. Most proudly, I am able to share my speech impediment success with my students who have similar challenges.

As with my stutter, I view the barriers of isolation and marginalization experienced as an Asian American as an opportunity to reach out beyond the walls of my university campus to connect, to network, to support others, to build alliances, and to inspire the next generation of leaders. While faculty women of color may experience isolation and marginalization in their academic departments and universities, in-person networking at conferences as well as virtually can help alleviate these issues while also being validating and promoting professional growth.

Isolation of Women of Color in Higher Education

Women of color in higher education face many seemingly insurmountable challenges. One of the challenges is being isolated in their departments, colleges/schools, universities, and their disciplines. This isolation makes it extremely difficult to navigate the tenure and promotion process. Even after being promoted to full professor, women of color continue to face challenges and difficulties, for example, not being considered for leadership roles and not being recognized for their professional contributions by their colleges and the universities as evidenced by Reis and Lu (2010): "Many women of the color faculty were recognized on a national level for their scholarship and work in the larger educational community. This was in contrast to little recognition at their home campuses."

Unfortunately, the sense of isolation and marginalization has been exacerbated by the pandemic. How do we emerge from this isolation and marginalization and achieve a sense of validation for our work and connectedness with other colleagues?

Networking as a Response to Isolation and Marginalization in the Academy

Obare (2020) reported that women are often encouraged to network; however; women are frequently not provided with instructions on how to network; what the expected outcome of the networking should be; how to make networking a win-win, value-added opportunity; how to grow and nurture one's own professional network; and how to organize/manage one's network. Many women leaders also report that they are excluded from informal networks (Rhode, 2017). Reflecting on my own networking journey, it took me many years to understand how to network effectively, how to ensure that the relationships the author was building were mutually beneficial to each person's professional career, and how to manage my professional network.

Reflecting on my academic journey, starting when I was in graduate school, my doctoral education prepared me well to be a researcher and a teacher, but not to be a "networker" or how to manage and grow a professional network. My doctoral professors did not advise me about the importance of networking and leadership. When I first started teaching in academia as a tenure track assistant professor in the Department of Instructional Technology, mentors suggested that I should start networking. However, they did not share how to network. Being an introverted person, I found it difficult to introduce myself to new people; further, as English is my third language, I am naturally self-conscious about my English and my Taiwanese accent. However, by observing colleagues, I began to step out of my comfort zone to meet new colleagues at professional conferences.

Most importantly, I volunteered to help others network and to make connections. For example, because I first came to the United States as an international student, I established a network of international students to facilitate our understanding of the American university's tenure and promotion process from the perspective of an international student. I offered workshops and hosted panels to discuss these important issues. As a university professor, I provide mentoring and coaching to new assistant professors and to graduate students who are interested in teaching in higher education. Although I lacked recognition on my own campus, my leadership and service were recognized at a national level. I was elected President of the International Division at AECT (Association of Educational Communication and Technology), the premier professional organization for educational technology faculty and business/industry practitioners.

Unfortunately, COVID-19 halted opportunities to network in person as conferences were canceled. Like most faculty, I was frustrated but focused on writing my research findings into manuscripts for scholarly journals. Participating in networks had allowed me to flourish outside of my university, and I sought ways to continue networking and having my voice heard. The result of this frustration is I-WIN, International Women's Innovative Network.

From Isolation During the Pandemic to I-WIN

Social distancing has been enforced among the general population to reduce the transmission of COVID-19, resulting in many people reporting loneliness and social isolation. Faculty are no exception (Razai et al., 2020; Hwang et al., 2020). As discussed in Narrative II, before the pandemic, women of color faculty reported experiencing isolation and invisibility in their own higher education institutions. I knew from earlier research that networking beyond one's home campus was a strategy for resistance for women faculty of color (Reis & Lu, 2010).

In June 2020, I attended a virtual international conference for women in leadership. Many virtual conferences I had previously attended consisted of a series of presentations/webinars delivering content with limited opportunities for discussion. Nevertheless, as a leadership scholar working on researching the topic of supporting university female students' leadership self-efficacy, I was eager to find opportunities where I could actually meet the presenters and other attendees for the purpose of building a new professional network. With encouragement from one of the conference leaders, I volunteered to host subsequent virtual meetings to discuss conference participants' research.

The group from this conference soon grew into a larger network where the women leaders had opportunities to be guest speakers. "Change a Mind--Change a Life: Transforming Core Beliefs to Shape Values and Enhance Effectiveness" and "Peer-to-Peer Women's Circles: Capacious, Inclusive, Professional Development by Women for Women" are just two examples of the many virtual presentations of participants' research. As a result of these virtual meetings about women in leadership, in October 2020, I founded I-WIN (International Women's Innovative Network). We offer a safe, virtual environment for a cross-generational men and women to learn, discuss, dialog, and network. This cross-generational dialogue is essential for leadership development, mentoring, coaching, and professional growth (Morris, 2017; Rudolph et al., 2018). We offer free, bi-weekly seminars and workshops for men and women, ranging in age from 17 to 78. We meet virtually on the first and third Thursdays of each month.

This professional network, I-WIN, has been extended to include a core administration team of four women in leadership. Within four months, our attendance has increased both in number and global participation. As of this writing, we celebrated our 20th consecutive meeting on January 7, 2021. We had 58 participants from such diverse countries as the United States, Canada, United Kingdom, and Botswana.

Supporting Undergraduate Students to Network Professionally

My primary motivation for building a virtual professional network was to address isolation and invisibility on my campus. However, this was also an opportunity to mentor my undergraduate students in building professional networks. Like myself, many of them are first generation, immigrant, and/or international students; and they range from undeclared freshmen to graduating seniors with diverse majors across campus. These students have always rated guest speakers highly and valued their information and knowledge, so I developed a plan for students to build and strengthen their own professional networks by adding assignments that would support their knowledge about how to build such networks.

Networking is an important skill for our students, and they need to be supported in understanding how to build their own professional and diverse networks. Before the pandemic, the world of digital media changed the way we work and network (Donelan 2016). To cope with the pandemic, we have changed again, even more significantly, the ways we work and communicate (Kaushik & Guleria, 2020). Badoer & Chester emphasize this (2020):

One major change in recruitment has been the shift from traditional hardcopy CVs, newspaper job advertisements, and attendance at job fairs, to the ubiquitous use of the Internet for many aspects of job recruitment and selection. Professional networking sites, such as LinkedIn, have quickly become an indispensable tool, presenting both challenges and opportunities for universities seeking to enhance graduate employability and better support student outcomes.

Undergraduate students should be encouraged to and mentored in the use networks, such as LinkedIn and I-WIN, to develop professional networks.

Recommendations for Building Networks

1. Encourage students to step out of their comfort zone and participate in networks. As a professor, give instruction and provide practice opportunities in networking properly. For example, informational interviews are a great opportunity to network. Practice with students to establish a list of questions they could use in the information interviews.
2. Be patient. The network you join or build does not have to happen immediately.
3. Build a network with a team to support others beyond your campus or institution.

CONCLUSION

One assumption of this chapter is that the stories of women of color in education, whether in higher education or in P-12 settings, share similarities in the barriers and challenges they face. It is important also to collect stories of their successes. These are the stories not often found in mainstream publications but are important to our understanding of racialized, gendered, and class experiences of people of color in education (Solorzano, 1997).

REFERENCES

Badoer, E., Hollings, Y., & Chester, A. (2020). Professional networking for undergraduate students: A scaffolded approach. *Journal of Further and Higher Education*, *45*(2), 197–210. doi:10.1080/0309877X.2020.1744543

Bartolome, L. (1994). Beyond the methods fetish: Toward a humanizing pedagogy. *Harvard Educational Review*, *64*(2), 173–195. doi:10.17763/haer.64.2.58q5m5744t325730

BBC News. (2020). *Black Lives Matter founders: We fought to change history and we won*. https://www.bbc.com/news/world-us-canada-55106268

Bell, E. L. J., & Nkomo, S. M. (2003). *Our separate ways: Black and white women and the struggle for professional identity*. Harvard Business School Press.

Capper, C. A. (2015). The 20th- year anniversary of critical race theory in education: Implications for leading to eliminate racism. *Educational Administration Quarterly*, *51*(5), 791–833. doi:10.1177/0013161X15607616

Clark-Louque, A., & Sullivan, T. A. (2020). Black Girls and School Discipline: Shifting from the Narrow Zone of Zero Tolerance to a Wide Region of Restorative Practices and Culturally Proficient Engagement. *Journal for Leadership, Equity, and Research*, *6*(2). https://journals.sfu.ca/cvj/index.php/cvj/article/view/95

Crenshaw, K. (1989). *Demarginalizing the intersection of race and sex: A Black feminist critique of antidiscrimination doctrine, feminist theory and antiracist politics*. https://chicagounbound.uchicago.edu/uclf/vol1989/iss1/8/

Dantley, M. E., & Tillman, L. C. (2010). Social justice and moral transformative leadership. In C. Marshall & M. Oliva (Eds.), *Leadership for social justice* (2nd ed., pp. 19–34). Allyn & Bacon.

Donelan, H. (2016). Social media for professional development and networking opportunities in academia. *Journal of Further and Higher Education, 40*(5), 706–729. doi:10.1080/0309877X.2015.1014321

Donthu, N., & Gustafsson, A. (2020). Effects of COVID-19 on business and research. *Journal of Business Research, 117*, 284–289. doi:10.1016/j.jbusres.2020.06.008 PMID:32536736

Douglas, M., Katikireddi, S. V., Taulbut, M., McKee, M., & McCartney, G. (2020). Mitigating the wider health effects of covid-19 pandemic response. *BMJ (Clinical Research Ed.), 369*, m1557. doi:10.1136/bmj.m1557 PMID:32341002

Flores, B., Cousin, P., & Diaz, E. (1991). Transforming deficit myths about language, literacy and culture. *Language Arts, 68*(5), 369–379.

Fuchs-Schündeln, N. (2020). *Gender structure of paper submissions at the Review of Economic Studies during COVID-19: First Evidence.* restud.com/wp-content/uploads/2020/05/FemaleSubmissionsCovid19.pdf

Furman, G. (2012). Social justice leadership as praxis: Developing capacities through preparation programs. *Educational Administration Quarterly, 48*(2), 191–229. doi:10.1177/0013161X11427394

Gover, A. R., Harper, S. B., & Langton, L. (2020). Anti-Asian hate crime during the COVID-19 pandemic: Exploring the reproduction of inequality. *American Journal of Criminal Justice, 45*(4), 647–667. doi:10.100712103-020-09545-1 PMID:32837171

Grissom, J. A., Egalite, A. J., & Lindsay, C. A. (2021). *How principals affect students and schools: A systematic synthesis of two decades of research.* The Wallace Foundation. https://www.wallacefoundation.org/principalsynthesis

Hargreaves, A., & Fullan, M. (2020). Professional capital after the pandemic: Revisiting and revising classic understandings of teachers' work. *Journal of Professional Capital and Community, 5*(3/4), 327–336. doi:10.1108/JPCC-06-2020-0039

Ho, J. (2021, January). Anti-Asian racism, Black Lives Matter, and COVID-19. *Japan Forum, 33*(1), 148–159. doi:10.1080/09555803.2020.1821749

Hwang, T. J., Rabheru, K., Peisah, C., Reichman, W., & Ikeda, M. (2020). Loneliness and social isolation during the COVID-19 pandemic. *International Psychogeriatrics, 32*(10), 1217–1220. doi:10.1017/S1041610220000988 PMID:32450943

I-WIN (International Women's Innovative Network). (n.d.). https://www.linkedin.com/company/international-women-s-innovative-network

Kaushik, M., & Guleria, N. (2020). The impact of pandemic COVID-19 in workplace. *European Journal of Business and Management, 12*(15), 1–10.

Kendi, I. X. (2019). *How to be an antiracist*. One World.

Khalifa, M. A., Gooden, M. A., & Davis, J. E. (2016). Culturally responsive school leadership: A synthesis of the literature. *Review of Educational Research, 86*(4), 1272–1311. doi:10.3102/0034654316630383

Kim, E., & Patterson, S. (2020). *The pandemic and gender inequality in academia*. Unpublished Manuscript, Vanderbilt University.

Lee, S. J., & Hong, J. J. (2020). Model minorities and perpetual foreigners: Stereotypes of Asian Americans. In J. T. Nadler & E. C. Voyles (Eds.), *Stereotypes: The incidence and impacts of bias* (pp. 165-174). Prager. https://publisher.abc-clio.com/9781440868672/

Martinez, M. A., Rivera, M., & Marquez, J. (2020). Learning from the experiences and development of Latina school leaders. *Educational Administration Quarterly, 56*(3), 472–498. doi:10.1177/0013161X19866491

McCollum, P. (2005). Review of literature of leadership- An excerpt from the new IDRA book, "The Ohtli Encuentro – Women of Color Share Pathways to Leadership." *IDRA Newsletter*. Retrieved from https://www.idra.org/resource-center/review-of-literature-on-leadership-part-ii/

Méndez-Morse, S., Murakami, E. T., Byrne-Jimenez, M., & Hernandez, F. (2015). Mujeres in the principal's office: Latina school leaders. *Journal of Latinos and Education, 14*(1), 171–187. doi:10.1080/15348431.2014.973566

Mendoza-Reis, N., & Flores, B. (2014). Changing the pedagogical culture of schools with Latino English Learners: Reculturing instructional leadership. In P. J. Mellom, P. P. Portes, S. Spencer & P. Baquedano-Lopez (Eds.), U.S. Latinos and Education Policy: Research-Based Directions for Change. Routledge.

Mendoza-Reis, N., & Smith, A. (2013). Re-thinking the universal approach to the preparation of school leaders: Cultural proficiency and beyond. In L. C. Tillman & J. J. Scheurich (Eds.), *Handbook of research on educational leadership for equity and diversity*. Routledge Press. doi:10.4324/9780203076934.ch28

Minello, A., Martucci, S., & Manzo, L. K. (2021). The pandemic and the academic mothers: Present hardships and future perspectives. *European Societies, 23*(sup1), S82-S94.

Morris, L. V. (2017). Reverse mentoring: Untapped resource in the academy? *Innovative Higher Education, 42*(4), 285–287. doi:10.100710755-017-9405-z

Murakami, E. T., Hernandez, F., Mendez-Morse, S. E., & Byrne-Mimenez, M. (2016). Latina/o school principals: Identity, leadership and advocacy. *International Journal of Leadership in Education, 19*(3), 280–299. doi:10.1080/13603124.2015.1025854

National Center for Statistics. (n.d.). *Fast facts: Race/ethnicity of college and university faculty.* https://nces.ed.gov/fastfacts/display.asp?id=61

News, N. B. C. (2021). *NBA's G League investigating after Jeremy Lin said he was called "Coronavirus" on the Court.* https://www.nbcnews.com/news/asian-america/nba-s-g-league-investigating-after-jeremy-lin-said-he-n1259073

Obare, S. O. (2020). Successful STEM women of color must network differently. In P. M. Leggett-Robinson & B. C. Villa (Eds.), *Overcoming barriers for women of color in STEM fields: Emerging research and opportunities* (pp. 82–99). IGI Global. doi:10.4018/978-1-7998-4858-5.ch004

Razai, M. S., Oakeshott, P., Kankam, H., Galea, S., & Stokes-Lampard, H. (2020). Mitigating the psychological effects of social isolation during the covid-19 pandemic. *BMJ (Clinical Research Ed.), 369*, m1904. doi:10.1136/bmj.m1904 PMID:32439691

Reis, N. M., & Lu, M. Y. (2010). Why are there so few of us? Counter-stories from women of color in faculty governance roles. *Educational Leadership, 20*(1), 61–97.

Rhode, D. L. (2017). *Women and leadership.* Oxford University Press.

Rudolph, C. W., Rauvola, R. S., & Zacher, H. (2018). Leadership and generations at work: A critical review. *The Leadership Quarterly, 29*(1), 44–57. doi:10.1016/j.leaqua.2017.09.004

Schwartz, H. L., Faruque, A., Leschitz, J. T., Uzicanin, A., & Uscher-Pines, L. (2020). *Opportunities and challenges in using online learning to maintain continuity of instruction in K-12 schools in emergencies.* Rand Corporation. https://www.rand.org/pubs/working_papers/WRA235-1.html

Solorzano, D. (1997). Images and words that wound: Critical race theory, racial stereotyping and teacher education. *Teacher Education Quarterly, 24*, 5–19.

Solorzano, D. (1998). Critical race theory, racial and gender microaggressions, and the experiences of Chicana and Chicano Scholars. *International Journal of Qualitative Studies in Education: QSE, 11*(1), 121–136. doi:10.1080/095183998236926

Solórzano, D., & Yosso, T. (2000). Toward a critical race theory of Chicana and Chicano education. In C. Tejeda, C. Martinez, Z. Leonardo & P. McLaren (Eds.), Charting new terrains of Chicana(o)/Latina(o) education. Hampton Press.

Solorzano, D. G., & Bernal, D. D. (2001). Examining transformational resistance through a Critical race and Latcrit theory framework: Chicana and Chicano students in an urban context. *Urban Education, 36*(3), 308–342. doi:10.1177/0042085901363002

Stanton-Salazar, R. D. (2011). A social capital framework for the study of institutional agents and their role in the empowerment of low-status students and youth. *Youth & Society, 43*(3), 1066–1109. doi:10.1177/0044118X10382877

Theoharis, G. (2007). Social justice educational leaders and resistance: Toward a theory of social justice leadership. *Educational Administration Quarterly, 43*(2), 221–258. doi:10.1177/0013161X06293717

Thompson, G., & Louque, A. (2005). *Exposing the "Culture of Arrogance" in the academy: A blueprint for increasing Black faculty satisfaction in higher education.* Stylus Publications.

UC-Riverside. (2021). *Survey Shows Anti-Asian Bias Rooted Perpetual Foreigner Stereotype.* https://socialinnovation.ucr.edu/news/2021/04/01/survey-shows-anti-asian-bias-rooted-perpetual-foreigner-stereotype

Viglione, G. (2020). Are women publishing less during the pandemic? Here's what the data say. *Nature, 581*(7809), 365–367. doi:10.1038/d41586-020-01294-9 PMID:32433639

Vincent-Lamarre, P., Sugimoto, C. R., & Larivière, V. (2020). *Monitoring women's scholarly production during the COVID19 pandemic.* http://projets.initiativesnumeriques.org/monitoring-scholarly-covid/methods_final.pdf

Whitford, E. (2020). *There are so few who have made their way.* Inside Higher Education. https://www.insidehighered.com/news/2020/10/28/black-administrators-are-too-rare-top-ranks-higher-education-it%E2%80%99s-not-just-pipeline

Yosso, T. (2005). Whose culture has capital? A critical race theory on community cultural wealth. *Race, Ethnicity and Education, 8*(1), 69–91. doi:10.1080/1361332052000341006

Chapter 4
Challenges Experienced by Women of Color in Educational Leadership

Ronald Morgan
National University, USA

Kitty M. Fortner
California State University, Dominquez Hills, USA

Kimmie Tang
California State University, Dominquez Hills, USA

ABSTRACT

There continue to be many issues women of color face as they pursue both an advanced education and leadership positions in education. There appears to be an increase in the number of women of color seeking advanced degrees and pursuing educational leadership positions, but the numbers are still small overall. While some educational stakeholders have worked to increase the number of women of color in educational leadership positions, it has been minimal. A central question that is often asked is, How does a school ensure that the educational leaders are capable of moving forward, with meeting the needs of a diverse student body? Many advocates say promoting a more diverse group of educational leaders, especially women of color, will only help increase student success. Increasing the number of women of color in educational leadership positions can help have a positive effect on the issues of racism, poverty, aggression, oppression, hostility, or even privilege.

DOI: 10.4018/978-1-7998-7235-1.ch004

INTRODUCTION

The content for this chapter primarily came from a conversation that led to a story that led to a research study. That initial conversation detailed the dissertation defense experience of two women of color and the challenges they endured. This led to exploring the experiences other women of color have had, with the hope of uncovering possible supports that could be provided to other women of color seeking leadership positions in the field of education. The participants in this study were all women of color who received their doctoral degree in educational leadership within the last 12 years and currently work as leaders in the field of education. Hopefully, understanding their stories will lead to safer passage for others on this journey. You will read about the many challenges and obstacles these women faced and the actions that helped them to navigate these struggles and emerge in the positions they wanted.

Throughout the process of interviewing these women, the following questions guided our understanding: 1) What challenges do women of color face when getting a doctorate degree and working in educational leadership? 2) What recommendations for doctoral programs are needed to support women of color as they enter and exit their programs? and 3) How did their doctoral program in educational leadership contribute to the attainment of educational leadership positions and promotions?

Women of color navigate a unique set of challenges and barriers in academia. For example, several scholars argue that women of color in academia have unique experiences, and despite higher numbers of women of color enrolled in degree programs, social attitudes create (and recreate) racist and gendered microaggressions (Collins, 1986). However, research regarding women of color in higher education largely examines the undergraduate experience. Literature concerning the experiences of women of color in graduate school is sparse. They continue to be underrepresented as doctoral students and faculty at the university level, especially in positions of educational leadership. As a result, women of color continue to be marginalized in educational leadership, leaving schooling in our society at a deficit (Felder, 2010; Gay, 2004; Hooks, 2015b). Using appreciative mixed-methods narrative inquiry, this study aimed to examine the experiences of women of color in educational leadership programs and the ways in which university systems support or constrain them based on the quality of faculty/student relationships, relevance of program curricula, quality of collegial relationships, and the attainment of educational leadership positions and promotions.

For this chapter, six women of color in educational leadership positions were surveyed, followed by semi-structured conversational interviews. The participants had earned doctoral degrees in educational leadership within the last 12 years. To gain a better understanding of this phenomenon, this research drew upon critical race theory, feminist theory, critical leadership, and transformative leadership to explore the intersection of race, gender, and class, and its overall impact on women of color in doctoral programs in educational leadership (Hooks, 2015b, Ladson-Billings & Tate, 2016, Santamaría & Santamaría, 2011).

BACKGROUND

Exploring the many issues women of color face as they pursued both a terminal degree and leadership positions in education illuminated the fact that obstacles and challenges block their paths, creating unnecessary stress and anxiety for many women of color. However, there was found to be minimal research on this subject. While there appears to be an increase in the number of women of color seeking advanced degrees and pursuing educational leadership positions, the numbers are still small overall. Some of the research centered on women of color being change agents in their educational leadership positions. Fullan (2001) believed an effective change agent possesses skills in three main capacities: developing relationships of trust, communicating the change vision effectively, and empowering others to take action toward change. With key stakeholders working to increase the number of women of color in educational leadership positions, the focus has been on a culture of shared leadership with distributed ownership and common communities of practice (Trybus, 2011).

Other research (Ogbu, 1995) suggests there is growing evidence that an increasing diverse student population needs an increase in diversity among educational leadership, especially women of color. With many of today's youth facing complex demands, academically, personally, and socially, it has never been more important for schools to increase diversity among the teachers, administrators, and staff. This will not only help educators understand the learning process better but also address the cultural needs of students. While most would agree on this benefit of increased diversity in educational leadership, it will also aid in providing important skills to students as they work on coping with the many issues, they face in 21st century schools.

However, a question that emerges is how does a school ensure that educational leaders are capable of moving forward with meeting the needs of a diverse student body, whether that is Pk–12 or higher education? Many of the issues students of color face are similar to what educational leaders of color face and often mirror one another. Many advocates say promoting a more diverse group of educational leaders, especially women of color, will only help increase student success, as they can help with teacher understanding and readiness of a culturally diverse group of students. Ebersole et al. (2015) suggested that "educators might re-conceptualize culture-based courses to deepen teacher perspectives rather than merely enhance teaching activities which support culturally responsive teaching and learning." One such framework is cultural proficiency, which according to Terrell and Lindsey (2009), "provides a comprehensive, systemic structure for school leaders to identify, examine, and discuss educational issues in schools." It is important to utilize the following when examining the cultural needs of a Pk–12 student: 1) Equity, 2) Advocacy, and 3) Social Justice (McAuliffe & Associates, 2013). By utilizing this type of cultural lens, one begins to understand if and how a student is affected by issues of racism, poverty, aggression, oppression, hostility, or even privilege.

Diverse educational leaders and, in particular, women of color can often work more effectively with the cultural needs of every student, whether at a school or college/university setting. According to McAuliffe and Associates (2013), the skills needed to work with students' cultural needs include "willingness to brook conflict, appreciation of diversity, openness to learning, the ability to engage in social critical thinking, having critical consciousness, and persistence." Additionally, those working with the cultural needs of students should above all be "critically alert" in order to have a cross-cultural connection. The question immediately arises as to how one learns to become critically alert and what training and/or skills are necessary for this to occur. The first step in this process of becoming critically alert involves equity and inclusiveness and is for everyone, not just a select few (McAuliffe & Associates, 2013.)

The participants who were interviewed for the study and then included in this chapter self-identified as Black (n=2), Latinx (n=2), and Asian (n=2). The following are the personal narratives of their experiences in doctoral programs and current leadership positions as women of color.

Personal Narratives

The following narratives will highlight six lived experiences of women of color, which focus on the issues, controversies, and challenges they faced while working in educational leadership positions. These narratives retell stories using a three-dimensional space narrative structure. In addition to a description of the participant, the following elements can be found in each of the narratives: 1) Interaction - the participant's look inward to internal conditions, feelings, hopes, and dispositions as well as to the existential conditions in their environment with other people, their intentions, purposes, assumptions, and points of view; 2) Continuity - The participants tell their story from their own understanding of the past, present, and future and how it applies to their situation; and 3) Situation - The participant shares their view of the context, time, and place situated in a physical landscape or in a setting bounded by characters, intentions, purposes, and different points of view (Creswell & Guetterman, 2019).

Participant 1 (Kathryn)

Kathryn identified as an African American woman in her 50's who is currently a school counselor and part-time adjunct instructor for a university counseling program. She received her doctoral degree in school leadership five years ago and in the interview discussed a number of obstacles she faced as a woman of color. She also discussed how she continues to face some of those same issues in her current school counseling position. Kathryn was quite detailed as she elaborated on what these issues were. She said her first and probably biggest obstacle was and continues to be the lack of support she receives as a woman of color. She often feels her voice is stifled or even ignored as she makes suggestions in meetings or other venues.

As Kathryn made the decision to pursue a doctorate, she said it was a personal goal of hers to achieve a terminal degree and also become proficient at conducting research. When she settled on the university she thought best suited her professional goals, she decided to apply and was accepted. Her doctoral cohort was about 50 percent people of color and 50 percent Caucasian, and evenly split between male and female. However, her doctoral faculty were all White and mostly male, and while she did not feel marginalized by any of them, she also did not feel institutionally supported by most of them. Additionally, she lost two chairs during her dissertation process but felt her third chair was very supportive and was instrumental in helping her complete the dissertation. She said she would recommend her doctorate program to other women of color but would like to see added institutional support for all doctoral candidates, especially those coming from underserved populations. Kathryn ended her comments about her doctorate program by stating, "it has opened doors for [her] in both K-12 school settings and higher education."

In her current position as a high school counselor, Kathryn is on the school's leadership team but is the only woman of color. She feels supported by her principal but often feels there are low expectations for her as a woman of color, and she is sometimes "underestimated" in what she can accomplish. She reported that her school began taking on diversity initiatives this past summer after the multitude of news reports of shootings of black men by police officers. She initially had low expectations of what these diversity initiatives might accomplish but has been pleased with the progress thus far and especially with the recent hiring of new minority candidates.

Kathryn has often felt that as a woman of color in both her doctoral program and in her current job that she has to be "twice as good" as her White counterparts. This idea of having to be better than others was instilled in this participant by her mother and is something she continues to believe in, even currently.

Participant 2 (Patricia)

Patricia is generation X, between 35 and 44 years of age, and identifies as an Asian American woman who has worked in the field of education for 14 years. Her parents are immigrants from Thailand. She is bilingual, but Thai is her first language, or her strongest language. She currently works as an assistant principal in a middle school in California. Prior to her current position and while she was in her doctorate program, she worked in a different district as a teacher on special assignment with the following responsibilities: Response to Intervention/Program Improvement Specialist, Data Specialist, and the Testing Site Coordinator. Before that position, she was a middle school math and science teacher in the same district for a short period of time. Patricia received her doctoral degree in leadership for educational justice at a university in California six years ago. She finished the three-year program focused on social justice in education in three years. Patricia entered the doctoral program with the desire to get her Administrative Services Credential and move into an administration position. She only investigated programs that offered the option for the credential. Additionally, she wanted a program close to her home, with a brick-and-mortar experience where she could interact in person, which she felt would keep her more accountable and help to build relationships.

Patricia described her doctoral program as having little diversity. Her program was a cohort program that was not very ethnically diverse, with over half of the cohort members being White. There was little ethnic diversity in the faculty also. There was one male professor who was African and one male professor who was Asian. Additionally, there were two female professors who were White. Patricia gave three strengths of the program. She felt the face-to-face component provided a space for relationship building, making connections, and deeper learning for her. She also felt the professor she worked closest with made extra effort to make himself available and give support whenever she needed it. She also talked about the emphasis on social justice and being in the forefront of the field at that time. She felt these aspects were valuable to her and others in the program.

One challenge that she noted was finding balance in her life. Going back to school as an adult was more difficult than she thought it was going to be. Organizing time and tasks from both personal and academic life was stressful and impacted her dissertation process. She felt that if not for the people in her cohort she may still be working on it. Additionally, another challenge she found with the program was around "White fragility." She stated, "So, it's like catered around that whole idea of opening the White person's eyes to how others feel or whatever and being sensitive to not making them feel guilty." She talked about how at times the teachers, specifically White teachers, would talk about race issues from the outsider perspective, as if they did not know that the people they were talking to had lived these experiences also.

She said this behavior annoyed her, as if the professors were "...talking to me like I'm White. Like I don't know these things already... because you're looking at your larger demographic. So once again minimizing the minority, right?" She felt that even though the emphasis was on social justice some professors did not recognize that what they were teaching connected to her in a different way.

The final issue Patricia observed was a sense of privilege that was exhibited by White students. She recalled how there were White students who seemed to have privileges as well as received recommendations and promotions quicker than the students of color. She recalls one incident specifically where a White student was late, left early, or just did not show up for class, and nothing was ever said, and when students of color missed a class or were late, comments were made, and they had to make up the work. It was a blatant display of racism by some professors. She stated she didn't recall any real supports that were targeted to help her specifically to navigate the program but that she made friends through the program who helped her to be and feel successful.

When talking about her work as an educational leader, Patricia stated she started immediately looking for an administrative position within her district. The district where she was working during her doctoral program was predominately White, with no people of color in leadership positions. She applied for several positions but was never chosen, even though she had been in the district seven years, had great reviews, and was working in a quasi-administrative position as a teacher on special assignment. She said, "I really felt like the district that I was in very much favors White people." She said she felt they would not hire an Asian woman in that district because there were so few women in administrative positions, and none were people of color. She recalled an experience where one of her friends, Kaye, a White female with less experience, was hired into a principal position. Kaye received her Administrative Services Credential by taking the California Preliminary Administrative Exam (CPACE) Exam and had never been out of the classroom, as opposed to Patricia, who had received her Credentials through an accredited program, completed her doctorate degree, and had three years' experience as an out-of-the-classroom leader in quasi-administrative roles. Patricia decided it was time to begin looking outside of her current district for a position because she knew that being a woman of color, she was not what the district was looking for. She was offered and accepted a position as a middle school assistant principal in another district about 40 miles away, to where she relocated to live in an area closer to her new district. Although this new district was also predominantly White with no diversity in the leadership, similar to the district that she moved from, Patricia needed to gain experience as an administrator in order to compete for other positions in the future.

As Patricia settled into her new district, she was forced to acknowledge the presence of challenges that undermined her authority and a lack of support for promotion. She shared that many of her co-workers at her site as well as at the district level refused to acknowledge she had a doctorate degree. She would send emails and sign with the title "Doctor" and would receive responses with the title changed to "Ms." or just her first name. Even intentionally correcting her name, she shared that four years later they are still not using her title correctly. She has also applied for six different positions to move up in administration from an assistant principal to a principal position and has to date not been chosen and sometimes not even given an interview. She sees the White males and females with less time in the district moving into these positions. She also believes that as a woman of color she has to work twice as hard to prove her worth.

Patricia talks about the heaviness of the load she carries as a woman of color trying to fit into a space that is not designed to accommodate her. She is skeptical of the leadership because they talk about social justice and implement programs that are supposed to promote equity and inclusion; however, the practice of the district is more exclusionary and marginalizing. Patricia is at the point of considering changing her career. Although Patricia has had many successes in the district, the load she carries as a woman of color has made her tired and weary. She says her culture is not celebrated in any way in her organization and that the struggle to be seen and acknowledged by her White leaders, peers, and subordinates has led her to think seriously about leaving education to look elsewhere for a career where her ethnicity, skills, and knowledge can promote her and reduce the stress she feels in education.

Participant 3 (Sylvia)

Sylvia identifies as a Latina Mexican American who is in her 50s and currently a program director of a university counseling program. She received her doctorate degree in educational leadership seven years ago and prior to that worked as a school counselor and also site administrator. She initially went into a doctoral program as a challenge to herself to see if she could do it, as no one in her family had an advanced degree. Her cohort began with 27 students and consisted of six Latinas and one Nigerian; the rest were Caucasian. The breakdown of male and female was about equal, and 23 of the 27 completed the program. Sylvia discussed a number of challenges as she went through her doctorate program, mainly consisting of very little institutional support. She said the six Latina students bonded together and became a type of support group for each other, which became the single biggest support for her in completing the degree. She also said being a self-advocate was instrumental in her completing the degree, which took her nine years from start to finish.

In her current position as an educational leader, Sylvia discussed a number of current and past challenges. She said she often feels like she is "presumed to be incompetent" in the face of others and said she would make a suggestion in a meeting, only to be ignored. Someone else would then make the same suggestion and people in the meeting will say "that's a great idea," leaving her to feel her ideas are basically ignored. She has heard from other women of color who say their ideas are often ignored in meetings in the same manner. Hence, Sylvia believes this not being heard is not unique to her but probably a pattern of occurrence for all women, especially those of color.

Sylvia sees herself as an advocate for women in leadership positions and will often speak out when she sees injustices occurring. After receiving her doctorate, Sylvia said she has more confidence in addressing race and gender inequities she comes across. She continues to champion the need for more diversity of thought and helping women of color advance into positions of educational leadership.

Participant 4 (Michelle)

Michelle identifies as a Black or African American woman who is currently serving as an assistant professor at the Department of Educational Leadership at a four-year university. Four years ago, in her late 30s, she received her doctoral degree in education. Prior to her doctoral program, she was a principal at a middle school. Initially, she pursued her doctoral degree to hold onto her position due to an increase of layoffs. The timing was just right for her to go back to school, although she had her third child during the program.

Michelle described her doctoral cohort as lacking diversity: "Whites (majority), followed by Hispanics/Latinos, and a few African Americans. There was a lack of Asian American students." The faculty was "more diverse in terms of ethnicity and sexual orientation than some of the other higher education institutions." Despite being a Hispanic-serving institution, the majority of the faculty were still predominantly White, with some Latinos/Hispanics and African Americans. However, it was a "challenge to keep African American faculties" as it is considered to be a "revolving door" position. In addition, there is a "noticeable lack of Asian American faculties" in that doctoral program.

Michelle shared that one of her personal goals was to pursue a higher education but did not realize the challenges. One of the biggest challenges was lack of transparency and communication between the school and her district. During her first two years, she lost her position as an administrator, along with her doctoral scholarship and paid teaching assistantship (TA). She had not received any communication, so she missed the deadlines for submitting her application and/or other paperwork. She felt she had to "hunt for information on how to access email that was being sent" and "find... basic information like [her] classes and financial aid package." For the first time, she started to question herself and her abilities and felt alone, frustrated, and unable to overcome the "institutional barriers." The rest of her cohort seemed to be doing well and did not appear to be experiencing similar challenges. When she sought assistance, she would often leave the room feeling "uncomfortable and confused." The message was clear: "you're lucky to be here…"

Another challenge Michelle faced was the lack of transparency of expectations from the instructor, especially in the area of scholarly writing. In one incident, she thought she had completed the assignment according to the rubric and expectation, only to learn later that it was incorrect. When she consulted with the instructor, she was told that she needed to "read beyond the instruction," did not "understand what it means to write at a doctoral level," and "was immediately referred to the writing center for support." This incident resulted in much unease and uncertainty.

Another obstacle was the lack of support for students who are pregnant and parenting. For example, it was difficult to engage in study groups where Michelle felt isolated from the rest of her cohort and "like they [her cohort] kind of chased [her] out." Oftentimes, her cohort would leave her out or "make the meeting times inflexible." She felt the institution lacked discourse and support for diversity, especially in the area of parents in the program. Although there were many obstacles she faced during her doctoral program, she shared that as she went through the program, she "really thought everything was the way it was supposed to be." She "didn't think anything of it" because she was "too busy trying to balance everything like trying to get [her] old position back as the principal, being pregnant, trying to figure out how to get back her scholarships and paid TA-ship back, and later, trying to prepare for a new job offer before graduating, working on her dissertation, and life obstacles in general."

Overall, Michelle felt she "had a good experience" in her doctoral program, aside from what has been mentioned, "especially after [she] had figured out how to navigate the system." She took initiative to learn about the system (e.g., "to get the funds, position and/or support you need, you need to go beyond filling out paperwork, you need to network and go directly to the right professor, the ones who are tenured"). She identified a faculty member who supported and helped her to navigate the system. She also actively participated in the students of color coalition and eventually created her own support group ("outcast group"). However, she wondered if she were younger, male, and had no children, would she still experience these same challenges?

In her current position, Michelle feels accepted and respected, but as a woman of color and parent, she often feels the need to prove herself. Specifically, she talked about having to publish more, be more active, and work harder "because of the stigma of both being Black and parenting four kids." She would often say "yes to everything" so no one would her "think less than capable." In addition, although the institution has a mission of equity and social justice, she felt more could be done. Specifically, she felt the institution as a whole should "walk the talk" and not just talk about being a socially just institution. In addition, she emphasizes the importance of using data to make sound decisions and be more vocal in advocating for meeting the needs of students and faculties alike. She is a strong proponent of social justice and equity for women of color in the professional fields.

Participant 5 (Kristie)

Kristie identifies as an Asian American woman who is currently serving as an adjunct faculty member at various universities. Ten years ago, in her mid-thirties, she received her doctoral degree in educational leadership. She was pregnant with her first child during the second year of her program. Prior to her doctoral program, she was an administrator at an elementary school. Initially, she pursued her doctoral degree with the goal of having a greater impact in the field of education.

Kristie attended a predominantly White institution, where the majority of her cohort members were White and/or Hispanics/Latinos, along with three African Americans, two Armenian Americans, and two Asian Americans. Her cohort of 30 only had six women. The majority of the faculty in the program were primarily Whites or Hispanics/Latinos and male. Her dissertation committees were made up of two White women and one Hispanic man.

Being the only Asian woman in her cohort, Kristie experienced many challenges. Most notably, she felt a continual need to prove herself with her peers. She recalled comments made throughout the program (e.g., "Are you sure you understand this?" or "Wow, I didn't think you got this."; "Did she really do this because it's really impressive"; and "Are you sure you can handle this kind of research for your dissertation?"). These reactions caused her to question her own work, abilities, and intelligence. As a result, she felt she had to work harder academically and professionally. She felt as though she was constantly "under a microscope," unable to let her guard down. She was afraid of making mistakes and had to choose her words carefully, as if she were "walking on egg-shells." In another example, her dissertation defense took two hours, while the majority of her peers completed their defense within 30 minutes. Her cohort could not understand why there were so many questions about her dissertation when they only had a few questions asked of them. A few of her peers thought it may have been her research topic, which focused on the gender discrimination and the education of Cambodian American students. A majority of Kristie's peers focused on specific topics more related to their chair's scholarship, such as the academic achievement among Hispanics/Latinos.

Kristie often felt invisible. On many occasions, she had to work hard to "get the attention of the instructor to call on her to respond and participate in class discussion." When given the rare opportunity, she felt the instructor did not really hear what was said. Yet, when others immediately repeated similar arguments, the instructor seemed more complimentary and acknowledging. Another incident occurred where the instructor announced and encouraged minority students who were interested in serving as his research assistant to apply. Specifically, the instructor stated that the only criterion is if the individual is interested in learning. As a result, a handful approached him for an application, but only Whites and Hispanic students were offered an application to complete. Giving the instructor the benefit of the doubt, she recalled approaching him to request an application in which he initially asked, "What's your name again?" and then he explained he was looking for someone who is bilingual in Spanish.

The school also lacked support for students who were expecting and nursing. Specifically, Kristie identified the challenges of needing to take frequent breaks (such as, restroom breaks, alternating sitting/standing breaks, nursing breaks) as instructors would "take deep sighs, roll their eyes, make 'a-hum' sounds." In addition, she felt uncomfortable "munching/snacking or drinking water" while lectures were given as she would hear comments like "really try to do those things during break times, okay?" As a result of feeling uneasy and uncomfortable, she had to adjust to minimize class disruption.

Although there were many obstacles Kristie faced during her doctoral program, she shared that overall, it was a "great program with some amazing classmates," and she "learned a lot." She stated that "in all honesty, [she] didn't have time to reflect on what's going on, grief, or let anything discourage [her] because [she] was too busy working full time during the day, part time as adjunct in the evening, taking care of the newborn, helping out at the family's shop, and pursuing a doctoral degree." As she reflected back to her doctoral experiences, she realized the challenges she went through and wondered, if she were born from a different ethnicity, different gender, and even different characteristics or attitudes, would she still experience similar issues or situations?

The need to prove herself also extended to Kristie's personal life. Having been raised in a traditional Asian family, it was a constant battle for her to break the cultural chain and stigma associated with females going to school and pursuing a career. She shared how difficult and challenging it was to convince her mother and brother to allow her to attend college, let alone pursue her doctoral degree. She was often reminded of her action being "disrespectful, selfish, and a disgrace" to the family. In addition, her intelligence and disposition were challenged daily. As a result, she had to prove to her family as well that she was capable of so much more than being just a daughter, wife, and mother.

In her current position, Kristie often feels the need to prove herself more than her counterparts because she is a woman of color, first generation college student, and mom of young children. Specifically, she mentioned she needed to publish more, be more outspoken to be taken seriously, be more active in everything, and work harder in order to be considered for a position. As an Asian woman, it is extremely difficult to move away from the stigma of being "Asian," and unfortunately, society perpetuates the cycle of "being voiceless." She felt that although the institution is willing to provide adaptations, it still lacks the discourse and support for diversity and social justice. She sees herself as an advocate, and a warrior of social justice and equitable change agent for all.

Participant 6 (Jennifer)

Jennifer, a first generation bi-lingual Millennial who identifies as a Hispanic/Mexican American woman, is currently a school board member in the Inland Empire in California. She received her educational doctorate in 2014, completing her three-year program in the three-year time frame. She has worked in the field of education for nine years and has been a member of a school board for two years of her four-year elected term. Her goal in getting a doctoral degree was to become a mentor for others who aspired to get a post-secondary degree. Her hope is that her success would act as a guide and motivator for other young people on the same journey.

Jennifer is the first person in her family to pursue a postgraduate degree. She stated she did not know any persons of color who had a doctoral degree when she made the decision to continue her educational journey for a post-secondary degree. As a person of color from a low-income family, she had worked hard to secure the grades needed for college but had not considered going on to a doctorate because of the financial obligation. While in high school, she received the Bill and Melinda Gates Foundation scholarship, which opened opportunities for her to consider bigger educational dreams. This scholarship paid for a 10-year education journey, which carried her through her doctoral degree. As a result of using the scholarship and continuing her educational journey before it expired, she was the youngest person in her cohort, and at the age of 28, she received her doctorate in leadership for educational justice.

Prior to starting her doctoral program, Jennifer was a counselor in a high school, serving high populations of Hispanic/Latino students. Her work was in supporting students to meet graduation requirements and get into college. After completing her doctorate, she continued to work as a counselor as she began to explore her next goal of becoming a trustee of a school board. She gained experience and understanding of how districts work by creating partnerships with county offices of education, districts, and others who could help her learn and grow her understanding of how to best serve students in the position of school board trustee.

Jennifer used three factors when choosing her doctorate program. Proximity was the first factor because she knew that she was going to stay in education and wanted to be close to her home and family, as they were her support system. The second factor was her desire to attend a private school. She had previously gone to a private school for her masters and felt the smaller class size allowed her to receive more attention from the professor. The final factor in her decision was that she had a short time left to use the scholarship money, and she did not want to waste the opportunity or support provided by the scholarship. When reflecting on the diversity of the program, Jennifer stated that even though the program was specifically designed to produce educational leaders focused on social justice, most of the professors were elderly White males, along with a couple of White female professors. She recalls two male professors of color: one Filipino and one African. The African professor was only there for one semester. Additionally, she said there were no women professors of color during the three years she was in the program.

A pleasant surprise came when she met her fellow cohort members, as they were a very diverse group. It was as if the professors had intentionally recruited and accepted a group of people who were diverse in ethnical background, generation, employment, and gender for the program. She believes the diversity of the group led to a richer and deeper learning experience. In her opinion, one of the greatest strengths of the program came from the richness of the conversation with the diverse group that was a part of her cohort. She is still close to six of the people from her program.

During her doctoral studies, her greatest challenge was connected to her understanding what a doctoral program entailed, organizing herself for success, and making the time to read and study. She states she would have benefited from having a mentor or counselor who assisted her with understanding the program and how to navigate. Initially, she said that it felt much like her high school, undergraduate, and master's programs, where she was the youngest and only Hispanic in the room. However, as she went through the program, she began to feel and see the cultural distance between the predominately White professors and the students of color. This resulted in a feeling of cultural dissonance with the professors and a stronger relationship with the other candidates in the program. The content taught in her program was in many ways detached from the professors teaching it. She stated that at times it felt as if the professors did not see the funds of knowledge and the lived experiences that students gave witness to and provided evidence for what they were reading in the content. Often the professors spoke at students rather than with the students and include them in the relevance of the conversation. She stated,

lectures were heavily theoretical with little practical application which is the reason many of the students joined the program. It was almost as if the professors only had head knowledge and no depth of understanding on the subjects or the work taking place in schools. And although there was learning taking place, it would have benefited us in the program to be more engaged in the work of leading for educational justice rather than just reading about it and discussing it.

When asked about support that was available for the student, specifically students of color, she did not recall any specific support that was offered or discussed with students in the program. One specific challenge where she would have liked to have support was in the writing component of the program. She felt her confidence when it came to writing was low, and being an English learner, she felt the writing assignments were often difficult and time consuming. Her suggestion of having a writing center or some type of writing support would have been helpful. Without this type of support, she spent long hours writing and rewriting assignments to ensure a passing grade.

As a current school board trustee, Jennifer uses her understanding of social justice from her doctoral program to advocate for the students in her district. She takes seriously the tasks of hiring, evaluating, and even firing, if necessary, the superintendent, who leads the schools in her district to success. She attributes her work to the mentoring she received during her doctoral program from one of the professors of color. He listened to her, encouraged her, and provided her insights into how to begin to pursue becoming a school board member. And although the board that she is a member of was predominately White at one time, since her election, there has been a shift in the demographics of the board, and now there are three Hispanic women, one White male, and one White female. In her campaign, she was up against the incumbent, an older White male, and even though it was a close race, she won, she believes, because she was what the people wanted. Although the current board of elected officials are diverse in ethnicity and gender, the school district itself continues to be predominately White. She stated that a challenge in the district is implicit bias in the hiring process and that the work of dismantling those procedures and reconstructing more equitable processes for hiring remains a difficult task.

SOLUTIONS AND PARTICIPANT RECOMMENDATIONS

Each participant shared stories of having feelings of invisibility, lack of recognition or acknowledgement, inability to find satisfaction or gratification, and feelings of self-doubt. Some talked about the pressure of the authoritarian regime that some found themselves participating in while others spoke about unconscious bias and forms of microaggressions that assaulted them daily. Other participants spoke about how they felt marginalized and silenced. All participants provided recommendations for doctoral programs, as well as the organizations where they worked, in relation to how women of color can disrupt these feelings. Through their experiences, they gained a clearer understanding of who they are, with hopes of supporting other women of color who find themselves on the same journey. In this final section, we discuss the common themes that emerged from the narratives and the various recommendations provided by the participants.

Invisibility

"Invisibility is an inner struggle with feeling that one's talents, abilities, personality, and worth are not valued or even recognized" (Franklin, 1999, p. 761). Franklin (2004) reported that the idea of mattering as a human, for Black females, is attached to recognition and acknowledgement. He found that the disregard that Black women and Black men felt because of their lived experiences over time has led to a sense of powerlessness in Black women (Franklin, 2004). Powerlessness stems from one's desire to be visible contrasted with the level of comfort society has with that visibility and leads to a decreased sense of belonging, and an increased sense of inferiority and self-hatred (Franklin, 1999). These experiences from childhood to adulthood forces Black women to change, conform, and accommodate to an ill-conceived sense of inferiority rather than living their lives as liberated people (Hooks, 2015b). Haynes et al. (2016) found that:

unless disrupted by counter-hegemonic teaching practice, academic transactions can promote a brand of invisibility marked by the effects of race or gender, which is conceivably symptomatic of the racialized sexism Black women and girls experience inside, and outside of the classroom. (p. 388)

Haynes et al. (2016) further reported that once participants discovered the connection between their past experiences and their present lives, they were able to recognize how the feelings of inevitability could render them helpless.

Kathryn shared that there is a need to improve our understanding of diversity issues that are taking place across the United States, and everyone, including university program faculty and doctoral candidates, need to join these efforts. Patricia stated you should not be afraid to move to other spaces where you can be seen. After staying in a district for over seven years, she was unable to move into an administrative position. She stated that leaving is scary but being in a place where one can be seen is important in her personal development. One recommendation from Jennifer is for doctorate programs to provide clear program guidelines and expectations for women of color seeking to enter their programs. It is important for women of color to investigate the programs they are considering. As they spend some time researching programs, there should be someone from the program to answer questions to help them better understand how the program works and what support is available for them. Women of color already feel invisible, and doctoral programs can counter these negative feelings by providing space for women of color to use their voices to advocate for their needs.

Authoritarian

Research has identified processes and barriers that disproportionately affect women and perpetuate a gender gap in leadership (Bear et al., 2017). Barriers such as discriminatory practices (Castilla, 2008); partiality among management for employing, advising, and supporting those who are similar to themselves (Gorman, 2006); ideas about the competency of women as less competent than men (Ridgeway, 2011); and procedural issues with recruitment processes continue to perpetuate the gender gap in leadership (Reskin & McBrier, 2000). Studies also show that the implementation of policies and procedures designed to disrupt gender inequities have little long-term effect (Kalev et al., 2006). While there were other common themes that came from the participants, one that was echoed by several was the issue of gender equity. According to Arriaga et al. (2020), true gender equity requires a "culturally proficient response." These authors went on to say that it also "means working together with female and male colleagues who are grounded in values for equity."

There are many examples of when an authoritarian issue takes place, but one that occurs the most often is when a male has a doctoral degree; Sylvia reported that in meetings men are addressed as Dr. "so and so." However, when she is addressed, she is often referred to to her by her first name or by "Ms." This also occurs in emails, as Patricia reported. This type of behavior not only represents an example of an authoritarian issue, but it also shows how cultural norms become accepted practice until they are challenged. Patricia suggests that universities consider hiring more women of color to teach courses because in her program the only professors of color were two-male professors, and she would have enjoyed learning from a woman of color who would bring a different perspective and type of support to the learning experience. Having a woman of color as a professor would also give the women of color a connection and a reference as they prepare to enter the leadership arena. Another participant stated universities should consider the way they mentor their candidates. Often White males are not the best mentors for women, especially women of color. This participant stated that White males can be great co-conspirators and use their social capital to support women of color going into leadership positions.

Unconscious Bias

This is characterized as behavior that is normalized through societal patterns and negatively affects others. People do not consciously know that they are doing it. Participants reported how unconscious bias often questioned their professionalism and abilities to perform the tasks required of them. Patricia stated she believes programs should consider ways to support the transition to leadership positions. She recalls candidates in the program who were White being invited to speak in various engagements and co-author manuscripts. She feels this is an unconscious bias that keeps Black candidates from excelling as quickly after the degree than their White counterparts. She states that she would have loved the opportunity to better understand what she could do with her degree and that it is important for women of color to have this information, as they may not have access to all the avenues available. Jennifer recommended that universities and organizations spend time and set procedures that help them to get to know each other. Her school board has put in place several procedures to help the members get to know each other better, and they work to be open and build trust in their communication about how words and actions affect them. One example is that they open their meetings with informal conversations, which helps them to see their similarities and build trust in their relationships.

Marginalized

"Marginalization is both a condition and a process that prevents individuals and groups from full participation in social, economic, and political life enjoyed by the wider society" (Alakhunova et al., 2015, p. 2). Generally, marginalization occurs when the power is taken or limited from a group of people because they are considered different from the dominant group. For example, Michelle shared:

I was marginalized from the study group just because I was pregnant during my doctoral program; and then, again in my job…this time, it was because of my kids… you know, me being Black and the stereotypes of having too many kids…so I'm often isolated and are [sic] not invited to anything.

Other participants—who also had young children—often felt their workplace was not designed to support professionals and often hear the message that "either you work as a professional or be a mom, you can't have both." As a result, the majority of the participants reported having to "work ten times harder to prove that [they are] more than capable to perform the job well" and felt they "could never say 'no' to anything that was asked of them." In addition, several participants discussed having low expectations placed on them by their supervisors, causing them to question their own abilities. As Kristie stated,

I remember in my old job, I would be the only one asked to perform high profile tasks, yet at meetings, I often hear my supervisor say, 'are you sure you can handle this?' to me, but never say it to anyone else. I would always wonder if it is because I was the only minority in that group.

These results confirm marginalization can manifest itself both subtly and overtly, and as a consequence, these feelings and experiences of being isolated and/or "picked on" are prevalent (Kersh, 2018).

Research highlights that women and minorities are more likely to experience marginalization in the workplace, and the institution has the ultimate responsibility to dismantle such practices (Falci & Watanabe, 2020). Michelle suggests there is a need to have more "substantial and real conversations about race and racism" in the workplace. She emphasizes, "it is only then we can hold ourselves and others accountable for the way we treat the experiences of people of color." Adding to this recommendation, Kristie believes it is important to create a work environment that welcomes and respects individuals to share their experiences openly, without judgement. As Michelle explained, "there's power in being able to tell your own story and being heard." Kristie suggests that everyone has a role to play: "walk… the talk, modeling what it is intended and said instead of just words on papers."

Silencing

Silencing is a powerful construct used to exclude one's participation in space where knowledge is defined, and the allocation of power occurs. Social groups who have been silenced have limited access to this space. Additionally, this space is controlled by the hegemonic rules of the dominant group (Spivak, 1988). Participants mentioned how they would often make a suggestion in a meeting and were ignored. A White male would then make a similar suggestion and then be commended for it. This ignoring type of behavior is an example of how women of color are often silenced, or they are made to feel their ideas are not important or relevant.

Kathryn shared that her doctoral program was a national degree program, and the instructors did not have any connection to the district where the student worked. This made it difficult to gain entry to gather data, and the candidate was met with a lot of resistance. Additionally, she found that when she would bring up concerns or issues, she felt silenced. She said that it felt as if she was being "ostracized," and that her power was being taken away. Kathryn also reported that she had to request permission to give advice or make suggestions that challenged the dominant norm.

Her recommendation for universities, organizations, and women of color who are moving forward to get their doctorate degree is to consider all options. She said the university needs to remember why students are coming into their programs and use these opportunities to get to know the students so they can provide equitable support, and not just implement programs because they need to use "some buzz words." Kathryn further advises organizations to include people of color in the development of programs that are going to affect their lives. She feels her organization jumped on the diversity and equity bandwagon and it was in word only, as the practices of the organization did not change. She felt even more silenced as the "facade" unfolded. She is planning to change districts in order to try and find a space where she is included, and she feels her voice will be heard.

Additionally, when talking about feeling silenced, one participant shared a story of how she actually watched her White counterparts receive opportunities that were never offered to her. Many of the White students were invited to co-author papers or co-present at conferences or were recommended for positions and committees to further their work. She did not have access to these types of opportunities and took a longer time to actuate her degree and still feels like she is on uneven ground. This participant was emotional when she spoke about having to navigate a new experience alone. She further stated that her first love is to write and feeling that her degree was supposed to help her to get someplace but because no one listened to her her dreams are yet to be actualized. She hopes programs will consider mentoring their graduates for a short time after the program is completed in order to support them in this new arena of work. This participant went on to recommend that women of color going into programs are diligent about making their voices heard and that they should be persistent in seeking out opportunities. She reported she is regretful that she did not do this herself. All of the women of color who participated in this study were happy and proud of themselves for completing their doctoral degrees. They all felt education opens doors to opportunities they would not have had otherwise. They encourage women of color to step into the postgraduate world and are open to making themselves available to support up-and-coming doctoral students in the future.

FUTURE RESEARCH

Follow up to this research will involve interviewing more women of color, including those who identify as Native American, LGBTQIA+, and those with a disability. To further explore the themes that have already been identified, we would expand on both our research and interview questions. These questions could include school and college experiences, as well as personal, cultural, and generational influences that may affect women of color and their decision making. Additionally, a comparative study should be conducted between women of color and their Caucasian counterparts to identify the challenges and similarities they may have. Furthermore, a comparative study involving men of color would provide additional information on their experiences to see if they were similar or dissimilar to women of color.

CONCLUSION

There are a number of significant conclusions that can be drawn from the "stories" provided by the women of color who were interviewed and shared their experiences for this chapter. Numerous avenues exist for universities and organizations to support women of color in their doctoral programs as well as in the work environment. Some of the participants' recommendations have led us to the following conclusions:

1. Universities can diversify their hiring practices to include women of color. This can include providing role models who may be willing to help promote or advance the support of women of color. This would mean going beyond traditional ways of recruiting women of color and being more intentional in their hiring practices.
2. Organizations and universities could play a more active role in promoting and supporting women of color by providing a more transparent and direct way of assisting women of color in their career paths and publications through co-authorship and mentorship. Women of color may or may not understand how to navigate the new opportunities in the field of education.
3. Offering institutional support for professionals with families of those targeted populations would be beneficial in a number of ways. This would not only help candidates balance their career with their personal lives, but it would also show a significant investment by the institution. Making a conscious effort to create and promote policies that are inclusive and consider the needs of professionals with families would be of great benefit to students as well as the institution.
4. Universities and organizations must work to create environments of respect and trust. This is accomplished by implementing policies and procedures that minimize shaming and promote spaces that are inclusive and accepting of diversity. To accomplish this, the work must be accepted and promoted by all involved.
5. Many university programs emphasize "social justice," but are predominantly led by Caucasian professors with classrooms filled with students of color. This does not mean the program or its courses are not valid. It does means there is an opportunity to provide a deeper learning experience. It is important that

professors acknowledge the lived experiences of the students they teach, which can enrich the learning and dynamics of courses.

As many institutions across the nation formalize ways to address systemic racism, microaggression, and inherent bias, there are still many issues facing people of color, specifically women of color, that need to be addressed. The preceding stories and recommendations are a beginning. These are not meant to be an ending point, but are ideas that can be used to create spaces where women of color, and all people, can feel valued, welcomed, supported, respected, and have a sense of belonging. To be successful in a doctoral program and in educational leadership positions, women of color would benefit from being seen as vital members "of the team," being given an opportunity to lead, being accepted for who they are, being included, and lastly, being heard.

REFERENCES

Admin. (2019, February 14). *From a nation at risk to a nation at hope.* http://nationathope.org/report-from-the-nation-download/

Alakhunova, N., Diallo, O., Martin del Campo, I., & Tallarico, W. (2015). *Defining marginalization: An assessment tool. A Product of the partnership between four development professionals at the Elliot School of International Affairs & The Word Fair Trade Organization-Asia.* The George Washington University.

Arriaga, T. T., Stanley, S., & Lindsey, D. B. (2020). *Leading while female: A culturally proficient response for gender equity.* Corwin.

Bear, J. B., Cushenbery, L., London, M., & Sherman, G. D. (2017). Performance feedback, power retention, and the gender gap in leadership. *The Leadership Quarterly, 28*(6), 721–740. doi:10.1016/j.leaqua.2017.02.003

Castilla, E. J. (2008). Gender, race, and meritocracy in organizational careers. *American Journal of Sociology, 113*(6), 1479–1526. doi:10.1086/588738 PMID:19044141

Collins, P. H. (1986). Learning from the outsider within: The sociological significance of black feminist thought. *Social Problems, 33*(6), S14–S32. Advance online publication. doi:10.2307/800672

Collins, P. H. (2015). *Black feminist thought: Knowledge, consciousness, and the politics of empowerment.* Routledge.

Creswell, J. W., & Guetterman, T. C. (2019). *Educational research: Planning, conducting, and evaluating quantitative and qualitative research* (6th ed.). Pearson.

Ebersole, M., Kanahele-Mossman, H., & Kawakami, A. (2015). Culturally responsive teaching: Examining teachers' understandings and perspectives. *Journal of Education and Training Studies, 4*(2). Advance online publication. doi:10.11114/jets.v4i2.1136

Falci, C. D., & Watanabe, M. (2020). Network marginalization of women in the workplace: A case in academia. *Journal of Women and Minorities in Science and Engineering, 26*(2), 155–175. doi:10.1615/JWomenMinorScienEng.2020029186

Felder, P. (2010). On doctoral student development: Exploring faculty mentoring in the shaping of African American doctoral student success. *Qualitative Report, 15*, 455–474.

Franklin, A. J. (1999). Invisibility syndrome and racial identity development in psychotherapy and counseling African American men. *The Counseling Psychologist, 27*(6), 761–793. doi:10.1177/0011000099276002

Franklin, A. J. (2004). *From brotherhood to manhood: How Black men rescue their relationships and dreams from the invisibility syndrome.* Wiley.

Fullan, M. (2001). *Leading in a culture of change.* Jossey-Bass.

Gay, G. (2004). Navigating marginality en route to the professoriate: Graduate students of color learning and living in academia. *International Journal of Qualitative Studies in Education: QSE, 17*(2), 265–288. doi:10.1080/09518390310001653907

Gorman, E. H. (2006). Work uncertainty and the promotion of professional women: The case of law firm partnership. *Social Forces, 85*(2), 865–890. doi:10.1353of.2007.0004

Haynes, C., Stewart, S., & Allen, E. (2016). Three paths, one struggle: Black women and girls battling invisibility in U.S. classrooms. *The Journal of Negro Education, 85*(3), 380. doi:10.7709/jnegroeducation.85.3.0380

Hooks, B. (2015a). *Ain't I a woman: Black women and feminism.* Routledge.

Hooks, B. (2015b). *Talking back: Thinking feminist, thinking Black.* Routledge.

Kalev, A., Dobbin, F., & Kelly, E. (2006). Best Practices or Best Guesses? Assessing the Efficacy of Corporate Affirmative Action and Diversity Policies. *American Sociological Review, 71*(4), 589–617. doi:10.1177/000312240607100404

Kersh, R. (2018). Women in higher education: Exploring stressful workplace factors and coping strategies. *Journal About Women in Higher Education, 11*(1), 56–73. doi:10.1080/19407882.2017.1372295

Ladson-Billings, G., & Tate, W. F. (2016). Toward a critical race theory of education. *Critical Race Theory in Education*, 10–31. doi:10.4324/9781315709796-2

McAuliffe, G., & ... (2013). *Culturally alert counseling: A comprehensive introduction*. Sage Publications.

Ogbu, J. U. (1995). Understanding cultural diversity and learning. In J. A. Banks & C. A. M. G. Banks (Eds.), *Handbook of research on multicultural education* (pp. 22–34). Macmillan Pub.

Reskin, B. F., & Mcbrier, D. B. (2000). Why not ascription? Organizations' employment of male and female managers. *American Sociological Review*, *65*(2), 210. doi:10.2307/2657438

Ridgeway, C. L. (2011). *Framed by gender: How gender inequality persists in the modern world*. Oxford University Press. doi:10.1093/acprof:oso/9780199755776.001.0001

Santamaría, L. J., & Santamaría, A. P. (2011). *Applied critical leadership in education: Choosing change*. Routledge.

Spivak, G. (1988). Can the subaltern speak? In C. Nelson & L. Grossberg (Eds.), *Marxism and the interpretation of culture* (pp. 271–316). University of Illinois Press., doi:10.1007/978-1-349-19059-1_20

Terrell, R., & Lindsey, R. (2009). *Culturally proficient leadership: The personal journey begins within*. Corwin.

Trybus, M. A. (2011). Facing the challenge of change: Steps to becoming an effective leader. *Delta Kappa Gamma Bulletin*, *77*(3), 33–36.

ADDITIONAL READING

Admin. (2019, February 14). *From a nation at risk to a nation at hope*. http://nationathope.org/report-from-the-nation-download/

Hensley, P., & Burmeister, L. (2009). *Leadership connectors: Six keys to developing relationships in schools*. Eye on Education.

Herzog, B. (2017). Invisibilization and silencing as an ethical and sociological challenge. *Social Epistemology*, *32*(1), 13–23. doi:10.1080/02691728.2017.1383529

Kroska, A., & Cason, T. C. (2019). The gender gap in business leadership: Exploring an affect control theory explanation. *Social Psychology Quarterly*, *82*(1), 75–97. doi:10.1177/0190272518806292

Chapter 5
Black Female Education Leaders and Intersectionality:
Leadership, Race, Gender, Power, and Social Justice

Alyncia M. Bowen
Franklin University, USA

Shaquanah Robinson
ⓘ https://orcid.org/0000-0002-3455-5851
University of Phoenix, USA

Jim Lane
University of Phoenix, USA

ABSTRACT

The pandemic has operated within a cultural movement opposing systemic racism. Redux of Black Lives Matter was spurred by the killings of George Floyd, Ahmad Aubrey, Rashard Brooks, Breonna Taylor, and others, and resulted in prolonged protests throughout the country. This caustic backdrop has created unique challenges for female Black educational leaders. Thus, they are compelled to navigate their already challenging duties among the intersections of leadership, race, gender, power, and social justice. Black female education leaders are challenged to courageously lead during an unprecedented era of disruption.

DOI: 10.4018/978-1-7998-7235-1.ch005

INTRODUCTION

At the time of this writing the United States is in the midst of the COVID-19 pandemic, super imposed within a cultural movement, fighting systemic racism. The pandemic has operated concomitantly with *Black Lives Matter (BLM)*. The escalation of BLM was spurred by the killings of George Floyd, Brianna Taylor, and others, and resulted in nationwide protests. This backdrop has created unique challenges for Black female education leaders, especially those who are mothers, sisters, aunts, and or friends of Black males. Days before the inauguration of Joe Biden as the 46th U.S. President and Kamala Harris as the first African American Vice President, the U.S. Capitol was invaded by domestic terrorists, many of whom touted Confederate flags and other icons of American White Supremacy.

These societal disruptions have intensified efforts to promote social justice. Throughout 2020 and into 2021, civic leaders participated in demonstrations that prompted heated discussions. Even during the funeral services that celebrated the life of John Lewis, US Congressman and civil rights leader, the comments were aimed at promoting civil rest during the period of unrest that was taking place. Throughout his life Lewis demanded social justice peacefully but forcefully, a definitive stance reflected in his signature epithet, *Good Trouble*. We believe this balance point of advocacy and opposition is the nexus at which the participants of our study find themselves.

Central to promoting causes of social justice are Black female education leaders who hold positions of influence and power in the schools they lead and the communities they serve. They face their own challenges and suffer their own racial abuses as they work to bridge the divide of racial and social injustice to create the most productive learning environment for their students. In this study, we learned and share the experiences of seven Black women who are education leaders in diverse institutional venues, including elementary, secondary, and university settings. Conversations with these Black female education leaders revealed that in their experiences, the rise of social justice issues stems from both overt and subtle abuses of power.

The challenge of Black female education leaders has been to courageously lead their institutions during an unprecedented era of disruption. This unique group has navigated their duties among the intersecting roles of *leadership, race, gender, power,* and *social justice.* The purpose of this study was to better understand how these intersections have shaped the identities of Black female education leaders during the *BLM* movement and COVID-19 pandemic.

BACKGROUND

Blalock & Akehi (2018) observed that "sharing stories, particularly when stories contain shared experiences, can further connect individuals around a commonality" (p. 90). Collaborative critical autoethnography invites personal and cultural critique (Boylorn & Orbe, 2014; Denzin, 2014) We used collaborative autoethnography to mingle our stories with those of our participants in an attempt to offer deep understanding into the lived experiences of school leaders. Collaborative autoethnography "invites the community to investigate shared stores and balances the individual narrative with the greater collective experiences" (Blalock & Akehi, 2018, p. 94). We provide autoethnographic reflections on our data following the discussion of our results.

The shared space of storytelling provided an infrastructure that empowered our participants to talk out loud in an environment of peers who could relate to their experience. Each participant was asked to share how leadership, race, gender, power, and social justice shaped her identity as a Black female education leader. They also were asked to describe how these intersections shaped their professional actions as Black female education leaders during the BLM movement and COVID-19 pandemic.

Black females make up approximately 13% of all public school principals (NCES, 2018) and 5% of all college presidents (Gray, Howard, & Chessman, 2018). These comprised the population of our study. We used purposive sampling to choose participants who could help us gain a deeper understanding of how Black female education leaders were influenced by the intersections of these roles. The sample population consisted of seven Black female education leaders who held a variety of leadership positions, including principals, college deans, and college presidents.

To capture the views of the participants, two focus groups were held using Zoom. The participants were audio recorded and their transcripts were provided for review. Each participant was asked to provide a reflective narrative of their experiences. This narrative was to include information that was not shared during the focus group but was relevant to the discussion.

Data was derived from transcripts of the focus group conversations and personal narratives. We asked participants to describe the ways that intersections of leadership, race, gender, power, and social justice have shaped their identities as Black female education leaders before and during the BLM movement and COVID-19 pandemic. The participants felt sharing their stories was therapeutic because they realized they were not alone in their experiences. As the reserchers facilitated the focus groups, it became evident that their stories were similar and worth sharing. Prior to conducting the focus groups, the researchers discussed the value and importance of sharing their stories with the participants. One leader who represented the thoughts of all appreciated the chance "to release some of this and know that what we are doing is right." In essence, this experience created a community, an environment that fostered connectivity in knowing that they had peers who had shared experiences.

RESEARCHERS AS PARTICIPANTS

The researchers participated in the study. The research team is comprised of two African American women and a white male. The two African American females provided insight into their roles within education. Both shared intricate details of experiences as it related to the study. While the white male co-researcher did not actively participate in the focus groups, his input was invaluable in managing the focus groups and in analyzing the data.

This study is a collaborative critical autoethnography that attempts to offer deep understanding into the lived experiences of female Black school leaders. We analyze overarching themes in autoethnographic narratives from seven Black female education leaders.

LEADERSHIP

The following is a brief review of scholars of educational leadership whose thoughts provide insight into the practices and motivations of the leaders in this study. Each is a transformational leader, pushing and pulling their schools forward to improve learning for their students while also changing the perceptions of their staff and breaking cultural norms along the way. They are motivated by an exceptional level of care that fuels these transformations, with an understanding that service to their students and community is the impetus for each action. They undergird this moral imperative with a strong faith that God will guide their path. This belief was shared by all of the participants. While spirituality was not a lens through which the researchers were evaluating, it did come up by all of the participants in their personal narratives. However, in this writing, spirituality is not explored.

Our participants seemed to consistently apply the tenets of transformational leadership, and ethical leadership in their decisions to shape their schools and educate their students. Indeed, these themes are so interwoven into their philosophies and actions that they cannot be separated. Burns described transformational leadership as focusing on "end values" such as justice and equality (1978, p. 425). Shields (2010) modified the moral impetus of school leadership through the concept of "transformative leadership" which "recognizes the need to ... to redress wrongs ... with regard to academic, social, and civic outcomes" (Shields, 2010, p. 572). Numerous scholars have discussed the importance of the ethic of care in shaping ethical school leaders. Noddings (1984, 2006) described care as an essential aspect of the education process and argued that humans innately feel sympathy for each other. Noddings further explained "a feminine" view of care "as a mode of experience" that men also share (2006, p. xvi).

Several scholars have argued that the demands of increasingly marginalized students require social justice as a moral focus. Starratt (2012) argued for an ethic of justice that balances the common good with individual rights. School administrators must make decisions within a milieu of historical and present social conditions. Shapiro &d Stefkovich (2011) asks "educators to deal with the hard questions regarding social class, race, gender" and focus on "concepts such as oppression, power, privilege, authority, voice, language, and empowerment" (p. 15).

We believe that the women in this study have intensely applied these concepts of care and justice while navigating the intersections of their unique roles as Black female education leaders as evidenced by their collective experiences. They have successfully navigated the influence of the BLM Movement and COVID-19.

STRONG BLACK WOMAN COLLECTIVE THEORY

In the U.S., the "controlling image of Black women such as the angry black woman" (Davis & Afifi, 2019, p. 1) influences the perception of how Black female education leaders lead. The Strong Black Woman Collective Theory "posits that Black women collectively re-appropriate the strong Black woman image to resist oppression and promote solidarity at the group level" (Davis & Afifi, 2019, p. 2). The findings in this study further advances the tenets of both of these theories and illustrates the experiences of Black female education leaders.

"Social theories emerging from and/or on behalf of US Black women and other historically oppressed groups aim to find ways to escape from, survive in, and/or oppose prevailing social and economic injustice" (Collins, 2000, p. 9). The participants in the study shared a prevailing theme of social injustices that influenced what schools they were assigned to. Most of the primary educators shared that they were assigned to schools that were typically located in areas of lower socio-economic standings and that most of the students that they served were black or brown.

The Strong Black Woman Collective theory has four positions: a) Black women communicate strength through the use of distinct communication practices; b) the assemblage of Black women who are communicating strength composes the strong black women collective; c) members of the SBWC participate in the collective by reinforcing each other's virtues of strength; and d) communication patterns of strength enable the SBWC to confront and retreat from oppressive structures outside, but also impede vulnerability and emotionality within, the collective (Davis and Afifi, 2019,

p. 4). We believe this theory provides understanding to the ways that our participants both applied their power and were misperceived by their colleagues and staff.

INTERSECTIONALITY

Crenshaw (1995) was an early discussant of the concept of *intersectionality* as an extension of Critical Race Theory (CRT). She explained, "The experiences of women of color are frequently the product of intersecting patterns of racism and sexism …. Because of their intersectional identity as both women *and* (sic) of color … (they) are marginalized within both" (Crenshaw,1995, p. 358). Collins (2020) observed, "Intersectionality is a way of understanding and explaining complexity in the world, in people and in human experiences" (p.2). Black female education leaders are compelled to navigate their challenging duties among the intersections of gender, race, power, and social justice. Hancock (2008) saw intersectionality as an analytic framework for examining "the relations between these concepts and the context within which they operate" (p.14).

Evocative stories "encourage us to compare and interrogate our own perceptions and reveal the challenges and opportunities we face in negotiating our worldviews with the understandings of others in our communities" (Boylorn & Orbe, 2014, p. 10). Boylorn further shares that intersectionality offers a multidimensional way for Black women to share their lived experiences. The researchers based their inquiries of intersections on the various roles of Black female education leaders.

BLACK WOMEN EDUCATIONAL LEADERS AND THEIR STORIES

Following is an introduction to the lives and careers of our seven participants. Five are K-12 public school leaders, one is a college dean, and one is a community college president. Here and in later sections, we tell their stories in their words. In this section we establish the context for our understanding of their stories. In later sections we discuss our results to show how we applied the intersectional lenses to better understand and describe their work.

Catherine

Catherine is a principal at a K-5 school in a large metropolitan area where she has served for seven years. She has worked as a principal for almost 20 years and has served as principal in several schools. She has worked in education for more than

20 years, previously serving in various roles including as a middle and high school teacher, a middle school teacher, and assistant principal. Her current school totals around 900 students. She explains that the demographics of the student population have changed during her current tenure. When she began working as a principal, the student population in her district was comprised of about 60% Caucasian and 30% Black. The mix is currently the opposite, with 60% African American and 20% White, with other ethnicities making up the balance.

She was the first African American to head this school, which she says is considered a "flagship school and a beacon in the community." Her students score well on the state assessments, and she regularly hosts tours of her school. She has enhanced her school's training programs to make her predominantly White staff more culturally sensitive. The dominant view of the faculty (in this participants opinion) has been that Black students can't or won't learn. Her battle is to show that, with understanding from their teachers, these students can and will succeed. Despite those efforts, the school has a high student turnover rate as White students continue to leave. She explains,

Some of the teachers don't want to work with the African American students. It's because of these misnomers, these misconceptions. That's why we had to have some culturally responsive training so that they will understand what is cultural versus what is stereotypical in their mind. Having to juggle all of that, I'm not as an African American female principal, just operating the school. I'm trying to put out some of these perceptions and misnomers and stereotypes and all of that and trying to get the teachers to understand where students need to come from. We have to meet these kids where they are. Some of them are in poverty. You don't know what's going on. Let's build and foster relationships.

Brenda

Brenda is in her tenth year as principal in a K-8 school in the inner city of a major metropolitan area. The student population totals nearly 900 students, and the population is classified as both high poverty and high performing. She has worked in education for over 15 years, also serving as an assistant principal, dean of students, and classroom teacher. When appointed principal it was noted that she was one of the youngest principals in her district. She explains, "I was young, I was a woman, I was Black, I was inexperienced as a leader, and I received one of the most challenging schools in all of our district." When she became principal, the school was rated "F" in the state's system, based on student standardized test scores. She remembers,

The classrooms were oversized, overpopulated with identified students... there was doubt, but I didn't feed into it. I knew what I could do. And I knew that the children who attended my school, despite their zip code, could learn. The turnaround for me was building relationships and building trust. The prior principal was an older Caucasian woman who had been there for over 25 years. And I think that it just became mundane and sort of this whole persona that because of where the children were from, they couldn't learn.

Because of the low ranking of the school, she was given the option of hiring a completely new staff. Instead, she decided to keep everyone. "I wanted to prove that it was leadership that starts at the top, not the students and not the staff. So same staff, same students, same parents." She knew she also had to gain the trust of her parents. "I began canvassing the neighborhood, walking through the housing development, just reaching out to them." That first year the school moved from an F to a C. The second year, the school moved to a B status, which it has maintained. The district rewarded Brenda's success by expanding the school from K-5 to K-8 and adding a variety of programs serving extremely disabled children. She explains,

I have severe and profound students on my campus that are bed ridden and chair ridden. With some of my student population, I'm just trying to keep alive throughout the day. When those programs expanded, I didn't get another nurse. I have kids that are getting tube fed, trached, diaper changed, bed ridden, but the healthcare staff did not expand; but it's okay, because I won every time, and that's what we do.

Linda

Linda is a principal at an inner-city elementary school with an enrollment of about 400 students. She has previously served as an assistant principal, teacher, and instructional leader. Prior to becoming the principal at her current location, she served a specialized population. This experience readied her for a school that was on the brink of failure. During the years she served as principal, she successfully turned the school around. She remembers, "I was ready to have my *Waiting to Exhale* moment" when she was transferred to another school with a high percentage of students with special needs. She remembers, "I grabbed my tears and just went on to do what they asked me to do and ran another school for two years and pulled those scores up from out of the pits of Hades." The district then turned that school into a magnet school and named her principal. Following success in that role, her superintendent placed her at the most challenging school in the district, which is where she serves today. When she received that assignment, she says

She, again cried some tears like Jonah not wanting to go to Nineveh, and God was like, I'll put you in the belly of the whale if you don't go. But I went. Some say I'm Mother Theresa, and that's probably a good thing and a bad thing all at the same time. But I have helped to pull that school up from an F to a C, with no newspaper articles or anything going out to explain what happened, but God knows, and so do I.

Sally

Sally is a principal in the largest school district in the Mid-West. She served as a high school principal for less than five years and is now serving as a K-5 principal.

One common element at all schools she served was the turnover rate of students. Twenty years ago, the school populations were predominately White with a sprinkle of Black. Today, she serves a school in which the ratio reflects a predominantly Black student population with a faculty that is predominantly White. She remembers,

Last year, I had a lot of struggles, a lot of fighting, with people accusing me of being racist. Teachers asked me, 'Are you saying I can't teach Black kids because I'm not like them?' I said, 'No, what I'm saying is that you need to remember that they are Black kids and there are some cultural differences you need to address and not blame the parents. We need to close that gap and address the needs in front of us.' We worked the whole year, and they got to know me, and at the beginning of my second year many of them came to me and apologized.

A key strategy she employed was implementing more culture building activities among the faculty. In addition, she began hosting a variety of academic and artistic events, including math and reading nights, musical performances, arts exhibitions, and a Fall Family Festival. As a result, she says, "We sat down together, we talked and we laughed, and we just enjoyed each other as people." Before those events, she said,

The parents were more observers of education, versus participators. And those are some of the things I worked to change. The teachers recognized that the passion that was driving me wasn't because I'm this hard Black woman that just wants to be in charge, but I'm someone who's driven by the need to move the kids. We made some great gains and people stopped looking at the person in charge and started listening to the vision. Once they started understanding my expectation, and I started giving them tools to show them how we could make a difference, we started more working together collaboratively in order to move the kids along.

Samantha

Samantha has served as President of a community college in the Northeast. At the time she was hired, she was the only full-time Black female professional at the college, with a total faculty diversity of less than 5%. That percentage has now increased to almost 10%. The student body includes about 15% students of color. She thinks she was hired to better serve those students. Despite that, she believes she must always be cautious in her words and actions. She explains,

As a black female leader, I always have to be cognizant of what I'm saying, how I'm saying it, what my approach is, not making people upset, not getting too, ahead of myself on issues such as Black Lives Matter. And that, that kind of takes away from my ability to get the work done as quickly as I'd like to get it done.

She cites as an example a study that illustrated disaggregated data – less than 5% of the Black freshmen were progressing academically. This was compared to the 40% White freshmen students who were progressing and, therefore, less likely to drop out of their programs. She shared that the mostly white faculty and staff started "making all of these assertions about Black students: They're not ready for college; they don't know how to study; and they're not used to it." She acknowledged that even the on-track data regarding the White students were not good, and she wondered why the White faculty did not understand that lapse as a problem for all students, not only those of color. She observed,

As a Black female in a predominantly white institution, it is very easy to find yourself alienated because people start taking personally what you're saying about the facts and the data in front of you. It has been a challenge, but one of the things I have decided is that I've been brought here for a reason. They knew what they were buying. And while I am certainly cautious, and oftentimes very reflective about my approach, I still believe that the work I was sent here to do needs to be done.

Paige

Paige is the dean of the College of Science, a post she has held for nearly five years. She has 20 years of experience in higher education and has advanced through the rank and tenure. Prior to earning the title of Dean, she was given another title as a means of proving she was ready to be called a dean. This was not the norm for her white male peers. Each had been promoted to Dean directly from their prior roles. When she asked the college president about the discrepancy, Paige says he replied,

"You know, everyone has to prove themselves in order to be called a dean." She explained her frustration:

As a black female leader, it was clear I had to become okay that they did not celebrate me. But it didn't change who I was. I couldn't let it show, so my motto became, I can show you better than I can tell you. I'm just going to show you who I am.

Later that year the president changed her title to Dean of the College of Science, commenting, "You are a fixer, you are a doer, you get things done." Although she was the first Black female dean in the college's history, the school did not share that news with the public in any press release. This was especially significant, she says, since the College of Science generates a significant portion of the university's income. At an internal celebration among staff, she says her colleagues praised her. Pleased but frustrated, she explained, "I'm sitting here thinking, 'You're so excited, but you won't announce it to anyone outside of the University.'" After she assumed the official position of dean, she encountered underlying racist and misogynistic attitudes among her White male colleagues. She explains,

We had good relationships before, so I assumed it would continue that way. And it did, for the most part; however, there were undertones against me as a Black female. Some said, "You don't have to prove yourself anymore. You're already a dean. So don't do anything else. You don't have to compete with us." And the fact that they said that showed they were intimidated, and that I would just have to continue to stand firm.

COVID forced a shutdown of on-ground classes at her university. Paige coordinated the move of her college to completely online learning. She also implemented regular online meetings with her and her faculty to discuss problems and, she says, "Make sure everyone was okay. Faculty loved the fact that they could talk about anything, and it never left that place." She was rewarded for her work in an email from the president, who wrote "We knew that you were good. But Wow."

RESULTING THEMES

Based on our understanding of our data, we revised the roles of our participants from the intersectionality frame we initially applied. We began viewing our data through the lenses of leadership, race, gender, power, and social justice. We have come to see these roles as intermixed and woven into the personal and professional fabric of each, rather than disparate elements. We don't believe this approach changes the applicability of the intersectionality model, since we see each role as representative of our participants. Each of our participants is a leader. Each is proactive in meeting the needs of her students. Each has power by definition of her position, although each agreed that her power is checked by her race in ways that would not be true if she were White. At the same time, race empowers each to act as a role model for not only students, but also parents and other stakeholders. Her race and cumulative experiences also fuel her passion for social justice. Thus, we find it difficult to parse these roles which we believe is the characteristic premise of intersectionality. With that, we follow with some specific examples that demonstrate the intersections of these roles.

Leadership

Key to this study is the understanding that each participant is a leader with influence over financial, capital, and human resources. They demonstrate both positional leadership and influence. Positional leadership denotes having an authoritative presence based on one's position within the organization. We do not see a reason to discuss differences between managers and leaders. Each is a leader who is passionate about changing her institution to best serve the needs of her students. We find it especially difficult to separate the role of leader from the other roles our participants assume, because we believe their leadership motivates every action they take. In effect, we could subsume this entire treatise under the topic and role of leader. Nonetheless, we follow with a few examples of strong leadership among the many that stood out.

The leaders in this study showed how they worked to mediate change within the school they served. Catherine stated,

I had to make sure we were transformational rather than transactional because schooling is no longer business as usual where we will just check a box. In this new way of learning, we purposely ensured we were giving the students everything we possibly could educational wise. Communication remains at the forefront of everything we do. With the demographics of students we serve, it was essential to contact parents to determine if students needed laptops, tablets, or hotspots. As a leader, I realize the only way to close the divide is to continuously push further and deeper than we would if we were in the building. We must close the gap.

Sally continued conversations about ways to meet the needs of the students outside of the school. She explained, "Just because we've closed the doors to the schools does not mean we have closed our hearts and minds to helping the disenfranchised of our population of students at our school." Brenda noted,

I think as black leaders and women attached to that, we're not afraid of hard work. You know, we are strong innately. But the buck has to stop somewhere. I think the stereotype that comes along with being a Black woman in leadership is that you can make it happen. You're strong enough to make it happen.

Race

We find *race* to be a significant intersectional factor in the lives of professional Black female education leaders. Being a Black female education leader influenced where they were placed as principals. Those locations were areas that experienced high diversity and high poverty. Catherine asked,

Why are all of the African American leaders always placed at the inner-city schools? And, you know, I don't take it as a negative, because I'm looking at that the opportunity to help students of color, students of my race in particular. I'm not going to look at it as this as a bad situation. But I just think there needs to be some more looking at by the school board of who they are placing in different situations and to make sure there is an opportunity for everyone to work in different environments and not just be relegated to one.

Race clearly intersected with the career paths of each of these leaders. Both Samantha, a college president, and Paige, a College of Science dean, are the first women of color to serve in their roles. Each principal works in a high-minority, high-poverty school. Each time Brenda exceeded expectations, the district expanded her school with more challenging students. She explained,

The district saw the quick school turnaround and added more to my plate. In addition to adding middle school, we expanded our Special Education population (SPED). So, the plate for me became full very quickly once I had shown what I could do. What I was being required to do wasn't as equitable as my colleagues who were older and white. No other campus had the number of SPED students that I had. I started voicing my opinion about why the school down the street wasn't required to open an additional SPED unit or why I have to add another grade level each year. So, you can say that there was some unfairness and inequality in that regard.

Sally conducted a survey of her faculty that illustrated the cultural inequality of students of color in her school. These findings required faculty to reject any prejudices that students of color were unprepared and consider the disparities of institutional systems that were keeping the students from succeeding.

Samantha shared several examples of systemic and individual racism she has encountered in her role as college president. In one, she discussed her self-imposed restrictions of talking about race in the community. She detailed her experience by saying,

It is somewhat of a challenge for me as a Black person in this community to talk about race. Many people I engage with state that racism is not a problem in our community. This is far from true. The truth is, there are not many people of color, so you don't see racism as much since there's not a lot of people to interact with those who are different from the majority.

She related that many of the students who served in the residence hall of her college were students of color. It became clear to her that that the students were appalled by the lack of official comments about the BLM movement following the George Floyd murder. Samantha remembered,

I was called out on social media and rightfully so. The callout prompted me to respond by having conversations on the campus. We also hosted forums with students, faculty, and staff about BLM, race, and racism in our country and community- specifically our college.

She concluded, "I have to encourage the conversations and do it in a way that perhaps a non-minority leader would not. But I also think that some of those issues probably would not have surfaced if the college had a non-minority leader."

In another experience, the board of directors automatically renewed the contract of my white male subordinates without my input. The individuals would not have been rehired if they had included her in the decisions. She concluded,

I'm almost feeling like we're back to the beginning with some of the progress that we've made in terms of race and race relations and figuring out how to live and work together. I think it's sad and its scary.

Power

Martin Luther King, Jr. defined power as "the ability to achieve purpose and effect change…the definition does not make the nature of power inherently good or bad" (Brown, 2018, p.95). Collins observed, "Power relations are never so absolute that they eliminate all dissent" (2019, p. 289). As evidenced by the participants in this research, their power, individual nor collective, eliminated the undertones of oppression. Nor did their positional power authorize them to wield it for bad.

Each principal implemented cultural awareness training to help their teachers understand the cultural milieu of their students. Brenda worked to stock her library with works written by authors of color. Catherine walked her neighborhoods to establish relationships with her parents. Samantha addressed the concerns of her Black students through social media posts. Paige initiated weekly faculty Zoom meetings. These were all demonstrations of the privileges of power that each used to accomplish their mission, that each agreed was to improve the lives, and the future, of their students. Catherine explained that "we must Maslow before we can Bloom." In other words, teachers must understand and address their students' physical and foundational needs. If students are hungry, they cannot hear their lesson over their growling stomachs.

These strong educators are caught between two pressures. They are leaders in their schools, and so possess the power to enact some change and promote social justice. At the same time, they tell repeated stories of how their power is shackled by their race and gender. Despite that, they work tirelessly to promote causes of social justice, which they see as central to their role as school leader.

SOCIAL JUSTICE

Leader as Role Model

Kelley (2012) suggests that the unique role that Black principals play in the lives of Black children can have a positive impact on their rate of success. While each action they take to promote the success of their students may be seen as an act of social justice, the concept of role modeling was significant throughout. Each sees herself as a model for both students and parents. These Black female education leaders often see themselves as role models, especially to those children who look like them. Linda explains,

I'll have my students, whether they're in trouble or not, to come sit behind my desk. I want them to know that you can go to school, finish high school, finish college and become a teacher and, become a principal if you like. I let them know, "You can do great things. But it first starts with the choices that you're making right now." I want them to say, "I want to be just like her when I grow up."

Sally remembered,

I saw the students gravitate toward the few black staff members that they had in the building. And there was me, an administrator, sitting in the seat or position

of authority. I let them know that I understood where they were coming from, but it was very important to me that set clear boundaries for them in the school and boundaries in society. I told them that I cared about them, that there were boundaries. And because of those boundaries, there were certain consequences that went along with their behavior.

Paige remembered the help she received from a vice principal who was a black woman when she was in high school.

I was very excited to have a black female vice principal. She really helped me a lot. There was an instance when I wrote an essay for my English class and was I told by the teacher that I had plagiarized because "people like you can't write like that." I did not understand what was going on. I shared this experience with my vice principal and she stepped in and helped to prove that I had indeed written the essay. That experience followed me throughout my educational journey, even when I earned my doctorate.

Leader as Teacher and Nurturer

Another element that emerged was the theme of teacher and nurturer, which seems concomitant with serving as a role model. We also have placed this under the role of practitioner of social justice. Catherine explained,

I think, you have to build this reputation of being an advocate for children. Once parents realize that you're an advocate for children, they will support you. So, it's important that I'm approachable, even in some of the most hostile situations. I've been able to get parents calmed down and get them on my side or on the side of understanding what's in the best interest of their child, understanding policy and procedures. Because a lot of times they just want to come in angry at the principal and saying that you're not being fair to their child. So, over the years, I've built that reputation of being a champion for students. And if you if you are truly who you say you are, as an educator, you are that champion for students, and parents can't help but to respect that, no matter when you have to sit in front of them, whether it's a suspension conference or whatever you're telling them, they are going to be more receptive.

Leader as Mother

While we did not initially search for it, the role of Mother emerged as infrequent but strong. We place this under the role of social justice, although it also could stand alone. We found two references to motherhood among our participants.

Brenda brought her son to school with her to prove her faith in the quality education her school was delivering. He's been tagging along with me since kindergarten going into his last year at the school for eighth grade. That was the personal decision that I made to ensure that what it was I was saying that I would do was good enough for my own son to receive.

As Linda was being transferred to an even more challenging school, her son became critically ill. She was faced with the challenge of being a good mother and a strong professional. She explained,

My son was very ill. In the meantime, another school was in need and I was told "That school needs you." I said I can imagine they do, but my son needs me. So long story short, where do you think they put me? At the school with the greatest academic need.

Spiritual Influence as Aspect of Social Justice

Religious faith emerged as a strong support and influence for our participants. We have chosen to subsume this under the role of practitioner of social justice, although believe this is another theme that could be identified as an additional role and form the basis of a future study.

Linda noted,

Without my faith, I would definitely be dealing with a lot of mental anguish, but we all have to have strong faith. The scripture that I stood on was that Philippians 4:13 I can do all things through Christ who strengthens me. If we all keep that in mind as leaders, we'll make it through anything, COVID-19, whatever it is. I just continue to pray and keep the faith and just know that what we do is a huge service to our community every single day. I feel like it's my opportunity to take what I learned at church and put it into action.

Catherine noted,

We've talked about some of the inequities and disparities, and it seems like they are throughout, but we're doing our part as educators in our God purposed role to fulfill those needs of the children and the public that we serve. We are public servants and we can feel comfort in knowing that, although it's challenging, we're doing the right thing. We're doing what's right in education.

Brenda reflected on her placements, explaining,

I knew whose I was and that with God I could do anything. I knew what he had prepared and planned for me. I always follow the biblical scripture of to whom much is given much more is required.

COVID-19 AND BLACK LIVES MATTER

We were surprised that neither COVID-19 nor the Black Lives Matter movement sparked significant discussion among these leaders. We suspect that is because as strong leaders they deal with constant challenges. We also believe that the precepts of BLM are endemic to everything they work for as Black education leaders. Some did address the issues directly, and we provide excerpts here.

Catherine observed,

I have seen some systemic inequities, throughout education and throughout just how our schools operate with resources, and I run a platform in my school based on diversity, inclusion and equity. And it's becoming harder and harder to ensure that all of those processes are in place, especially now, in light of COVID-19 in light of Black Lives Matter.

Sally reflected,

I was a student of the inner city, and I knew the power of having strong educators in front of the kids to show them that they too could do it. And so, in light of the Black Lives Matter movement, it just resonates with me so much, because these Black students in front of you, these students of color, they matter.

Samantha was able to confer her philosophy of cultural oppression in the wake of the Black Lives Matter movement by recognizing an opportunity for a partnership, through dialogue, between the college and the community. She explained, "We didn't talk about Black Lives Matter as much as we should have because the community at large is just so white." She further reflected,

COVID did not create the problems. Outside of the public health issue, the other problems that we have seen as a result of COVID, or what we think is a result of COVID, it really just magnified those problems that we've had. The problem of racism has been a problem for us before. But because we're in this crisis mode in our country, these ugly things are starting to come out. And this is one of them. And we have to address this issue and address it now. And I'm going to tell you something else. If we don't do it because it's the right thing to do, we need to do it because it is the economically smart thing to do. Because we know that people of color, there are more of us now than ever. We are starting to hopefully make some, some progress on wages and things like that, but at some point, we're going to have to address the fact that as we have more people of color, we've got to invest in getting them educated, getting them employed, getting them paying taxes, getting them being solid citizens in our communities, because it makes economic sense for us.

PERSONAL REFLECTIONS

In the following section we offer our own perspectives regarding the issues and roles we asked our leaders to discuss.

Shaquanah

It has always been my intention to inspire students to do the unthinkable. Every year, I share my story of my childhood, growing up in the 'hood' yet persevering and pushing past obstacles that should have stopped me from fulfilling my dream. I share with students the one thing that makes me proud of my accomplishment: being the first doctor in my family. Since I've moved out of my parents' home, my neighborhood has started to deteriorate but that did not stop me from going back to celebrate. When I decided to take graduation pictures after completing my doctorate, it was important to me to have pictures taken on the street I grew up. I keep these pictures on my desk to show students that if I can do it, so can they.

BLM and COVID have forced me to reflect on the way I show compassion to others. Being a task driven individual, I have to remember to separate my focus on the individual before the task. COVID has required me to spend more time checking on the mental well-being of individuals and addressing those needs first. With the social disconnect we are all experiencing. I am learning to listen more. As a leader, I want to hear what teachers have to say. I want to know what concerns them, what scares them, what encourages them, and what disappoints them about this shift we have experienced. I am a teacher at heart so I know when teachers are heard, the atmosphere and energy tend to shift in a different direction.

As a mother, I don't have the privilege of just imagining atrocities that plague society. As a mother, I have to live through those experiences and try to teach my son strategies that will just get him home alive if he was to have interactions with officers. If you have never had to tell your child, "just do what they tell you to do so you can make it back to me", then lucky you. I'm not that lucky. If you watched George Floyd's death and didn't struggle to find the words to explain to your child what happened to cause Floyd's death and how you can avoid the same treatment, then you cannot relate to me as a Black mother.

Alyncia

Growing up it was never an option, I was expected to continue my education. Earning my doctorate was a rewarding experience for me and my family. I was the first female in my family to earn a doctorate and to earn one in business. My lineage is that of religious leaders, so earning a doctorate in theology was expected.

My parents divorced when I was young and society suggested that I would not graduate from high school let alone matriculate through college. I was blessed to have my mother as a strong role model. She worked diligently and went to school so that we could live a very middle-class life. I recall sitting in the hallway while she was in her classes. Some of her peers would stop by to help me with my homework. Exposure to the college life was priceless. When my mother became ill at the young age of 35 many thought we would not make it, but we did with the help of God and strong influencers such as my mother, grandmother, Superintendent Gene Harris, State Representative Otto Beatty and Waldo Tyler, an area pharmacist who saw my future and privileged me to learn more about medications.

Even though my mother attempted to shield me from racism and racial injustice, at a young age I learned very quickly that there were differences between me and many of my classmates. And while we witnessed the murder of George Floyd and so many others, it is still a life journey for equality in all areas of life.

Jim

I know that as a White male born into the middle class, I have been given privileges of which I am unaware. I know I am often blind to implicit and endemic racism that the others in this study, including my fellow researchers, face. I know my role group has been part of a privileged class in American culture, and I know that my perceptions are filtered through this prism.

My heritage is rooted in the Deep South. A few years ago, my wife and I visited a family cemetery hidden in a Georgia wood. Among the graves of my ancestors rested several who had fought for the Confederate States of America, the iron CSA insignia attached to the tombstone. Did those guys fight to defend slavery? In the archives, the family history, I haven't found any evidence to support that. I know that goes against the conventional argument. Does that make me bad? I am a white, middle class male. Am I the enemy?

One of the great honors of my life has been to participate in the discussion with these strong Black women. I have been humbled and inspired by each story. My goal is to work to tell their stories so that others can understand. Through increased understanding, perhaps we can all become better and our culture, seemingly fractured, can coalesce and rise to its promised heights.

CLOSING

Everyone has a story to tell. The data supporting this study illustrated the intersectionality of race, gender, power and social justice. The strong, wonderful women who agreed to share their stories with us showed how their professional identities were shaped through the intersections of their diverse roles and how these intersections influence their personal and professional decisions. We agree with Collins that "intersectionality offers a window into thinking about the significance of ideas and social action in fostering social change" (Collins, 2019, p. 288).

Participants felt sharing their stories was therapeutic. One leader appreciated the chance "to release some of this and know that what we are doing is right." Our results reinforce the need for further research. The voices of strong women of color must be heard. One shared, "I tell my stories to make sure people see that I'm human. It doesn't matter what color you are. Your blood doesn't come out green."

Subtle signs of racism are on display in many professional work environments. These signs may manifest themselves in passive aggressive words to colleagues or inequitable actions of discrimination. Schools are microcosms of society, and so are rife with endemic racism. Catherine explained,

Have we heard of white flight? Let me explain it to you. That is when they walk out of the door, and this is not only the teachers, but the students and their families because of the color of your skin.

Samantha observed,

The voices and experiences of black people need to be heard. They need to be understood and validated. The actual work of deconstructing the institutional and organizational systems of oppression, really, I think, is the work of white people. The problem with really getting to eradicating racism, would really mean that we would have to strip our country down to the very studs of the power who created it, in order to really see a post racial society. And we as Black people do not have the power to do that. That's why we need white people to help us with that we need people who are saying that "this is not what we believe in, and this is not going to help us."

In closing, we return to Catherine's statement: "We must Maslow before we Bloom. We've got to meet these kids where they are."

REFERENCES

Blalock, A. E., & Akehi, M. (2018). Collaborative autoethnography as a pathway for transformative learning. *Journal of Transformative Education*, *16*(2), 89–107. doi:10.1177/1541344617715711

Boylorn, R. M., & Orbe, M. P. (2014). *Critical autoethnography: Intersecting cultural identities in everyday life*. Left Coast Press.

Brown, B. (2018). *Dare to lead: Brave work, tough conversations, whole hearts.* Random House.

Burns, J. M. (1978). *Leadership. Harper. Collins, P. H. (2000). Black feminist thought: Knowledge, consciousness, and the politics of empowerment* (2nd ed.). Routledge.

Collins, P. (2019). *Intersectionality as critical social theory*. Duke University Press. doi:10.1215/9781478007098

Crenshaw, K. (1995). *Critical Race Theory: The Key Writings that formed the Movement*. The New York Press.

Davis, S. M., & Afifi, T. D. (2019). The Strong Black Woman Collective Theory: Determining the prosocial functions of strength regulation in groups of Black women friends. *Journal of Communication*, *69*(1), 1–25. doi:10.1093/joc/jqy065

Denzin, N. (2014). *Interpretive autoethnography* (2nd ed.). SAGE Publications, Ltd. https://www.doi.org/10.4135/9781506374697

Gray, A., Howard, L., & Chessman, H. (2018). *Voices from the field: Women of color presidents in higher education*. Retrieved from: https://www.tiaainstitute. org/sites/default/files/presentations/2018- 12/TIAA%20Womens%20Forum%20 President%20Interviews%20-%20ACE2.pdf

Hancock, A. M. (2008). Intersectionality, multiple messages, and complex causality: Commentary on *Black Sexual Politics* by Patricia Hill Collins. *Studies in Gender and Sexuality*, 9(1), 14–31. doi:10.1080/15240650701759359

Kelley, G. J. (2012). *How do principals' behaviors facilitate or inhibit the development of a culturally relevant learning community?* (Unpublished doctoral dissertation). Indiana State University, Terre Haute, IN.

NCES. (2018). Retrieved from: https://nces.ed.gov

Noddings, N. (1984). *Caring: A feminine approach to ethics and moral education*. University of California Press.

Noddings, N. (2006). *Caring: A feminine approach to ethics and moral education* (2nd ed.). University of California Press.

Shapiro, J. P., & Stefkovich, J. A. (2011). *Ethical leadership and decision making in education: Applying theoretical perspectives to complex dilemmas* (3rd ed.). Routledge.

Shields, C. (2010). Transformative leadership: Working for equity in diverse contexts. *Educational Administration Quarterly*, 46(4), 558–589. doi:10.1177/0013161X10375609

Starratt, R. A. (2012). *Cultivating an ethical school*. Routledge. doi:10.4324/9780203833261

Chapter 6

The Room Is Crooked AF:
Black Women, Resistance, and Leadership

Portia Newman
 https://orcid.org/0000-0002-7991-1389
Virginia Commonwealth University, USA

ABSTRACT

Societal perceptions of Black women are challenged by Black women's ability to survive in spaces that have historically been uninviting. Black women's leadership practice has developed in response to their racialized and gendered lived experiences. Through analyzing studies of Black women leaders, research suggests Black women have a strategic set of skills and practices that can be used to advance their leadership positionality. This chapter will describe the ways Black women operate at the intersection of resistance and leadership. Their leadership has become a skill, a practice, and a tool that creates space for themselves.

INTRODUCTION

March of 2020 prompted an urgent reaction to a global health crisis, and at the same time, the world reached a tipping point in response to hundreds of years of racial injustice in the United States. This double pandemic (COVID-19 and racism) further complicated the way people experience the world. These two pandemics brought a heightened sense of awareness of the place and space of Black people within society. Critical discourse between scholars and world leaders as well as activists focused on the value of Black life in America.

DOI: 10.4018/978-1-7998-7235-1.ch006

First, public health data provided statistical evidence of how the coronavirus was negatively impacting Black lives and doing so at alarming rates. News headlines featured issues on the social determinants of health that disproportionately affected Black communities, resulting in high rates of maternal mortality and stress-induced illnesses. Not only were health and environmental disparities exposed, but it sparked a greater discourse around barriers to healthy life outcomes and the connection to opportunity the policing of and bias directed toward Black communities. Black death at the hands of the police or citizens who believed they had the authority had become commonplace and reached a tipping point leading to acts of resistance all over the United States. In public demonstrations in many cities, Black people were negotiating their health and livelihood to be active agents for change. Black people used their voices and took to the streets in a fight to break the cycle of survivorship and grief. The increased visibility of Black death in the media related to Covid-19 and racism, exposed the anti-black impressions of our institutions. Media outlets prompted a nationwide response resulting in hashtags like #sayhername, #blacktranslivesmatter, #blacklivesmatter, and #blackmomsmatter. News outlets and social media pages (i.e., Facebook, Twitter, Instagram) activated a charge for the nation to pay more attention to Black communities, Black people, and Black humanity. This resulted in a growing number of organizations and companies focusing their efforts or creating more inclusive workspaces. There was an increase in appointments to leadership roles while also general commitments related to diversity metrics as a way to confirm the awareness of Black people, more specifically Black women's roles in society.

The increased tension caused by both pandemics signaled that there would be lasting effects causing drastic transitions in both professional and personal environments. Public intellectuals used their platform to support and critique the Black Lives Matter movement that then prompted emerging discourse on the diversity of organizational leadership. The current socio-political climate has Black people, specifically, Black women, reclaiming spaces as leaders. Black women are being highlighted for managing their roles and taking on more responsibility while navigating predominately white professional spaces. Harris-Perry (2011) describes the workplace as "fraught terrain for Black women" who are constantly navigating preconceived notions and bias (p.91). In a study of Black women principals by Newcomb & Niemeyer, (2015) they describe how these leaders are exhausted of resources and lack access to support mechanisms. In a study conducted by Mays et al., (1996) the researchers discuss the negative health outcomes of workplace challenges like discrimination, that inherently increase the burden and pressures as an employee. These noted challenges are deeply rooted in Black women's herstory and research providing evidence of the broad range of experiences. For Black women, the arduous path toward leadership is riddled with opposition. This impacts how they negotiate their space and position themselves to acquire the support they need to experience inclusivity and belonging. As an outcome of the heightened awareness of Black women's experience, more Black women continue to think critically about their racialized and gendered experiences and the impact it has within the workplace. According to the Center for American Progress (2019) Black women are directly impacted by societal influences challenged by both race and gender which have direct impact on roles, responsibilities and pay.

The interconnectedness of race and gender in addition to other identities, add a layer of complexity to Black women's existence. Early discussion and analysis of intersectionality emerged after Crenshaw's (1989) work that was further validated by Collins' (2000) work on Black Feminist Thought. Both scholars used their research to investigate how Black women construct their gendered and racialized identities. These factors influencing their leadership identity have been explored in several studies introducing many adverse experiences. Those experiences are underscored by the ways both pandemics have disproportionately impacted Black women's roles. Race and gender complexify the experience of leadership for Black women; therefore, Black women employ various strategies to navigate leadership spaces (Oikelome, 2017).

Black women leaders leverage skills that were developed in response to their lived experiences including adversity, challenges and resistance (Newman, 2021a). A considerable amount of literature has been published on the barriers to leadership for Black women and on the skills used to navigate leadership spaces. These studies highlight examples of code switching, nurturing workplace relationships, leading with a community centered approach and other strategies that shape their leadership practice (Aaron, 2020; Greaux, 2010; Nelson et al., 2016; Sakho-Lewis, 2017). This is evidence of Black women's leadership "survival techniques" used to sustain their leadership efforts across industries and in different roles and positions (Rosser-Mims, 2010, p.7). The notion of survival within professional spaces suggests that the work-spaces mirrored the socio-political context of Black women in the world. This was evident in the ways the pandemic has made hyperaware Black women's place and space – or lack thereof in the work place. There is evidence of the inequitable and oppressive systems and structures that were exacerbated by the pandemic yet impacts Black women's leadership.

CROOKED ROOM

Naming the systems at play help to frame what Black women are experiencing as leaders during this time. As media raises questions about their roles, positions and contributions, there is context provided in the literature as to why Black women have been forced to navigate spaces as they have. Melissa Harris-Perry (2011) in *Sister*

Citizen, references an analogy of the "crooked room" describing the rigid space constructed by the rules of hegemony and maintained by the inaction of the most privileged. Harris-Perry (2011) states "When they [Black women] confront race and gender stereotypes, Black women are standing in a crooked room, and they have to figure out which way is up" (p.29). Under a strict scope of whiteness, Harris-Perry (2011) uncovers the many ways white dominant culture influences people's beliefs, ultimately dictating how Black women are seen. In a speech, Malcom (1962) declared that Black women were the most disrespected and condemned group in America. The truth in that statement is piercing, yet he is straightforwardly describing the conditions that Black women develop their identity.

Current literature continues to unpack the relationship between Black women and the socio-political context of their existence. Representation of Black women as domestic leaders, with political voices with influence suggests that despite the challenging perceptions, Black women are a critical part of society. The crooked room is defined by the negative perceptions and adopted identities forced upon Black women making it difficult to identify their true selves. The crooked room is a direct product of a history of marginalization, racial, and gendered oppression directly supported by ideas of Black inferiority stemming from white dominant beliefs. As a result, Black women's existence has become a constant struggle to provide a counter-narrative to their own story.

White Racial Frame

Harris-Perry (2011) connects history to the present by discussing the politicized and complex roles and positions of Black women. Yet, understanding Feagin's (2010) idea of the White Racial Frame as the foundation to the analogy of the crooked room is imperative. The White Racial Frame (WRF) illustrates the endemic nature of racism and discrimination deeply rooted in the systems and structures of society. The ideological frame of Whiteness is institutionalized within our policies, practices, and personal beliefs. The WRF is founded on two sub-frames: (1) Whiteness as a virtue and (2) negative stereotyping of Black and Brown people (Feagin, 2010). The integration of these two subframes is maintained by five components: (1) racial stereotypes; (2) racial narrative and interpretations; (3) racial images; (4) racialized emotions; and (5) inclinations to discriminatory actions (Feagin, 2010, p. 10). With the two subframes as pillars within this framework, they work together to create underlining policies and behaviors that maintain the marginalization Black women. Subsequently, the policies and practices are set to impede Black women's progress toward opportunity and access within the workplace. Feagin's frame incorporates the ideas of racial discrimination and difference that fuel stereotypes about Black women. For example, the "intentional misrecognition of Black women" as leaders and active agents in society leads to shame, forced identities of being strong and extreme self-sacrifice (Harris-Perry, 2011, p. 22). Feagin (2010) extends the evidence of the WRF by discussing the use of racial imagery to influence the perception of people of color. As a tactic used in political movements, this continues as images of Black people in distress, images of single-motherhood and Black women with negative emotions are displayed across media outlets. Such passive efforts to misframe the narrative of Black women's experience has a lasting and broad impact on how an employers and colleagues may perceive them.

To sustain divisions and otherness, the WRF operates to maintain the status quo, or marginalization of Black and Brown people; an understood social order sustained by "social-reproduction" upholding hierarchical differences through systemic and institutional racism (Feagin, 2010, p.35). The WRF is then both a theory and a practice that is used to permeate the idea of white superiority and fuels anti-black sentiments. To understand the Black women's presence and practice, one must challenge how systems and structures have shaped their development overtime.

Intersection of WRF and the Crooked Room

Historically, harmful stereotypes have been used to describe Black women's features, attitudes and behaviors which are used to build the crooked room. For example, media images and public perceptions misrepresent Black woman's' identity. Black women are not seen as expansive but rather stifled for many years as they were delegated to low-wage roles in agriculture, caretakers (of white families) and domestic service (Banks, 2019). In addition, Gomez et al. (2019) describes how the WRF influences discrimination within media and policy by operating as a control function, victimizing the lives of Black and Brown people. Gomez et al. (2019) uses an example of how Black women celebrities too are subjected to the negative stereotyping despite having reached high levels of fame and fortune. This is done by distorting images of Black women in the media, problematizing them in professional spaces, and blaming them for their lived experiences (Harris-Perry, 2011). In other instances, Black women's experience within the labor force is rooted in Black women's labor that historically was focused on the respectability of white women's domesticity. Michelle Alexander (2012) author of The New Jim Crow, writes that the deliberate measure of former President Reagan's crime and welfare campaign that portrayed Black women as co-dependent of federal assistance, exacerbate the negative image of the working class and its evolving existence as property for labor during slavery. Then this imagery shifted in the 1980s transitioning the image from lazy to necessary to the workforce. These images played out in the media, complicating Black women's lived experience, and leading to a sense of even greater inferiority, further proving the impact of white superiority, to which, all others are compared.

In addition, Black women's attitudes and behaviors were and are often viewed as promiscuous, angry, and lacking critical skills (Harris-Perry, 2011). The WRF criticizes Black women's use of language, community building practices and other forms of expression. These negative perceptions of Black women's identity have reinforced the discriminatory practices against Black women in the labor force (Banks, 2019). As a result, generations of Black women have been under paid and unassigned to critical roles within the labor force.

Organizational Containment

At the same time diversity policies have had a turn in the experience but have not completely invested in Black women as employees who should be engaged at every level. Decades of legislation created incremental advancements in careers for Black women yet, there are currently still extreme limitations and barriers to success. For example, in professional spaces, negative stereotypes often limit opportunities for upward career mobility. Berry, (2014) describes these restrictions as organizational containment; a set of systemic barriers experienced in pursuit of access to organizational resources critical to effectiveness and advancement. The factors contributing to these barriers like race, gender and socio-cultural experiences limit exposure and opportunity. Negative stereotypical imagery from early century writers and scientist that described Black people as lazy, criminal, or unintelligent has informed our institutions to date (Feagin, 2010). Black women continue to navigate professional spaces that assent to white virtues, power, and privilege. The high value on education, social networks, and lack of accountability to whiteness is a permission not afforded to Black women. Although there have been many Black women who have achieved high levels of education and developed their networks, that did not come without adversity. To operate in professional spaces that uphold white virtues and overwhelmingly benefits white women, Black women are met with some passive and historical and institutional barriers. Evidence of century old institutional structures that prohibited the advancement of Black women continue to exist in present day with regards to wealth attainment, family structures, job, and educational access. Thus, the WRF is a complex frame of systemic oppression forcing Black women to see their leadership skills and practice as resistance.

CROOKED ROOMS AND PANDEMIC PROBLEMS

According to the US Bureau of Labor Statistics, Black women represent 53% of the Black labor force. Within the total labor force Black women represented 36% of the management, professional, and related occupations (positions with the highest earned wages) (*Women in the Labor Force*, 2019). When aggregating data by industry, Black women represent 40% of education and health services. The labor force has shifted since spread of Covid-19 causing a decrease in employment rates. The US Bureau of Labor Statistics charts the changes which highlight how Black people have disproportionately been impacted as many service -oriented (non-healthcare) jobs have been eliminated. When coupling the challenge with securing work due to a global pandemic with the intuitional biases related to access and opportunity, there is a larger issue as Black people, more specifically Black women are in a precarious situation.

As critical employees during the pandemic, Black women are serving in hospitals, schools and other service industries. With roles in warehouses, the postal service and in food services, there is a large concentration of Black women in low wage-earning positions. Contrary to that, executive leaders of big businesses have gross underrepresentation of Black women on their teams. As the literature base explores the racialized and gendered experiences of Black women leaders, statistical data about the roles and positions they occupy are proof that Black women are not advancing to leadership roles at the same rate or in the same numbers as their white counterparts. Job function statistics suggests that Black women make up less than 2% of executive leadership and less than 5% of college presidents (Gagliardi et al., 2017; Ngue et al., 2020). Executive teams in education and across industries are largely occupied by white employees and subsequently those who earn the highest wages. This exemplifies how the most worked, highly exposed to Covid-19 and underpaid group -- Black women, continue to provide great contributions despite being undercompensated or protected.

As frontline workers, navigating not only the impact of Covid-19, Black women are aware of the threat to their job security. While working, they also contend with the workplace culture that comes with working in predominately white spaces like hospitals and schools. No matter the industry, being Black and a woman doesn't change how pervasive the negative stereotypes of Black women shape their professional experiences. Black women continue to find ways to navigate the inequities of the workforce as poignant reminder of the impact of both pandemics on the labor force and their presence as critical employees.

Both pandemics have raised issues with the systems, policies and practices and how they have impacted leadership in multiple spaces. While Black women are navigating these spaces there is an opportunity explore how Black women's identities, lived experience and conditions inform their leadership practice. In *A Love Letter to This Bridge Called My Back,* one of the chapters opens with the reflection below. It *read:*

I am 90 days into a pandemic and media outlets are flooded. There are protests for Black liberation, demonstrations for justice for Black death (Mr. George Floyd, Ahmaud Arbery, Breonna Taylor...a never-ending list of names) and I am exhausted by briefings on our public health crisis that is disproportionately killing Black folks. I AM TIIIIIIIIIRED. I don't think I can handle any more "Are you ok?" or "I can't believe this is happening!" commentary from my colleagues. I posted my "away message" on my email as an act of resistance and it read, "Caring for myself is not self-indulgence, it is self-preservation, and that is an act of political warfare." (Audre Lorde, 2017) ...and so here I am (Newman, 2022).

This excerpt explicitly names the experiences of many during these pandemics. Both pandemics have surfaced the experience of Black women by noting the ways they continue to resist and employ skills and practices necessary to their survival and resilience. One of part of that reflection raised this idea that Black women in the workplace have to carve out time to take care of themselves in order to preserve their energy when navigating what is happening in the world and processing how it directly impacts them emotionally and psychologically.

Black and Woman

Crenshaw's (1989) concept of intersectionality can be used to explain how both race and gender shape the nuanced identities of Black women. The entanglement of race and gender described as double jeopardy measures the impact of race and gender on career advancement exposing how Black women are having different experiences in professional spaces compared to their counterparts (Grant, 2016; Jean-Marie et al., 2009). Black women leaders are navigating organizations while also negotiating their layered identities. Black women are subjects of race and gender-based politics and practices. Black women are often directly impacted by the decisions related to reproduction, wealth attainment, and workforce development and opportunity (Beal, 2008). All areas that have been impacted by the outcomes of both pandemics. Black women employees see themselves as Black and work to counter the negative stereotypes about their race by adopting a sense of imperviousness. In research on the strong black women schema, we see how the effects influence Black women's identity development (Harris-Perry, 2011). Collins (2000) states, "contemporary U.S. Black women intellectuals are engaged in the struggle to reconceptualize all dimensions of the clash of oppression and activism as it applies to African-American women" (p.13). Being Black and a woman extends, if not inflamed as these women become leaders in organizations where they are few in number.

White Space

Segregation and marginalization have manifested a division between Black and White, orchestrating an overwhelming sense of "White Space" in schools and in workplaces (Anderson, 2015, p. 10). "White Space" is the structured existence of Whiteness where Black people exist within white dominant structures forcing them to navigate spaces never designed for their presence. White space has direct implications to the theory of organizational containment as a system that perpetuates the division and limits mobility but lacks the structures to advance inclusivity in the work environment. The nature of white space presents itself as organic and innate, and that it has normalized a culture of homogeneity within society. This white space can be used to understand and compare the inequities of Black women's experience in the work environment

Historically, in white spaces, such as industry and school district leadership, Black women worked as middle managers, administrators, and teachers. These roles do not describe the executive leadership as those spaces were originally created by white men for white men; thus, creating barriers to advancement for Black women. For instance, as executive leadership in fortune 500 companies, Black women do not advance in their careers at the same rate as white women, make less than their white counterparts, and are not afforded the same opportunities for support (Ngue et al., 2020). This is similar to what Feagin (2010) describes as the systems that operate within the WRF, thus upholding the idea of the crooked room. In addition, for Black women leaders, white spaces also expose them as targets of racism and sexism.

Black Women in White Spaces

Black women have learned to navigate the inequalities within white spaces. There is a heightened sense of awareness of being Black and a woman that informs their daily leadership practices. In a 2019 study conducted by the Korn Ferry Institute, exploring the experiences of Black P&L Leaders, insights suggest that Black leaders focused on both overperformance in their work while outperforming their white colleagues. The overperformance demonstrates Black leaders are capable, thus allowing them and to take charge of their careers. Not only are Black leaders exhausting all their work ethic, but they are doing so in the name of all the Black leaders in their respective spaces. The study further explains that without Black executives, companies are missing an important source of leadership that ultimately impacts a culture of inclusivity. For other Black employees this is critical in their work experience. Harvard Business Review describes how Black women's' existence as leaders are tied to the collective experiences of other Black people suggesting that they are "viewed through a larger filter of race and class" (Cheeks, 2018, p.

4). This filter is often misrecognized as a monolithic Black experience but does explain the interconnectedness of Black people and their lived experiences. This occurs because of the lack of diversity in many institutions and white spaces. The lack of Black people, more specifically Black women in leadership across institutions and industries have created a damaging culture centered around white supremacy thinking that is rooted in the norms, standards, and practices of an organization (Okun, 2020). As superintendents, principals, and executive level leaders in various industries there are psychological costs to being in the racial minority (Wingfield, 2015). The coping mechanisms and strategic leadership behavior employed becomes a necessary practice to alleviate the ramifications of discrimination.

CHALLENGES WITHIN LEADERSHIP

Stereotypes

The literature also provides examples of long-standing tropes of Black women including that of being angry or strong. Forced by the need to survive, Black women have had experiences with aggressors who trivialize their place and are then blamed for their response. Jones and Norwood (2017) attempted to dismantle the "angry Black woman trope" by raising the point that anger is an emotion or a state of being. As an emotion, anger can be expressed when one is triggered or disrespected which may result in a direct response. Black women are not "innately angry or angrier than any other person" and it is unfair when they are perceived as such (Jones & Norwood, 2017). It becomes response to Black women without holding the aggressor responsible for the harm done. In an attempt debunk the myth of the negative stereotypes about Black women, one must grapple with the historical context of seeing Black women as the other. History has settled with the extreme characterization of Black women, calling them Mammy, Jezebels and Sapphires. These names paint an image of oversexualized or overwhelmingly domesticated women who live in service to others (Harris-Perry, 2011). Navigating professional spaces becomes more about how to navigate the short-sighted ideas about behaviors and attitudes while working to present themselves as intelligent and capable. The respectability politics that Black women are held accountable to are an underhanded approach to force them to conceal the fullness of their racialized and gendered identities. Research suggests that across industries Black women deeply understand the perceptions of racial stereotypes and have consistently developed practices to circumvent the negative impact.

The leadership skills and practices of Black women are influenced by their racialized, gendered, and cultural experience. Counter to their own narratives are the interpretations of their identities managed by the WRF. As a critical element of the frame, negative stereotyping is representative of the way Black women are "racialized, sexualized, minimized and demonized in popular discourse and media" (Gomez et al., 2019, p. 2). For instance, commentary about being aggressive, critiquing body size, making broad generalizations about their knowledge based off where they are from or the schools they attended, and calling attention to hair styles are all rooted in negative perceptions of Black women. The attempt to socially control Black women through attacks on their image and intellect positions them as targets of workplace policies having to always "contend with the hypervisibility imposed by their lower social status" in ways their colleagues do not (Harris-Perry, 2011, p. 39). Evident in board rooms and on teams, Black women leaders are navigating the new territory of leadership and meet resistance by their colleagues. Microaggressions fixed on degrading commentary or dismissive actions regarding language, presentation or other identities are harmful to Black employees. Black women experience daily discrimination at higher rates than their white counterparts (LeanIn.org). With such unrest as an employee, Black women find the compounding incidents to be stirring and having lasting health effects (Dickens & Chavez, 2018).

Communication

Communication is a necessary part of leadership; however Black women are challenged by the use and delivery of language. Jones and Norwood (2017) explained how the angry black women trope is weaponized in professional and social settings. In many instances, direct speech or quick responses by Black women are perceived as expressing anger or aggression. Although the history of Black women's positionality could easily trigger that emotion, it is not typically Black women's disposition. In those moments, the choice of words and the delivery of responses can be alarming. This is also true in non-confrontational moments when Black women are engaging with their colleagues. Jean-Marie et al. (2009) describes how Black women in the study developed a practice of collaboration and consensus building as way to evoke a sense congeniality. The anticipated response would be a more welcoming audience or increased interest in the Black women's instruction. Such navigational tools exemplify an unassertive yet powerful positionality for Black women leaders. The need to navigate the fragility of their white counterparts with pleasantries and light instructions as to not alarm their white colleagues (DiAngelo, 2018).

Communication practices are also impacted by both gender and racialized stereotypes, it subject to regional or linguistic biases. The culturally relevant speech of Black people, described as speech patterns manipulated by regional dialects and colloquialisms becomes a point of tension within the WRF (Feagin, 2010; Rickford, 1999). With regards to communication as a way to display strength and ingenuity,

Black women have established code-switching as a coping strategy used to shift identities, sometimes losing their own true identities (Harris-Perry, 2011; Richie et al., 1997). As a result, Black women are forced to negotiate their identities in search of a balance between personal and organizational culture (Santamaría & Santamaría, 2015). For example, Black women are constantly reframing their ideas and recharacterizing themselves.

The outcomes of this is present in the way Black women have led movements and organizations with a level of linguistic dexterity necessary for survival and success (Newman, 2021b). Lorde, (2017) describes self-preservation as the intentional efforts to resist as protection from socio-political pain and challenge of one's lived experience. Black women have done so by employing a leadership approach and technique radically different from their white counterparts (Santamaría, 2014). The long-term effects of socializing in this way impacts Black women's self-perception and the reach of their work.

Effective Communication Through Language in Leadership

The way Black women extend their reach within their function is due to the extensive nature of their language. Language is a necessary part of one's leadership practice used to engage others and deliver messages to and about stakeholders. Language is expansive and can be described as a traditional practice of connecting stories and experiences across generations and periods of time (Sakho-Lewis, 2017). Black women use language in many forms. In some cases, it is a direct use of verbal interactions while in others they use nonverbal communication like with body language to strategically communicate with others. As language is both necessary and vital to the work as a leader, Black women have found ways to express themselves across lines of power, roles and in different environments. This is an important skill to have and use especially when there are so many negative ideas about the way Black women engage impacting how they are perceived as leaders.

BLACK WOMEN, RESISTANCE AND LEADERSHIP

Black women are showing up as leaders in social justice movements and in traditional industry spaces. At the nexus of Black women's leadership is their experience with history and present-day influence of their multiple identities (Alston, 2012). The power in Black women's leadership can be found in their multilingualism, people management skills and collective power of community. Black women exercise leadership skills and practices as a strategy to resist systems and advance as leaders.

Despite having challenges, in many ways Black women have acquired a set of people-centered beliefs and practices balancing position and power.

History of Leadership Studies

Racist institutional structures and beliefs are barriers that make Black leadership a struggle and Black women are forced to lower positions in society" (Feagin, 2010; Rosser-Mims, 2010). Early scholarship on leadership has mainly focused on white male leaders in roles in spaces such as education and business. As the field of leadership has expanded, scholars extended the scope of leadership to include the gendered experiences across industries and introduced literature including race as a factor (Alexander, 2010; Shakeshaft, 1989). For instance, Shakeshaft (1989) stated that academic research, the funding of the work and the subject of study had been centered around white-males. Consequently, the outcomes of that work have presented a limited representation of leadership theory and practice. Alexander (2010) continued to highlight this gap by raising awareness of critical Black women leaders who were trailblazer in leadership and opportunity. The evolution of these works seeks to bridge together a single gendered experience to a more complex view include race and culture. Leadership studies continue to include intersecting identities like race, gender, and culture, noting the impact of these identities on the leadership experience (Yammarino, 2013). In Yammarino's (2013) discussion of new areas for leadership studies, she suggests that the future of this work will focus less on traditional identities but on culture differences toward inclusivity. Furthermore, Santamaria (2014) describes this emerging leadership practice connected to ideas of social justice and applied leadership. The ways leadership studies continue to evolve merges the idea of theory and practice and is informed by the varying identities of current leadership.

Resistance

Collins' (1986) reference to Black women as "outsiders within" demonstrates how Black women have learned to navigate white spaces (p.15). As an often underrepresented and misrepresented group, restricted by the aforementioned stereotypes, Black women have developed a set of skills and strategies to resist the negative perceptions of who they are. Resistance becomes a practice of dissent. Black women introduce intentional skills and strategy in their practice as a complex approach to resistance as leaders; and as they navigate White spaces, they continue to resist the negative stereotyping at the same time (Bonaparte, 2016; Santamaría, 2014).

W.E.B. Du Bois, (1903) coined the term, double consciousness to describe the duality of identity for Black people. This is also true for Black women as they present differently at work and in other spaces. Black women's resistance to negative stereotypes and perceptions of who they are happens by adopting a "culture of dissemblance" that they use as a form of protection and survival (Harris-Perry, 2011, p. 58). As leaders, Black women learn to navigate their roles with high levels of adaptability and hyper- aware of the challenges they may face (Evans-Winters, 2019); an ongoing practice for Black women in any leadership space.

Black women's active refusal to resist the structures and negative perceptions of the white dominant culture is necessary for their career mobility (hooks, 2014). Yosso, (2005) names navigational capital as the ability to maneuver systems and institutions that did not traditionally welcome Black and Latinx people. To be successful in these spaces, Black women participate in what Sakho-Lewis (2017) calls "veil walking" or the act exchanging knowledge across different internal institutions and roles (p.13). The ability for Black women to have a keen sense of understanding of the unwritten rules and policies within a system is critical for their ability to navigate spaces.

In a review of several qualitative studies, researchers identified common resistance practices, focused on communication, and leadership strategies to advance as leaders (Bonaparte, 2016; Oikelome, 2017; Sakho-Lewis, 2017; Santamaría, 2014). Themes from the research highlighted Black women's application of critical leadership strategies employed to engage teams and external stakeholders to increase congeniality among professional colleagues (Santamaria, 2014). In a national study by Leanin.org, Black women described their experience with discrimination and ways they overcompensated by being highly ambitious and involved in their work. Other strategies included ways Black women build consensus and are willing to engage in critical conversations as a way to share power and establish community (Bonaparte, 2016; Oikelome, 2017; Santamaria, 2014). Black women are often direct in this as circumvent barriers by identifying opportunities that they want and creating the space for themselves with the help of support through mentorship to reach their goals (Oikelome, 2017).

In a particular study of college presidents, participants identified mentorship as a common practice to navigate their roles and functions (Oikelome, 2017). Through these relationships, Black women learned about the nuances of their profession or gained insight into the unnamed procedures of their roles. Black women move through the white dominant systems and structures of organizations with a familiar strategy noted as "playing the game (Davis, 2012, p. 165). As leaders they use the social norms to strategically develop relationships with their peers, inviting colleagues to engage in the decision making, and involving themselves in internal groups and organizations (Davis, 2012; Santamaria, 2014). As many of the studies involved Black women across industries and in different regions, their navigational strategies prove to expand across many circumstances.

FOLLOW THE LEADER

The study of leadership becomes more inclusive as the research addresses the experiences of Black women as critical leaders. There is evidence of Black women serving as educational leaders, business leaders, and lead agents of change within the Civil Rights movement and in Black communities dating as far back as the 1700s (Barnett, 1993; Franklin, 1990). Black women leaders like Harriet Tubman, Sojourner Truth and many others highlight the impact of their political power and advocacy due to their Black womanhood. Noted scholars of Black feminism and critical pedagogies used to narrate the experiences of Black women are foundational to understanding their place as leaders. Yammarino (2013) highlights the works of Patricia Hill Collins, Anna Julia Haywood Cooper and Jill Nelson among many others as literature that explore Black women's lived experience. This is the framework for Yammarino's (2013) qualitative study of Black women presidents exploring womanhood, scholarship and strategies for increasing their presence in executive level higher education roles.

Deeply understanding the pervasive nature of the WRF and the historical and structural context of this lens has the potential to further transform leadership spaces. Black women leaders directly impact and inform critical decisions as demonstrated by their application of strategies and approaches to leadership practice (Alston, 2012). The ways Black women adjust, readjust and shift, sparks a conversation amongst aspiring leaders about ways they can resist oppressive narratives. Harris-Perry (2011) references the many labels forced upon Black women like Mammy and Jezebel; yet, highlights the way Black women have redefined those labels. Black women are learning from these experiences within the crooked room and are developing a unique set of leadership skills and practice. This is also true as they navigate the challenges of the pandemics. Leadership for Black women is a practice, a tool, a way of life for so many. Despite the underrepresentation in cross-sector spaces Black women continue to operate with intentional strategies for survival and to exist within the culture of organizations and systems (Apugo, 2019; Silver & Jansen, 2017).

Revolutionary Leaders

Freire, (1972) writes in the Pedagogy of the Oppressed, about the revolutionary leader as an active participant in the transformation of communities, people, and place. Freire's work is foundational to Black women's leadership practice and approach.

Revolutionary leaders are not individuals promoting individual interests, rather they radical leaders advancing community growth. For instance, amidst the protests and violence against Black bodies, there was a spike in interest around literature that discussed the impact of racism and bias (León et al., 2020). During this time many Black authors and activists saw an increase in the public's interest in their writing. As literary agents of change, they are responsible for providing content that was relevant and necessary to the current state of affairs. Authors who whose books had been on the shelf re-emerged to the New York Time's Bestsellers list. According The Guardian (2020), authors such as Michelle Alexander, Ibram X. Kendi alongside activist leaders like Bryan Stevenson and Brittney Cooper made the list. Without concrete data on the racial demographics of the consumers, it is clear there was a greater interest in understanding and action toward anti-racist behaviors. The topics ranged from police brutality, inequities in access for Black people and ideas on ways to change mindsets. The literary power of these texts is evidence of how these authors acts as change agents. There work charges a community of people, of leaders across industries, to commit to change with lasting impacts. Revolutionary leaders have a sense of responsibility for others and this is evident in the way Black women employ mothering techniques as a form of care and leadership (Sakho-Lewis, 2017). Revolutionary leadership practices have proven to be timely, radical and relevant particularly in the fight for social justice. Black women like Bree Newsome, sacrifice freedom for the movement of civil rights and humanity. Similarly, leaders within organizations are making hard decisions to challenge power systems and advocate for equity across teams and programs.

More specifically, Freire describes the liberatory "theory of action" of revolutionary leaders that creates opportunities for those who have been historically marginalized. Even within the systems and structures designed to limit access, the justice-oriented approach of revolutionary leaders pushes them to occupy spaces of possibility. In Horsford's (2012) study, the research describes the practice of "bridge leadership" as an effective model for Black women's leadership practice. It recounts their ability to make connections across lines of difference, in service to others across various environments. Freire's charge for these leaders to focus on the collective being of communities and support in finding solutions to their problems. As targeted as Black women leaders are in the workspace, they still find time to support others and display a level of concern that is often other directed (Harris-Perry, 2011). The selflessness of their practice further commits them to ideas of hope and possibility that can only be images within the context of their lived experience.

Hope Dealers

As detailed by the work of bell hooks (2003) a pedagogy of hope includes the ways leaders practice care and vision setting linked to a strategic leadership approach. This practice forces leaders to engage with people across lines of difference, work toward understanding and empathy while providing guidance. This is necessary as Black women leaders understand from a personal experience what it means to be invisible or neglected. Considering their lived experience, Black women leaders extend love and hold themselves responsible for the well-being of the people they serve. Hope as a leadership skill is the applied energy of emotion and thinking necessary to motivate others toward a goal (Snyder et al., 1991 as cited in (Helland & Winston, 2005). Connected to the field of positive psychology, hope becomes a strategy to engage teams and advance goals employed strategically by leaders. Hope involves a future orientation that is important to the effectiveness of the leader (Helland & Winston, 2005)

Black women leaders who participate in activism understand how to sustain efforts toward a better future. Historical figures like Angela Davis and Shirley Chisolm who were able to demonstrate their leadership through vision setting were paramount. These Black women, among others, believed in the possibility of the future and a revolutionized state of being. As industry professionals, this is evident in Black women's ability to set strategic direction and goals toward organizational progress. For Black women leaders, the aspirational beliefs are connected to ancestral traditions of hope, spiritual morals, and joy (Alexander, 2010). By exercising these beliefs, Black women are employing engagement practices that are rooted in humanity (Sakho-Lewis, 2017). The immensity of hope for Black women leaders transcends the barriers they face. It is with their leadership prowess, that Black women continue to define and shape their leadership identity.

LEADERSHIP IN ACTION

Black women's leadership in action can be described by the complexity of their practice as educational leaders, health policy experts and community activists. Black women's leadership during these times is a result of their "racialized, gendered and cultural experiences and presents their skills and practices as grounded in experience, calculated, and deliberate (Newman, p.72, 2021b). This becomes a critical part of their leadership craft and necessary to navigate all of the crooked spaces they occupy. To further explore the actions taken in a qualitative grounded theory study by Newman (2021b), there are seven notable skills listed as inherent to Black women's practice. Those skills include; community acumen, strategic prowess, moral direction, foresight, endurance, communication aptitude and empathy. Through the analysis of that study, these specific skills were identified as critical "to navigate their organizations, meet role expectations, and help with sustaining their existence in their role.

Of the skills identified, three are most relevant to navigating the current socio-political climate include: community acumen, foresight, and empathy. Community acumen is defined by "A community-centered approach leveraging a collective mindset toward making judgements and decisions; intentional relationship building to serve others and also in service to self; identifying personal needs" (Newman, 2021b, p. 85) This is important to understanding the community most impacted by the pandemics but also aware of the experiences of these groups with a focus on providing equitable solutions. Black women employ this practice as a way to center others in their work. Harris-Perry (2011) notes that this common practice for Black women as their work is always other -directed. This practice is also consistent with the roles and positions Black women have occupied in the pandemic as both caretaker and teachers, frontline workers and in many service-oriented roles. To add to this skill, foresight was defined as the "ability to "see around the corner"- identify trends, forecasting and to prepare for/build, create, share possibilities" (Newman, 2021b, p.85). The associated behaviors include how Black women leaders in this environment can radically imagine new ways for us to service and evoke change. The creativity in their work is solidified by their intuitive nature. There is evidence of some socio-cultural practices and traditions like space holding that speaks to Black women's ability to engage without judgement across space, place and time (Sakho-Lewis, 2017). In these times, this is critical in being able to reimagine what futures could look like on the other side of a global health pandemic and when their racial equity present in our systems and institutions.

Another related skill to Black women's leadership during this time of reckoning is empathy. In the study, it was defined as "the practice of intentional care for others with attention to and with responsibility of their well-being" which is center around care, concern and compassion (Newman, p. 85, 2021b). In this study it was described as a critical tool holding these leaders responsible for their actions and engagement with others. The ways in which empathy shows up in political and social movement is concentrated on efforts to galvanize groups and seeing the humanity in those people. This approach moves the work along and creates space for all people to become agents of change. This research not only provides language for those skills and practices but allows for Black women to reframe their contributions to change.

FUTURE RESEARCH AND DIRECTION

Continued research on the impact of the WRF on the experiences of Black women leaders, lends itself to a deeper understanding of their place and space. Further research on the impact of gendered and racialized experiences on the development of their skills and practices is necessary to learn more about the ways Black women exist as leaders. Additionally, further research on other intersecting identities that may influence their practice could provide more information on the development of their leadership skills and practice. Throughout this chapter, the focus has been on the historical implications of racism and how in the present day, those beliefs, and morals manifests in organizations and within movements for justice and racial equity. With the current climate and opportunities that exist to increase the presence of Black women leaders it is important that Black women can operate as leaders with little resistance. This is made possible by acknowledging the institutional biases, negative stereotypes and developing skills to dismantle those systemic barriers. Opportunities for future research could address the following questions:

1. What other factors influence Black women's leadership skills and practice?
2. How do Black women sustain their revolutionary and hopeful efforts as leaders?
3. If Black women leaders have made a practice out of care of others, who will extend love, empathy, and hope for them?

There are many perspectives of Black women's leadership skills and practice; they continue to be a group of leaders who will work to occupy leadership spaces inside and outside mainstream environments. The impact of further research only supports the practical implications for leadership development and promotion. Additionally, the study of leadership theory and practice will expand to include the complexities of Black women leaders.

CONCLUSION

The White Racial Frame is a theoretical concept that explains how Black women are seen in society and how this is exhibited within professional spaces (Feagin, 2010). The WRF creates a restricted perception of Black women, and limits how their contributions are perceived. Black women's resistance to the WRF is evident in their skills, practice, and presence as leaders. In response, Black women occupy leadership spaces and employ strategies necessary to their professional survivorship. While navigating the interconnectedness of race, gender and culture, Black women's leadership practice is an act of resistance. Black women leaders, operating in roles on and tangential to white dominated leadership spaces, develop and use a complex set of skills to sustain their place and space. These efforts are powerful navigational tools in roles across industries and outside mainstream spaces. This further supports the ideas that Black women can adapt to the socio-political identities forced upon them and thrive as critical and complex leaders.

REFERENCES

Aaron, T. S. (2020). Black Women: Perceptions and Enactments of Leadership. *Journal of School Leadership*, *30*(2), 146–165. doi:10.1177/1052684619871020

Alexander, M. (2012). *The new Jim Crow: Mass incarceration in the age of colorblindness*. New Press.

Alexander, T. (2010). Roots of Leadership: Analysis of the Narratives from African American Women Leaders in Higher Education. *International Journal of Learning*, *17*(4), 193–204. doi:10.18848/1447-9494/CGP/v17i04/46973

Alston, J. A. (2012). Standing on the promises: A new generation of Black women scholars in educational leadership and beyond. *International Journal of Qualitative Studies in Education: Emerging African American Women Scholars*, *25*(1), 127–129. doi:10.1080/09518398.2011.647725

Anderson, E. (2015). The White Space. *Sage (Atlanta, Ga.)*, *1*(1), 10–21. doi:10.1177/2332649214561306

Apugo, D. (2019). A Hidden Culture of Coping: Insights on African American Women's Existence in Predominately White Institutions. *Multicultural Perspectives*, *21*(1), 53–62. doi:10.1080/15210960.2019.1573067

Banks, N. (2019). Black women's labor market history reveals deep-seated race and gender discrimination. *Economic Policy Institute*. https://www.epi.org/blog/black-womens-labor-market-history-reveals-deep-seated-race-and-gender-discrimination/

Barnett, B. M. (1993). Invisible Southern Black Women Leaders in the Civil Rights Movement: The Triple Constraints of Gender, Race, and Class. *Gender & Society*, *7*(2), 162–182. doi:10.1177/089124393007002002

Beal, F. M. (2008). Double Jeopardy: To Be Black and Female. *Meridians (Middletown, Conn.)*, *8*(2), 166–176. doi:10.2979/MER.2008.8.2.166

Berry, R. (2014). Identifying organizational containment and its effect on the career paths of black educators. *Theses and Dissertations*. doi:10.25772/034A-Y804

Bonaparte, Y. (2016). Leaning In: A Phenomenological Study of African American Women Leaders in the Pharmaceutical Industry. *Advancing Women in Leadership, 36*. https://vcu-alma-primo.hosted.exlibrisgroup.com/primo-explore/ fulldisplay?docid=TN_proquest1827617820&context=PC&vid=VCUL&lang= en_US&search_scope=all_scope&adaptor=primo_central_multiple_fe&tab=all &query=any,contains,Leaning%20In:%20A%20Phenomenological%20Study%20 of%20African%20American%20Women%20Leaders%20%20in%20the%20 Pharmaceutical%20Industry

Cheeks, M. (2018, March 26). How Black Women Describe Navigating Race and Gender in the Workplace. *Harvard Business Review*. https://hbr.org/2018/03/how-black-women-describe-navigating-race-and-gender-in-the-workplace

Collins, P. H. (1986). Learning from the Outsider Within: The Sociological Significance of Black Feminist Thought*. *Social Problems, 33*(6), s14–s32. doi:10.2307/800672

Collins, P. H. (2000). Black Feminist Thought: Knowledge, Consciousness, and the Politcs of Empowerment (Revised 10th Anniversary). Routledge.

Crenshaw, K. (1989). *Demarginalizing the Intersection of Race and Sex: A Black Feminist Critique of Antidiscrimination Doctrine, Feminist Theory and Antiracist Politics*. Academic Press.

Davis, D. R. (2012). *A Phenomenological Study on the Leadership Development of African American Women Executives in Academia and Business.* ProQuest LLC. http://search.proquest.com/docview/1697499660/69FDEFC14CB84EC1PQ/13

de León, C., Alter, A., Harris, E. A., & Khatib, J. (2020, July 1). 'A Conflicted Cultural Force': What It's Like to Be Black in Publishing. *The New York Times.* https://www.nytimes.com/2020/07/01/books/book-publishing-black.html

DiAngelo, R. (2018). *White Fragility: Why It's so Hard for White People to Talk About Racism*. Beacon Press.

Dickens, D. D., & Chavez, E. L. (2018). Navigating the workplace: The costs and benefits of shifting identities at work among early career U.S. Black women. *Sex Roles, 78*(11–12), 760–774. doi:10.100711199-017-0844-x

Du Bois, W. E. B. (1903). *The Souls of Black Folk: Essays and Sketches*. A.C. McClurg.

Evans-Winters, V. E. (2019). *Black Feminism in Qualitative Inquiry: A Mosaic for Writing Our Daughter's Body Futures of data analysis in qualitative research* (illustrated ed.). Routledge.

Evelyn, K. (2020, June 11). Black US authors top New York Times bestseller list as protests continue. *The Guardian*. https://www.theguardian.com/books/2020/jun/11/new-york-times-bestseller-list-black-authors

Feagin, J. R. (2010). *The white racial frame: Centuries of racial framing and counter-framing*. Routledge. doi:10.4324/9780203890646

Franklin, V. P. (1990). "They Rose and Fell Together": African American Educators and Community Leadership, 1795-1954. *Journal of Education*, *172*(3), 39–64. doi:10.1177/002205749017200304

Freire, P. (1972). *Pedagogy of the Oppressed*. Herder and Herder.

Frye, J. (2019, August 22). *Racism and Sexism Combine to Shortchange Working Black Women*. Center for American Progress. https://www.americanprogress.org/issues/women/news/2019/08/22/473775/racism-sexism-combine-shortchange-working-black-women/

Gagliardi, J., Espinosa, L., Turk, J., & Morgan, T. (2017, June). *American College President Study 2017 | TIAA Institute*. https://www.tiaainstitute.org/publication/american-college-president-study-2017

Gomez, R., Rascon-Canales, M., & Romero, A. (2019, February 5). We See You, Hermana—At All of Your Powerful Intersections! The White Racial Framing of Serena Williams. *Latinx Talk*. https://latinxtalk.org/2019/02/05/we-see-you-hermana-at-all-of-your-powerful-intersections-the-white-facial-framing-of-serena-williams/

Grant, C. M. (2016). Smashing the Glass Ceiling. In *Responsive Leadership in Higher Education* (pp. 167–179). Routledge.

Greaux, L. (2010). *A Case Study of the Development of African American Women Executives*. ProQuest LLC. http://search.proquest.com/docview/870283884/69FDEFC14CB84EC1PQ/7

Harris-Perry, M. (2011). *Sister Citizen: Shame, Sterotypes and Black Women in America* (6th ed.). Yale University Press.

Helland, M. R., & Winston, B. E. (2005). Towards a Deeper Understanding of Hope and Leadership. *Journal of Leadership & Organizational Studies*, *12*(2), 42–54. doi:10.1177/107179190501200204

Hooks, B. (2003). *Teaching Community: A Pedagogy of Hope*. Psychology Press.

hooks, b. (2014). *Yearning: Race, Gender, and Cultural Politics*. Routledge.

Horsford, S. D. (2012). This Bridge Called My Leadership: An Essay on Black Women as Bridge Leaders in Education. *International Journal of Qualitative Studies in Education: QSE, 25*(1), 11–22. http://dx.doi.org.proxy.library.vcu.edu/10.1080/09518398.2011.647726

Jean-Marie, G., Williams, V. A., & Sherman, S. L. (2009). Black Women's Leadership Experiences: Examining the Intersectionality of Race and Gender. *Advances in Developing Human Resources, 11*(5), 562–581. https://doi.org/10.1177/1523422309351836

Jones, T., & Norwood, K. J. (2017). Aggressive Encounters & White Fragility: Deconstructing the Trope of the Angry Black Woman. *Iowa Law Review, 102*(5), 2017–2069. http://proxy.library.vcu.edu/login?url=http://search.ebscohost.com/login.aspx?direct=true&AuthType=ip,url,cookie,uid&db=a9h&AN=124842614&site=ehost-live&scope=site

Korn Ferry. (2019). *The Black P&L Leader: Insights and Lesson from Senior Black P&L Leaders in Corporate America*. Korn Ferry Institute. https://www.kornferry.com/content/dam/kornferry/docs/pdfs/korn-ferry_theblack-pl-leader.pdf

Lorde, A. (2017). *A Burst of Light: And other essays*. Izia Press.

Mays, V. M., Coleman, L. M., & Jackson, J. S. (1996). Perceived race-based discrimination, employment status, and job stress in a national sample of Black women: Implications for health outcomes. *Journal of Occupational Health Psychology, 1*(3), 319–329. https://doi.org/10.1037/1076-8998.1.3.319

Nelson, T., Esteban, C., & Adeoye, C. (2016). *Rethinking Strength: Black Women's Perceptions of the "Strong Black Woman" Role*. https://journals-sagepub-com.proxy.library.vcu.edu/doi/full/10.1177/0361684316646716

Newcomb, W. S., & Niemeyer, A. (2015). African American women principals: Heeding the call to serve as conduits for transforming urban school communities. *International Journal of Qualitative Studies in Education: QSE, 28*(7), 786–799. https://doi.org/10.1080/09518398.2015.1036948

Newman, P. (2021a). *The Bloomsbury Handbook of Gender and Educational Leadership and Management* (V. Showunmi, P. Moorosi, C. Shakeshaft, & I. Oplataka, Eds.). Bloomsbury Academic.

Newman, P. (2021b). *Leading in Crooked Rooms: Race, Gender, Culture and Black Women's Leadership Skills and Practices*. Virginia Commonwealth University.

Newman, P. (2022). Ruminations of Black Womanhood, Leadership and Resistance. In G. Wilson, J. Acuff, & A. Kraehe (Eds.), *A Love Letter to This Bridge Called My Back*. University of Arizona Press.

Ngue, P., Saddler, R., Miller-Surratt, J., Tucker, N., Long, M., & Cooke, R. (2020). *Working at the intersection: What Black Women are up against*. Lean In. https://leanin.org/black-women-racism-discrimination-at-work

Okun, T. (2020). *White Supremacy Culture*. DRworksBook. https://www.dismantlingracism.org/

Richie, B., Fassinger, R., Linn, S., Johnson, J., Prosser, J., & Robinson, S. (1997). *Persistence, connection, and passion: A qualitative study of the career development of highly achieving African American–Black and White women*. https://psycnet-apa-org.proxy.library.vcu.edu/fulltext/1997-08136-003.html

Rickford, J. R. (1999). Suite for ebony and phonics. In *African American Vernaculuar English: Features, evolution, educational implications* (pp. 320–328). Blackwell Publishers.

Rosser-Mims, D. (2010). *Black Feminism: An Epistemological Framework for Exploring How Race and Gender Impact Black Women's Leadership Development*. Academic Press.

Sakho-Lewis, J. R. (2017). Black Activist Mothering: Teach Me About What Teaches You. *The Western Journal of Black Studies*, *41*(1/2), 6–19. http://proxy.library.vcu.edu/login?url=http://search.ebscohost.com/login.aspx?direct=true&AuthType=ip,url,cookie,uid&db=sih&AN=128902077&site=ehost-live&scope=site

Santamaria, L. (2014). Critical Change for the Greater Good: Multicultural Perceptions in Educational Leadership Toward Social Justice and Equity. *Educational Administration Quarterly*, *50*(3), 347–391. https://doi.org/10.1177/0013161X13505287

Santamaría, L., & Santamaría, A. (2015). *Culturally Responsive Leadership in Higher Education: Promoting Access, Equity, and Improvement*. Routledge.

Shakeshaft, C. (1989). The Gender Gap in Research in Educational Administration. *Educational Administration Quarterly*, *25*(4), 324–337. https://doi.org/10.1177/0013161X89025004002

Silver, N., & Jansen, P. (2017). The Multisector Career Arc: The Importance of Cross-Sector Affiliations. *California Management Review*, *60*(1), 33–55. https://doi.org/10.1177/0008125617725290

Wingfield, A. H. (2015, October 14). *Being Black—But Not Too Black—In the Workplace*. The Atlantic. https://www.theatlantic.com/business/archive/2015/10/being-black-work/409990/

Women in the labor force: A databook : BLS Reports: U.S. Bureau of Labor Statistics (No. 1084). (2019). https://www.bls.gov/opub/reports/womens-databook/2019/home.htm

X, M. (2008). *1962 L.A. Police Killings* (Vol. 2) [Audio recording]. spotify:track:1UNfkEgBaIXaBBSEbJ2hh1

Yammarino, F. (2013). Leadership: Past, Present, and Future. *Journal of Leadership & Organizational Studies*, *20*(2), 149–155. https://doi.org/10.1177/1548051812471559

Yosso, T. (2005). Whose culture has capital? A critical race theory discussion of community cultural wealth. *Race, Ethnicity and Education*, *8*(1), 69–91.

Chapter 7
Black and Brown Women Fostering Authentic Activism in Counseling Programs Amid Social Unrest

Monique Willis
California State University, Dominguez Hills, USA

Jotika Jagasia
Lamar University, USA

Ada Robinson-Perez
Binghamton University, USA

ABSTRACT

The COVID-19 pandemic, racial injustice, and civil unrest of 2020 disproportionately impacted Black and Brown communities jolting "progressive" academic systems and exposing inherent inequities. Such inequality warrants authentic activism to promote social awareness and facilitate a culture of collaboration, respect, and inclusivity. This chapter centers on three early-career Black and Brown women leaders associated with counseling programs who voice their positionality statements, experiences, and views to align with relevant theoretical concepts. Black feminism, postcolonial feminism, and critical race theory pedagogies serve as the authors' foundation, highlighting race, culture, gender, and intersectionality to unmask cultural oppression in higher education. Committed to their lives' work as academics, researchers, and mental health practitioners, the authors assume substantial professional responsibilities and engage in emotional labor adopting a sense of family and mothering to support students. Finally, the authors provide suggestions to undo injustices during turbulent times.

DOI: 10.4018/978-1-7998-7235-1.ch007

INTRODUCTION

Two thousand and twenty involved significant turmoil, incited by the global COVID-19 pandemic, political strife, and civil unrest, resulting in increased fear, uncertainty, and distress in racial and ethnic minority communities. The CDC (2020a) recognizes that minorities, specifically Black and Brown communities, including people of color with diverse backgrounds and experiences, are disproportionately impacted by COVID-19, as evidenced by poor access to essential, appropriate, and culturally responsive health care. This time also marked senseless killings of Black men and women, including George Floyd and Breonna Taylor, at the hands of law enforcement, capturing an all too familiar occurrence. The discontent that followed these atrocities sparked outrage, followed by protests across the globe. Consequently, never has there been such a necessary time to turn one's attention to sources that can provide guidance and fortitude to unify and organize social and racial justice. This moment calls for an activist movement to mobilize change to preexisting American norms and bring about justice for marginalized communities. Higher education reflects such standards, the "ivory tower," a breeding ground for great minds, knowledge, and opportunity. Yet, the history of academe reveals that many of the premier institutions benefited from the labor of slaves (Wilder, 2013).

While academic institutions no longer use slave labor, Black and Brown students and faculty, especially women, continue to be negatively impacted by inequality, reflected in poor retention rates and high service responsibilities (Walkington, 2017). Per the authors, Black and Brown leaders should use their voice as a collective to educate and stand against microaggressions and other practices that may be invisible but still impede actual progress in the academy. Black and Brown female leaders must transform higher education institutions to embody antiracist practices to foster all students' knowledge and cultural influence. The authors of this chapter assume authentic and transformative leadership in their roles to bridge our ancestors' struggles with efforts to foster intergenerational dialogue with future generations (Generett & Welch, 2018). Transformation of the academy necessitates deconstruction of hegemonic ideologies imposed upon Black and Brown women throughout history to allow Black and Brown women leaders to center their voices unapologetically, honor truth, and manifest their excellence and beauty within academic spaces.

BACKGROUND

As the world faces the devastation of the coronavirus (COVID-19) pandemic, the economic, physical, emotional, and psychological impact on individuals, families, and communities is extensive. Explicitly, the Black and Brown communities experience disproportionate rates of COVID-19 related deaths, infections due to deficiencies in access to healthcare, and underlying conditions such as hypertension, diabetes, respiratory illnesses, obesity, and other social determinants of health (CDC, 2020a; CDC, 2020b). Specific to social determinants of health, individuals who already struggle with mental illness or substance abuse face additional challenges, including unemployment, housing insecurities, and inaccessibility to behavioral healthcare (SAMHSA, 2020). In mid-December 2020, the nation's number of COVID-19 related deaths was more than 318,000 and climbing (Stobbe, 2020). Although COVID-19 vaccinations are well underway for administering in the United States (CDC, 2020a), "vaccination fear" among Black and Brown communities is prevalent because of the nation's history of deceit, exploitation, and inequitable care from the government medical and research communities (Jones, 2020).

In addition to the severe impacts of COVID-19, violence and death also ravaged Black and Brown communities. Hate speech, a type of terrorism targeting individuals or groups following an incident or triggering an event of terrorism aimed to hurt or disrespect, based on a person's identity (Chetty & Alathur, 2018), surged against Asian American communities in 2020. Beliefs that the COVID-19 began in Wuhan, China, in December 2019 resulted in xenophobic hate speech and physical crimes against Asian American communities (Gover, Harper & Langton et al., 2020). Between March 19, 2020 and February 18, 2021, Stop AAPI Hate reported 3,795 hate crimes against Asians (Kulkarni et al., 2021), traditionally unreported due to language barrier, fear of immigration status, or distrust of law enforcement (Gover et al., 2020). Cries against these injustices enkindled Stop Asian Hate rallies. Despite the demonstrations, hate speech towards South Asians continues to proliferate in 2021 on social media platforms due to increased COVID-19 cases in India, blaming the Indian community for spreading the infectious virus variant (Prakash et al., 2021).

In March 2020, a Black woman, Breonna Taylor, was killed as law enforcement executed a search warrant in her home (Oppel et al., 2021). Ms. Taylor, a young woman who served her community as an emergency medical technician, lay in bed alongside her boyfriend when police in Louisville, Kentucky, raided her home (Coates, 2020). Matters worsened as the nation witnessed the senseless and brutal deaths of George Floyd and Ahmaud Arbery (Dennis, 2020). The killing of George Floyd, a Black man, while detained on suspicion of using a $20 counterfeit bill in May 2020 played out on social media months following Taylor's death. In September 2020 (Burrell, 2020), a grand jury trial did not charge two police officers for Breonna Taylor's killing. These events' culmination ignited a national and international movement over racial injustice, creating a broad alliance for the Black Lives Matter Movement.

The historical violence against communities of color has persisted for over 400 years. Profound racism and oppression continue to inundate our Black and Brown communities during these difficult times. The toll of systemic racism has a ripple effect across student populations. The consequences include the burden of physical and mental health ailments disproportionately impacting underrepresented minority (URM) students and their families. As practitioners and scholars, the authors recognize the magnitude of these health and social problems and seek to improve them in the academy. Women of color (WOC) in leadership in the academy must "lean in" more deeply to advocate for systemic change. Scholars' ethical and moral duty is to effectively teach and shape the next generation of professional therapists, counselors, and social workers eager to serve vulnerable communities, families, and individuals ravaged by the dual impacts of the COVID-19 pandemic and racism. Leading and persevering amid injustices and social unrest is undoubtedly not a new phenomenon. However, as emerging leaders, an emphasis on the significance of transformative leadership during this historical time in the academy to engage in critical discourse is necessary for structural change.

In response to the racism and racial discourse reflected in the use of color-based racial designations in the United States (Harpalani 2015), the authors deconstruct the binary of "Black" and "White." The analysis and deconstruction process requires reflexivity in defining racial concepts not to categorize or divide but to unite in solidarity and honor the tapestry of our racial and ethnic identities. Throughout the chapter, references to "Black" include persons who identify their ethnicity within the African diaspora, and "Brown" includes but is not limited to the Latinx community. Brown may also refer to our non-White sisters who identify as Asian, Asian American, and Pacific Islander (AAPI). Harpalani (2015) notes that South Asian Americans are "a group of people that does not" fit neatly within the prevailing racial groupings of Black and White and historically have maintained "racially ambiguous identities within the United States" (p. 610). The following positionality statements provide more meaning to our ethnic identities and social locations.

Positionality Statements

As collegiate scholars and practitioners in the counseling fields, marital and family therapy, and social work, the authors, referred to as "we" in this statement, recognize that the gravity of our lived experiences and intersectional identities as Black and Brown women profoundly enriches our pedagogy. We ascribe to the ideologies of Black feminism while embracing ideas of postcolonial feminism that address the complexity of our global and diverse cultural contexts in America. In capturing *Black Feminist Thought*, the convergence of race, class, and gender oppression describes how the United States constituted slavery in its fabric, subsequently influencing Black women's relationships with their families, communities, employers, and one another (Collins, 2000). We are Black and Brown women who live within, between, and at the margins with diverse backgrounds. Historically, feminists of color in

America addressed colonization to describe the appropriation of their experiences by "hegemonic White women," yet when expanded transnationally, it has been used to categorize "economic and political hierarchies" and specific discourses of the "third world" (Mohanty, 1988). Postcolonial feminists criticize Western feminism and seek to dismantle or deconstruct the homogeneity and systemization of different women globally. Audre Lorde's (1984) work frames our differences as Black and Brown women as powerful, stating:

Advocating the mere tolerance of difference between women is the grossest reformism. It is a total denial of the creative function of difference in our lives. For difference must be not merely tolerated but seen as a fund of necessary polarities between which our creativity can spark like a dialectic (p. 99).

As the political, collectively, we reflect nuanced experiences of race, culture, national origin, gender, kinship, ideology, and leadership. Some of our locations include more recent histories of immigration to the United States, third-culture persons, and women attempting to integrate multiple cultural identities (Horne & Arora, 2013). Being Black and Brown women writers, we seek to pursue a movement outside the dominant discourse, referred to as "migratory subjectivity," as we assume agency while refusing subjugation (Davies, 1994).

Through our work as feminist researchers and transformational leaders, we seek to achieve ways to "undo" inequality, whether "in small or big ways" (Kleinman, 2007, p.7), and promote agency and resistance to economic and political hierarchies and structural domination (Mohanty, 1948). We work to achieve egalitarian collaboration and alliance building (Zerbe Enns et al., 2020) among Black and Brown communities to endeavor critical consciousness and social change. In solidarity against oppressive structures, we share our voices as Black and Brown women leaders.

Monique: I am an early career academic serving as an assistant professor and administrator of a couples and family therapy program in a Hispanic serving institution and a mental health clinician. I am keenly aware of the complexity of my identity that reflects marginalized experiences and positions of privilege. I identify as an educated, first-generation, Black Belizean American, cis-gendered female, wife, mother, and caregiver of a multigenerational household. My identity as a Black Woman "opened doors" to the halls of higher education. I moved through the highest level of academia. Within those chambers, I quickly learned that uniqueness often is not valued while conformity is. Well-intentioned assessors punctuated my experiences, highlighting my ability to engage in their world, only to be momentarily crippled by haunting doubts that my aptitudes perhaps are fantastical. Committed to the higher education vision, I pursued research, an academic position, and family therapy to address disparities among and improve marginalized groups' overall well-being. Even within my short career, I have experienced discrete and overt acts of racism meant to silence my voice and privilege the structures of those in power. My responsibility to activism and social justice propels me to stand up to the systems that perpetuate acts of racism, genderism, classism, ableism, and other isms. I stand up for and with silenced and marginalized students; I speak up for them as my ancestors worked tirelessly for me, hoping that future generations will benefit from my struggles.

Jotika: I identify as a bilingual, Brown, Hindu South Asian Indian migrant (immigrant) cis-gender female, mother, caregiver, therapist, and first-generation researcher with a Ph.D. in Marriage and Family Therapy from a historically White American institution. One could speculate that earning a doctorate from a well-respected research institution would naturally make the American dream accessible. Unfortunately, due to visa bureaucracies, I yo-yo between India and the USA, which has hindered my ability to work consistently and access relevant jobs in this country. In addition, my "volunteer" uncompensated research makes me think that I do not belong in academia. Nonetheless, I am a marriage and family therapist (MFT) with a research focus on culturally appropriate MFT practices with the Indian (South Asian) population. I have encountered microaggressions of sexism, racism, and classism and have internalized much of the oppression around me.

Ada: I am an African American female assistant professor in social work at a moderate-sized public, historically White institution. My intersectional identity includes my cis-gender status as a mother of two sons and one daughter. I am also a first-generation doctoral graduate who earned a Ph.D. in 2019 while working full-time in a state university leadership role. In juxtaposition to a university administrator (associate director of Employee Assistance Program) and adjunct professor, I was one of few Black female doctoral graduates of an interdisciplinary program. I experienced microinsults and microinvalidations in both roles while steadily navigating my responsibilities within an institution that reminded me of my social location. Despite the structural inequalities that discouraged or attempted to silence me, I was uniquely aware of my influence, physical presence, and voice in these academic spaces. As a leader, I continue to support black and brown students who engage in activism. I have observed student protests with sit-ins, die-ins, and marches that speak out against bigotry, systemic racism in national alliance with the Black Lives Matter Movement to challenge the institution's cadre of leadership to promote positive change for minoritized students, faculty, and staff. I situate my activism in the form of resistance and advocacy that empowers individuals and groups in boardroom meetings, classrooms, and counseling sessions with clients.

Collectively, we are in an era requiring us to center our diverse voices and take our rightful place unapologetically while also seeking ways to effectively advocate for sustainable systemic, equitable, and inclusive practices. As authors, we write this chapter to bring ourselves to the forefront explore and investigate our relationships to "advanced" institutions from a historical and contemporary viewpoint. We aspire to strengthen our capacity to grow and advance ourselves by embracing transformational leadership principles in solidarity as women of color.

LEADERSHIP AND FEMINIST ACTIVISM

Race operates as a barricade and a syndicate of inequality for both students and faculty wherein the effects of the color of our skin are more than skin-deep. In addition to color-based racial designations, the manifestation of gender goes beyond traditional roles and expectations, further deepening injustices and prejudice. The perpetuation of sexism further exacerbates when systems draw in the intersectionality of race and ethnicity into focus. Higher education institutions often label themselves as color and genderblind, promoting diversity, inclusion, and equal opportunity (Hsieh & Nguyen, 2020). Yet, the threat of racism and sexism within American remains and infiltrates the same institutions that value a patriarchal system (Kelly et al., 2019; Moorosi et al., 2018). These systems of oppression compound the privilege afforded to them by headship, further intersecting with social class, sexuality, culture, and language in the workplace (Moorosi et al., 2018; Sabharwal & Varma, 2017).

The stratification of color in the United States commands that Black and Brown faculty consistently maintain lower positions than their White counterparts, consequently compromising the value of their scholarship and their status as scholars within their departments (Lim, 2006; Rockquemore & Laszloffy, 2008). Social stratification can offer a sense of belonging to White faculty members and, at the same time, make WOC feel as if they are just being tolerated or do not belong.

Monique: As a first-year assistant professor and director of the University Clinic, I was eager to practice and implement teaching and program development cherished in my doctoral and postdoctoral experience. However, it was clear within months that the institutional systems did not welcome strategies that promote equity and techniques to advance and evaluate the program. In entering the academe, I maintained that education was a pathway to liberation (Lim, 2006; Rockquemore & Laszloffy, 2008). This opportunity, I believe, should be afforded to all students, especially first-generation graduate students of color. In accordance, I advocated for access for all admitted students and engaged in innovative student-centered learning, understanding that a solid educational foundation in family therapy could serve students for the remainder of their careers. The system could not tolerate my work and presence, but my inclusive strategies provided a haven for students silenced by the system and my White counterparts. White faculties' opinion is valued, and their effort recognized, and consequently, White faculty may more readily receive acceptance, while women of color experience institutional segregation, isolation, alienation, hostility, devaluation, marginalization of scholarship, and intimidation (Rockquemore & Laszloffy, 2008).

Unfortunately, being Black is stereotypically associated with intellectual mediocrity. The Black professor must prove their authority, integrity, intelligence, and experience to the students in the class where the slightest apparent error reads as incompetence (Rockquemore & Laszloffy, 2008). Foreign Brown faculty face similar challenges about credibility due to their accent and being nonnative English speakers. Women of Color from AAPI are traditionally stereotyped as passive and submissive to authority (Hsieh & Nguyen, 2020), leading to instruction where systems of oppression maintain Brown faculty instructors as nonconfrontational and uncritical of mainstream America (Asher, 2006). Further, sexual objectification can lead to sexual harassment and derogatory behavior towards Asian female faculty rooted in the docile lotus flower or Geisha stereotype (Li & Beckett, 2006, Mukkamala & Suyemoto, 2018). The construction of White institutions not intended for people of color's success maintains uniform standards for "all," wherein Black and Brown women must succeed irrespective of the inequities. To make visible the invisible predicament, faculty of color must choose between professional success and losing personal integrity (Rockquemore & Laszloffy, 2008).

MENTORSHIP AMONG WOMEN OF COLOR

There is a dearth of research on the intersectionality of race, gender, language, culture, and class for Black and Brown women in leadership roles in academia (Hune, 2011; Li. & Beckett, 2006; Moorosi et al., 2018; Sabharwal & Varma, 2017) and, further, the importance of women of color as role models (Hsieh & Nguyen, 2020; Hune, 2011). Despite the variances in identities, positionalities, and challenges, women of color in academia can provide identity-informed mentorship, promoting socialization/ acculturation for other women of color (Hsieh & Nguyen, 2020).

Ada: I have seen the harsh realities of the academy undergirded with racism and sexism that often pushed talented and educated Black women leaders out of the institution due to the devaluation of their skills and contributions to their respective fields. These racialized experiences inflict emotional scars and ultimately compromise both the physical and mental health of Black women. Academia claims to value the concept of "diversity," which often tends to feel equivalent to tokenism, contributing to or worsening colorblind racism. I am a Black female academic faculty seeking tenure through a historical tradition that undervalues service in this era. This service value helps keep underperforming minority students enrolled in university through mentorship and affirming students to remind them that they belong in college, hoping they do not withdraw or transfer due to not having a sense of belonging. My service also includes promoting and researching the significance of Black mental health and mental wellness so that students, faculty, and staff of color can understand the adverse effects of racial microaggressions and the concept of racial battle fatigue to heighten their consciousness and to take radical steps to protect their emotional health. I am proud to be part of a collective movement that aims to rebuild and change systems, educational institutions, and counseling services intended to uplift. Still, I recognize that these systems have historically profited and exploited Black and Brown people's labor in this country, often inflicting more harm than good. As a form of empowering support, mentorship serves as a tool to insulate students and faculty from and navigate the academy's course.

Black and Brown faculty should cultivate at least three support systems to succeed (Rockquemore & Laszloffy, 2008; Rong & Preissle, 2006) to combat the risk of racial insensitivities and prejudices that may result in demotion, isolation, and estrangement.

1. Supportive on and off-campus social relationships where differences among women of color can be engaged productively and promote solidarity will reduce the impact of racial insensitivities and prejudices that may result in demotion, isolation, and estrangement.
2. Professional mentors who identify and nurture relationships (Rong & Preissle, 2006) recognize, validate, and encourage their diverse perspectives and experiences as assets rather than liabilities to their work and offer sponsorship to pursue professional and social development.
3. Accountability partners to supportive relational networks to foster optimal faculty success (Rockquemore & Laszloffy, 2008) is vital for collective success.

According to Hua (2018), women of color faculty meet or exceed teaching, publishing, and service demands, increasing the impact of professional vitality in ways not required of others. Although WOC faculty have the status as professors, which implies social and cultural power, their identity in the classroom leaves them vulnerable to existing cultural biases. Colleagues and students can mar Black and Brown women's successful leadership by internal sabotage. The dynamics of structural intersectionality, historic slavery mentality, internalized racism, sexism, disregard for their position, and undermining their authority can lower self-esteem (Hua, 2018; Lim, 2006; Sabharwal & Varma, 2017). The combination of being in a vulnerable position as both a woman and a racial minority has led many WOC to sacrifice everything: their relationships, voice, and integrity in pursuit of a promotion (Rockquemore & Laszloffy, 2008). Scholars must reinforce transformational leadership (Fluker, 2015) to create righteousness and benevolence in communities.

The Emotional Labor and Identity Taxation of Women of Color in Academia

Black legal scholar Kimberlé Crenshaw (1989) said, "As a Black woman, my labor is always used while my voice and intersectional experience is invisible." Black and Brown women faculty benefit the institution as they contribute to the diversity of the university. However, universities likely view their teaching as service rather than skilled labor due to the inordinate energy invested in supporting URM students. Cottingham and colleagues (2018) found double standards, feelings of heightened scrutiny in White institutions, racial slurs, anger, frustration in having their authority questioned, and self-doubt in legitimizing feelings of rage resulted in an encumbering "double shift" on women nurses of color. Padilla (1994) coined "cultural taxation" to describe the extra burden of service responsibilities placed upon minority faculty. The authors' positions align with Padilla's (1994) point of view, stating: "We frequently find ourselves having to respond to situations imposed on us by the administration, which assumes that we are best suited for specific tasks because of our race/ethnicity or presumed knowledge of cultural differences" (p. 26).

This type of taxation takes on many forms for Black and Brown scholars. Some examples include serving on diversity committees and search committees to provide racial representation and requests to teach multicultural or diversity-focused courses (Perry, Moore, Edwards, et al., 2010. Faculty and student relationships are also a critical necessity that may also exacerbate cultural taxation. Othermothering, a historical concept (Collins, 2000) researched as a pedagogical practice, involves faculty of color, typically women, who offer care to Black students. Although research indicates some benefits to this dynamic, othermothering may also create a strain or become an emotional burden as relationship boundaries may become blurred or complicated (Mawhinney, 2011). Black and Brown female faculty often feel obligated to engage in othermothering with URM students to support and advocate as a parallel form of resistance to the racism and sexism mutually experienced within the academy (Guiffrida, 2005; Mawhinney, 2011).

Ada: I recall a recent experience with a Black male student who transferred to this institution and disclosed a history of trauma and recent episodes with racial microaggressions. I committed to meeting with this student regularly after class to connect him to campus counseling services and a Black male mentor program on campus. The student stated to me, "I don't think I belong here." Convincing the student otherwise was frustrating and incredibly sad. This young man's perseverance included growing up in foster care in NYC, graduating from high school, and earning a seat in a Research I university. My instinct as a mother, social worker, and educator "kicked in" as I eagerly sought to help restore his self-confidence as I also took exception to my own racialized experiences as a Black female professor at this PWI. This form of cultural taxation includes the need to speak up in faculty meetings when Black students report bias and microaggressions. White faculty often react by minimizing and invalidating these experiences instead of practicing empathy or affirming the impact of racialized experiences. In my leadership role, I fervently involved myself in organizing a process to engage professional staff and faculty in having these critical conversations about the intersections of race, gender, racism, and other systems of oppression to provoke change in the academy to support URM students while becoming better human beings.

Hirshield and Joseph (2012) expanded upon the concept of cultural taxation by introducing "identity taxation" to further emphasize the unique challenges faced by women of color. WOC should respond to this need with a deep sense of "cultural obligation" (Padilla, 1994). This sense of obligation is often rooted in our intersectional identities as mothers, with unique cultural backgrounds valuing collectivism and mutual support. As scholars, we understand these values as antithetical to the outdated tenure and promotion practice that anchors values in individualism linked to the self-aggrandizing nature of research while dismissing the importance of service that often influences the retention of URM students.

Although colleges and universities in the United States have slowly become more diverse, the number of underrepresented faculty in higher education has not kept up with the increased enrollment of underrepresented minority students (Kyaw, 2021; Southern Regional Education Board (SREB), 2021). In addition to underrepresentation, female academic leadership and salary equity deficiencies persist (Johnson, 2017). In addition, work-life balance seems to be an implausible concept and a figment of the imagination for many female academics with families. The American Council on Education Center for Policy Research and Strategy (2020) published an update on the status of women in higher education. It is not a coincidence that the rate of ascension to leadership occurs more frequently for men than for women. In contrast, women disproportionately carry entry-level service and teaching-only positions (Johnson, 2017). Furthermore, the data indicate that women who have ascended into leadership roles (e.g., presidents) compared to men were less likely to be married (90% male vs. 71% female), have children (90% male vs. 72% female), and more likely to have altered their careers to care for a dependent spouse/partner parent (19% male vs. 27% female) (Johnson, 2017).

These factors are even more disparate for women of color in faculty positions. Since 2006, women have earned half of all doctoral degrees compared to men (U.S. Department of Education, National Center for Education Statistics, 2014). However, the rate of promotion and salary equity continues to lag. Male faculty salaries are $13,616 higher than female faculty in public institutions and $17,843 higher in private institutions (U.S. Department of Education, National Center for Education Statistics, 2014). Intragroup numbers of rank among Black, Indigenous, People of Color (BIPOC) are also disparate by gender. For example, the tenured professor status for men of color outranked women significantly across different races *except* in the levels of associate professor, assistant professor, and instructor positions, which generally have lower salaries. Ranks are represented in Table 1.

Table 1. Number of Full-time faculty in degree-granting postsecondary institutions, by race/ethnicity, sex, and academic rank: fall 2018

Rank	Black Male	Black Female	Hispanic Male	Hispanic Female	Asian/ Pacific Islander Male	Asian/ Pacific Islander Female	Native American Male	Native American Female	Total of All Races
Professors	4,091	2,914	4,222	2,604	14,401	5,328	351	255	185,758
Associate Professor	4,282	4,914	4,117	3,567	10,963	7,733	279	299	159,135
Assistant Professor	4,334	7,294	4,227	4,686	10,987	10,421	295	368	181,239
Instructors	2,616	4,609	3,497	4,388	2,624	3,541	384	402	98,798

Note: This table was prepared June 2021from Digest of Educational Statistics by the U.S. Department of Education, National Center for Education Statistics, Integrated Postsecondary Education Data System (IPEDS), Fall 2015, fall 2017, and fall 2018. In the public domain.

Without adequate support and attention to cultural taxation and systemic inequities, retaining and achieving tenure and promotion is less likely for female faculty of color. In a study on African American female social work educators in predominantly White institutions (PWI), Edwards and colleagues (2008) cite studies in the literature review dating back to 1974 to substantiate systemic concerns of bias and discrimination in higher education. Research shows that African American faculty were likely to leave their positions because of perceptions of racial discrimination and the constant challenge of barriers to mobility (Durr & Harvey Wingfield, 2011). In addition, Black women experience exclusion from collaborative research projects with their peers, a lack of sponsorship, and a lack of access to research funding (Edwards et al., 2008; Higginbotham, 1981; Moore, 1981; Moore & Wagstaff, 1974). Black and Brown women face frustrations with discrimination and the pressure to advocate for themselves and URM students. They often experience the weight of being "present" to be heard and to represent diverse voices so that institutions meet their interests and needs. This emotional labor in the academy is an exhaustive sacrifice that many women of color persist through as an act of resistance to racism and sexism deemed necessary for community advancement.

Although Black and Brown women faculty overwork without compensation and contribute to university operations at the expense of their emotional labor, Black and Brown women also rely on this emotional labor to survive or to create opportunities, even though universities exploit this work (Evans & Moore, 2015; Kelly et al., 2019). As a result of systems of oppression, WOC has a sense of increased responsibility and expectation of perfection in their career, homelife, and familial relationships. The system expects Brown women from collectivist cultures and traditions to assimilate into an individualistic value system in the United States to fulfill numerous multifaceted roles of a minority faculty, researcher, teacher, wife, daughter, and mother (Asher, 2006; Li & Beckett, 2006). Maintaining this perfection is exhausting and leads to burnout (Crenshaw, 1989; Evans & Moore, 2015). Women of color carry the "Sacrificial Lamb Syndrome" and feel the need to suppress the desire to succeed. The outcome of the endless demands on their time, tolerance, and competence without regard to their welfare can lead to poor health outcomes and impede academic success (Rockquemore & Laszloffy, 2008).

Black and Brown women must employ more emotional labor and hyper-surveillance in the workplace to survive historically White spaces (Durr & Harvey Wingfield, 2011; Kadowaki & Subramaniam, 2014). Black women are seen by institutions as "space invaders" while experiencing overt forms of sexism, racism, and microaggressions (Kelly et al., 2019) that force them to manage feelings and hostile environments. Many professional Black women must simulate the White penchant to be welcomed, accepted, and advance in their workplaces (Durr & Harvey Wingfield, 2011), thus facing the double disadvantage of gendered racism.

Furthermore, sexuality and class also serve as pointers of privilege for heterosexual and middle-class women of color and creates a divide for those with economic and sexual freedoms from working-class and gay women of color (Hua, 2018). The tax of embodied racialized and gendered history and the accompanying unrecognized emotional labor it exacts on Black women's psychology in leadership is of utmost importance. Scholars, practitioners, trailblazers, and activists should institute transformative leadership to impact today and future generations significantly.

THE MENTAL HEALTH IMPACT ON BLACK WOMEN WEATHERING COLORBLIND RACISM IN THE IVORY TOWER

In an era when affirmative action policies are under threat, the notion of colorblind racism, a contemporary concept, continues to reinforce and complexify the social construction of race and gender (Collins, 2000; Nayak, 2015) that maintains power structure and preserves White elitism in the ivory tower (Campbell, 2014; Wilder, 2013). The academy, a defender and beneficiary of the enslavement of African and genocide of Native Americans, destructive tyranny in America, is a space that was certainly never designed for or intended to support women in leadership, especially Black women. Academe has been a persistent purveyor of implicit and explicit discrimination towards students, faculty, and staff of color throughout history. Such bias is evident in the racial and ethnic diversity of college and university administrators, faculty, and staff that has not kept pace comparable to the student body's growth.

According to the U.S. Department of Education Postsecondary Education System, in 2015-2016, approximately 45% of all undergraduate and 32% of all graduate students were people of color. However, in 2017, 72.6% of all faculty were White while 21.5% were faculty of color, 9.5% Asian, 5.7% African American/Black, and 4.8% Hispanic/Latino (American Council on Education, 2020, p. xviii). The data from 2018 to 2019 shows, White faculty represented nearly all academic heads. Women of color department heads were prominent in ethnic, cultural, gender, and group studies. Furthermore, the most significant gender gap among Black and African American full-time faculty occurred in family and consumer science and human services. Women represented 6.7% compared to men at only 1.1%. (American Council on Education, 2020). As scholars, practitioners, and transformative leaders, we center our voices in this paper to examine the insidiousness of racism and its covert effects on Black women's mental health while reinforcing the need to execute the changes we want to see in tandem. Kessler et al. (1999) found that racial discrimination is significantly related to adverse mental health consequences (Constantine & Sue, 2007; Williams & Mohammed, 2013).

Pertinent to this chapter, the authors use critical race theory to emphasize the association between psychological distress and systemic racism by examining wellness by applying the Sojourner Syndrome and Strong Black Woman Schema. Critical race theory also underpins the conceptual framework of strategic mothering and validates the significance of intersectionality and the need to uplift voices of color as emerging transformational leaders.

Critical Race Theory in Higher Education

In vocalizing our concerns about leadership struggles in the academy, the authors employ Critical Race Theory (CRT) tenets as a tool for inquiry and praxis. Although CRT in educational leadership is not primarily studied, few studies examine how racism and White privilege operate together to dominate institutions, manifesting its educational policy elements through colorblind language (Crenshaw et al., 1995; Davis et al., 2015). CRT developed in the 1970s from critical legal studies during the post-civil rights era asserts that racism is endemic and ingrained in the American systems interwoven into the existing power structures (Delgado & Stefancic, 2001) as seen in higher education. Researchers have applied this theoretical framework to multidisciplinary fields, such as education, healthcare, and counseling professions (Abrams & Moio, 2009; Acheampong et al., 2018; Solórzano & Yosso, 2001). Namely, CRT has been used to examine the manifestation of racism throughout various care systems that have historically marginalized and oppressed Black and Brown people in this country. It has also provided a framework to think about and challenge the contemporary politics of racial domination (Crenshaw et al., 1995). This critical discourse engages our understanding of and affirms ourselves as transformational leaders, female educators of color within the counseling fields, scholars, mothers, wives, and community leaders with an intentional effort to protect and preserve our mental health.

Jotika: My story is of resistance and unsettling ambiguity, where I do not feel like I belong entirely to Indian or American culture. I straddle these two worlds. As a student, researcher, and therapist, I realized early in my journey that although we regard academia as institutions that condemn cultural and racial injustices, they reinforce internalized oppression by not recognizing the interracial, intercultural, and gender bias from a global context. I maintain a stance of being ethically oriented towards a world that may not be ethical because it seeks to silence my experience as an Indian woman in America. Although being quiet is comfortable, it merely maintains the status quo. I am beginning to sort out my various selves, embracing my experience's intersectional nature. It is time for a transformation, and my fight is for ending racial apartheid and for respect and acceptance that, as a deserved woman of color, I strive for greater freedom and rights for WOC. I am here to "thrive," not merely "survive" in a country filled with abundance and opportunity. As a woman of color, I never want to forget the sacrifices that paved the way for my advancement and the corresponding responsibility I bear to do my part to make choices that will extend these opportunities to those who follow me.

Preservation is essential to function in more influential positions to support students of color whose experiences may also be marginalized, dismissed, or rejected. The underpinnings of CRT provide the authors with a foundation in this endeavor. The authors following CRT tenets to this work: racism as ordinary, differentiation of racism, intersectionality, and uplifting voices of color through counter-stories. Delgado and Stefancic (2001) and other leading CRT scholars update these tenets in seminal writings in their respective disciplines. CRT is the framework applied to address resilience fatigue and increase racial battle fatigue that leads to exhaustion (Smith, 2004) and sojourner syndrome (Mullings, 2002), all of which may lead to poor mental health outcomes.

Racism as Ordinary

Racism is ordinary, is not an aberration but is a pervasive condition in this nation that is difficult to address and cure (Delgado & Stefancic, 2001). Racism has played a central role in the structuring of schools and schooling practices. In higher education, colorblind racism is often cloaked in the myth of meritocracy within the tenet of liberalism with a message that implies, "if you work hard enough, you will earn recognition, prestige, and the honor that is due" (Alexander, 2010; Bonilla-Silva, 2006). Due to racism's insidiousness, it is also challenging to address because it evolves (Delgado & Stefancic, 2001). Colorblind racism emerged due to the progress made in law reform from the Civil Rights movement, restored, and maintained a hierarchical power. As Black and Brown women refuting subjugation to the oppressive forces of colorblind racism, we name our reality by acknowledging that this form of patriarchal control has inflicted racial pain requiring acknowledgment and healing (Williams & Mohammed, 2013). By identifying the requisite changes in higher education, the authors propose a leadership model that, through our collective strength, will make meaningful changes within the spheres of influence occupied both in the classroom and in our communities.

Differential Racialization

Differential racialization is common in higher education, where institutions racialized minority groups differently and at varying times in response to the everchanging needs for the benefit of Whiteness (Delgado & Stefancic, 2001). Therefore, stereotypes of minority groups shift over time. Women of color must often push against both gendered and racial stereotypes. This pressure creates tension and division among Black and Brown women in leadership. For example, within the labor market, the "model minority" stereotype, as a concept, usually refers to people of Asian descent. It implies this group has a disciplined "work ethic," submissive to authority, and naturally more intelligent (Cho, 2003). Blacks, specifically African American women, have endured negative images that have stereotyped them throughout time; specific periods often mark these historical stereotypes. For instance, during the slavery period, White America perceived Black women as unintelligent, shiftless (Constantine & Sue, 2007), and a motherly slave or "mammy" (Abdullah, 2012; Johnson, 2003).

Black women were hypersexualized and dehumanized for capitalistic gains and White dominance that began with the history of chattel slavery (Bailey, 2017). Black women have also faced the stereotypes of being perceived as angry, domineering, impenetrable, and unable to feel pain (Overstreet, 2019; Smith, 2004). Black women specifically face occupational stereotypes representing subservient and subordinate roles such as caregivers, cleaners, or cooks, serving those in power. These perceptions negatively impact the way colleagues and students treat Black women and may affect advancement opportunities. African American women professors are more likely to be evaluated more harshly by students than their White counterparts due to perceptions of lower competency, legitimacy, and interpersonal skills (Bavishi et al., 2010). Higher education perpetuates differential racialization based on the devaluation of women of color. As Black and Brown women, we remain committed to redefining our narratives that embrace our cultural roots and traditions that help shape our scholarship, pedagogy, leadership style, and approaches to counseling.

Intersectionality

Intersectionality recognizes that no person has a single identity. The significance of multiple identities underpins the roles of mothers, wives, women of color, and scholars from various class, cultural, ideological, and linguistic backgrounds. This position acknowledges that race and gender have historically served as axes of oppression. Black and Brown women are not a monolithic group but have thrived despite varying degrees of discrimination in the United States and globally. Collins and Bilge (2016) apply intersectionality as an analytical tool to grapple with the complexities of racism hinged on race, class, and gender. Crenshaw et al. (1995) state that "identity can be a site of resistance for members of marginalized groups and at this point in history the most critical resistance strategy for disempowered groups is to occupy and defend a politics of social location" (p. 375). As women of color in the academy and emerging transformative leaders, precisely due to the offenses in 2020, we unite our diverse voices to address and promote antiracist and antisexist ideologies. We honor our intersectional identities in the spaces that we move, teach, counsel, and lead.

Uplifting Our Voice Through Counter-Stories

Counter-stories shared through a CRT lens recognize that the dominant group's power has silenced oppressed groups' voices and distorted historical truth. CRT advocates for retelling or rewriting history by allowing those oppressed to share the reality of their lived experiences from their lens. (Abrams & Moio, 2009). A plethora of studies (Constantine & Sue 2007; Hunn et al., 2015; McGee & Stovall, 2015; Nadal et al., 2014) considers the impact of racial microaggressions on mental health. Counter-narratives, a liberatory methodology, can help faculty, students, and clients of color share their experiences about racial microaggressions by unsilencing their voices and creating a space to unpack racialized experiences that imposed psychological and emotional harm. Counter-storytelling is also an analytical tool and argues that people of color's experiential knowledge must be recognized (Hubain et al., 2016; Solórzano & Yosso, 2002). Black and Brown women possess different histories and experiences with the oppression that only we understand and can communicate to Whites (Delgado & Stefancic, 2001). As the second author, I name incidents of microaggression as a valid counter-story:

Jotika: When I taught undergraduates as a teaching assistant during my doctoral program, I experienced multiple microaggressions inflicted by my White students, such as mispronouncing my name repeatedly even after calling out these errors and writing my name down. As a result, they renamed me (replacing) my name with Jo (White name). Correcting them meant having to challenge structures of oppression personally, getting low scores on end-of-year student reviews, which could mean the program did not renew my scholarship/assistantship for the following year. The assistantship was my only way to support myself in the USA. In other instances, people spoke very slowly to me based on the racialized assumption that I had poor English skills as a South Asian. With their incorrect grammar, students have asked me, "How did you grow up in India when you speak good English?" After living in the United States, I am a perpetual foreigner (U.S. citizenship and immigration services provide most immigrants an Alien Number). Giving me a mark as an alien serves to delegitimize my humanity.

Notions of power, leadership, and intelligence have been defined and shaped by colonialism, White supremacy, globalization, patriarchy, and sexism (as well as ableism, ageism, cis-centrism, and heteronormativity). Historically, White America overlooked and ignored women of color from mainstream leadership conceptualizations. In some respects, the authors believe our absence from mainstream leadership is advantageous because what a person idealizes as "truth," they eventually become. History has shown that Eurocentric leadership cloaked in patriarchy, colonialism, and imperialism serves to oppress, possess, and control resulting in dismantled families and communities worldwide. Black and brown women have been anchors to their families throughout history in response to and resisting oppressive systems to preserve their family and dignity. Doing otherwise would lead to an early demise, physically, emotionally, psychologically, and spiritually. Strength and fortitude are necessary for preserving current and future generations, as it was for their foremothers. The activism of women of color not only serves as a racial uplift for communities but can also serve to change Whites' perspectives (Barnes, 2016). Black women have always had to operate and lead with an Ethic of Care, a practice handed down since slavery. That is how systemic changes move forward with progress. However, as authors, we would be remiss if we did not explicitly speak to the cost of this resistance to power.

Resilience Fatigue and Racial Battle Fatigue

Resilient strength is considered an attribute among women; however, the need to keep up this relentless comes at the expense of emotional and physical fatigue that permeates their entire being (Abrams et al., 2014). Black and brown women "weather" and withstand constant scrutiny with impossible demands that force them to endure pseudo-Superwoman capes and for Black women adhere to the image of the "Strong Black Woman" schema with mental toughness (Abrams et al., 2014; McGee & Stovall, 2015; Overstreet, 2019). Although the Black woman's body bears a close resemblance to the (White) female, the Black woman epitome is masculine with an aggressive and overly assertive temperament; therefore, not wholly female (Corbin et al., 2018). In a study conducted to examine the "Strong Black Woman" schema, scholars explain that when faced with extreme pain and fear, Black women seldom, if at all, have the luxury to express their emotions. They understand that displaying any emotion could indicate weakness and inadequacy (Abrams et al., 2014; Beauboeuf-Lafontant, 2007). These impressions lead to the stereotype of a "Do-it-all" Strong Black woman who can bear all the pain without complaints. The

"Strong Black Woman" trope creates a double-edged sword, leading to double-binds for Black women in higher education (Corbin et al., 2018). Among brown women, the exotic "Geisha" and "worker bee" stereotype for Asians leads to the belief that they are submissive and can work quietly as part of the team but are incapable of leading (Mukkamala & Suyemoto, 2018). The authors recognize that the need to exercise resistance to vulnerability can result in difficulty asking for assistance when we are overwhelmed or handling demanding tasks. Possessing this mental psyche over time causes and exacerbates the psychological strain and distress often.

Working with dignity and strength means running the risk of being labeled a troublemaker, someone difficult, or even angry. Black women frequently face the media-perpetuated misogynoir scripts of "Angry Black Woman" prevalent in popular USA culture (Corbin et al., 2018). Asian women who speak up about injustices they face are stereotyped as manipulative and untrustworthy "Dragon Ladies" (Mukkamala & Suyemoto, 2018). Women of color face these stereotypical representations and must endure racial prejudice and microaggressions. Black and Brown women cope with gendered racial microaggressions, which are emotionally draining, leads to racial battle fatigue, affect their life quality, and ultimately impact their success. Microaggressions are committed based on perceptions of race intersected with gender, class, sexuality, immigration status, which physiologically and psychologically tolls people of color (Cottingham et al., 2018, Evans & Moore, 2015). Offenders often carry out gender microaggressions through verbal and nonverbal onslaughts in elusive, impulsive, or oblivious forms. A woman of color must consistently defend, validate, and explain her position while making herself vulnerable to the risk of abandonment and isolation. This sense of everlasting injustice leads to hypervigilance, self-policing, exhaustion, and increased racial battle fatigue even within the academy (Smith, 2015). Despite these challenges, women of color (WOC) also engage in everyday micro-endurances that empower them to succeed in racially oppressive institutions without compromising their dignity. In addition, women from marginalized groups in White spaces need access to mentors, sponsors, and advocates who can defend, protect, and empathize with them against misogynoir. We believe that mentors support acculturation in the academy, necessary for women of color (Hsieh & Nguyen, 2020).

Sojourner Syndrome: Assuming the Roles of Service

To analytically interpret our lived experiences' meaning, the authors examine our individual and collective identities also through Strategic Mothering and Sojourner Syndrome frameworks. Black feminist scholars before us have analyzed the social constructs of interlocking identities and relational categories as a tool to interpret the ways that Black women have survived and thrived in society for the betterment of ourselves and community (Abrams et al., 2014; Collins & Bilge, 2016; Mullings, 2002). Sojourner Syndrome, developed by Leith Mullings (2002), connotes a survival strategy symbolic of both constraint and activism through her analysis of disparate rates of health problems among Black women. The syndrome describes Isabella Van Wagenen, a slave born in Ulster County, New York. During her enslavement, she endured physical and sexual violence, having her children stripped from her and sold into slavery. After being released from bondage, she ultimately named herself Sojourner Truth and received her spiritual calling to advocate for racial and gender reform (Washington, 2013). Sojourner traveled around the country to promote Black liberation following the passing of the New York State Emancipation Act of 1827. The Sojourner syndrome, seeded in the understanding that Black women could not rely on the patriarchal protection from the government, the women's suffrage movement, or the institution of marriage, forced Black women to rely on their strength and propensity to care for themselves and their families' communities (Barnes, 2016; Painter, 1996).

Barnes (2016) applies Sojourner syndrome as a parallel to her strategic mothering framework, which she developed and employed in her ethnography, "Raising the Race." This study examines Black professional women navigating marriage, motherhood, and community from a cultural model. Barnes (2016) analyzes how Black women employ specific strategic mothering practices to ensure familial and communal survival (Barnes, 2016, p. 6). The authors identify with the strategic mothering framework as we examine our transformational leadership roles in higher education. Simultaneously, we adhere to a womanist tradition of caring rooted in our cultural histories, family therapy, and social work (Beauboeuf-Lafontant, 2007).

Monique: Caring for those who can't and those who are able is a part of my existence and how future generations can strive. Through strategic mothering, I sow seeds within students in the academy as future clinicians and individuals who will ease the traumas in our local community. The pandemic quickly made clear the impacts of many disparities for not only our students and the local community. One experience stands out as I engaged in research with a Black female student. We addressed our research aims in communing while simultaneously transforming our talk space to process and support her during difficult times. Through strategic mothering, I tapped into her "Strong Black Woman" and her struggles to keep it all together, which she did in the past. In these small moments, she allowed me to care, be vulnerable, and show her asking for help is acceptable when we simply cannot do more. She, in my eyes, is an emerging authentic transformative leader that requires profound support and mothering to manage academia and sustain herself.

There is a necessity to invest deeply in our families while also constructively extending ourselves with caring through our pedagogy, recognizing that strategic mothering practices will evolve based on various social structures as done throughout history (Barnes, 2016). For example, as discussed previously, the perpetuated myth of the "Strong Black Woman" conveys that she can overcome hardships, move through obstacles, become a matriarchal leader in her family and the community while managing racism and sexism, all without complaint (Overstreet, 2019). "Being strong" is an essential and effective coping strategy that enables Black and Brown women to deal successfully with life's adversities. Unfortunately, most Black and Brown women internalize stereotypical myths, believing that they possess greater emotional strength than other women. As a result, they are more likely to set high expectations of their abilities to manage life's problems.

Although there is great benefit in "pressing" through complex challenges, research indicates that African Americans who experienced gendered racism were likely to have psychological distress (Tomas et al., 2008). In addition, due to coping styles that prevent women from seeking help related to their psychological pain, they often present depressive or anxiety symptoms and neglect their need for mental health counseling (Tomas et al., 2008).

Maintaining the "strong woman" role can lead to poor mental health outcomes, a recognized byproduct of Sojourner syndrome. The only way to protect Black and Brown women and subsequent generations is to abandon the Strong Black women's facade. Research is needed to determine how principles of racism as ordinary, differentiation of racism, intersectionality, counter-stories, racial battle fatigue, and sojourning impact Black women's willingness to seek professional mental health. As women of color who lead, teach, and conduct research in counseling, we maintain and understand the importance of combating racial injustice and the responsibility to engage our past and present to reverse the damage of racism and discrimination.

FUTURE DIRECTIONS: "UNDOING" INJUSTICE

Black women in the academe benefit greatly from relational connections centered on mutual empathy and mutual empowerment (Edwards et al., 2008). The importance of relationships is firmly rooted in the value Black women place in the community. Through our sisterly relationships and our communities, the authors seek and work to bring about change. In the following sections, we expound on strategies to resist and dismantle the discriminatory practices in higher education. In addition, we stress the importance of caring for our mental health to foster environments that harness equity and respect. Amidst COVID-19, following George Floyd and Breonna Taylor's deaths, White America may be at a reckoning point with their morality. Given the agitation, transformational leadership in higher education is needed more than ever.

For some institutions and organizations, efforts to improve their position and stance on diversity initiatives are likely performative, resulting from #Black Lives Matter's social and economic pressure. Still, our fight to center our voices is the same yet different, notwithstanding the enlightened gaze that emerged in the summer of 2020. Research indicates that vigorous systemic changes effectively dismantle racism (Griffith et al., 2007). We implore college administrators to engage in bold initiatives such as expanded diversity recruitment and retention strategies (Edwards et al., 2008) and implicit bias training. Such programs are essential for Black and Brown faculty to navigate the tenure process, adjust to the campus culture, and address sociopolitics in the campus's climates. Undoing injustices include accessing diversity grants and fellowships to help with research funding and protect time to engage in research and writing throughout the publication process (Young & Anderson, 2019). Above and beyond, higher education institutions must designate importance to service. Women of color engage in extensive service experiences in addition to formal academic responsibilities; institutions do not value service, as they value research and associated publications. Beyond efforts to recruit and appropriately weigh women of color's work, institutions must create spaces that fortify them.

As women of color, we have assumed our seats at the table in the ivory tower. This seat creates space for our presence but can yield discomfort and burnout, such as when colleagues overlook our ideas or occurrences of microaggression. In exploring options for substantive change, we must attend to the Black and Brown faculty holistically. We recommend options for counter-spaces/affinity groups for Black faculty and staff to affirm our Blackness and validate our worth (Jones & Rolón-Dow, 2019). Faculty/Staff of Color affinity groups can help provide mutual support and help recruit and retain underrepresented groups to build morale. Our final recommendations emphasize the importance of emotional and psychological health. For example, the COVID-19 restrictions require that women work from home or give up their careers due to the necessity to care for their children. Instead, as women, we need efforts that prioritize work-life-family balance, refocus, and prioritize the family that may require a flexible work schedule.

Faculty and Staff/Employee Assistance Programs are at increased risk of being outsourced to managed care companies, providing less individualized care for faculty coping with racialized experiences. Principally, we recognize deficiencies in ethnically diverse clinicians' availability to match Black and Brown female's requests. Internal, external, and affiliate Employee Assistance Programs must have culturally responsive clinicians who can recognize and respond to traumatic racism by applying a trauma-informed approach in practice (Bryant-Davis & Ocampo, 2005; Jacobson Frey, 2020). There is a need for effective counseling, and we seek to increase clinicians' proficiencies to work with Black and Brown faculty. We suggest that mental health training must include the unique needs of People of Color. Curriculum and clinical practice need to ensure that counseling students graduate with specific expertise in understanding Black and Brown communities without increased burdens on faculty of color. We suggest that counseling programs require coursework and practicum specialties to support students of all backgrounds and identities and develop the skill to address racial and social justice.

Black and Brown female faculty require supportive social relationships on and off-campus. Namely, these relationships must focus on mentors that identify and nurture relationships with sponsorship and accountability vital to foster optimal faculty success. For example, even though our affiliations with different academic institutions across the USA, a Black female mentor who valued sponsorship and understood the importance of supportive relationships brought the authors together. What grew out of this small group moved beyond the academic and professional collaboration and became an encouragement space. Engaging in what began as bi-weekly writing meetings quickly became a space to process the world's ills and injustices, share strategies to address systems of oppression embedded in the academy, and develop forthcoming generation practitioners and academics.

To connect the past and present to build a future, we believe that mentoring future clinicians and academics is critical for community building, advancing counseling and human services, and academic success. Faculty and student relationships can affect student satisfaction (Guiffrida, 2005) and retention rates. Our collective work as transformational leaders involves employing strategic mothering practices in our roles with students, specifically students of color underrepresented at the institutions we serve. Minority mentoring helps validate and address challenges specific to identity, invisibility, and exclusion (Hughes et al., 2012). There is often an absence in senior minority faculty at PWIs for mentorship with junior faculty resulting in a domino effect for limited mentors to help guide URM students through their academy experience. Although mentoring is vital, there is a tension between service and the formal work standards required for tenure. This disproportionate service labor common for minority faculty can result in burnout and lower attentiveness to research and grant writing demands. Academic institutions must provide training opportunities for nonminority senior faculty in cultural sensitivity to understand the issues related to minority scholars and to participate in culturally responsive mentoring with minority faculty and students (Hughes et al., 2012).

Opportunities to mentor and engage in intergenerational dialogue with students of color are prized experiences where leaders can engage in transformative and authentic practices. In their respective academic institutions, both Monique and Ada engage in mentoring Black women students.

Monique: I identified a skillset and aptitude in a first-year MFT student during a foundational summer course. I explicitly connected with the student to discuss her interests and identify opportunities for mentorship and sponsorship. We worked together to determine her interests, needs, and goals and invited her to research women of color in leadership. Throughout our exchanges, I relayed scholarship and grant opportunities that aligned with her interests. However, most importantly, the mentor relationship revealed a critical component of her need as a Black woman moving beyond academe to address her overall well-being. COVID-19 wreaked havoc on many, and students, particularly students of color, experience additional stresses. Attempts to connect were mindful of these possibilities and explored how the pandemic had shaped her daily life and ability to manage and engage in school.

CONCLUSION

During 2020, we partook in historical endeavors to change the higher education landscape in response to COVID-19 and the national outcry for racial and social justice. The impacts were evident as both faculty, staff, and students endured the emotional stressors related to COVID-19. With heightened concerns for Black and Brown students, programs still needed to ensure that students remained engaged while pursuing matriculation through their college courses. Students were forced or opted to take their college courses online due to safety concerns for themselves and their family members; they faced several challenges and obstacles to success. Many underrepresented minority students chose to remain in their hometown, often in urban centers where the COVID-19 rates were higher instead of their college campus. This decision to stay in their homes was sometimes met out of obligation to care for family members who had experienced illness or were susceptible to the disease due to health risks or occupational risks. We became aware of intimate and personal details of students' lives, such as contending with limited space in small living quarters with large family households and limited access to technology. We observed these experiences to be mentally exhausting for students already overwhelmed with college life's daily stressors while also contending with everyday forms of racism. Students also encountered the pressure of working more hours to contribute to their households due to parental loss of employment. As a result, we worked more intensely with students to ensure their success through mentoring to offer support and guidance. We remain committed to our multiplicity of roles from a strategic mothering framework during these challenging times.

As scholars in marital and family therapy and social work, the authors recognize the profession's commitment to children, families, and the global community. We seek to honor these characteristics in our leadership and pedagogy. We invest deeply in our family network and our community of students, the next generation of family therapists, social workers, and academicians who will emerge as transformational leaders. We believe that an explicit and authentic commitment to equity and inclusion and a family-friendly institutional climate will ensure faculty success. We recognize that while our efforts are valid and our approach to leadership has the power to facilitate change, continued work is needed. Future research requires efforts to understand the pandemic and unrest implications better to support change and give voice to marginalized voices. These studies need to explore Black and Brown faculty and students' mental health needs to refine clinical support.

REFERENCES

Abdullah, M. (2012). Womanist mothering: Loving and raising the revolution. *The Western Journal of Black Studies, 36*(1), 1–21.

Abrams, J. A., Maxwell, M., Pope, M., & Belgrave, F. Z. (2014). Carrying the world with the grace of a lady and the grit of a warrior: Deepening our understanding of the "Strong Black Woman" schema. *Psychology of Women Quarterly, 38*(4), 503–518. doi:10.1177/0361684314541418

Abrams, L. S., & Moio, J. A. (2009). Critical race theory and the cultural competence dilemma in social work education. *Journal of Social Work Education, 45*(2), 245–261. doi:10.5175/JSWE.2009.200700109

Acheampong, C., Davis, C., Holder, D., Averette, P., Savitt, T., & Campbell, K. (2019). An Exploratory Study of Stress Coping and Resiliency of Black Men at One Medical School: A Critical Race Theory Perspective. *Journal of Racial and Ethnic Health Disparities, 6*(1), 214–219. doi:10.100740615-018-0516-8 PMID:30039499

Alexander, M. (2010). *New Jim Crow, the mass incarceration in the age of colorblindness.* Perseus Books LLC.

American Council on Education. (2020). *Race and Ethnicity in Higher Education 2020 Supplement.* https://www.equityinhighered.org/

Asher, N. (2006). Brown in black and white: On being a South Asian woman academic. In G. Li & G. H. Beckett (Eds.), *Strangers" of the academy: Asian women scholars in higher education* (pp. 163–177). Stylus Publishing.

Bailey, A. (2017). *The weeping time: Memory and the largest slave auction in American history.* Cambridge University Press. doi:10.1017/9781108140393

Barnes, R. J. (2016). *Raising the race: Black career women redefine marriage, motherhood, and community*. Rutgers University Press.

Bavishi, A., Madera, J. M., & Hebl, M. R. (2010). The effect of professor ethnicity and gender on student evaluations: Judged before met. *Journal of Diversity in Higher Education, 1*(12), 245–256. Advance online publication. doi:10.1037/a0020763

Beauboeuf-Lafantant, T. (2007). You have to show strength: An exploration of gender, race, and depression. *Gender & Society, 21*(1), 28–51. doi:10.1177/0891243206294108

Bonilla-Silva, E. (2006). *Racism without racists: Colorblind racism and persistence of racial inequality in the United States*. Rowman & Littlefield.

Bryant-Davis, T., & Ocampo, C. (2005). The trauma of racism. *The Counseling Psychologist, 33*(4), 574–578. doi:10.1177/0011000005276581

Burrell, X. (2020, September 30). Two officers shot in Louisville protests over Breonna Taylor charging decision. *New York Times*. https://www.nytimes.com/2020/09/23/us/breonna-taylor-decision-verdict.html

Campbell, E. (2014). Using critical race theory to measure "racial competency" among social workers. *Journal of Sociology and Social Work, 2*(2), 74-86. doi:. v2n2a5 doi:10.15640/jssw

Centers for Disease Control. (2020a). *Health equity considerations and racial and ethnic minority groups*. https://www.cdc.gov/coronavirus/2019-ncov/community/health-equity/race-ethnicity.html

Centers for Disease Control. (2020b). *Non-Hispanic Black people disproportionately by COVID-19 hospitalization in CDC Data*. Author.

Chetty, N., & Alathur, S. (2018). Hate speech review in the context of online social networks. *Aggression and Violent Behavior, 40*, 108–118. doi:10.1016/j.avb.2018.05.003

Cho, S. K. (2003). Converging stereotypes in racialized sexual harassment: Where the model minority meets Suzie Wong. In A. K. Wing (Ed.), *Critical Race Feminism* (2nd ed., pp. 349–366). NYU Press.

Coates, T. (2020, September). A beautiful life. *Vanity Fair*, 72-81.

Collins, P. H. (2000). Black feminist thought: Knowledge, consciousness, and the politics of empowerment (2nd ed.). Routledge.

Collins, P. H., & Bilge, S. (2016). *Intersectionality*. Polity Press.

Constantine, M. G., & Sue, D. W. (2007). Perceptions of racial microaggressions among Black supervisees in cross racial dyads. *Journal of Counseling Psychology, 34*(2), 142–153. doi:10.1037/0022-0167.54.2.142

Corbin, N. A., Smith, W. A., & Garcia, J. R. (2018). Trapped between justified anger and being the strong Black woman: Black college women coping with racial battle fatigue at historically and predominantly White institutions. *International Journal of Qualitative Studies in Education: QSE, 31*(7), 626–643. doi:10.1080/0 9518398.2018.1468045

Cottingham, M. D., Johnson, A. H., & Erickson, R. J. (2018). I can never be too comfortable": Race, gender, and emotion at the hospital bedside. *Qualitative Health Research, 28*(1), 145–158. doi:10.1177/1049732317737980 PMID:29094641

Crenshaw, K. (1989). Demarginalizing the intersection of race and sex: A Black feminist critique of antidiscrimination doctrine, feminist theory and antiracist politics. *University of Chicago Legal Forum, 140*, 139–167.

Crenshaw, K., Gotanda, N., Peller, G., & Thomas, K. (Eds.). (1995). *Critical race theory: The key writings that formed the movement*. The New Press.

Davies, C. B. (1994). *Black women, writing and identity: Migrations of the subject*. Routledge.

Davis, B. W., Gooden, M. A., & Micheaux, D. J. (2015). Colorblind leadership: A critical race theory analysis of the ISLLC and ELCC Standards. *Educational Administration Quarterly, 51*(3), 335–371. doi:10.1177/0013161X15587092

Delgado, R., & Stefancic, J. (2001). *Critical race theory: An introduction* (2nd ed.). New York Univ. Press.

Dennis, A. (2020, June). Anguish in America: A nation torn apart. *People*, 35–45.

Durr, M., & Harvey Wingfield, A. M. (2011). Keep your 'N' in check: African American women and the interactive effects of etiquette and emotional labor. *Critical Sociology, 37*(5), 557–571. doi:10.1177/0896920510380074

Edwards, J. B., Bryant, S., & Clark, T. T. (2008). African American female social work educators in predominantly White schools of social work: Strategies for thriving. *Journal of African American Studies, 12*(1), 37–49. doi:10.100712111-007-9029-y

Evans, L., & Moore, W. L. (2015). Impossible Burdens: White Institutions, Emotional Labor, and Micro-Resistance. *Social Problems, 62*(3), 439–454. doi:10.1093ocpropv009

Fluker, W. E. (2015). Now we must cross a sea: Remarks on transformational leadership and the civil rights movement. *Boston University Law Review. Boston University. School of Law*.

Frey, J. J. (2020, October 14). How employee assistance programs can help your whole company address racism at work. *Human Resource Management*. https://hbr.org/2020/10/how-employee-assistance-programs-can-help-your-whole-company-address-racism-at-work?ab=hero-subleft-1

Generett, G. G., & Welch, O. M. (2018). Transformative leadership: Lessons learned through intergenerational dialogue. *Urban Education, 53*(9), 1102–1125. doi:10.1177/0042085917706598

Gover, A. R., Harper, S. B., & Langton, L. (2020). Anti-Asian hate crime during the COVID-19 pandemic: Exploring the reproduction of inequality. *American Journal of Criminal Justice, 45*(4), 647–667. doi:10.100712103-020-09545-1 PMID:32837171

Griffith, D. M., Mason, M., Yonas, M., Eng, E., Jeffries, V., Plihcik, S., & Parks, B. (2007). Dismantling institutional racism: Theory and action. *American Journal of Community Psychology, 39*(3-4), 381–392. doi:10.100710464-007-9117-0 PMID:17404829

Guiffrida, D. (2005). Other mothering as a framework for understanding African American students' definitions of student-centered faculty. *The Journal of Higher Education, 76*(6), 701–723. doi:10.1353/jhe.2005.0041

Harpalani, V. (2015). To be white, black, or brown? South Asian Americans and the race-color distinction. *Washington University Global Studies Law Review, 14*(4), 609. https://link.gale.com/apps/doc/A452881504/AONE?u=csudh&sid=bookmark-AONE&xid=a69c00cf

Higginbotham, E. B. (1981). Is marriage a priority? Class differences in marital options of educated Black women. In P. Stein (Ed.), *Single life* (pp. 259–267). St. Martins.

Hirshfield, L. E., & Joseph, T. D. (2012). 'We need a woman, we need a Black woman': Gender, race, and identity taxation in the academy. *Gender and Education, 24*(2), 213–227. doi:10.1080/09540253.2011.606208

Horne, S. G., & Arora, K. S. K. (2013). Feminist multicultural counseling psychology in transnational contexts. In C. Z. Enns & E. N. Williams (Eds.), *Oxford library of psychology. The Oxford handbook of feminist multicultural counseling psychology* (pp. 240–252). Oxford University Press.

Hsieh, B., & Nguyen, H. T. (2020). Identity-informed mentoring to support acculturation of female faculty of color in higher education: An Asian American female mentoring relationship case study. *Journal of Diversity in Higher Education*, *13*(2), 169–180. doi:10.1037/dhe0000118

Hua, L. U. (2018). Slow feeling and quiet being: Women of color teaching in urgent times. *New Directions for Teaching and Learning*, *153*(153), 77–86. doi:10.1002/tl.20283

Hughes, A. K., Horner, P. S., & Ortiz, D. (2012). Being the diversity hire: Negotiating identity in an academic job search. *Journal of Social Work Education*, *48*(3), 595–612. doi:10.5175/JSWE.2012.201000101

Hune, S. (2011). Asian American Women Faculty and the contested space of the classroom: Navigating student resistance and (re)claiming authority and their rightful place. *Journal of Diversity in Higher Education*, *9*, 307–335.

Hunn, V., Harley, D., Min, W. E., & Canfield, J. P. (2015). Microaggression and the mitigation of psychological harm: Four social workers' exposition for care of clients, students, and faculty who suffer 'a thousand little cuts.'. *The Journal of Pan African Studies*, *7*(9), 42–54.

Johnson, H. L. (2017). *Pipelines, pathways, and institutional leadership: An update on the status of women in higher education*. American Council on Education.

Johnson, P. C. (2003). At the intersection of injustice: Experiences of African American women in crime and sentencing. In A. K. Wing (Ed.), *Critical race feminism* (2nd ed., pp. 209–218). NYU Press.

Jones, J. M., & Rolón-Dow, R. (2019). Multidimensional models of microaggressions and microaffirmations. In G. C. Torino, D. P. Rivera, C. M. Capodilupo, K. L. Nadal, & D. W. Sue (Eds.), *Microaggressions theory: Influence and implications* (pp. 32–47). John Wiley & Sons, Inc.

Jones, R. (2020, December 21). Understanding COVID-19 19 vaccine hesitancy in the Black community. *News & Politics*. https://wearyourvoicemag.com/understanding-covid-19-vaccine-hesitancy-in-the-black-community/

Kadowaki, J., & Subramaniam, M. (2014). Coping with emotional labor: Challenges faced and strategies adopted by instructors. *Understanding and Dismantling Privilege, 4*(2).

Kelly, B. T., Gardner, P. J., Stone, J., Hixson, A., & Dissassa, D.-T. (2019). Hidden in plain sight: Uncovering the emotional labor of Black women students at historically White colleges and universities. *Journal of Diversity in Higher Education*, *14*(2), 203–216. doi:10.1037/dhe0000161

Kessler, R. C., Mickelson, K. D., & Williams, D. R. (1999). The prevalence, distribution, and mental health correlates of perceived discrimination in the United States. *Journal of Health and Social Behavior*, *40*(3), 208–230. doi:10.2307/2676349 PMID:10513145

Kleinman, S. (2007). Feminist fieldwork analysis. *Sage (Atlanta, Ga.).*

Kulkarni, M., Choi, C., & Jeung, R. M. (2021, March). How to stop the dangerous rise in hatred targeted at Asian Americans. *USA Today.* https://www.usatoday.com/story/opinion/2021/03/30/how-stop-rise-hatred-aimed-asian-americans-column/7044033002/

Kyaw, A. (2021, April 25). Report: Faculty diversity falling behind student diversity. *Diverse Issues in Higher Education.* https://diverseeducation.com/article/212463/

Li, G., & Beckett, G. H. (2006). Reconstructing culture and identity in the academy. In G. Li & G. H. Beckett (Eds.), *Strangers" of the academy: Asian women scholars in higher education* (pp. 1–14). Stylus Publishing.

Lim, S. G. (2006). Identities Asian, female, scholar: critiques and celebration of North American academy. In G. Li & G. H. Beckett (Eds.), *Strangers" of the academy: Asian women scholars in higher education* (pp. xiii–xviii). Stylus Publishing.

Lorde, A. (1984). *Sister outsider: Essays and speeches.* Crossing Press.

Mawhinney, L. (2011). Othermothering: A personal narrative exploring relationships between Black female faculty and students. *The Negro Educational Review, 62-63*(1-4), 213-232. http://gateway.proquest.com/openurl?url_ver=Z39.88-2004&res_dat=xri:bsc:&rft_dat=xri:bsc:rec:iibp:00417280

McGee, E., & Stovall, D. (2015). Reimagining critical race theory in education: Mental health, healing, and the pathway to liberatory praxis. *Educational Theory*, *65*(5), 491–511. doi:10.1111/edth.12129

Mohanty, C. (1988). Under Western Eyes: Feminist Scholarship and Colonial Discourses. *Feminist Review*, *30*(1), 61–88. doi:10.1057/fr.1988.42

Moore, H. A., Acosta, K., Perry, G., & Edwards, C. (2010). Splitting the academy: The emotions of intersectionality at work. *The Sociological Quarterly*, *51*(2), 179–204. doi:10.1111/j.1533-8525.2010.01168.x

Moore, M. (1981). Mainstreaming Black women in American higher education. *Journal of Societies of Ethnic and Special Studies*, *5*, 61–68.

Moore, W., & Wagstaff, L. (1974). *Black educators in White colleges*. Jossey-Bass.

Moorosi, P., Fuller, K., & Reilly, E. (2018). Leadership and intersectionality: Constructions of successful leadership among Black women school principals in three different contexts. *Management in Education*, *32*(4), 152–159. doi:10.1177/0892020618791006

Mukkamala, S., & Suyemoto, K. L. (2018). Racialized sexism/sexualized racism: A multimethod study of intersectional experiences of discrimination for Asian American women. *Asian American Journal of Psychology*, *9*(1), 32–46. doi:10.1037/aap0000104

Mullings, L. (2002). The Sojourner syndrome: Race, class, and gender in health and illness. *Voices,* 32-36.

Nadal, K. L., Griffin, K. E., Wong, Y., Hamit, S., & Rasmus, M. (2014). The impact of racial microaggressions on mental health: Counseling implications for clients of color. *Journal of Counseling and Development*, *92*(1), 57–66. doi:10.1002/j.1556-6676.2014.00130.x

Nayak, S. (2015). *Race, gender and the activism of Black feminist theory: Working with Audre Lorde*. Routledge.

Oppel, R. A., Taylor, D. B., & Bogel-Burroughs, N. (2021, April). What to know about Breonna Taylor's death. *New York Times*. https://www.nytimes.com/article/breonna-taylor-police.html

Overstreet, M. (2019). My first year in academia *or* the mythical Black woman superhero takes on the ivory tower. *Journal of Women and Gender in Higher Education*, *12*(1), 18–34. doi:10.1080/19407882.2018.1540993

Padilla, A. M. (1994). Ethnic minority scholars, research, and mentoring: Current and future issues. *Educational Researcher*, *23*(4), 24–27. doi:10.2307/1176259

Painter, N. (1996). *Sojourner Truth: A life, a symbol*. W. W. Norton.

Prakash, P., Choi, C., & Jeung, R. M. (2021, May). Global spread of COVID-19 variant first detected in India brings with it fears of anti-Indian racism. *Scroll*. https://scroll.in/global/995805/global-spread-of-covid-19-variant-first-detected-in-india-brings-with-it-fears-of-anti-indian-racism

Rockquemore, K. A., & Laszloffy, T. (2008). *The Black academic's guide to winning tenure—without losing your soul*. Lynne Rienner Publisher, Inc.

Rong, X. L., & Preissle, J. (2006). From mentorship to friendship, collaboration, and collegiality. In G. Li & G. H. Beckett (Eds.), *Strangers" of the academy: Asian women scholars in higher education* (pp. 266–288). Stylus Publishing.

Sabharwal, M., & Varma, R. (2017). Are Asian Indian scientists and engineers in academia faced with a glass ceiling? *Journal of Ethnographic and Qualitative Research*, *12*, 50–62.

Smith, W. A. (2004). Black faculty coping with racial battle fatigue: The campus racial climate in a post-Civil Rights Era. In D. Cleveland (Ed.), A long way to go: Conversations about race by African American faculty and graduate students (pp. 171-190). Peter Lang Publishing Inc.

Smith, W. A. (2015). Foreword. In R. Mitchell, K. J. Fasching-Varner, K. Albert, & C. Allen (Eds.), *Racial battle fatigue in higher education: Exposing the myth of post-racial America* (pp. xi–xii). Rowan & Littlefield Publishers.

Solórzano, D. G., & Yosso, T. J. (2002). Critical race methodology: Counter-Storytelling as an analytical framework for education research. *Qualitative Inquiry*, *8*(1), 23–44. doi:10.1177/107780040200800103

Southern Regional Education Board. (2021, April). *Student and faculty diversity in SREB states*. https://www.sreb.org/diversityprofiles

Stobbe, M. (2020, December 22). More than 3 million people died in 2020 - the deadliest year in U.S. history. *USA Today*. https://www.usatoday.com/story/news/nation/2020/12/22/2020-deadliest-year-united-states-coronavirus/4006270001/

Substance Abuse and Mental Health Services Administration. (2020). *Double jeopardy: COVID-19 and behavioral health disparities for Black and Latino communities in the U.S.* https://www.samhsa.gov/sites/default/files/covid19-behavioral-health-disparities-black-latino-communities.pdf

Thomas, A. J., Witherspoon, K. M., & Speight, S. L. (2008). Gendered racism, psychological distress, and coping styles of African American women. *Cultural Diversity & Ethnic Minority Psychology*, *14*(4), 307–314. doi:10.1037/1099-9809.14.4.307 PMID:18954166

U.S. Department of Education, National Center for Education Statistics. (2014). *Digest of Educational Statistics, Table 316.10. 201*. https://nces.ed.gov/programs/digest/d14/tables/dt14_316.10.asp?current=yes

U.S. Department of Education, National Center for Education Statistics. (2018). *Digest of Educational Statistics, Table 315.20*. https://nces.ed.gov/programs/digest/d19/tables/dt19_315.20.asp

Walkington, L. (2017). How far have we really come? Black women faculty and graduate students' experiences in higher education. *Humboldt Journal of Social Relations*, *39*, 51–65.

Washington, M. (2013). "Going where they dare not follow": Race, religion, and Sojourner Truth's early interracial reform. *Journal of African American History*, *98*(1), 48–71. doi:10.5323/jafriamerhist.98.1.0048

Wilder, C. S. (2013). *Ebony & ivy: Race, slavery, and the troubled history of America's universities*. Bloomsbury Publishing.

Williams, D. R., & Mohammed, S. A. (2013). Racism and Health I: Pathways and Scientific Evidence. *The American Behavioral Scientist*, *57*(8), 1152–1173. doi:10.1177/0002764213487340 PMID:24347666

Young, K., & Anderson, M. R. (2019). Microaggressions in higher education: Embracing educative spaces. In Microaggression Theory: Influence and Implications. Hoboken, NJ: John Wiley & Sons, Inc.

Zerbe Enns, C., Díaz, L. C., & Bryant-Davis, T. (2020). Transnational feminist theory and practice: An introduction. *Women & Therapy*. https://doi-org.libproxy.csudh.edu/10.1080/02703149.2020.1774997

KEY TERMS AND DEFINITIONS

Authentic Leadership: Authentic leadership is a leadership theory that focuses on transparency, morals, and ethics to promote trustworthiness, balanced decision-making, and self-awareness to improve followers' well-being.

Black Feminism: A philosophy that concentrates on Black women's experiences and viewpoints.

Black Strategic Mothering: A philosophy that identifies how Black women make decisions in their couples' relationship, family, and profession with a more significant focus on the Black community's survival.

Critical Race Theory: A theoretical lens that explores race/culture and racism in the dominant discourse and attends to how perceptions of race impact victims.

Cultural Taxation: A term coined by Amado Padilla in 1994 describes the extra burden of service responsibilities placed upon minority faculty and staff to serve as ethnic representatives as unofficial diversity consultants within the university setting.

Emotional Labor: The practice of understanding, managing, and expressing feelings to elicit the desired disposition in others.

Intersectionality: The interconnection and overlapping systems of multiple social identities, including but not limited to race, ethnicity, nationality, gender, ability, sexual status, sexual orientation, etc.

Microaggression: A common, indirect, subtle, intentional, or unintentional discrimination interaction or behavior against persons of a marginalized group.

Postcolonial Feminism: A feminist perspective developed in response to Western feminism that focused on Western women's experiences to categorize women in other countries.

Racial Battle Fatigue: A cumulative response to racial oppression coined about people of color in historical White institutions.

Resilience Fatigue: A cumulative response to prolonged or complicated or traumatic stresses.

Sojourner Syndrome: A process that describes the multiple roles and social identities of Black women to foster resilience in oppressive occurrences.

Transformative Leadership: Transformative leadership is a leadership theory that focuses on inspirational motivation, intellectual stimulation, individual consideration, and idealized influence to promote trust and loyalty among leaders and followers.

Chapter 8
Othering, Intersectionality, and Americanism:
Examining How People of Color Navigate Leadership in Counseling

John J. S. Harrichand
https://orcid.org/0000-0002-3336-2062
The University of Texas at San Antonio, USA

S. Anandavalli
Southern Oregon University, USA

Cirecie A. West-Olatunji
https://orcid.org/0000-0001-9261-2650
Xavier University of Louisiana, USA

ABSTRACT

Black and Brown leaders in the counseling profession continue to be minoritized as they navigate a White dominant profession. It is important that the counseling profession take steps to empower Black and Brown counseling leaders with the tools needed to effectively and confidently lead. The authors examine the socially just and culturally responsive counseling leadership model (SJCRCLM), the inclusive leadership model (ILM), and culture-centered leadership models (CCLM) using personal narratives. Black and Brown counseling leaders at different levels of leadership (i.e., beginner, intermediate, advanced) are provided with recommendations for navigating life in the US and specifically a profession that is dominated by Whiteness.

DOI: 10.4018/978-1-7998-7235-1.ch008

INTRODUCTION

The American Counseling Association (ACA, 2020a) is the world's largest counseling association representing over 50,000 professional counselors. Founded in 1952, the ACA is a non-profit professional and educational organization. Since its inception, 19 of the first 20 presidents have been White men, and although the profession strives to promote multicultural competence, it continues to experience challenges in seeing diverse individuals represented in leadership (Meyers, 2017). According to Meyers (2017, para. 4) "many [members] feel that the counseling profession is still largely dominated by White culture."

In this chapter we draw attention to the challenges experienced by Black and Brown leaders in the counseling profession as they navigate "White Supremacist America" (Inwood & Alderman, 2016). Particularly, we situate this dialogue within the context of the ongoing dual pandemic, wherein the COVID-19 health crisis and heightened racial tensions exacerbate issues of White Supremacy, racist nativism and leadership. We begin the chapter by identifying the socio-political environment in the United States (US) and its impact on the profession of counseling. Next, we operationalize the meaning of the phrase "Black and Brown leadership" in relation to social identities and minoritized statuses. Following this, we outline three leadership models that specifically center Black and Brown leadership approaches. Additionally, each author adopts one model and offers personal narratives of how characteristics of the model fit their personal journey of leadership in the counseling profession. Finally, Black and Brown counseling leaders are provided with practical leadership applications that can be incorporated in a White-dominated profession.

Our aim is to equip and empower Black and Brown counseling leaders with the tools needed to lead effectively and confidently in their spheres of influence while in environments that question their Americanness and simultaneously assign them 'Other' (non-white) identities. The chapter examines the Socially Just and Culturally Responsive Counseling Leadership Model (SJCRCLM; Peters et al., 2020), the Inclusive Leadership Model (ILM; Victorian Equal Opportunity and Human Rights Commission, 2013), and a Culture-Centered Leadership Model (CCLM; Metz, 2018).

Objectives

- Identify the socio-political environment in the US and its impact on the profession of counseling.
- Learn the meaning of the phrase Black and Brown leadership as explained in terms of social identities and minoritized status (i.e., othering, intersectionality, Americanism).

- Evaluate leadership models by comparing them with the lived experiences of the authors.
- Identify practical leadership applications that Black and Brown counseling leaders can incorporate in a White dominated profession, especially during times of tumultuous change and social unrest.

THE STATE OF AFFAIRS: REVIEW OF SOCIO-POLITICAL CONTEXT IN THE US

In 2019, Horowitz and colleagues stated that although over 150 years after the 13th Amendment abolished slavery in the US, a large proportion of Americans hold the belief that Black people continue to be negatively impacted by the legacy of slavery. In a national Pew Research Center survey of 6,637 adults conducted between January 22 and February 5, 2019, researchers commented that four out of 10 Americans believe the US has not made enough progress in the area of racial equality. 56% of participants believe that President Trump and his administration have worsened race relations in the US since taking office. In addition, approximately 75% of Americans surveyed stated that President Trump's leadership has normalized the expression of racist views in the US (Horowitz et al., 2019).

The recent murders of George Floyd, Breonna Taylor, and Ahmaud Arbery among others builds the article by Horowitz and colleagues (2019), further exposing systemic racism in the US at the hands of police (Arredondo et al., 2020), as historian Arica Coleman terms "modern-day lynching" (Brown, 2020, para. 2). The disproportionate deaths of Black and Brown people in the US at the hands of police is not new; "African American men and women, American Indian/Alaska Native men and women, and Latino men face higher lifetime risk of being killed by police than do their White peers" (Edwards et al., 2019, p. 16793). More specifically, as of December 8, 2020, 28% of people killed by police identified as Black, even though Black communities account for only 13% of the population ("Mapping Police Violence," 2020).

According to Arredondo and colleagues (2020), the pandemic of White racism and White supremacy is the beating heart of the resistant behavioral, emotional, and psychological injustices and racial tensions evidenced in the US. The sad reality is that the effects of White racism and White supremacy remain linked to the profession of counseling and unfortunately, they continue to be experienced by Black and Brown counseling leaders (Arredondo et al., 2020; Meyers, 2017).

The second pandemic impacting our world and way of life is the coronavirus disease (COVID-19). It has exposed racial disparities in the US where culturally and ethnically minoritized individuals are disproportionately hospitalized and/or dying at a rate of 1.1 – 2.8 times higher than their White counterparts (Centers for Disease

Control and Prevention [CDC], 2020a). According to Schild and colleagues (2020), COVID-19 is the largest pandemic event of the 21st century. As of June 9, 2021, approximately 173.7 million cases of COVID-19 and more than 3.74 million deaths have occurred globally (World Health Organization, 2021). COVID-19 statistics for the US stand at over 33 million confirmed cases and over 592,600 deaths. Litam and Hipolito-Delgado (2021, p. 3) state that COVID-19 has exacerbated "preexisting racial and ethnic disparities …[and] have negatively affected communities of color that tend to be overrepresented in lower socioeconomic groups, have limited access to health care and education, have an undocumented status, and work in jobs considered 'essential.'" In addition, the Trump administration used the pandemic as a tool to disproportionately affect the safety and wellbeing of international students in the US (Anandavalli et al., 2020; Anandavalli et al., 2021). Of importance is the reality that ethnic minority groups, i.e., groups with which Black and Brown counseling leaders identify and support, are the communities that have evidenced higher rates of COVID-19 infections, deaths, loss of income, and psychological distress (CDC, 2020b). In the next section we specifically examine the influences of the dual pandemics on the counseling profession.

Impact on Profession of Counseling

Leadership is an important role that members of the counseling profession, specifically counselor educators, embody as part of their identity (Council for Accreditation of Counseling and Related Educational Programs [CACREP], 2015). The experience of Black and Brown leadership in the counseling profession gained a more challenging form in the context of the double pandemics gripping our nation – COVID-19 and racial inequity – both of which have been compounded by the economic crisis taking place. This is in part due to the reality, as experienced by the authors, where Black and Brown counseling leaders are simultaneously offering support to their professional communities while wrestling with the impact of the current state of affairs on their own mental health and wellbeing (Hunter et al., 2020; Litam et al., in press; Smith & Roysircar, 2010). Within the counseling profession, the ACA's (2014) *Code of Ethics* instructs counselors-in-training (CITs), counselors, supervisors, and educators to be social justice agents (i.e., *ACA Code of Ethics Preamble*, #3, p. 3). To realize the task of being social justice agents, CITs and professional counselors are provided with the Multicultural and Social Justice Counseling Competencies (MSJCC; Ratts et al., 2015) and ACA Advocacy Competencies (Toporek & Daniels, 2018) as resources. However, the preceding issues appear to be affecting the mental health and wellbeing of our counselors, including our Black and Brown counseling leaders, who are meeting the needs of a hurting society (Litam et al., 2020). The following section provides a review of literature on Black and Brown leadership in the counseling profession, highlighting statistics and challenges.

BLACK AND BROWN COUNSELING LEADERS

The lived experiences of leaders, while somewhat comparable, are impacted by the identities they embody. Situated in the critical feminist paradigm, the intersectionality framework highlights how the lives of individuals are constantly shaped by the socio-cultural identities they embody along the dimensions of race, gender, sex, and other related dimensions (Crenshaw, 1989, 1991; Shin et al., 2017). Moreover, intersectionality of identity also connotes the necessity of taking social action against this social and cultural hegemony. According to Storlie and colleagues (2015) the counseling profession acknowledges the importance of multicultural leadership, seeing it as "vital to the professional role and expectations of counselor educators that ultimately impact the students they will teach, advise, mentor, and supervise" (p. 156). As of December 2020, over 52,000 counselors (i.e., professional, retired) and students hold membership in ACA – data on sex is not available, and although information on ethnic identity is requested, it is not required. Based on the current data, only 8,347 members specified their ethnic identity, with approximately 80% (6,703 members) identifying as White/European Ancestry and the other approximately 20% (1,644 members) identifying as non-White/European, i.e., Asian, Black or African American, Hispanic or Latinx, Native/Indigenous, Two or More Cultural Identities, and Other (ACA, 2020b). Even with this ethnic diversity, the counseling profession continues to be challenged, i.e., dominated by the hegemonic White culture when it comes to representativeness in its leadership (Arredondo et al., 2020; Chan et al., in press; Meyers, 2017). Using the intersectionality framework, we note that the representation within the ACA membership is disproportionate and potentially indicative of larger narratives around leadership in the American society, which are grounded in White, male ideals (Chan et al., in press). Thus, Black and Brown counseling leaders are likely to feel especially isolated, marginalized, and that their legitimacy in the leadership positions is questioned. More specifically, Black and Brown professionals navigating the counselor education community are 'Othered' on a regular basis (Bryant et al., 2005; Chan et al., in press).

In many ways the lack of equitable representation of Black and Brown leadership in the counseling field is indicative of larger Americanism, wherein dominant ideals of the US culture grounded in race, gender, and socio-economic status determine the larger values, practices and rituals (Ricento, 2003). This reality was captured in a seminal piece in ACA's flagship journal, *Counseling & Development* by Dr. Beth A. Durodoye (1999), who chronicled her own experiences of overt and covert racism as a Black woman, counselor educator, and leader in the counseling profession. She documents the double standards existing for her as a Black woman that Black and Brown counseling leaders continue to be held to today. Her article provides a quality list of experiences related to being "Othered," i.e., feeling as an outsider, minimized, and of little significance in social spaces, within higher education and the field of counseling. Durodoye (1999) documents a few notable examples of being "Othered" including: (1) being ignored for making a point of consequence only to see a White colleague recognized for referencing the same point; (2) being questioned on how she held the position she did; (3) being questioned by campus police for exiting a building late at night; and (4) being asked during a national conference presentation how her proposal got accepted instead of being questioned on the presentation itself. Dr. Durodoye's persistence, strength, and character is captured in the response she offers to incidents of racism: "the little indignities ... [faced daily] do not deserve my attention. I ... fight ... battles ... worth fighting and let go of those that have little bearing on the goals I have set out to achieve in the field" (1999, p. 46).

Building on Durodoye's (1999) piece, Bryant and colleagues (2005) chronicled the value of African American women in the counseling profession, noting that although they (i.e., African American female counseling professionals) have and continue to significantly contribute to its multicultural growth, they continue to be minoritized and Othered by the same profession they helped and continue to help build. Some of the challenges Black and Brown counseling leaders continue to experience, as outlined by Bryant and colleagues (2005), include, *invisibility*, where Black and Brown counseling leaders are often excluded from general conversations and only approached when issues of multiculturalism and diversity are addressed. Another challenge is *overvisibility* or *tokenism*, what Bryant and colleagues (2005) refer to as the assumption that African American and People of Color who are hired for faculty positions in higher education, and specifically counselor education, are not hired for their intellectual merits but to meet the diversity quota of their respective institutions. Bryant and colleagues (2005) also identify *alienation and devaluation* as a challenge experienced by African American female counselor educators, which is referred to as "the distance between [the Black and Brown counseling leader] and their colleagues that is created due to a feeling of not knowing, understanding, or caring about what [the Black and Brown counseling leader] wants" (p. 316). More specifically, devaluation of Black and Brown counseling leaders refers to minimizing and/or disrespecting their accomplishments in higher education, and the belief that their scholarship related to multiculturalism and diversity issues might be insular and/or not scholarly enough, especially in relation to the tenure and promotion process (Bryant et al., 2005). Based on the lived experiences documented within the counseling profession, one is left with the questions of whether or not Black and Brown counseling leaders are having to navigate unwritten rules as they serve a White-dominant profession, the impact this has on their leadership, and how their White colleagues view and experience them as leaders. In the next section, we provide insights into our lived experiences as captured by three leadership models that specifically center Black and Brown leadership approaches.

LEADERSHIP MODELS

This section provides a review of three specific leadership models that center Black and Brown counseling leaders. Each author adopts one model and closely examines how their lived experience as a counseling leader can be conceptualized using personal examples to enhance the readers' understanding.

Socially Just and Culturally Responsive Leadership Model (Peters et al., 2020)

According to Peters et al. (2020, p. 955) "[s]ocial justice and culturally responsive leadership mirrors the scholarship on cultural responsivity and social justice." In other words, culturally responsive leadership is said to utilize a culturally responsive framework to theorize leadership, utilize a culturally responsive lens to interpret one's leadership, and engage in leadership that is culturally responsive (Lopez, 2015, 2016). This model seeks and demands social change by challenging and dismantling systemic powers (i.e., Eurocentric, heteronormative, cisgender) that negatively exert toxic effects on all communities, but unjustly impacts minoritized communities, i.e., the communities where Black and Brown counseling leaders exist. The components of the Socially Just and Culturally Responsive Leadership Model (SJCRLM) by Peters and colleagues (2020) are summarized below.

Causal Conditions

The first component of the SJCRLM (Peters et al., 2020) addresses *causal conditions* that allow leaders to engage in SJCRL. These conditions include personal or observer experiences and identities that inform individuals to engage in leadership. Another causal condition that informs leadership engagement is awareness and knowledge of different social-cultural, institutional, and organizational structures, especially those that privilege some and oppress others. Affective experience, i.e., emotions that impact and/or challenge leaders to engage in SJCRL is another causal condition. Sense of calling and/or duty is a fourth causal condition, which speaks of the individual's personal and professional compass or duty calling them to engage in SJCRL. A final causal condition, environmental stimuli, accounts for the landscape or climate that the individual interacts, which influences their engagement in SJCRL.

Contextual Factors

According to the SJCRLM, *contextual factors* are conditions, patters, and properties that include action strategies by individuals engaging in SJCRL. The first contextual factor is bidirectional points of entry and influence, including ecological systems (e.g., privilege and marginalized identities) that the individual engages in and is influenced by while participating in SJCRL. A second contextual factor is counseling leadership pillars: community, counseling, teaching, scholarship, service, and supervision through which individuals navigate when engaging in SJCRL in organizations and higher education settings. A third contextual factor is dimensions of consideration which encompass conditions (i.e., history of cause, stakeholders, future actions) or processes that the individual intentionally reflects on before engaging in SJCRL.

Intervening Conditions

Within the SJCRLM, *intervening conditions* represent overarching structural factors that impact the SJCRL action strategies used. The first condition focuses on obstacles, which includes the issues/barriers that the individual might encounter when seeking to enact SJCRL (i.e., challenging people, socio-cultural and/or systemic barriers). A second condition is group-system dynamics, which include implicit and explicit behaviors and dynamic characteristics of leadership between and within groups and systems, (i.e., norms, decision making, capital, atmosphere, safety, acceptance, belonging). A third condition is conflicts, (dis)agreements, and change that operate on a continuum (positive – negative) and are characteristic to human relationships.

Actions

Another component of the SJCRLM is *actions* and includes all the activities that are visible or invisible in addition to interpreting events. Personal actions focus on intrapersonal behaviors or inquiries used by counseling leaders to justify SJCRL (i.e., personality dispositions, personal strengths, congruent theoretical lens, self-reflection, self-accountability). Skill-oriented actions associated with leadership include counseling skills and flexibility.

Relational-Oriented Actions

Relational-oriented actions focus on the value of relationships, trust and connection, and holding a critical view of leaders using SJCRL related to successful actions and uptakes (i.e., collaborating, mentoring). Community cultural actions highlight the behaviors counseling leaders participate in that support diversity, equity, and justice within minoritized and privileged cultures and communities (i.e., challenging, disrupting, advocating, centering). Group-system actions encompass the intentional behaviors that counseling leaders employ when addressing between and within group system interactions, norms, and processes.

Phenomenon, Consequence, and Core Category

Within the SJCRLM, the *phenomenon* symbolizes the process of channeling and integrating social justice, cultural responsivity, and counseling leadership, including the actions, context, and intervening conditions impacting the representation of SJCRL. On the other hand, *consequences* denote "pathways that foster, hinder, or stagnate in five domains: equity, inclusion, and representation; access and opportunity; distribution and mobility; participation and engagement; and relationships, connections, and belonging" (Peters et al., 2020, p. 974). Finally, the *core category*, i.e., connectivity, is the most frequently occurring concept and main finding within the SJCRLM, impacting all aspects of leadership for counseling leaders utilizing this theoretical framework.

Personal Narrative: Dr. John Harrichand

As president-elect for a state counseling organization, I have found Peters and colleagues' (2020) SJCRLM helpful in depicting my experiences as a Brown leader in a profession that is predominantly White and heavily influenced by policies and practices rooted in Americanism. My journey into counseling leadership stems from *causal conditions* and *contextual factors* focused on acknowledging the lack of representation in Black and Brown counseling leaders as a doctoral student attending a national emerging leaders program. It also comes from hearing from a group of White leaders who shared that their journeys into leadership stemmed from other White leaders mentoring them. This experience made me assess my privilege (i.e., an awardee) and marginalized identities (i.e., Indo-Chinese Guyanese, queer person of Color). I then asked myself who the Black and Brown counseling leaders are that I can draw from as sources of inspiration based on the counseling leadership pillars. Thankfully, there were a *distant* few, including Catharina Chang, Cirecie West-Olatunji, and Gargi Roysircar. I took stock of my position and desire to exact change acknowledging the conditions that existed (*actions* and *intervening conditions*) based on the dominant discourse of Americanism. Some of those appear to disproportionately favor my White peers when it comes to awards and job selections within our counseling profession, over Black and Brown individuals. However, my desire to be part of the change process was momentarily eclipsed by my insecurities of being an unknown statistic within the counseling profession. I had fears of being targeted/ostracized by current counseling leaders for "calling out" the disparity captured in pieces by Arredondo and colleagues (2020), Chan and colleagues (in press), and Meyers (2017). My insecurities were captured by W.E.B. Du Bois, and reworded by Ibram X. Kendi (2019, p. 29) "To be American is to be White. To be White is not to be [a Person of Color]." I was caught in a state of "dueling consciousness" as noted by Kendi (2019), i.e., looking at myself through my own eyes (racial relativity), thinking I am good enough to be a leader in the counseling profession. While simultaneously looking at myself through the eyes of White America (racial standards), I was thinking that I would never be good enough (i.e., White enough, American enough) to be a leader in the counseling profession. Fortunately, I was employed at a public institution, and found community in a department of peers who are committed to equity, diversity, inclusion, and social justice (*relational-oriented actions*). One of my colleagues, a Black-Jamaican woman and leader in the state counseling organization, recognized my strengths and abilities and welcomed me into the organization. Through our relationship built on trust, respect, and connection (*core category*), we continue to create space for diverse voices within the state counseling organization, while advocating for systemic change and dismantling racist policies and ideas associated with Americanism (*consequences*). As Black and Brown counseling leaders, our focus, i.e., *phenomenon*, is on centering the voices of people of color (BIPOC) communities while prioritizing their access to mental health services. Through connection with other Black and Brown counseling leaders and White co-conspirators, my resolve has been strengthened. I am committed to being an SJCR leader, peer, and mentor for other Black and Brown leaders and emerging leaders focused on fostering community and sustaining a vibrant pathway for greater representation of Black and Brown counseling leaders in a profession that I dearly love.

Inclusive Leadership Model (Victorian Equal Opportunity and Human Rights Commission, 2013)

As leadership approaches around the world move toward a new shift, the Inclusive Leadership Model (ILM) by Victorian Equal Opportunity and Human Rights Commission (VEOHR, 2013; Dillon & Bourke, 2016) created by Deloitte, a private company headquartered in the UK, considers leaders' inclusivity and responses to diversity as central to effective leadership. The authors of the submitted report argue that as the demographics of employees move toward greater representativeness, it is imperative that leaders are equipped to model values of social justice and equity. They identified six key characteristics that define a highly inclusive leader. These six characteristics are discussed below.

Commitment

Researchers found that inclusive leaders were *committed* to incorporating diversity in the organizations they lead and treated members with fairness and respect. They strived to understand the uniqueness of each team member and took action to ensure that members felt included and connected to the organization. Furthermore, the leaders were committed to diversity and inclusion as an organizational priority and allocated resources towards improving diversity within their community.

Courage

The researchers also believed *courage* was an important trait found among inclusive leaders. Inclusive leaders are not afraid to speak up, challenge the status quo, and demonstrate their allegiance to issues of diversity by holding others accountable when they engage in non-inclusive behavior. They challenge organizational practices that perpetuate homogeneity and find ways to draw strengths from diverse individuals. Additionally, they are courageous enough to admit their mistakes when wrong and take necessary actions to rectify.

Cognizance of Bias

Inclusive leaders are aware of personal and organizational *blind spots and biases*, engaging in meaningful self-regulation to help ensure "fair play" for all members. Highly inclusive leaders are receptive to feedback and make necessary changes in their thinking and actions when offered constructive feedback regarding their blind spots and biases. At an organizational level, they identify and challenge practices that minimize merit of individuals. Highly inclusive leaders engage in transparent and informed decision making regarding recruitment and retention. Their decisions are grounded in objective rationale that reinforce inclusivity at an individual and organizational level.

Curiosity

Highly inclusive leaders maintain an *open mind* and engage in meaningful, convergent thinking. They desire to learn more about how others think and experience the world. Highly inclusive leaders are better with ambiguity and pursue opportunities to connect with a diverse range of communities.

Cultural Intelligence

Highly inclusive leaders demonstrate *confidence and effectiveness in cross-cultural interactions*. They take a deep interest in learning more about cultures other than their own and further their knowledge by pursuing opportunities to immerse in culturally diverse environments. They experience self-efficacy in leading cross-cultural teams. Highly inclusive leaders work efficiently with individuals from various cultural contexts and present themselves as flexible to adapt to changing cultural contexts.

Collaboration

Highly inclusive leaders are committed to empowering individuals from diverse backgrounds and build *meaningful collaborative relationships* with diverse communities. Furthermore, they build safe environments wherein people feel comfortable to speak up and intentionally include all members in dialogue and decision making.

Personal Narrative: Dr. S Anandavalli

As I reflect on my journey in the field of counseling and counselor education, I recognize that I am an anomaly in the dominant notion of Americanism and American leadership. With the prevailing and historical events sharply favoring a prototype that embodies male, heterosexual, White, middle class, Christian, and US citizen identities when it comes to leadership, I stand in stark contrast as a foreign-born Asian Indian, Hindu woman. The intersecting identities I embody disturb the established notions of leadership and Americanism. Hegemonic notions of Americanism were offered to me at various junctures in my professional development. In many ways, counselors are leaders of social justice and advocacy in their communities. However, in the past, several clients of mine would be suspicious of my presence and my background, even before the first word was uttered in our professional relationship. Their images and projections on who can be seen as a mental health leader and who cannot strongly informed their attitudes and biases against me. It disturbed their schemas to see me in a leadership position.

A comparison of attitudes can be made between my former clients at the internship site and the counseling professionals I encountered at regional conferences. Although many of them have been extremely supportive and have continued to offer their wise mentorship to me to this day, I do recall instances when people would smirk at my pronunciation during presentations and ignore my questions during networking meetings. There were at least two regional conferences that I attended one year when I don't think I saw a single person who looked like me. Thus, early on, I was made aware of my outsider status in the profession. The limited presence of *collaboration*, *cultural intelligence*, and *curiosity* among the leadership and professional members in those organizations had a dramatic impact on me. In retrospect, I recognize the power of internalized racism because by the end of my graduate level training, I had come to accept and believe in my outsider status within the local community and the larger mental health profession.

However, entering the national-level organizations for counseling certainly changed my perspective. Although notions of Americanism, and conventional prototypes of leadership persist in the larger organizations as well, I came to learn that there was also a longer legacy of inclusive leadership pockets spread throughout various counseling divisions. It was by sheer chance that I encountered a call for emerging reviewers for the *Journal of Multicultural Counseling and Development*, led by Dr. Cirecie West-Olatunji. I immediately applied for the position as I had heard of the editor's inclusive leadership style. The culture within the editorial board was one of deep mutual respect and *commitment* to maintain the intellectual and demographic diversity. During our annual meetings, everyone on the board had a chance to share their feedback, including constructive comments. I recall this one moment when I was speaking about my experiences as a doctoral student of Color and the entire room went silent to empathetically listen to what I had to say. The team's sense of *curiosity* regarding my experiences, strong affiliation to support one of their members and commitment was evident to me at that moment. From then on, I have gone on to collaborate with various members of the board in research, scholarship advocacy, and service.

The explicit and *courageous* ILM planted a seed of leadership within me. Over the last two years of my leadership within the Association for Multicultural Counseling and Development, I have strived to carry forward the model. As I work with graduate students, mentees, and colleagues, I attempt to build a meaningful relationship with them, one that communicates that I value their humanity and unique contributions to the team. I have also recognized that as with all humans, I too come with my own internalized *biases*. Thus, I have moved toward a community style leadership, wherein I invite another professional and create a co-leadership model. Having a reliable and supportive team allows me to be cognizant of my biases. I have also carried my experiences with the journal into my own scholarship. Incorporating values of *courage* and *curiosity*, I have published several articles that further reiterate my *commitment* to inclusive leadership in the mental health profession. My journey continues as an emerging professional in the counseling and counselor education profession; I seek to continue to grow as an inclusive leader who contributes in shifting the tone of the profession, and communicates that all are welcome and valued in this field.

Culture-Centered Leadership Models

While scholars in the area of counseling have begun to develop frameworks for leadership identity within the discipline, there is insufficient discussion about leadership models that do not rely on traditional Eurocentric values and worldviews. In order to support the assertion that more Black and Brown counselor leaders should exist within professional organizations, it is important to begin by deconstructing our understanding of existing conventional frameworks, followed by exploring scholarship that promotes leader identity and development from a culture-centered perspective. Several scholars have offered examples of leadership identity from Asian-centered (Kodama & Dugan, 2019), Indigenous-centered (Sandefur & Deloria, 2018), Latinx-centered (Estepp et al., 2016), and African-centered perspectives (Metz, 2018). All of these frameworks provide a rationale for why it is so important to employ cultural values and worldviews outside of Eurocentric or Western ideology in order to facilitate effective leadership for Black, Indigenous, and People of Color (BIPOC) in counseling and other disciplines. Issues, such as interdependence vs. independence and radical humanism vs. transactional humanism are hallmarks of BIPOC leadership models. *Radical humanism* reflects a mandated emphasis on wellness of the whole as an end unto itself, whereas *transactional humanism* focuses on teamwork to benefit the individual with outcomes for the whole.

In formulating an African theory on leadership, Metz (2018) suggested that communitarianism is a salient feature in which the moral ethic of *ubuntu* (I am because we are) reflects the idea that our highest moral obligation is to become more fully human. By focusing on communion, individuals can achieve self-realization through a sense of belonging and acting for the common good. Thus, unlike servant leadership (Greenleaf, 2008), a commonly cited leadership framework in counseling (Herr, 2010), an Afro-communal ethic eschews teamwork efforts that support individualism and competition that predominate Eurocentrism. Rather, the *Afro-communal ethic* promotes leadership principles that facilitate communion as a means in of itself, representing the ultimate form of humanism.

Afro-Communal Ethic of Leadership

Based upon a review of the literature and discussion with a leadership scholar (C. Southwell, personal communication, December 22, 2020), we offer an alternative conceptualization of leadership identity in counseling that is founded upon *communal ethical leadership, i.e., Afro-Communal Ethic of Leadership*. Figure 1 presents a visual representation of the Afro-Communal Ethic of Leadership model. The leadership model is represented by X and Y axes in which the X-axis refers to a continuum of leadership attitudes and behaviors, from hegemonic to decolonizing. The Y-axis denotes the concept of interpersonal sense of belonging, from individualism to communitarianism. Within each quadrant are characteristics of leadership based upon the interaction of the two lines. Significantly, the quadrants are encased in two circles. The inner circle represents Afrocentricity as an identity, mission, and commitment that prioritizes the critical needs of Black and Brown communities. The outer circle denotes the organization's mission and goals specific to the leadership context.

The *first quadrant (Q1)* represents the blending of decolonization and communitarianism wherein the leadership characteristics are interdependence, responsibility to the whole, and being future-focused. *Colonialism* refers to the pervasive political, economic, social, cultural, and legal influence and dominance of one nation over another (Chilisa, 2016). On the other hand, *decolonization* refers to a deliberate and ongoing practice of deconstructing and dismantling ideologies that perpetuate notions of Western colonial superiority. In other words, decolonization is an act of rebellion in countering forces that reiterate White imperialist dominance (Chilisa, 2016). Some of the outcomes of operating from this framework are humanizing relationships and self-affirmations. Examples of existing theories reflective of this quadrant are womanism, Afrocentricity, and critical inquiries. This quadrant has a low Eurocentric dominance risk because of its focus on deconstructing the denigrating view of self and other forms of internalized oppression.

In the *second quadrant (Q2)*, leadership representing the interaction between hegemony (cultural dominance) and communitarianism, the leadership characteristics are utilitarianism and cooperation. Leaders using this framework typically demonstrate dependency and hoarded authority. Some examples of leadership frameworks from this perspective are servant leadership, teambuilding leadership, relational cultural theory, and feminism. This quadrant has a cautionary Eurocentric dominance risk that is represented by paternalism, fear of open conflict, and a leader who believes in only one right way.

The *third quadrant (Q3)* provides characteristics of hegemonic-individualistic leadership. The leadership characteristics from this framework are predominantly hierarchical and the effects are dehumanizing, marginalizing, and privileging. Some

Figure 1. Afro-communal ethic of leadership model

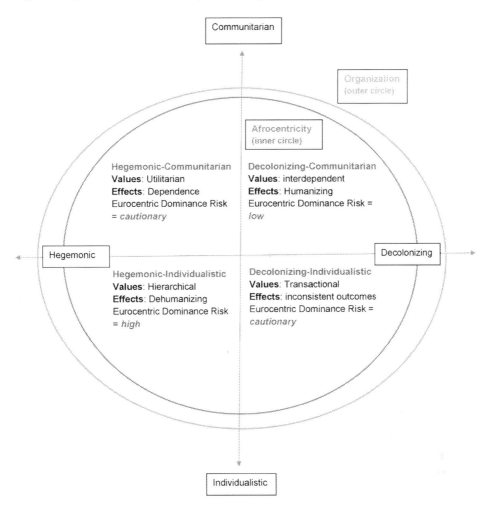

examples of this leadership style include trait leadership as well as style and skills approaches. The risk of Eurocentric dominance using this perspective is high due to the emphasis on individualism, dialectical (either/or) thinking, and perfectionism.

The *fourth quadrant (Q4)* represents a decolonizing and individualistic leadership style. The values from this particular perspective are humanitarianism, transactionalism, idiosyncrasy, and responsibility to the partial whole. The effects of this leadership style are fleeting outcomes and inconsistency. Some existing frameworks are situational leadership and leadership member exchange. The Eurocentric dominance risk for this quadrant is cautionary because of the emphasis on paternalism, the right to comfort, and power hoarding.

Organizations should not require that Black and Brown counselors who seek to become leaders adopt Eurocentric values in order to acquire effective leadership skills. However, the first step is to examine, evaluate, and address Eurocentrism in counselor training. Black and Brown emerging leaders need to become much more knowledgeable about their own cultural values and then seek culture-centered leadership models. In this case, we are presenting an alternative to Eurocentric leadership identity in counseling and other disciplines. It is imperative that those seeking leadership positions acknowledge that counselor training, both pre-service and in-service, needs to incorporate more cultural perspectives on leadership. To that end, it is necessary to engage in research on culture-centered leadership in order to propose and disseminate alternative models of leadership for Black and Brown counselors.

Personal Narrative: Dr. Cirecie West-Olatunji

As the editor-in-chief of an academic journal, I found it important to lead the editorial team using the lens of *Afro-communalism*. At the start of my tenure, I found that there was minimal communication between the readership and the editorial team as well as among the editorial team members. This may have accounted for the lack of a sense of relationship and responsibility to the whole. In particular, I found that there were a high number of negative responses to invitations to review papers by the editorial review board members. Additionally, there was not a clear understanding of the roles of the emerging reviewers and consulting elders. In considering an Afro-communal leadership framework, I sought to facilitate a *sense of community* in which we were all contributing to the whole. Here, the process (our relationships) was just as important as the product (publication of articles). Over the course of my time serving as editor, we were able to build strong relationships in which *mentoring* occurred at every level that increased the quality of the journal output, enhanced transparency, and augmented communication within and beyond the editorial team. Thus, by increasing the sense of belonging, not only did the journal become more self-actualized, we did too individually and collectively.

RECOMMENDATIONS

In this section, we discuss our recommendations for counseling professionals and the larger leadership within the profession. These recommendations are based on an extensive literature review and our professional leadership experiences.

1. **Deconstruct Eurocentric ideologies:** In order for Black and Brown leaders to be effective, it is important that they deconstruct the Eurocentric ideologies that are embedded within our education and training. We need to excise the cultural hegemony that serves as a foundation for our conceptualizations of individuals and institutions. The Eurocentrism in our training is so deeply embedded in our thinking that it can be difficult to critically deconstruct the self-alienating, culturally hegemonic ideology that may have become all too familiar at this point. Decolonizing our leadership frameworks might be the first step toward becoming an effective leader in counseling as well as in other disciplines.

2. **BIPOC knowledge systems:** We need to aggressively seek new knowledge that is framed within Black, Indigenous, and People of Color (BIPOC) cultural worldviews. Given the plethora of knowledge disseminated within our traditional educational and academic contexts, this is not an easy task. However, there are scholars who are theorizing and engaging in research that is culture-centered and counters Eurocentric philosophies. Black and Brown leaders and emerging leaders in counseling need to engage in critical dialogue about existing leadership frameworks and establish new frameworks for leading organizations and institutions, particularly those impacting Black and Brown communities. Transformative leadership models, such as Afro-communal ethics, emphasize the need for epistemic change, resulting from social action. It is for the good of the whole.

3. **Speaking out:** Black and Brown counseling leaders need to avoid being silent/complicit when it comes to witnessing, experiencing, and/or hearing of issues related to discrimination and marginalization. It is important that we speak out against such acts of aggression, and when other Black and Brown counseling leaders, especially early career/untenured, speak out (i.e., go against Eurocentrism of the profession). We as a community need to support them as the support is greater when seasoned, tenured Black and Brown leaders come alongside them and/or add their voices to the call for justice. As Arredondo and colleagues (2020) state, we as a counseling profession, including Black and Brown counseling leaders, need to be social justice advocates, actively seeking to unmask White supremacy and White racism within our profession. After all, "silence is violence."

4. **Reflection:** We recommend that you pause and take inventory of the situation or your experience (including your emotional experiences of anger, sadness, etc.) related to your identity being minoritized, minimized, or Othered. In this moment of reflection, rest, take care of your mental and physical health and wellness, then re-engage in the vital work of challenging, disrupting, and rewriting the narrative of White America, inviting other BIPOC voices to the

conversation and the solution of building a "United" America (Durodoye, 1999).

5. **Mentorship:** Extant evidence in counseling literature indicates that relational, and supportive mentorship can prove to be critical for emerging scholars. West-Olatunji and Anandavalli (in press) discuss that mentees benefit from relationship-building strategies that foster greater trust, community, and investment in the organization. We invite established Black and Brown leaders in the field to initiate and expand on mentorship opportunities to connect with emerging scholars in the field. Established leaders in the field may provide pivotal guidance for scholars who may experience isolation, stress, and frustration due to racial disparities within and outside of the profession.

6. **Community cultural wealth:** Yosso's (2005) scholarship on community cultural wealths indicate that Black and Brown communities often rely on unique cultural assets to navigate a biased and racialized system. She identifies several capitals including social capital, wherein individuals draw strength from their communities to persist and thrive in a highly stratified society (Yosso, 2005). We invite Black and Brown leaders in the counseling field to advantage their social capital through building networking platforms, community circles, and fellowship. Social capital can potentially offset experiences of isolation and marginalization in the profession and help individuals support other Black and Brown leaders in meaningful ways. In the second author's personal experience, a Black and Brown community was developed during her doctoral training to offer and leverage support to students of Color.

7. **Pay it forward:** We request Black and Brown leaders to pay it forward. Given the relatively fewer mentors of Color in the profession (as compared to White identifying mentors), we invite Black and Brown leaders to support emerging scholars in diverse ways. These measures may include developing scholarship funds that support Black and Brown scholarships, inviting emerging Black and Brown scholars to collaborate on research work, offering service and leadership positions to deserving Black and Brown professionals and students, and advocating for change in the profession at a larger level as well.

CONCLUSION

In this chapter, we identified three models of Black and Brown counseling leadership that specifically center values of inclusivity, social justice, and decolonization in response to Othering and Americanism. Through our personal narratives that reflect our unique intersecting identities, we examined our journeys as beginning, intermediate, and advanced leaders in the counseling profession. Critical incidents throughout the dual pandemic and an extensive literature review indicated to us that scholarship in Black and Brown leadership is needed in the counseling and allied professions. We invite scholars to pursue scholarships examining the leadership experiences of Black and Brown leaders using culturally responsive methodologies, which can serve as a pipeline in advancing counseling as an inclusive and equitable profession.

REFERENCES

American Counseling Association. (2014). *ACA code of ethics*. Author.

American Counseling Association. (2020a). *About us*. https://www.counseling.org/about-us/about-aca

American Counseling Association. (2020b). *Membership report*. Author.

Anandavalli, S., Borders, L. D., & Kniffin, L. E. (2021). "Because here, White is right": Mental health experiences of international graduate students of color from a critical race perspective. *International Journal for the Advancement of Counseling*. Advance online publication. doi:10.100710447-021-09437-x PMID:34054168

Anandavalli, S., Harrichand, J. J. S., & Litam, S. D. A. (2020). Counseling international students in times of uncertainty: A critical feminist and bioecological approach. *The Professional Counselor*, *10*(3), 365–375. doi:10.15241a.10.3.365

Arredondo, P., D'Andrea, M., & Lee, C. (2020, September 10). Unmasking White supremacy and racism in the counseling profession. *Counseling Today Online*. https://ct.counseling.org/tag/topic-ct-multiculturalism-diversity/

Brown, D. L. (2020, June 3). 'It was a modern-day lunching': Violent deaths reflect a brutal American legacy. *National Geographic: History & Culture – Race in America*. https://www.nationalgeographic.com/history/2020/06/history-of-lynching-violent-deaths-reflect-brutal-american-legacy/

Bryant, R., Coker, A., Durodoye, B., McCollum, V., Pack-Brown, S., Constantine, M., & O'Bryant, B. (2005). Having our say: African American women, diversity, and counseling. *Journal of Counseling and Development*, *83*(3), 313–319. doi:10.1002/j.1556-6678.2005.tb00349.x

Centers for Disease Control and Prevention. (2020a, August 18). *COVID-19 hospitalization and death by race/ethnicity*. https://www.cdc.gov/coronavirus/2019-ncov/covid-data/investigations-discovery/hospitalization-death-by-race-ethnicity.html

Centers for Disease Control and Prevention. (2020b, June 25). *COVID-19 in racial and ethnic minority groups*. https://stacks.cdc.gov/view/cdc/89820/cdc_89820_DS1.pdf

Chan, C. D., Harrichand, J. J. S., Anandavalli, S., Vaishnav, S., Chang, C. Y., Hyun, J., & Band, M. P. (in press). Mapping solidarity, liberation, and activism: An autoethnography of Asian American and Pacific Islander (AAPI) leaders in counseling. *Journal of Mental Health Counseling*.

Chilisa, B., Major, T. E., Gaotlhobogwe, M., & Mokgolodi, H. (2016). Decolonizing and indigenizing evaluation practice in Africa: Toward African relational evaluation approaches. *The Canadian Journal of Program Evaluation*, *30*(3), 313–328. doi:10.3138/cjpe.30.3.05

Council for Accreditation of Counseling and Related Educational Programs. (2015). *2016 CACREP standards*. http://www.cacrep.org/wp-content/uploads/2017/07/2016-Standards-with-Glossary-7.2017.pdf

Crenshaw, K. (1989). Demarginalizing the intersection of race and sex: A Black feminist critique of antidiscrimination doctrine, feminist theory and antiracist politics. *University of Chicago Legal Forum*, *140*, 139–167. https://chicagounbound.uchicago.edu/cgi/viewcontent.cgi?article=1052&context=uclf

Crenshaw, K. (1991). Mapping the margins: Intersectionality, identity politics, and violence against women of color. *Stanford Law Review*, *43*(6), 1241–1299. doi:10.2307/1229039

Dillon, B., & Bourke, J. (2016). *The six signature traits of inclusive leadership: Thriving in a diverse world*. Deloitte University Press. https://www2.deloitte.com/content/dam/insights/us/articles/six-signature-traits-of-inclusive-leadership/DUP-3046_Inclusive-leader_vFINAL.pdf

Durodoye, B. A. (1999). On the receiving end. *Journal of Counseling and Development*, *77*(1), 45–47. doi:10.1002/j.1556-6676.1999.tb02416.x

Edwards, F., Lee, H., & Esposito, M. (2019). Risk of being killed by police use of force in the United States by age, race-ethnicity, and sex. *Proceedings of the National Academy of Sciences (PANS) of the United States of America, 116*(34), 16793–16798. 10.1073/pnas.1821204116

Estepp, C. M., Velasco, J. G., Culbertson, A. L., & Conner, N. W. (2017). An investigation into mentoring practices of faculty who mentor undergraduate researchers at a Hispanic Serving Institution. *Journal of Hispanic Higher Education*, *16*(4), A338–A358. doi:10.1177/1538192716661906

Greenleaf, R. (2008). *The servant as leader*. The Greenleaf Center for Servant Leadership.

Herr, E. H. (2010). *Leadership: A position paper*. https://cdn.ymaws.com/www.csi-net.org/resource/resmgr/research,_essay,_papers,_articles/leadership_herr_position_pap.pdf

Horowitz, J. M., Brown, A., & Cox, K. (2019, April 9). Race in American 2019. *Pew Research Center: Social & Demographic Trends*. https://www.pewsocialtrends.org/2019/04/09/race-in-america-2019/

Hunter, E. A., Hanks, M. A., Holman, A., Curry, D., Bvunzawabaya, B., Jones, B., & Abdullah, T. (2020). The hurdles are high: Women of color leaders in counseling psychology. *Journal of Counseling Psychology*. Advance online publication. doi:10.1037/cou0000526 PMID:32584056

Inwood, J., & Alderman, D. (2016). Taking down the flag is just a start: Toward the memory-work of racial reconciliation in white supremacist America. *Southeastern Geographer*, *56*(1), 9–15. doi:10.1353go.2016.0003

Kendi, I. X. (2019). *How to be an antiracist*. One World.

Kodama, C. M., & Dugan, J. P. (2019). Understanding the role of collective racial esteem and resilience in the development of Asian American leadership self efficacy. *Journal of Diversity in Higher Education*. Advance online publication. doi:10.1037/dhe0000137

Litam, S. D. A., Ausloos, C. D., & Harrichand, J. J. S. (in press). Stress and resilience among professional counselors during the COVID-19 pandemic. *Journal of Counseling and Development*.

Litam, S. D. A., Harrichand, J. J. S., & Ausloos, C. D. (2020, September 11). *The effects of COVID-19 related stress on a national sample of professional counselors* [Conference session]. Association for Assessment and Research in Counseling (AARC) 2020 Online Summit.

Litam, S. D. A., & Hipolito-Delgado, C. P. (2021). When being "essential" illuminates disparities: Counseling clients affected by COVID-19. *Journal of Counseling and Development*, *99*(1), 3–10. doi:10.1002/jcad.12349

Lopez, A. E. (2015). Navigating cultural borders in diverse contexts: Building capacity through culturally responsive leadership and critical praxis. *Multicultural Education Review*, *7*(3), 171–184. doi:10.1080/2005615X.2015.1072080

Lopez, A. E. (2016). *Culturally responsive and socially just leadership in diverse contexts: From theory to action.* Palgrave MacMillan. doi:10.1057/978-1-137-53339-5

Mapping Police Violence. (2020, December 8). https://mappingpoliceviolence.org/

Metz, T. (2018). An African theory of good leadership. *African Journal of Business Ethics, 12*(2), 36–53. doi:10.15249/12-2-204

Meyers, L. (2017, October 25). Making the counseling profession more diverse. *Counseling Today.* https://ct.counseling.org/2017/10/making-counseling-profession-diverse/

Peters, H., Luke, M., Bernard, J., & Trepal, H. (2020). Socially just and culturally responsive leadership within counseling and counseling psychology: A grounded theory investigation. *The Counseling Psychologist, 48*(7), 953–985. doi:10.1177/0011000020937431

Ratts, M. J., Sing, A. A., Nassar-McMillan, S., Butler, S. K., & McCullough, J. R. (2015). *Multicultural and social justice counseling competencies.* https://www.counseling.org/knowledge-center/competencies

Ricento, T. (2003). The Discursive Construction of Americanism. *Discourse & Society, 14*(5), 611–637. doi:10.1177/09579265030145004

Sandefur, G., & Deloria, P. J. (2018). Indigenous leadership. *Dædalus: Journal of the American Academy of Arts & Sciences, 147*(2), 124–135. doi:10.1162/DAED_a_00496

Schild, L., Ling, C., Blackburn, J., Stringhini, G., Zhang, Y., & Zannettou, S. (2020). *"Go eat a bat, Chang!": An early look on the emergence of sinophobic behavior on web communities in the face of COVID-19.* https://arxiv.org/pdf/2004.04046.pdf

Shin, R. Q., Welch, J. C., Kaya, A. E., Yeung, J. G., Obana, C., Sharma, R., Vernay, C. N., & Yee, S. (2017). The intersectionality framework and identity intersections in the journal of counseling psychology and the counseling psychologist: A content analysis. *Journal of Counseling Psychology, 64*(5), 458–474. doi:10.1037/cou0000204 PMID:29048193

Smith, M. L., & Roysircar, G. (2010). African American male leaders in counseling: Interviews with five AMCD past presidents. *Journal of Multicultural Counseling and Development, 38*(4), 242–256. doi:10.1002/j.2161-1912.2010.tb00134.x

Storlie, C., Parker-Wright, M., & Woo, H. (2015). Multicultural leadership development: A qualitative analysis of emerging leaders in counselor education. *Journal of Counselor Leadership and Advocacy*, 2(2), 154–169. doi:10.1080/232 6716X.2015.1054078

Toporek, R. L., & Daniels, J. (2018). *American counseling association advocacy competencies*. https://www.counseling.org/docs/default-source/competencies/aca-advocacy-competencies-updated-may-2020.pdf?sfvrsn=f410212c_4

Victorian Equal Opportunity and Human Rights Commission. (2013). Waiter, is that inclusion in my soup? A new recipe to improve business performance. *Deloitte*. https://www2.deloitte.com/content/dam/Deloitte/au/Documents/human-capital/deloitte-au-hc-diversity-inclusion-soup-0513.pdf

West-Olatunji, C. A., & Anandavalli, S. (in press). It's all about mentorship. In J. M. Swank & C. A. Barrio Minton (Eds.), *Critical incidents in counselor education: Teaching, supervision, research, leadership, and advocacy*. Wiley.

World Health Organization. (2021, June 9). *WHO coronavirus disease (COVID-19) dashboard*. https://covid19.who.int/

Yosso, T. J. (2005). Whose culture has capital? A critical race theory discussion of community cultural wealth. *Race, Ethnicity and Education*, 8(1), 69–91. doi:10.1080/1361332052000341006

Chapter 9
The Transformational Change Agent Equation:
Reziliency of Native American Women in Leadership Roles in Higher Education

Tamara C. Cheshire
Folsom Lake College, USA

Crystal D. Martinez-Alire
Folsom Lake College, USA

Vanessa Esquivido
California State University, Chico, USA

Molly Springer
California State University, San Bernardino, USA

ABSTRACT

As Native women professors, counselors, and administrators within higher education, the four authors will focus on transformational change within oppressive environments, addressing institutionalized racism stemming from a colonial history of education. The authors will discuss identified barriers including operating in an oppressive work environment which can sometimes render us invisible and silent for self-preservation, threats to our positions from taking a stand against racial or cultural inequity, and resisting assimilation strategies created by structural racism. It is important to share experiences with working in systematically oppressive environments and the covert ways in which Black, Indigenous, People of Color (BIPOC) are transformational change agents, leaders against racial and cultural oppression.

DOI: 10.4018/978-1-7998-7235-1.ch009

INTRODUCTION

We have always been very resilient—but our resilience doesn't mean that our lives are ever easy. - Benaway, Seven Quotes About Resiliency from Black and Indigenous, Queer, Trans, Women

Note. Gwen Benaway identifies as a "trans girl of Anishnaabe and Métis descent."

As Native women professors, counselors, and administrators within higher education, the prior quote about resiliency and our lives being anything but easy, rings true. Transformational change within oppressive environments and addressing institutionalized racism inherent within the colonized system of education is never easy, but it is needed and necessary for Black, Indigenous, People of Color (BIPOC) student success.

The four Native women professionals writing this chapter have identified several barriers to transformational change in higher education. Barriers identified include (a) operating in a hostile, oppressive work environment which can sometimes render BIPOC professors, counselors, and administrators invisible and silent for self-preservation or challenge these professionals to resist, further taxing their mental health; (b) assimilation strategies to prevent transformational change; and (c) threats to positions and livelihood from taking a stand against racial or cultural inequity. The authors have offered their professional experiences throughout the chapter. It is important to share experiences from working in systematically oppressive environments and the ways in which BIPOC are transformational change agents/ leaders against racial and cultural oppression. The recent emergence of defining Black and Indigenous representation is called into focus through the acronym BIPOC rather than POC which indicates non-white individuals. Therefore centering Black and Indigenous voices is a politic the authors are asserting in this chapter.

The authors discuss efforts to resist assimilationist strategies historically driven to crush creativity and halt transformational change and propose a transformational change agent equation. The transformational change agent equation is based on the needs of transformational leaders being met, minus barriers inherent within higher education, plus Native American *reziliency* (Belcourt-Dittloff, 2006), and strategies to combat the barriers inherent with the colonized system, resulting in transformational change to the institution.

TRANSFORMATIONAL CHANGE AGENT EQUATION

Met Needs – Barriers + Rezilience + Strategies = Transformational Change

The foundational framework of this chapter centers on the areas of the transformational change agent equation which include: met needs (self-care), a description of some of the significant barriers to change, discussion of Native "reziliency" (Belcourt-Dittloff, 2006), and highlighting strategies for change. Each section will address the transformational change agent equation and will be described in further detail. For the authors to share their professional experiences and narratives in the sections identified, the history of racism within the educational system must be examined in the proceeding section.

History of Education Colonized

In order to speak truth to power, one must first enable oneself to see the truth, the truth of the profoundly damaging legacy of colonization (Seward, 2019, p. X).

Structural Racism and Violence

Structural racism exists in all areas of education, and it is based in oppressive settler colonialism and pervasive in policies and practices. Structural and systemic racism is inherent in the very framework of educational institutions, making it difficult for Black, Indigenous People of Color (BIPOC) to lead (Archuleta et al., 2000; Brave Heart & DeBruyn, 1998; Conley, 2008; Deyhle & Swisher, 1997; Wolfe, 2006; Wright & Tierney, 1991). Colonial educational institutions have been created to be oppressive in order to prevent BIPOC entry into middle- and upper-class status, thus perpetuating the systems of class, race, and gender oppression. Lomawaima (1999) suggests that educational institutions were created to propagate stereotypes, inequitable treatment, and the domestication of Native peoples in order to transform and eradicate Indian self government, self determination and self-education (pg. 3).

Structural violence is defined by Norwegian sociologist Johan Galtung, as "meaningful as a blueprint, as an abstract form without social life used to threaten people into subordination" (Galtung, 1969, p.172). Structural racism and violence have inherently been and continue to be a part of the educational system for Native Americans. The Native American experience within American education has largely been one of assimilation, betrayal, and oppression (Adams, 1995; Lowamaima, 1999; Reyhner & Dodd, 1995; Stemlau, 2005; Szasz, 1999; Trennert, 1988).

Boarding Schools: Foundation of Structural Racism and Violence

Education itself and educational institutions (prek-12, community college and 4-year colleges and universities) are continuously oppressive environments for Native American students, faculty, counselors, staff, and administrators. It has been argued for many years the colonial system of education is based on a foundation of oppressive ideologies of assimilation, civilization, and Christianization that align to the dispossession of Indigenous Peoples lands, cultures, spiritual, economic, and societal structures (CCEAL, 2019; Jackson et al., 2003; Smith, 1999, 2012). Empirical evidence suggests the United States educational system has long been an oppressive agent in the continued subjugation of Native peoples (Braveheart, 1999; Deyhle & Swisher, 1997; Esquivido, 2019; Guillory & Wolverton, 2008; Lomawaima, 1999; Pavel & Padilla, 1993; Springer, 2015).

It is important to consider context as it relates to how Native American people feel toward the United States education system. For example, the boarding school experience was an instrument of colonization that had an extremely negative impact on Native American society, culture, families, and overall wellness. As a result, boarding school systems left a generation of American Indians traumatized (Braveheart, 1999; Deyhle & Swisher 1997) and not apt to trust American formal systems of education (Springer, 2015). The damage resulted in intergenerational trauma that continues to greatly impact many Native people today (Martinez-Alire, 2013). The remaining effect has been an overwhelming critique of the United States education system by generations of Native Americans, claiming that the system of education is not only hegemonic, but oppressive, culturally unresponsive or invalidating of Native epistemologies (Black, 2002; Brayboy, 2005b; Cajete, 2005; Lowamaima, 1994; Stephen, 1999).

By understanding the historical mistrust of the educational system, these Native authors working within the higher educational institutional settings are able to provide support to Native students who have a tendency to be reluctant in trusting others. This history clearly impacts today's Native students (CCEAL, 2019). Establishing healthy relationships with Native students can build trust and help students feel connected to the college campus, ideal for student success (Springer, 2015).

The next section addresses the importance of met needs, specifically self-care, as a segment of the transformational change agent equation, which can be used against the barriers of working within higher educational systems.

Transformational Change Agent Equation - Met Needs (Self Care)

These are the tools that we [Native]...people use to build a decolonizing praxis that shows how ceremony is theory and knowledge embodied through song, dance, and movement. (Baldy, 2018, p. 126)

To take care of others, a leader must first take care of themselves (Williams, 2020). For Native women, taking care means many things, including healing from historical trauma (Braveheart & DeBruyn, 1998), an ongoing process; practicing cultural and spiritual traditions (Risling Baldy, 2018); attending cultural celebrations and community gatherings; and taking time to build and maintain affective relationships with children, families, community members, professional colleagues, and ourselves (Gunn Allen, 1992). As professionals there are expectations to fulfill responsibilities to the Native community by participating in ceremony and caretaking of elders, children, and families. These obligations can be jeopardized by spending additional time at work.

Author's Experience

I think the added work of being a BIPOC and the only BIPOC of a specific racial/ ethnic group, is something that we do automatically because we care about the success of students of color; but it can also be harmful to us, our jobs and our health. Being asked to do too much is sometimes overwhelming and can be harmful to our health. We have to know when and how to strategically say no in certain circumstances for our own mental health and well-being.

A level of involvement and service is expected from every college or university employee. If an individual is the only or one of a few Native people on campus, colleagues and supervisors pull at their time and energies, wanting them to serve on committees and workgroups. Native counselors, faculty, staff, and administrators are often taken advantage of and there are high incidents of burnout, which inevitably either hinders or prevents transformational change. As agents of change, Native professionals must be aware of this dilemma that can prevent them from being granted tenure or longevity because of over commitment. Non-Native allies on campus can be of assistance by running interference and external Native organizations can place pressure on the college institution to support Native employees. Additional external support can provide an opportunity for the Native employee's voice to be heard. Having tribal agencies and governments involved in a partnership with the college can help build support for Native employees working within the higher educational system. Other examples and personal narratives within the college setting follow.

Author's Experience

Racial and cultural oppression are foundationally built into the workspaces in universities. The conscious defunding of Ethnic Studies departments across the nation for years is systematic and structural racism. California passed legislation AB 1460 to force state universities to require students to take an Ethnic Studies class in order to graduate. As of fall 2020, each California State University (CSU)—23 CSU's in total—are scrambling to pass resolutions to implement this new law on their independent campuses. BIPOC in Ethnic Studies departments are now having to work harder than ever to protect this requirement in Ethnic Studies. For example, BIPOC are continuously sought out to be on every committee demonstrating each University's "dedication" to diversity, BIPOC are often small in population. Specifically, with CSU's there is a lack of California Indian representation who are indigenous to the land on which every CSU campus is situated. BIPOC are now taking on implementation of this AB 1460 bill with no extra compensation, no release time, and more workload. This is racial and cultural oppression in the workspace. As BIPOC we often experience "burn out" too quickly and then are told by our white colleagues to say "no" to things. This is not our reality. If we do not show up to these meetings, we do not get a voice. We don't want people speaking for us, but when there is so little representation, this kind of work is never-ending. This labor without recognition falls on BIPOC repeatedly within institutions. Yet, BIPOC are taxed for time and continue to advocate for more BIPOC to be hired within their colleges and universities, and often are unheard. There needs to be a change within the educational system to grant release time and recognize that the community work is of high value.

Self-care and support from family, the Native community, Native colleagues, and tribe are important factors that help Native professionals endure the hardships they face in this environment, but family can also bring challenges.

Author's Experience

Another tricky peril of being a Native professional is the reality that many of us have children and spouses who also happen to be Native and with that comes a myriad of cultural obligations and other issues that are embedded in things like healing, trauma, and spirituality. It's difficult to know that family members are not well, and you are working to serve students and help them through a myriad of challenges, meanwhile you cannot help cousin Joe with his alcohol codependency or sister Sue who tried to commit suicide last year because of her past sexual trauma. It makes you feel like a failure some days.

Non-Native allies can be supportive in a number of ways. These include (a) serving as a soundboard to hear and understand the frustrations suffered by Native professionals in a hostile environment; (b) acting as a buffer to the racist attacks on Native professionals; (c) calling out microaggressions; (d) advocating for Native voices to be heard; and (e) aiding in the tenure process and longevity of Native professionals and supporting transformational change recommended by Native professionals in higher education.

This comprehensive support system consisting of family, Native colleagues, Native community, tribe, and non-Native allies assists in the needs of Native professionals being met and can help to combat the oppressive barriers that exist in higher education. The next section will focus on identifying barriers within the change agent equation.

Transformational Change Agent Equation – Barriers

Leaders who do not act dialogically, but insist on imposing their decisions, do not organize the people–they manipulate them. They do not liberate, nor are they liberated: they oppress. —Paulo Freire, Pedagogy of the Oppressed

As discussed earlier in this chapter, structural racism and violence persist in higher education, creating inherent barriers perpetuated by the system to prevent change and maintain the status quo. Identifying these said barriers is a first step to addressing the outright oppression that exists for BIPOC professionals to change the system and transform higher education. In this section, the authors identify common barriers known in BIPOC spaces for combating structural racism and violence as part of the equation for transformational change.

Operating in an Oppressive Work Environment

Working in a structurally oppressive environment that is intended to be supportive of diversity and inclusivity can take its toll on an individual's mental health. This type of environment can insist on the assimilation of the Native professional, which can render them invisible and silent for self-preservation purposes or trigger resistance; both are taxing to physical and mental health (Wood & Harris, 2021).

Author's Experience

As a Native American woman college administrator, it's been a difficult journey to be working for a field with a sordid past in supporting Native peoples. I doubt many Native educators, administrators, etc.; work in education because they love the system of education; in fact, it's often the opposite. We go into the field to change it for the better for Native students. So, we throw ourselves into the battlefield, and are often on the front lines of an epistemological war zone. It feels fatiguing in that way.

Paulo Freire (Freire & Ramos, 1970) mentioned structural oppression can be so overwhelming that it prevents people from reaching their potential as transformational change agents. Native professionals are also relying on their positions to financially support their families and contribute to their communities. Threats to these positions are meant to prevent Native professionals from taking a stand against racial or cultural inequity and making transformational change.

Hiring Processes

Colonialism is inherent within the American education system, and this system manifests racial and cultural oppression within hiring procedures impacting everything from student services to curriculum development and teaching practices used within the classroom (Springer, 2015). It is rare when BIPOC professionals are hired within higher education but even more unlikely that Native American professionals are hired within these systems.

The hiring process that limits the number of BIPOC at any given college or university campus also systematically reduces BIPOC support at these institutions. When hiring committees are comprised of the same people who perpetuate colonialism within the learning environment, we cannot expect this system to change.

When BIPOC professionals are hired and volunteer for hiring committees, the trauma they experience being threatened with their livelihood or job to go with the flow of the committee is immense. Unless systems of support are created within the institution of higher education to challenge the structure, it is a dangerous environment for newly hired BIPOC and those working within the system (in a bubble of sorts surrounded by a few allies) to maintain their positions at all costs to make change after achieving position security or academic tenure.

Tokenism

Few—if any—Native American professionals are hired within the higher education setting (Tierney, 1991). Those who are hired have often experienced being a token. Tokenism occurs when one individual is held responsible for representing an entire group of people. Tokenism (Kanter, 1977) can lead to quick burnout (Hassell et al., 2011) through the additional responsibilities that Native women assume in order to educate not only students, but their colleagues. Tokenism removes the ability for Native women to have the impact on transformational change that is needed because Native women are often called upon for specific limited roles. For example: being asked to speak only on Indigenous People's Day. It is difficult to enact change in existing oppressive policies and practices in the first place, let alone with this additional burden.

Author's Experience

When there are limited BIPOC faculty and staff within institutions and having the responsibility to be on every committee, a way to discredit them is by calling them a "token." This is an oppressive tool that many of us fall into, a way to point the finger and blame some of the only BIPOCs we have on campuses. To tokenize is to oppress. Many of us, BIPOC, know what that feels like to be the only one in the room, or the only one on emails being consulted, the only one who is experiencing the workplace in this way. This is a great amount of pressure to perform in a certain manner because if not it can create unfair expectations and set a precedent for new Native employees' coming into the college setting.

There are certain ways a leader can identify if they are viewed as a token versus a transformational leader. One way is how administrators, faculty, and other key members on campus approach them, such as when suggestions are glazed over or not heard. The authors of this article are women of color and have experienced being viewed as token leaders, which has carried a heavy cultural tax. For example, being one of few limited Native American women within a higher educational campus or educational setting can create a dynamic in which a person is called upon to represent not only their voice, but that of an entire Native community.

Author's Experience

As a leader, one barrier was being one of few full-time faculty members identified as Native American, so most of the work fell to one person. There have been times when certain campus events occur yearly (e.g., Native American month or California Indian Day) and being from the Native American population or community, it is assumed that a specific individual will take on any extra workload or be the main contact for the entire population. Whenever there is Native American reference, the Native person is brought into the discussion which can lead to faculty burnout if that individual is the only one being called upon. In the planning of campus events, such as bringing in Native American guest speakers or dance groups, the Native person at the college is the one to reach out usually and becomes the main point of contact for the college and they are expected to have recommendations or connections to the entire Native community. This is just one example in which a leader from a specific ethnic community can be viewed as token vs. transformational.

Being expected to contribute to the higher education setting is one thing, but after contributing time and energy to various committees and projects to transform the college, being made invisible and ignored once more is an overt act of aggression and a persistent barrier.

Multiple barriers exist for BIPOC in systems of higher education. Operating in an oppressive work environment, making sure hiring processes are fair and equitable to BIPOC professionals and tokenism are just a few discussed in this chapter. The next section will focus on the transformational change agent equation variable, reziliency (Belcourt-Dittloff, 2006).

Transformational Change Agent Equation – Reziliency

It is this spirit of hope, determination, bravery, courage, and ferocious love that creates resilient people and resilient recovery from loss and trauma. It is this spirit that will help American Indian people today and tomorrow. (Belcourt-Dittloff, 2006, p. 107)

According to Waller et al. (2002), American Indian communities have social and cultural capital, which promote educational resilience and persistence (Starks, 2010). American Indian individuals and communities have overcome harsh conditions through what Belcourt-Dittloff (2006) calls reziliency. Reziliency means resiliency factors, skills, and processes used to cope with oppressive conditions from a Native lens (Belcourt-Dittloff, 2006). With a nod to reservation survival, reziliency theory is not exclusive: Belcourt-Dittloff did not mean for the term to pertain specifically to American Indians living on reservations, partially because a majority of Native peoples live in urban areas and partially because she wanted to coin a term that would encompass the psychological ways in which both reservation and urban Natives adapt in positive ways to adversity or trauma.

In experiencing structural racism throughout their lifetime, Native professional leaders have employed reziliency strategies to manage the stressors of structural racism to cope. The reziliency theoretical framework provides a basis for the aforementioned transformational change agent equation derived from Cheshire's (2013) student success equation, based on needs being met minus barriers, plus resiliency characteristics, which equal student success. This equation is rooted in TribalCRT, i.e., Tribal Critical Race Theory (Brayboy, 2005a), with institutional barriers identified as deficit model thinking, assimilation strategies, lack of cultural competence or understanding, and institutional racism stemming from colonialism, applied to students and BIPOC professionals. Brayboy (2006) addresses the continued impact of colonization on Natives and further explains how colonization equates to European American thought, knowledge, and power structures present in modern day United States society, government, politics, law, and education. Native professionals in higher education develop forms of resistance against oppression, discrimination, and assimilationist strategies created by structural racism and are often pressured into taking a stand against racial or cultural inequity, which often jeopardizes positions.

Author's Experience

To strategically obtain support from allies. To listen to advice from other BIPOC in the same organization. To weigh costs vs. benefits scenarios. To learn how to play chess. We often have to make sacrifices that others in our positions never have to make and this means that we might have to stop advocating for change in one area, to obtain change in another.

Allies can be of help in this instance, running interference, listening to our concerns, and advocating that our voices be heard, but resilience and persistence come from our cultural and professional experiences fighting against oppression and discrimination, maintained by structurally racist institutions. The development of strategies to persist and cope is imperative under these circumstances. In the next section, the authors will describe and focus on the strategies for transformational change.

Transformational Change Agent Equation – Strategies

We are not re-creating rote actions that are divorced from our understanding of the complex epistemologies that make up our cultural ceremonies; instead, these ceremonies allow us an embodied theoretical framework for healing, reclaiming Native feminisms, and effecting decolonization. (Baldy, 2018, p. 126)

Becoming a catalyst for transformational change is difficult; it takes strategy. One must navigate how to enact and create certain policies and practices to support transformational change. Coming from a distinct disadvantage as a BIPOC makes this application even more difficult as the target of the discrimination. This section will focus on the professional experiences of Native women, provide definitions, and identify strategies to implement transformational change.

Decolonization as a Strategy

Colonization is when a dominant group or system takes over and exploits and extracts from the land and its Native peoples (Smith, 2013). Colonialism and imperialism are built within education and help maintain the educational system in the United States (Lomawaima, 1999); this system manifests racial and cultural oppression within hiring procedures, impacting everything from student services to curriculum development and teaching practices used within the classroom.

Anti-colonial thought calls for a critical awareness of the social relations and power issues embedded in the ways of organizing the production, interrogation, validation and dissemination of knowledge in order to challenge social oppression and subvert domination. It also calls for acknowledging accountability and power (Dei & Kempf, 2006).

Decolonization is a strategy for how BIPOC in higher education can thwart structural racism. Yet, decolonization is not a single event or prescribed blueprint but a complex and contested process of unlearning and undoing centuries of colonial ideas, desires, and infrastructures (Stein & Andreotti, 2016). It can be part of the transformational change applied to dismantle structural racism and violence, but it is a lengthy process. An example of how organizations have embraced decolonization as a theory of change would be how the American College Personnel Association has included a more extensive acknowledgement on their conference site and now has a "Strategic Imperative for Racial Justice and Decolonization" and accompanying syllabus (ACPA, 2018). It takes time to decolonize a campus because structural racism is embedded in the architecture of the campus; from the way the buildings are built, to the layout of the desks in a classroom which influences and is influenced by the curriculum content and how that is taught; the efforts to decolonize are immense and can be overwhelming. The strategy is to take one day at a time to begin to dismantle the structural racism that is inherent in the system and to recruit allies to help in this process.

BIPOC Representation

Having diverse representation through hiring BIPOC professionals in tenure track and more secured, tenured positions in higher education leads to creating an inclusive environment that is significant within the educational setting (Paradiso, 2020). Adjunct, part time, or temporary positions do not lead to long term, sustainable changes within the system. Equitable hiring processes and procedures are essential to a diverse employee workforce as well (Wood & Harris, 2021). Another way to address racial inequity is to ensure there is diversity on campus committees. A leader, working at the college should be active in committees like curriculum, matriculation, budget, equity, and academic senate to address issues on a broader scale. Having diverse representation leads to creating an inclusive environment that is significant within the educational setting (Paradiso, 2020).

Creating a Supportive Environment for BIPOC

Creating a supportive environment in which BIPOC professionals work is imperative to transformational change. As a transformational leader, it is important to inspire, motivate, and appeal to followers through high expectations in accordance with a supportive environment (Nevarez & Wood, 2010). Creating a welcoming and inclusive culture for everyone enriches the environment, enhances student learning and opportunities, and builds a support network for BIPOC leaders. There should be a support network within the organization where BIPOC leaders can make change without being threatened, employee voices can be heard, and strategies for change can be recommended.

Behaviors that do not support racial identity need to be addressed at the leadership level and requires institutional administration to listen and acknowledge those employees who are BIPOC and their contributions. Native allies are integral to creating a "safe space" and being of support against the overt and covert oppression and micro/macro aggressions experienced daily. External Native organizations made up of Native colleagues can also provide support to Native professionals in higher education (Sacramento Native American Higher Education Collaborative, 2021, Vision & Goals).

Leaders can effectively take a stand against racial or cultural inequality by bringing awareness to what is occurring on campus. A critical component of leadership is not to be afraid of taking risks and being willing to discuss racism (Nevarez & Wood, 2010). Having uncomfortable and courageous conversations about inequity, like calling out racist behavior, is one way to ensure equity. Another significant element of transformational leadership, according to Bottomley et al. (2015), is when the leader helps to support intellectual stimulation, which encourages followers to challenge previously held assumptions and beliefs. In doing so, it is anticipated that followers will become more creative in their approach, and where understanding the importance of change within an organization is key. The transformational leader encouraging intellectual stimulation allows followers to analyze information in a new way without upholding status quo within an institution. As mentioned several times in this chapter, non-Native Allies with power and privilege are important to the longevity and sustainability of Native professionals on campuses of higher education because without the power of alies, the Native voice continues to be marginalized and devalued.

Policy Change

Another strategy of transformational leadership (Nevarez & Wood, 2010) is enacting policy change. One example of change to a policy within the higher education system is the creation and adoption of the land acknowledgment statement that honors the local Native American tribal community. Creating the land statement is not a simple task, as this should include several key stakeholders—college administration and tribal leaders— involved in the process, taking time to ensure all cultural language and historical information is included in the statement. Having the college adopt a land statement formally is an important part of acknowledging the respect that is owed to Indigenous tribal communities; however creating this statement, although a bold move, can receive some push back from members of the campus community who are not aligned with the values of equity and diversity.

Author's Experience

There was pressure from the community to ensure that the land statement was an accurate reflection of the Native history and tribal community in the regional area. There were supportive individuals from the campus that helped to get the buy in from the other campus community stakeholders and helped to explain the significance of adopting a land statement. There were several meetings held with the college president and tribal leaders to discuss the land statement and to create a draft that honored the community and college partnership. After the draft was written it then was taken to the campus committees of shared governance for approval and adoption. There were concerns about the language in the statement itself, those were worked through and communicated during the meetings. It was instrumental having the voice of a local Native person from the community to help provide context behind the acknowledgment. The final land statement was then approved and posted on the college website.

Overall, it is critical to bring in key stakeholders to help support the initiative for policy change (Nevarez & Wood, 2010). It was also important for the campus to recognize the time commitment from not only the faculty member, but from the local Native community to make sure the land statement was done in the best way that reflected the Native American voice. Creating a land statement and honoring the first people of this land that many of the higher educational institutions are built on gives respect to the Native community, which is why these land statements are so vital to society. Native Americans are the experts at being Native American, and thus, their voices must be heard when creating policy that can directly or indirectly affect their educational lives (Tierney, 1990).

Author's Experience

Our people are our greatest resource! I have always said this and will always say it. It wasn't until a Native woman administrator was hired by the college where I worked for 20 years, that we were able to make changes in policies and divert resources to Native students. This major change did not take place until this time, no matter all the work I did at the faculty level with writing curriculum (Ethnic Studies) and serving on the academic senate and on the curriculum committee, it wasn't until there was someone in a position of power (administration), that institutionalized change could take place.

One of the best practices as a transformational leader in education is understanding the institutional history and being aware of the process for policy change. By understanding the process of the higher education institution, a leader can learn how to change educational policy and identify best practices. Nevarez and Wood (2010) suggested leaders become familiar with the codes of ethics that guide a profession as this will help the leader to understand the standards of behaviors. Every leader should be aware of the environment and observe the institution before taking risks and making changes to policy.

A few recommendations for Native colleagues:

- Take time to work on personal healing from historical and institutional trauma.
- Be kind and compassionate; sometimes it is not the person, but the system that has created a lack of education about Native peoples.
- Be patient with colleagues who have not been educated about race consciousness, also recognizing this is part of the structural racism experienced being BIPOC.
- Help others learn to decolonize their thinking by being inclusive and supportive, (Colonial thinking is deficit minded.)
- Remember being strategic, intentional, and confident is about building healthy, authentic relationships with others.
- Stay grounded and connected to community.
- Serve on hiring committees.

CONCLUSION

Institutional racism and on-going oppression must be addressed, and a paradigm shift is needed. Furthermore, there is continued need for on-going self-reflection and assessment by professionals in the field. (Lara-Cooper & Walter Lara, 2019, p. 25)

This chapter focused on major topics relating to structural racism and violence inherent in educational environments for BIPOC, specifically Indigenous/Native peoples, and on strategies for transformational leadership. Through the lived experiences of Native women authors within higher education, this chapter proposes a transformational change agent equation, which provides strategies to support BIPOC resiliency within higher educational workspaces (Shanker & Sayeed, 2012). Lessons learned by the authors support the creation of transformational change for BIPOC leaders and can be employed by other readers to create safe spaces, support systems, and ultimately, change within higher education.

A social and racial justice reckoning is happening now in the wake of the public lynchings of George Floyd, Brianna Taylor, Stephon Clark, Elijah McClain, and many more murders of Black Lives by the hands of police. The Black Lives Matter (BLM) movement has continued to be a cornerstone for change that has reverberated beyond the Black community (Esquivido et al., 2020). Many of our stagnant Native American issues have now begun to move forward because of the BLM movement's momentum. Making transformational change within a system inherently built to oppress and assimilate targeted populations is overwhelming. Support and care from supervisors and allies make a positive impact on Native women professionals which empowers them to feel valued and respected in workspaces within higher education (Zimmer, 1988). It is critical for transformational leaders to identify key relationships and build support systems with allies.

Community and stakeholder trust is significant when trying to implement change, especially to policy. It is important to facilitate a collaborative approach for stakeholder buy-in when making changes to policy and procedures within the organization. Although it will take time to make changes in policy, it is imperative as BIPOC leaders to not give up and to continue to make change one step at a time.

The most effective way to become a catalyst for change is to bring decolonized solutions to higher education. Offer these solutions as counters to the traditional methodology. Sway colleagues to consider their positionality and to decolonize their thinking. Provide support to colleagues, build relationships, be kind, and compassionate even when frustrated with the lack of critical consciousness. These are inequitable systems that have been built and adhered to for many years. The systems were not built in a day, and they will not be dismantled in a day. Set goals for dismantling oppression and racism. What needs to happen now, versus what can happen next year and the year after. Build on top of what has occurred, remind your organization of the land that it sits upon, and the debt owed to the community. Help leadership rethink student "success." Join a committee and set a plan toward decolonization and equity.

As Native women faculty, counselors, and administrators, the authors are dealing with not just historical trauma, but with fresh trauma, racism, and implicit bias we must face every day from our students, colleagues, and supervisors. Sometimes it is hard to get up every day and fight the good fight. Without self-care and support from other Native women, Native organizations, and tribal communities, it is almost impossible to get this work done. However, Native women leaders in higher education persist in making change, often with great sacrifice, that will impact future generations.

REFERENCES

Adams, D. W. (1995). *Education for extinction: American Indians and the boarding school experience, 1875-1928*. University Press of Kansas.

American College Personnell Association. (2018). *Strategic Imperative for Racial Justice and Decolonization.* http://convention.myacpa.org/houston2018/sirjd-syllabus/

Archuleta, M., Child, B. J., & Lowamaima, K. T. (2000). *Away from home: American Indian boarding school experiences, 1879-2000.* Museum of New Mexico Press.

Belcourt-Dittloff, A. E. (2006). *Resiliency and risk in Native American communities: A culturally informed investigation* (Unpublished doctoral dissertation). University of Montana.

Black, J. E. (2002). The "mascotting" of Native America: Construction, commodity, and assimilation. *American Indian Quarterly*, *26*(4), 605–622. doi:10.1353/aiq.2004.0003

Bottomley, P., Mostafa, A. M., Gould-Williams, J. S., & León-Cázares, F. (2015). The impact of transformational leadership on organizational citizenship behaviours: The contingent role of public service motivation. *British Journal of Management*, *27*(2), 390–405. doi:10.1111/1467-8551.12108

Brave Heart, M. Y. H. (1999). Oyate Ptayela: Rebuilding the Lakota Nation through addressing historical trauma among Lakota parents. *Journal of Human Behavior in the Social Environment*, *2*(1-2), 109–126. doi:10.1300/J137v02n01_08

Brave Heart, M. Y. H., & DeBruyn, L. M. (1998). The American Indian holocaust: Healing unresolved historical grief. *American Indian and Alaska Native Mental Health Research*, *8*(2), 56–78. https://pubmed.ncbi.nlm.nih.gov/9842066/ PMID:9842066

Brayboy, B. (2005a). Toward a tribal critical race theory in education. *The Urban Review*, *37*(5), 425–446. doi:10.100711256-005-0018-y

Brayboy, B. (2005b). Transformational resistance and social justice: American Indians in Ivy League universities. *Anthropology & Education Quarterly*, *36*(3), 193–211. doi:10.1525/aeq.2005.36.3.193

Brayboy, B. M. (2006). Toward a Tribal Critical Race Theory in Education. *The Urban Review*, *37*(5), 425–446. doi:10.100711256-005-0018-y

Cajete, G. (2005). American Indian epistemologies. In M. T. Fox, S. C. Lowe, & G. S. McClellan (Eds.), New directions for student services (No. 109, pp. 69–78). / doi:10.1002s.155

CCEAL. (2019). *From boarding schools to suspension boards: Suspensions and expulsions of Native American students in California public schools.* https://cceal.org/wp-content/uploads/2019/09/Suspension-Boards-Final.pdf

Cheshire, T. (2013). *Barriers & bridges: American Indian community college student success*. Lap Lambert Academic Publishing.

Conley, E. (2008). *Exploring barriers to education for Native American Indians: A Native perspective* [Doctoral dissertation, Florida Atlantic University]. http://fau.digital.flvc.org/islandora/object/fau%3A2811

Dei, G. J., & Kempf, A. (2006). *Anti-colonialism and education: The Politics of Resistance* (Vol. 7). Sense Publishers. doi:10.1163/9789087901110

Deyhle, D., & Swisher, K. (1997). Research in American Indian and Alaska Native education: From assimilation to self-determination. *Review of Research in Education, 22*, 113–194. doi:10.2307/1167375

Esquivido, V. (2019). *Fighting for Federal Recognition: A Nor Rel Muk Wintu Ethnohistory* [Unpublished doctoral dissertation]. University of California, Davis.

Esquivido, V., Esquivido, M., & Gali, M. S. (2020). Black Lives Matter on Indigenous lands: Solidarity in Sacramento. *News of Native California, 34*(1), 20–24. https://newsfromnativecalifornia.com/

Freire, P., & Ramos, M. B. (1970). *Pedagogy of the oppressed*. Seabury Press.

Galtung, J. (1969). Violence, peace, and peace research. *Journal of Peace Research, 6*(3), 167–191. doi:10.1177/002234336900600301

Guillory, R. M., & Wolverton, M. (2008). It's about family: Native American student persistence in higher education. *The Journal of Higher Education, 79*(1), 59–87. doi:10.1353/jhe.2008.0001

Gunn Allen, P. (1992). *The sacred hoop: Recovering the feminine in American Indian traditions*. Beacon Press.

Hassell, K., Archbold, C., & Stichman, A. (2011). Comparing the workplace experiences of male and female police officers: Examining workplace problems, stress, job satisfaction and consideration of career change. *International Journal of Police Science & Management, 13*(1), 37–53. doi:10.1350/ijps.2011.13.1.217

Jackson, A. P., Smith, S. A., & Hill, C. L. (2003). Academic persistence among Native American college students. *Journal of College Student Development, 44*(4), 548–565. doi:10.1353/csd.2003.0039

Kanter, R. (1977). *Men and women of the corporation*. Basic Books.

Lara-Cooper, K., & Lara, W. J. (2019). *Ka'm-t'em: A journey toward healing*. Great Oak Press.

Lomawaima, K. T. (1999). The un-natural history of American Indian education. In K. Swisher & J. Tippeconnic (Eds.), *Next steps: Research and practice to advance Indian education* (pp. 1–31). ERIC Clearinghouse on Rural Education and Small Schools., https://files.eric.ed.gov/fulltext/ED427903.pdf

Lowamaima, K. T. (1994). *They called it prairie light: The story of Chilocco Indian school*. University of Nebraska Press.

Martinez-Alire, C. (2013). *The perceptions of tribal leadership and the impact of education and cultural knowledge: Examining tribal leadership and education within California Native American communities* [Doctoral dissertation, California State University, Sacramento]. Sacramento Doctoral Dissertations.

Nevarez, C., & Wood, L. (2010). *Community college leadership and administration*. Peter Lang Publishing. doi:10.3726/978-1-4539-1712-1

Paradiso, A. (2020). The importance of inclusion in the workplace. *Engage: Employee Engagement Blog*. https://www.achievers.com/blog/the-importance-of-inclusion-in-the-workplace/

Pavel, D. M., & Padilla, R. V. (1993). American Indian and Alaska Native Postsecondary Departure: An example of assessing a mainstream model using national longitudinal data. *Journal of American Indian Education, 32*(2), 1-23. https://www.jstor.org/stable/24398302?casa_token=3EkZZHYOOrUAAAAA%3AXWwQGlinj-oJCYixNWMLc91qIRVDSVnl-l2ykC39BuxvI2lYnwtorPDTJNMqSBUoHWjmQxPtLp8UsC9M2U8qe2uxuiFgAIOyVoEWBED0WRMgc5WqJ2Fc&seq=1#metadata_info_tab_contents

Reyhner, J., & Dodd, J. (1995). *Factors affecting the retention of American Indian and Alaska Native students in higher education*. https://jan.ucc.nau.edu/~jar/Factors.html

Risling Baldy, C. (2018). *We are dancing for you: Native feminisms and the revitalization of women's coming-of-age ceremonies*. University of Washington Press.

Sacramento Native Higher Education Collaborative. (2021). *Vision and goals*. Author.

Seward, M. S. (2019, April 2). Decolonizing the classroom: Step 1. *NCTE Standing Committee on Global Citizenship*. https://ncte.org/blog/2019/04/decolonizing-the-classroom/

Shanker, M., & Sayeed, O. (2012). Role of transformational leaders as change agents: Leveraging effects on organizational climate. *Indian Journal of Industrial Relations, 47*(3), 470–484. http://www.jstor.org/stable/23267338

Smith, L. T. (1999). *Decolonizing methodologies: Research and Indigenous peoples.* University of Otago Press.

Smith, L. T. (2012). *Decolonizing methodologies.* Zed Books.

Smith, L. T. (2013). *Decolonizing methodologies: Research and indigenous peoples.* Zed Books.

Springer, M. (2015). *Native student organizations as a high impact practice: Native students perceptions of the effects of participation in a Native student organization on their academic and personal success at predominately white institutions* (Publication No. 3742179) [Doctoral dissertation, New England College]. ProQuest Dissertations Publishing.

Starks, J. E. (2010). *Factors influencing the decisions of Native Americans to attend or not attend college or vocational school: A phenomenological study* (Publication No. 3433010) [Doctoral dissertation, College of Saint Mary]. ProQuest Dissertations Publishing.

Stein, S., & Andreotti, V. D. O. (2016). Decolonization and higher education. Encyclopedia of Educational Philosophy and Theory, 10, 978–981. doi:10.1007/978-981-287-532-7_479-1

Stephen, M. (Ed.). (1999). *Indigenous community-based education.* Multilingual Matters.

Stremlau, R. (2005). "To domesticate and civilize wild Indians": Allotment and the campaign to reform Indian families, 1875-1887. *Journal of Family History, 30*(3), 265–286. doi:10.1177/0363199005275793

Szasz, M. (1999). *Education and the American Indian: The road to self-determination since 1928.* University of New Mexico Press.

Tierney, W. G. (1990, May). *American Indians and higher education: A research agenda for the 90s.* Paper presented at the Opening the Montana Pipeline: American Indian Higher Education in the Nineties Conference, Montana State University, Bozeman, MT.

Tierney, W. G. (1991). Native voices in academe: Strategies for empowerment. *Change, 23*(2), 36–45. doi:10.1080/00091383.1991.9937678

Trennert, R. A. Jr. (1988). *The Phoenix Indian School: Forced assimilation in Arizona, 1891-1935.* University of Oklahoma Press.

Waller, M. A., Okamoto, S. K., & Hankerson, A. A. (2002). The hoop of learning: A holistic, multisystemic model for facilitating educational resilience among Indigenous students. *Journal of Sociology and Social Welfare*, *29*(1), 97–116. https://heinonline.org/HOL/LandingPage?handle=hein.journals/jrlsasw29&div=9&id=&page=

Williams, M. T. (2020). Microaggressions: Clarification, evidence, and impact. *Perspectives on Psychological Science*, *15*(1), 3–26. doi:10.1177/1745691619827499 PMID:31418642

Wolfe, P. (2006). Settler colonialism and the elimination of the Native. *Journal of Genocide Research*, *8*(4), 387–409. doi:10.1080/14623520601056240

Wood, L., & Harris, F. (2021). *Racelighting in the normal realities of Black, Indigenous, and People of Color (Scholarly Brief) Community College Equity Assessment Lab*. http://bmmcoalition.com/wp-content/uploads/2021/03/Racelighting-BRIEF-2021-3.pdf

Wright, B., & Tierney, W. (1991). American Indians in higher education: A history of cultural conflict. *Change, 23,* 11–18. https://naspa.tandfonline.com/doi/abs/10.1080/ 00091383.1991.9937673?journalCode=vchn20

Zimmer, L. (1988). Tokenism and women in the workplace: The limits of gender-neutral theory. *Social Problems*, *35*(1), 64–77. doi:10.2307/800667

ADDITIONAL READING

Annie E. Casey Foundation. (2008, February 9). *How families survive and thrive in the American Indian and Alaska Native community. Seeing the protective rainbow: Family resiliency in Native American communities*. https://www.aecf.org/resources/how-families-survive-and-thrive-in-the-american-indian-and-alaska-native-co/

Baldy, C. R. (2018). *We are dancing for you: Native feminisms and the revitalization of women's coming-of-age ceremonies*. University of Washington Press.

CCEAL. (2019). *From boarding schools to suspension boards: Suspensions and expulsions of Native American students in California public schools*. https://cceal.org/wp-content/uploads/2019/09/Suspension-Boards-Final.pdf

Lara-Cooper, K., & Lara, W. J. Sr. (2019). *Ka'm-t'em: A journey toward healing*. Great Oak Press.

Nevarez, C., Wood, J. L., & Penrose, R. (2013). *Leadership theory and the community college: Applying theory to practice*. Stylus Publishing.

KEY TERMS AND DEFINITIONS

Affective Relationships: Refers to interpersonal relationships that fulfill personal needs for emotional interactions with specific people in our lives including family, community, tribe, and colleagues; these relationships include the need for giving and receiving emotional support, attention, and supportive nurturing behavior.

BIPOC: The recent emergence of defining Black and Indigenous representation is called into focus through the acronym BIPOC rather than POC (People Of Color) which indicates non-white individuals. Therefore, centering Black and Indigenous voices is a politic the authors are asserting in this chapter.

Boarding Schools: Enacted as part of United States government assimilationist policies in the late 1800's; was the outright kidnapping of Native American children from their families to assimilate and indoctrinate them into 'white' society, resulting in intergenerational traumatic experience. The boarding school experience was an instrument of colonization that has long lasting negative impacts on Native American society, culture, families, and overall wellness today.

Reziliency: A specific type of resiliency Native people possess related to specific types of oppressions experienced by Native people (e.g., boarding schools; stolen colonized land base; reservations; forced removal).

Structural Racism: Exists in all areas of education and it is based in oppressive settler colonialism, and pervasive in policies and practices. Structural and systemic racism is inherent in the very framework of educational institutions, making it difficult for Black, Indigenous and People of Color (BIPOC) to lead.

Structural Violence: Violence inherent in colonized systems, like education; used to threaten BIPOC into subordination or inaction to prevent transformational change. The Native American experience within American education has largely been one of assimilation, violence, and oppression.

Transformational Change Agent Equation: An equation developed to identify and connect specific variables including met needs of the Native professional, barriers, Native Reziliency, strategy, and change.

Transformational Leadership: A leader who can motivate with a high degree of emotional intelligence and can inspire change that transforms previously held organizational culture normatives.

Chapter 10
What Do You Do When Silence Is No Longer Golden?

Darlene E. Breaux
Alief ISD School Board, USA

ABSTRACT

For decades, the voice of Black Americans has been systematically silenced: from the beginning, when African ancestors were ripped away from their home shores of Senegambia and West-Central Africa, through the civil rights movement of the '50s and '60s, to current civil unrest after America witnessed the murder of George Floyd. The Black Lives Matter movement's rise is a direct result of Black people who are sick and tired of being silenced. The purpose of this chapter is to describe four personalities—mediator, advocator, agitator, and activator—, the situations in which each would be appropriate, and the lessons learned through these experiences. This chapter will cover a brief personal narrative of the author growing up and taught to be seen and not heard and how the sheer notion of silence is golden is no longer appropriate in times of social unrest and when lives are at risk. The author highlights the cognitive dissonance felt as a school board member amid the new social justice movement of the late 2000s.

INTRODUCTION

In 1619, more than 20 enslaved Africans landed in Virginia, and since that time, slavery has impacted every facet of the cultures and traditions found within the United States of America (Jones, 2019-present). For centuries, the voices of Black people have been systematically silenced or erased from United States history. However, it is imperative for Black people to collectively use their voices to hold America

DOI: 10.4018/978-1-7998-7235-1.ch010

accountable for its promises. Otherwise, silence becomes an instrument of violence (Kinouani, 2020). Silence serves as a tool to strip away the voices and remove from recognition the humanity of cultural groups being pushed to the margins by the power dominant cultural groups.

Silence suggests the old African Proverb that reads, "until the lion learns to write, every story will glorify the hunter," has merit. Every moment offers the power to create a narrative that dictates not the accurate representation of events but the perceptions people hold about what happened (Trouillot, 1995). This use of perceptions over facts occurred as early as the beginning of America's founding when Christopher Columbus was said to have "discovered" a land that was currently inhabited by indigenous people living on an island, an island we now know was the United States territory of Puerto Rico (Trouillot, 1995). The resulting representation of Columbus's discovery silenced the voices and the lived experiences of the indigenous inhabitants of North America and the Caribbean Islands.

Regardless, Black people continue fighting for the human right to have their experiences shared, understood, valued, and reflected in social justice policy and practice. This ongoing fight is evidenced by the civil rights movement of the 1950s and 1960s to the current civil unrest after America witnessed the murder of George Floyd. The rise of the Black Lives Matter movement is a direct result of Black people reclaiming their voice and the right to matter on American soil.

In my personal experience as an educational leader, I have often been in spaces where my voice is the only one that speaks up for the students and families not represented at the table. Ironically, I grew up being taught that it is appropriate to be seen and not heard, but the notion that silence is golden no longer sits well with my soul. I asked myself, who am I in this space? Am I a mediator, an advocator, an agitator, or an activator? I struggled as I came to terms with these multiple personalities and the cognitive dissonance I experience as a school board member, leader, and parent. Amid this new social justice movement, I began the process of finding my voice. I recognized "the calling to speak is often a vocation of agony, but we must speak. We must speak with all the humility that is appropriate to our limited vision, but we must speak" (King, 1957). In this recognition, four roles emerged as necessary for promoting change as a leader. These roles were mediator, advocator, agitator, and activator.

Mediator

Mediation is a process for resolving disputes where an intermediary guides conflicting parties to have a conversation to jointly resolve their concerns (Beer et al., 2012; Fisher et al., 2011). Conflicts are fueled by social, economic, and political elements that influence the outcome of the resolution (Cloke, 2013). Specifically, conflicts within social movements are commonly resolved or suppressed by highly destructive methods such as apathy, suppression, avoidance, and enforced silence (Cloke, 2013).

A mediator is an intermediary who facilitates communication between two parties to bring about an agreement, compromise, or resolution (Beer et al., 2012; Harvard Program on Negotiation, 2020). Mediators hold open the line of communication between disputing parties and empower them to focus on the overarching goals and underlying interests. The role of a mediator is fulfilled by an impartial person who brings people or organizations together to discuss an issue and resolve a conflict.

During the Civil Rights Movement, the two leaders who rose to prominence were Dr. Martin Luther King, Jr., and Malcolm X. Although both men's fathers were preachers and politically active, Malcolm X and Dr. King had vastly different approaches to addressing social injustices. Dr. King chose the nonviolent approach of civil disobedience, while Malcolm X chose a system to achieve equality "by any means necessary" and did not abhor or discourage violence. However, these two leaders did not mediate solutions.

There was a little-known figure in the civil rights movement named Whitney Moore Young, Jr., a social worker and an expert in race relations who led the National Urban League's entrance into the Civil Rights Movement. Young was not seen at the forefront during the Civil Rights Movement as Dr. King and Malcolm X were. Instead, Young served as a mediator operating in the background between White businessmen and community leaders to help Black people pursue and attain employment and full access to their human rights and Constitutional liberties (Gladden, 2018). Young learned the skills to prevent, resolve, transform, and transcend conflicts and to examine and address the context in which these conflicts occur, as recommended by Cloke (2013).

Stephan and Thompson (2017) explored connections between civil resistance and conflict resolution. They found that combining the power of activism and peace mediation empowers people to resolve conflicts. In the quest for sustainable peace as a solution to political and social conflicts, conflict resolution specialists like Young use negotiation. In contrast, grassroots-level movements like those led by King use nonviolent civil resistance. Success with resolving conflict and finding peace involves identifying the issues, understanding and empathizing with each party's position, and working authentically to resolve the conflict. These elements can generate a win-win solution when the individuals involved in the dispute share equal power for using their voices (Stephan & Thompson, 2017).

Silence supports the continuation of division. A school board member who is complacent or silent does not facilitate change. School boards that create a space for voices to be heard can realize a more just educational environment. The Texas Association of School Boards (TASB, 2021) stated that school board members form a link for mediating between the school system and the public. As mediators, school board members promote continuous, productive discussion.

Currently, I serve on a school board that convenes to make the best and most just decisions for the more than 46,000 students and their families served by our district. We are fortunate to embrace a part of the city containing the International District. The diversity of our community is why the school board's decisions come with heavy responsibility. It is vital that the school board serves the constituents and values and embraces the benefits of diversity to effectively meet the needs of all sectors of the community.

During the 2020-2021 school year, COVID-19 swept through our nation. Its effects forced all educational leaders to rethink how education can be effective in this new normal where schools transitioned from on-campus, in-classroom learning to online educational delivery. We had to ask, "Who are we in this pandemic?" Our community was torn between keeping our students and staff safe and serving our students' academic and social-emotional needs in this unprecedented time. Both parents and teachers alike stood frozen and looked to us school board members as educational leaders to do the right thing. Our area of the city had some of the highest rates of COVID-19 infections.

The topic of conversation across the nation involved determining when and how we would safely bring our students and staff back to on-campus learning. Education, as we knew it, was going through a transformation. Our approach to resuming in-person learning meant carefully considering both safety and academic support and balancing the two issues. Above all, we remained committed to being flexible, proactive, creative, and nuanced in our planning.

Weeks were spent listening to medical officials, scientists, the governor, the Texas Education Agency (TEA), our parents, and our employees. Many of these stakeholders had very different priorities, and the struggle to understand each other's perspectives was evident. Stepping back from my leadership role and listening as a neutral party helped me understand each party's interest in the issues. Since I did not have the answers, I had to help each stakeholder understand each other as a mediator. I had several opportunities to host listening sessions with various stakeholders and to ensure each party's voice would be heard for developing the opportunity to form a win-win solution. I used these listening sessions to mediate the constituents' concerns. Because of inclusive participation in the process, we presented our solution to state legislators. This process was beneficial because it highlighted the need to facilitate conversations that enabled everyone to speak and listen. I learned to value my role as a mediator who facilitated progress toward the desired outcome.

Advocator

An advocator is a person who pleads the causes of and supports or promotes the interests of another person or group (Merriam-Webster, n.d.a). One of the most compelling stories about advocacy has been conveyed about a young Pakistani girl, Malala Yousafzai, who was shot in the head by the Taliban on her way home from school because of her fierce advocacy for the education of girls (Yousafzai, 2013). Malala survived the shooting and was undeterred from her mission of fighting for the rights of young women to be educated. There was an international outpouring of support for Malala that led to her becoming the youngest person to receive the Nobel Peace Prize in 2014 (Kettler, 2020). She has continued to travel around the world as an advocate and an activist bringing awareness to the basic rights of women to be educated (Kettler, 2020). One would expect that being a young woman living in Pakistan facing threats from the Taliban would force Malala into silence and retreat to space where her community has historically placed women and girls. Malala chose to stand up and speak out for herself and all of the other young women who were depending on her to amplify their voices.

As a child in a household of seven children, silence was appreciated, but while growing up in the segregated North, silence was survival. My parents were trying to blend into, instead of sticking out, in our primarily White neighborhood. Their silence was necessary for my family's wellbeing and taught me that I can support a cause from the sidelines rather than from the public eye. I was slowly learning that my voice that can bring about change can also cause destruction. My parents saw firsthand what happens to Black people vocal about injustices, and therefore they chose to remain silent. My parents quietly cheered on the movement but remained passive bystanders for fear of their safety. By observing my parents' acquiescence to the status quo, I learned was that being Black meant that I was expected to be quiet because my thoughts and opinions would not be valued by the people who held power.

At the time of this chapter's writing, my father was 94 years old. He had worked 6 days a week until he was 92 as a barber in the shop he owned for 60 years. He was a veteran of the segregated U.S. Army and World War II. His primary customer base at the barbershop was White men; consequently, he had mastered what I call *color-blind conversations* involving topics deemed "safe" to discuss in mixed company, like sports and the current weather. My siblings and I learned that when we leave the house, we represent the family. We understood that anything we did could impact my father's business. We, too, learned to master the art of color-blind conversations, to speak in generalities, never have a strong opinion on anything, and to go along to get along. So, what do you do when those color-blind conversations gnaw at your soul, and your silence is no longer golden? You find your voice.

In the Spring of 2020, there was an epidemic of instances where Black men and women lost their lives or liberty to complete everyday tasks. Their experiences moved me to use my voice to support the 54-million Texas students' right to exist in this country. I spent the summer of 2020 reflecting on my position, my "why," and my own childhood that taught me to internalize silence as beneficial to survival and success. Nonetheless, as a leader, I understood my responsibility to speak up and advocate for the rights of students. I remember that I was compelled to act, to advocate, to use my voice. I recognized "the calling to speak is often a vocation of agony, but we must speak. We must speak with all the humility that is appropriate to our limited vision, but we must speak" (King, 1957). At that time, I didn't know what that something I would speak about was, but I had made up my mind that it was not the time to remain silent.

Over the next couple of days, right after the killing of George Floyd by police officers went viral on social media, a group of students marched in protest. These were young people who did not ask permission; they did not ask for help; they organized their march on their own and made it happen. The pictures and the videos on social media caused me to reflect on how often I overthought decisions and choosing to stick to safe color-blind conversations because I worried about what people would say and whether speaking out would be politically correct.

Well, I concluded that sometimes, it is necessary to step away from the noise of the crowd and learn about myself—my values and beliefs—in the midst of chaos and confusion. The least seen and heard need advocates even when they do not ask for help. I chose to be that person to advocate for the students making the news instead of being cautious and silent. During graduation that year, even with it being scaled-down and socially distant, the students' eyes exemplified hope, confidence, and the courage to embrace the uncertainty of their future. At that moment, the words by 18th-century William Henry of "the eyes shout what the lips fear to say" became a real flashpoint in my journey toward finding my voice.

When the announcer stated, "Please stand for the pledge" during graduation, I could not. I glanced to my left and looked straight at the school board president. I spoke no words, but I made my intentions clear and kneeled firmly into my decision. I lowered myself to my knee on the floor of the stage. I looked out among the students and saw students of every race take a knee as well. Some held fists up in silent protest, some stood without covering their hearts, and some sat quietly in their seats.

My choice did not fare well with one of my fellow school board members, a veteran. He saw choosing not to stand as disrespecting the flag. I shared with my colleague an earlier conversation that I had with my father, the World War II veteran. I had asked my father how he felt about the protest and the flag. He told me he did not fight for the United States flag because it was just a piece of material, but he had fought for a better life for himself and our family. However, when he returned from his World War II post in Okinawa, Japan, he still did not feel free in the country for which he had been willing to give his life. He understood the fight on American soil was for the ideals of the flag. Now, in the 21st century, people of color continue fighting the war for their freedom and liberty and property rights, just as my father was fighting for democracy in the first half of the 20th century. In my case, taking a knee was using my voice to fight. My action was silent, but the message I conveyed very publicly was quite loud.

For educational leaders, advocacy leadership should move beyond the occasional trip to the state capital to lobby for a policy or resources and should shift its focus to advocacy for students (Anderson, 2009). Those who lead through advocacy understand the systemic issues that impact the classroom, district, and community. They seek to address the cause of inequitable policies through understanding the power of influence that individuals have (Anderson, 2009). As a board member, I was compelled to ensure that I used my position as a catalyst for greater advocacy and change. I did not allow silence to become a barrier to the forward progress of our students.

Agitator

According to Merriam-Webster dictionary (n.d.b), an agitator is someone who stirs up public feelings on controversial issues to support an effort to change. An essential skill of an agitator is to bring awareness to an issue and stir people to bring about change through corrective action and collective work (Nobel, 2017). Looking back into the histories of Black and Brown people, there have been times where the inaction has become so uncomfortable that action was the answer. For instance, the Montgomery bus boycotts happened because Black people could no longer accept their status as second-class citizenship with inequitable access to transportation. The Civil Rights Movement protest of citizens refusing to ride the city buses in Montgomery, Alabama, dealt a significant financial blow to the city's economic welfare. The boycott highlighted the agency of everyday people and their respective communities in the struggle for liberation (Alderman et al., 2013). The Montgomery bus boycott has been regarded as one of the first mass protests in the United States and set the stage for other large-scale actions that ushered in change for Black people as the Civil Rights Movement gained traction. By this historical period, the status quo of segregation was unbearable both to Black and White people and caused ordinary, everyday citizens to be agitated into uncommon action.

Another way to agitate for change is through the political process. In Texas's 87th Legislative session, a contentious bill, House Bill (HB) 3979, was presented. As Governor Abbott signed HB 3979 into law on June 15, 2021, he promoted it as a "strong move to abolish critical race theory in Texas" (p. 1) and to limit how

Texas teachers can talk about current events, race, and racism in the classroom. The bill also prohibited students from receiving credit for participating in civic activities such as political activism or speaking to elected officials on a particular issue. Lastly, the bill prohibited any teaching of the *New York Times Magazine's* 1619 Project as a tool to examine the country's foundation based on the first slaves arriving on North American soil.

I felt the need to ensure that more people were aware of the bill and its ramifications, so I reached out to my network of educators and curriculum experts. I encourage them to contact their local officials regarding the stance that should be taken on the bill. I worked with a senator to provide talking points on how the bill would be detrimental to the gains recently achieved through the approval of an African American studies course for the state of Texas. In addition, we discussed ways to amend the bill if indeed it did pass by adding language to the bill that would require students to read stories and study writings from multiple women and people of color. Multiple alerts for a call to action went out from teachers, education advocacy groups, and even legislators. The amended language was stripped from the bill at the last moment, and the bill passed in its original form. Although we were not successful in our efforts to kill the bill, we did not waste our time. This bill represented a clear example of how institutional practices silence honest conversations about the role that race and racism play in Texas and American society. Because of bills like HB 3979, I must continue to use my role as a school board member to agitate and promote change when policies create barriers and narrow the educational curriculum to silence and marginalize the voices of people who do not hold social or political power, such as our Black and Brown students and their families.

To elevate the voice of one group does not diminish the existence of the other group. Emerson and Yancey (2011) shared the following:

From a White person's perspective, it is not easy to be White these days. Often when the subject of race comes up, it feels to White people that they are the objects of blame, anger, misperception, and ridicule. Whites are often put on the defensive. Second, given programs such as affirmative action, it also seems as if preferential treatment is given to anyone who is not White. In this vein, it might look like society is racialized, but in the sense that it favors non-Whites. "Why can't we just get over this race thing and live as Americans?" Whites in the United States often think. "Why does it have to be so complicated? Sure, there may be a few racist people, but they are about a tiny percentage. Society is open to any and all who want to put the time and effort into achieving their dreams. So, let's stop talking about race and living in the past; let's move on and get to eating some of the fruits of the American way of life. (p. 9)

Emerson and Yancey (2011) added that scholars studied what it means to be White in America and described White privilege using the following three dimensions:

1. White structural advantage,
2. White normativity, and
3. White transparency.

White structural advantage occurs when White Americans sit in the seat of advantage to disproportionately influence the sociopolitical institutions controlled by the government, the legal and political system, industry, businesses, and so on. These structural advantages afford White people what is known as *privilege*. Privilege means a person simply benefits from liberties, opportunities, and dispensations that are unearned and based solely on the status of their color as White.

Emerson and Yancey (2011) defined White normativity as the dominant standardization of White cultural practices, ideologies, and proximity within the racial hierarchy, such as society following how White people do things; understand life, society, and the world; and hold a dominant social location over other racial groups which is accepted as "just how things are." Finally, White transparency arises from the inability of White people to think about issues such as White norms, behaviors, and perspectives, or even White-specific experiences versus the specific experiences of persons of other races and cultures (Flagg, 1993).

However, White educators can be allies to support the plight of Black and Brown leaders. To this point, a fellow White educator posted this on her social media on May 29, 2020,

Rage baking because the Black women in my life are exhausted and in pain.

Rage baking because there is fear and anger and frustration and deep hurt in the Black community.

Rage baking because I can't sit still with all that's happening around us,

Rage baking because I can text and call and check-in, but I can also deliver cookies.

Rage baking because enough is enough.

The dehumanization of Black bodies has to end.

Rage baking because there is fear for the Black men in my life and anger for what they experience.

238

Rage baking because that's all I know to do at this moment.

If you are White and you don't understand how people could turn to rioting and burning down cities, D.M. me.

No, I don't want that either, but at some point, after lots of peaceful protesting and no change, what is expected?

If you are a White educator, I BEG you to read (many lists are being shared), to check your own biases and beliefs.

Listen to interviews.

Listen to the deep cries of Black people. And then ACT.

It's not enough to say we love kids if we keep going forward with the same policies and ways of doing things at school.

We have to value them as a whole, human beings, as equal, as worthy of being fought like hell for, of being taught to the highest potential no matter what apartment complex they live in.

We have to call out racism on our campuses.

We can't keep expecting Black folks to do this fight peacefully, and us sit by in silence.

I am rage baking tonight because I've run out of rage tears for the moment. (R. Bitter, personal communication, May 29, 2020).

This post was a salient reminder that systemic racism affects everyone, regardless of race, ethnicity, or color. The post served as a reminder of the importance of understanding the long-standing history of racism affecting this country and the need to focus on ensuring social justice within this country.

As a board member of a Texas public school district, I am also a member of TASB. TASB's (2021) mission is to promote educational excellence for Texas schoolchildren through advocacy, visionary leadership, and high-quality services to school districts. School board members can engage with TASB through being a part of its Board of Directors, an annual Delegate Assembly, and through a powerful grassroots process. TASB's Advocacy Agenda is developed and instituted through the grassroots process throughout Texas; however, the Delegate Assembly is the policy-making body of TASB. The decisions made during the Delegate Assembly are translated by TASB's Board of Directors into actionable items for all school board members across Texas.

As a delegate at the 2020 Delegate Assembly, the expectations required my active participation as a voice for districts and communities. This role was critically important because what we discussed and voted on at the Delegate Assembly became TASB's Advocacy Agenda. This agenda represented the guiding document followed throughout the 2020-2021 school year as the organization and board members spoke to elected officials in Austin during the 2021 Texas legislative session. I also had the opportunity to submit requests for changes to any of TASB's proposed priorities before the assembly day. During the Delegate Assembly, TASB's (2021) proposed advocacy priorities included directing the Texas Legislature:

To combat systemic racism by supporting diversity and cultural awareness initiatives throughout districts through staff and student education and restorative teaching and disciplinary practices that treat all students equally and focus on building relationships.

A delegate sent a request to remove the phrase "combat systemic racism" from this statement. This delegate made a statement that "systemic racism does not exist." I spoke up for all 5.4-million Texas schoolchildren and educated those delegates who chose to turn a blind eye to the reality of systemic racism. I drew upon my need to be an agitator and rouse my fellow delegates' feelings regarding this controversial issue. I requested to speak to provide an opposition to this gentleman's request. My statement is as follows:

I disagree with the proposed priority to strike-throughs from the primary amendment. To remove these statements is to remove the acknowledgment of the existence of systematic racism in our educational system and to turn a blind eye to the value of relationships. This very act of refusing to acknowledge the existence gives districts the excuse not to address it. By acknowledging that systemic racism exists does not suggest that we are personally responsible but more so that these disparities are unacceptable realizations. And the ownership lies with the policies and practices that have caused these unintended consequences and not the responsibility of our students. Students deserve to be educated in environments that value and respect them as individuals, including recognizing and appreciating their racial, ethnic, and social diversity. Understanding how education intersects with race, culture, language, social-economic status, learning ability, and gender helps remove the blinders to the root causes of the inaccurate portrayal of educational competence.

In the end, the vote not to remove the phrase "combat systemic racism" passed with 148 yeas to 102 nays, but fewer than 50 votes separated us. These numbers were a reminder that there is still much work to be done to end racism. The impact that including this statement has for advocating for a more just policy is that it shares a foundational understanding and belief that the TASB Governance recognizes the role that historical and institutional racism has had in the education of our most disadvantaged students. No longer will this system of oppression be ignored. TASB Governance opened the doors for school boards across Texas to begin lifting their voices by having those difficult conversations.

Activator

The leader who takes thoughts, ideas, and concepts and turns them into actionable steps to make things happen is an activator (Rath, 2007). Activators inspire, encourage, and promote leadership in others simply by doing. A great skill that activators possess is galvanizing the talent around them to quickly implement a plan. Stacey Abrams fought against voter suppression during her 2020 campaign for Governor of Georgia. While she was not elected, the grassroots movement and subsequent nonprofit continue to address voter suppression. As an activator, Stacey Abrams used her campaign for governor to encourage more turnout and connected with individuals, inspiring them to get involved. Her story represented failure as an opportunity to rebound and even push further action.

Whether leading through politics or in the local school board, the need to activate positive changes exists. Leaders must often take a stand on certain positions even when they can be contentious (TASB, 2020). For school board members, action is most often done through the TASB Delegate Assembly and through issuing resolutions. Often people attempt to play the middle to be safe but straddling the fence does not support meaningful change (TASB, 2020). Leaders, specifically board members, are called to listen to both sides of an issue; however, in the end, decisions must be made that will best support students.

To understand these issues at a deeper level as a school board member, I lean into spaces where people have those difficult conversations about race, equity, and systematic racism. This experience inspired me to lead my district through a series of events and establish its first-ever equity policy. Sustainable changes to systems take persistence and focus on the hoped-for outcomes. The collaborative work with the school board and superintendent's cabinet worked to create a shared understanding and definition of equity for our district. The change process included accepting that I may not be the expert even though I am committed to learning and finding support when necessary. The school board committed to a comprehensive equity audit that resulted in a report and recommendations for professional development.

Also, our school board chose to hold ourselves accountable by creating board goals aligned to this work. I have included an excerpt from our actual policy designed to advance racial and social equity in the educational setting and improve academic achievement for all district students. Thus, the Alief Independent School Board (2020) established the following goals:

1. The district shall identify and eradicate all barriers that have persisted and caused achievement gaps between various ethnic groups, students with and without disabilities, or any other marginalized groups; and commit to closing the achievement gaps to ensure all students reach their fullest academic and social potential.
2. The district shall improve student preparation for college and career by removing any barriers that would prevent the district from providing every student with equitable access to a high-quality and value-focused culturally relevant curriculum, instruction, resources, support, and facilities.
3. The district shall maintain a safe and orderly environment by providing professional development and other learning opportunities that focus on developing an understanding of the following;
   a. Implicit Bias – The attitudes or stereotypes that affect our understandings, actions, and decisions in an unconscious manner
   b. Micro Aggressions – Indirect, subtle, or unintentional discrimination against members of a marginalized group
   c. Cultural Competence – The awareness of one's own cultural identity and world views while developing positive attitudes towards cultural differences.
4. The district shall recruit, develop, and retain racially and linguistically diverse and culturally competent administrative, instructional, and support staff, and shall provide professional development and other learning opportunities that will support the deep understanding and skill attainment for eliminating racial, ethnic, and socioeconomic disparities in achievement and discipline representation among various groups.
5. The district shall build positive relationships with stakeholders as valuable contributors in the education of every student by welcoming and empowering students and their families regardless of their first language, national origin; gender; gender identity; family structure; or cultural, racial, or ethnic diversity.

Educational equity in the district means striving for the absence of disparities so all students can excel and succeed in a rigorous learning environment. Equity is achieved through transparent evaluation of stated goals and continuous progress. Assessing equity requires comparing data, research, and social determinants among the more and less advantaged groups to assist the district in creating programs, policies, and fair allocation of finances and resources to give all students equitable opportunities to succeed. The board shall hold all Board Members, the superintendent, and all school personnel accountable for the implementation of this policy through the District's Board and Administration Core Beliefs, Commitments, Priorities, and Equity scorecard, as well as performance objectives included in the superintendent's contract. (pp. 2-3)

This policy has been a game-changer for the district. Our school board members now use the lens of equity to examine our policies and practices to ensure that all our decisions serve the best interest of all our students and do not create any unintentional barriers. Many of our teachers and campus leaders have expressed appreciation to the school board for our commitment to support their efforts to access needed resources for their students in a more equitable manner. Finally, this policy has produced a safe space in which school board members can dialogue with our students, staff, and community to have those tough conversations about diversity, equity, and the inclusion of all our students. Leaders as activators do not have all of the answers at the start of producing change, but the passion activators have for changing the status quo motivates others to join the effort. The activator begins the process of change, but the resulting momentum found within the collective group brings about the change.

CONCLUSION

When I was young, I watched a cartoon called the Wonder Twins. The Wonder Twins' names were Zan and Jayna. The twins were aliens from the planet Exxor with a shapeshifting ability activated only when they touched each other's hands. Zan held the ability to morph into any form of water, while Jayna could transform into any animal. I found it interesting that they could not activate their powers unless they reached out to one another and connected to each other physically. Nowadays, I believe each of us holds the ability within ourselves to significantly impact our relationships and surroundings. Reaching out to those who share similar goals and committing to getting the work done does accelerate success toward any much-needed change.

As I revisit the question of leadership and change in a post-Floyd era of social unrest, I hope leaders will learn from my experiences of navigating hostile spaces when seeking change in the mindsets of others by acting in the roles of mediator, advocator, agitator, and activator. Leadership through mediation puts the power for activating the solution in the hands of each party. Indeed, the mediator has the opportunity to gain insight into the perspectives and priorities of others and to show empathy for bringing people together to achieve the same goals. Leaders benefit their constituents when they embrace new information, even if it challenges their worldviews, become an informed voice for addressing the needs of the people they serve, and mediate between the various worldviews their constituents hold.

Leaders as advocates know when it is necessary to amplify the voices of others. They know when silence is no longer golden and agitate others into action when policies need to be addressed for ensuring the wellbeing of others. Leaders never pass up a chance to use their voices with courage, even when unsure whether others will comprehend the rationale for the advocacy and agitation.

Finally, leaders are activators. They know and understand their networks and galvanize support to get the work done. Action serves as the leader's voice. Remember, in the end, it is not what a person says alone that moves the needle of change. However, it is what a leader both says and DOES that activates change.

My self-talk served to agitate me as I advocated for the change to myself. This self-mediation pushed me past my complacency into the role of activator. I must admit that initially, I had found safety and security in staying quiet, but I knew that my silence served no one. I followed the 1957 guidance by Dr. Martin Luther King, Jr., summing up all these roles as necessary for producing change: "In the end, we will remember not the words of our enemies but the silence of our friends." In closing, I implore you: Never allow the golden glow of your silence to diminish the realization of the power of your voice.

REFERENCES

Abbott, G. (2021, June 15). *State of Texas office of the governor: Message*. https://gov.texas.gov/UPLOADS/FILES/PRESS/FILING_STMT_HB_3979_critical_race_theory_IMAGE_06-15-21.pdf

Alderman, D., Kingsbury, P., & Dwyer, O. (2013). Reexamining the Montgomery bus boycott: Toward an empathetic pedagogy of the civil rights movement. *The Professional Geographer*, *65*(1), 171–186. doi:10.1080/00330124.2012.658728

Alief Independent School District. (2020). *AE(local) – educational philosophy*. https://pol.tasb.org/Policy/Download/584?filename=AE(LOCAL).pdf

Anderson, G. L. (2009). *Advocacy leadership: Toward a post-reform agenda in education*. Routledge. doi:10.4324/9780203880616

Beer, J., Stief, E., & Stief, E. (2012). *The mediator's handbook* (4th ed.). New Society.

Cloke, K. (2013). *The dance of opposites: Explorations in mediation, dialogue and conflict resolution systems design*. Good Media Press.

Emerson, M. O., & Yancey, G. (2011). *Transcending racial barriers: Toward a mutual obligations approach*. Oxford University Press.

Fisher, R., Ury, W., & Patton, B. (2011). *Getting to yes: Negotiating agreement without giving in* (3rd ed.). Penguin Group.

Flagg, B. (1993). "Was blind, but now I see": White race consciousness and the requirement of discriminatory intent. *Michigan Law Review*, *91*(5), 953–1017. https://repository.law.umich.edu/cgi/viewcontent.cgi?article=2408&context=mlr. doi:10.2307/1289678

Gladden, J. (2018). *Social work leaders through history: Lives and lessons*. Springer. doi:10.1891/9780826146458

Harvard Program on Negotiation. (2021). *Mediation*. Harvard Law School. https://www.pon.harvard.edu/category/daily/mediation/?cid=11411

Hickman, G. R. (Ed.). (2016). *Leading organizations: Perspectives for a new era* (3rd ed.). Sage.

Jones, N. H. (Host). (2019-present). The fight for a true democracy [Audio podcast]. *The New York Times*. https://www.nytimes.com/2020/01/23/podcasts/1619-podcast.html

Kettler, S. (2020). *Malala Yousafzai biography*. https://www.biography.com/activist/malala-yousafzai

King, M. (1957, November 17). *The trumpet of conscience*. Paper presented at Dexter Avenue Baptist Church, Montgomery, AL.

King, M. (1967, April 4). *A time to break silence*. Paper presented at a meeting of Clergy and Laity Concerned at Riverside Church, New York, NY.

Kinouani, G. (2020). Silencing power and racial trauma in groups. *Group Analysis*, *53*(2), 145–161. doi:10.1177/0533316420908974

Kirwan Institute for the Study of Race and Ethnicity. (n.d.). *Defining implicit bias*. The Ohio State University. http://kirwaninstitute.osu.edu/research/understanding-implicit-bias/ https://www.texastribune.org/2021/05/28/texas-critical-race-theory-greg-abbott/

Merriam-Webster. (n.d.a). Advocate. In *Merriam-Webster.com dictionary*. Retrieved June 15, 2021, from https://www.merriam-webster.com/dictionary/advocate

Merriam-Webster. (n.d.b). Agitator. In *Merriam-Webster.com dictionary*. Retrieved June 15, 2021, from https://www.merriam-webster.com/dictionary/agitator

Neck, C. P., Manz, C. C., & Houghton, J. D. (2016). Self-leadership: The definitive guide to personal excellence. *Sage (Atlanta, Ga.)*.

New York Times Magazine. (2019). *1619 project*. https://www.nytimes.com/interactive/2019/08/14/magazine/1619-america-slavery.html

Nobel, C. (2017). The three types of leaders who create radical change. *Working Knowledge Business Research for Business Leaders*. https://hbswk.hbs.edu/item/the-three-types-of-leaders-who-create-radical-change

Northouse, P. G. (2015). *Leadership: Theory and practice* (7th ed.). SAGE.

Rath, T. (2007). *Strengths finder 2.0*. Gallup Press.

Stephan, M. J., & Thompson, T. (2017, August 10). Connecting civil resistance and conflict resolution: 'People power' activists and peace mediators combine to build a stronger peace. *The Olive Branch*. https://www.usip.org/blog/2017/08/connecting-civil-resistance-and-conflict-resolution

Texas Association of School Boards. (2021). *TASB mission and values*. https://www.tasb.org/about-tasb/mission-and-values.aspx

Trouillot, M.-R. (1995). *Silencing the past: Power and the production of history*. Beacon Press.

Yousafzai, M. (2013). *I Am Malala: The girl who stood up for education and was shot by the Taliban*. Little, Brown.

Chapter 11

Racialization of Religion:
Making Space for Counter-Narratives of Muslim American Youth

Noor Ali
Northeastern University, USA

ABSTRACT

Muslim American high school seniors navigate their educational spaces at a time when the 2016 Election has unleashed a rhetoric that is riddled with Islamophobia. The experiences of four female participants engages us in their counter-narratives, debunking stereotypes and assumptions that exist about their demographic. The formal and informal experiences of the educational journeys of these participants help us explore the role of family, faith-based education, mosque, and community in the lives of these students. The social and academic learning opportunities for these participants showcased instances of inclusion and marginalization, where there were times when the students underwent a double consciousness. Transitioning from faith-based schools to the public education system became easier when positioned in a climate of diversity. Muslim American students experience a dichotomous pull between religious values and American culture and remain cognizant of these differences. Muslim educational leadership will find the study insightful.

INTRODUCTION

Criminalized for the crimes of others, Muslim youth face repercussions in society where they are consistently judged for not being American enough if the label of religion is tagged to them. Carrying the burden of guilt by association when acts of

DOI: 10.4018/978-1-7998-7235-1.ch011

terror are perpetrated, Muslim American youth face experiences that are particular to their demographic. Regardless of their differences based on language, culture, ethnic origin, etc., Muslim American youth are bracketed as "designated Others" due to their religious identity and made "targets of reflexive hatred" by the mainstream (Suarez-Orzoco in Sirin & Fine, 2008, p. xiii). According to Sirin and Fine (2008), in the post 9/11 context, the "two cultural identities, "Muslim" and "American" were reinvented" (p.11). In the light of the attacks on the twin towers the possible multiplicity of identities of Muslim Americans was not only questioned, but also sabotaged as they were demonized for their religious association.

The last few years have seen a 78% increase in Islamophobic attacks on Muslim Americans due to the political climate of bigotry during the 2016 presidential campaign which is representative of a continued demonization of this population (Lichtblau, 2016). The rising voiced bigotry against Muslim Americans was witnessed again at a Trump rally, where the President paused his speech for 14 seconds to allow the audience to chant slogans saying "send her back" about the Muslim American elected Representative Ilhan Omar. Each time there is a mass shooting or terrorist attack, the immediate concern of the Muslim American population is not where and how it occurred, but an internal plea that it's not a Muslim who perpetrated it, as that translates itself in a blanket demonization of everyone with that religious association.

This chapter explores insights from four female Muslim American high school students into how school leadership can create spaces for the counter-narratives that exist within this demographic. It allows for an understanding of the currently underrepresented educational experiences of Muslim youth that would enable a development of means by which they can be empowered to becoming visible citizens of their country with the pivotal role that leaders can play in making that a reality. Muslim American youth find themselves navigating their identities in a time of hostility and support without light being shed on their educational experiences that are particular to them. Educators and school leadership, curriculum experts and counsellors must be equipped with an understanding offered here towards achieving true inclusion in the educational system. When students' experiences lie at the heart of teaching, their learning becomes relevant and meaningfully connected to their personal and public lives (hooks, 1994).

BACKGROUND

Through his ecological theory, Bronfenbrenner (1979) posits the inter-relational impact of the macro, exso, meso, and micro in creating a multifaceted and interdependent identity and experience for individuals (also Hernandez, 2016). In a context where white mainstream is the acceptable definition of American, and often promulgated as being antithetical to all else that is non-white, an identity dichotomy is assumed. Muslim American youth have their narratives to share in their particular experience of being the demonized non-white. The role of leadership in enabling Muslim American Youth towards creating counter-narratives that are not sabotaged by whiteness is a task that requires mindful deliberation, while remaining centered in the voice of the youth itself. It is often the case, that adults in the community hijack the narrative of youth to tell it in and on their own terms. It remains imperative that in the narrative of Muslim American youth itself the role of leadership finds a pivotal place that best lends itself to support youth.

The Burden of Hyphenation

Muslim American youth today continue to face a dilemma of twoness similar to that which DuBois (1903) explicated more than a century ago in his discourse on race and national identity, where being Black and being American were antithetical to each other and extolled a continuous effort on the part of the marginalized demographic to consistently prove how these two aspects of one's identity could be present in any one individual. Being a young Muslim American today necessitates forging "collective identities that honor both their parents' culture of origin as well as their home" here in America, all the while walking a "tightrope of scrutiny" of their own community and the larger mainstream (Suarez-Orozco in Sirin & Fine, 2008, p. xiii). The Muslim American experience similarly evokes practicing a hyphenated identity that questions the legitimacy of nationality because of the religious guilt by association tag attached to it (McCloud, 2010). How one can be truly American if they are Muslim as well is a question that faces this demographic because of the presumed exclusivity of these two titles. More than a hundred years ago DuBois wished "to make it possible for a man to be both a Negro and an American" for he had no desire to "Africanize America", nor "bleach his Negro soul in a flood of white Americanism" (1903, pp. 1-4). Muslim American youth stand at similar crossroads, where they need to legitimize aspects of their religiosity within the Muslim community and their national pride to mainstream America.

"Double Consciousness" and Oppression of Muslim Americans

In coining the term "double consciousness", DuBois (1903) offered critical race theorists a platform to situate the conversation about the identity of marginalized people. Lewis detailed DuBois's concept of double consciousness as one in which the individual "dwelt equally in the mind and heart of his oppressor as in his own beset psyche" (as cited by Dixson, Anderson, and Donnor, 2017, p. 14). In other words, being a marginalized individual entails a daily practice of seeing oneself through one's own eyes as well as through those of the oppressor, and often times, standing at the crossroads of this very dichotomy. Black (2012) explicates a representation of double consciousness "when being an "American" means African Americans have to be integrated, assimilated or marginalized for subordination and invisibility instead of their being included as full citizens on their own equally negotiated terms" (p. 6). The predicament that emerges is the contradiction that may occur in how one perceives herself personally and publicly due to the superimpositions by the mainstream white (Black, 2012).

Similar to African-Americans, other people, who sit outside of the norm of the mainstream United States culture, face a similar struggle of justifying the harmlessness or authenticity of their identity to the dominant. An example of a group who fits this characteristic would be Muslim Americans. Regardless of whether Muslim American youth were born before or after 9/11, or that they have no association to the 9/11 atrocities personally, they are demonized by virtue of holding a Muslim name, or their parents' country of origin, or their choice of clothing (Sirin & Fine, 2008). Levinson (2011) urges us to consider "double consciousness" not as an ailment, but as a perspective that allows us to see the multiplicity that exists in identities that are not monolithic, but rather boldly intersectional and multi-faceted, where it is possible to be Muslim American unapologetically. Whether marginalized Muslim American students navigate their identities with this "gift of second sight" (Black, 2012) that celebrates this multiplicity, or grapple with the struggles of situating themselves, can best be learned through their own story-telling. It is in this story-telling that lay seeds for Muslim American educational leadership to be shaped effectively.

Racism and Religious Oppression

According to the National Research Council (2006), racial discrimination also includes "differential effect or treatment on the basis of factors other than race". This component of the definition "broadens its scope to include decisions and processes that may not themselves be racially motivated, but have the ultimate consequence of systematically disadvantaging minority groups" (Pager, 2006, p.2). In other words, multiple types of oppression can be understood through the use of racism as a framework, because it hinges on the presence of discrimination which is common to such experiences.

Religious bigotry, like racism, promulgates supremacist tendencies seeking to dominate all others that may represent fear or threat for the mainstream due to their difference as "Others" (Lorde, 2007). According to Choper, (1994) even though "race may seem to be a more immutable condition than religion, and religious belief systems may appear to have a more interwoven effect than race on the conduct of people's lives, both traits have been the object of public (and private) stereotyping, stigma, subordination and persecution in strikingly similar ways" (p. 492). More specifically, while one's race may lie on a color binary and therefore evoke stereotypical prejudice, religious markers also are treated with similar discriminatory reaction. Comparing prejudice based on religion and race, Choper states succinctly, "intentionally disadvantaging individuals because of their religion is the constitutional and moral equivalent of invidiously discriminating against people because of their race" (p. 501).

Muslim Americans are a diverse group that represent a makeup of multiple genders, races, languages, cultures, ethnicities, and nationalities. Despite these differences, due to the discrimination based on their religion, they share a common experience (Tindongan, 2011). Simpson and Yinger (1985) in their analysis of prejudice towards racial and cultural minorities shed light on the commonalities of different minorities' experience in their interaction with the mainstream. They state that minorities share these experiences because they are a non-dominant group that holds on to identifiable cultural traits and practices, which are held in low esteem by the mainstream. In this sense, Muslim Americans also share the experience of oppression with other oppressed groups in the United States. As Simpson and Yinger (1985) suggest, "relations among [different] races have a great deal in common with relations among groups that think of themselves as different on other grounds- culture, nationality, religion" (p. 24). The markers and implications of prejudice remain the same whether the target is racially or religiously centered. Prejudice seeks to generalize about a group, stereotyping and misjudging all in one broad stroke (Choper, 1994).

Experiences in Educational Settings

The founding principles of this nation are a testimony to the ideal of creating a society that guarantees freedom and justice for all (Dorn, 2014). These ideals also translate into our educational system's stated goals to provide a relevant and appropriate education to all students, regardless of their differences (Calbos, 2014). However, we notice that in reality some students' experiences continue to be nullified and they remain marginalized (Reyes III, 2007). If authentic democracy is to flourish, and the principles of social justice and equity truly realized, then all students, regardless of demography, need to be given a voice and space (Brown, 2006; Shields, 2004).

Systemic Discrimination

Institutionalized oppression against Muslims ranges from microagrression, microassaults, and microinvalidations to outright violence and blatant bigotry (Bonet,

2011; Sue, 2010). Being born or growing up in a country that seeks to avoid, ignore, invalidate, and demonize one's experiential narrative is akin to being shunned to a life of invisibility or consistent apologetics (Sirin & Fine, 2008; Shields, 2004). The political climate in the post-2016 Election where media and presidential rhetoric have unleashed an irresponsibly Islamophobic campaign are testimony to the exacerbation of this social injustice of institutionalized oppression that had increased dramatically post-9/11 (McCloud, 2010; Kimberly, 2011; Sarwar & Raj, 2016; Said, 1997).

As a religious minority, Muslim Americans define themselves as a duality, a "hyphenated identity", in a consistent effort to bridge the gaps created by bias (Sirin & Fine, 2008, p. 195). While other religious groups living in this country may refer to themselves as Buddhist, Jewish, Christian, Sikh, or Hindu with ease, Muslims are wrought in a cycle of apologetics where they define themselves as Muslim American to assure society that they are safely patriotic and not of a singular religious identity (McCloud, 2010). Muslim American youth navigate through acculturation, marginalization, demonization, sometimes experiencing micro and macro aggressions, at other times choosing self-invalidation upon finding their experiences irrelevant to the mainstream.

LESSONS FROM THE NARRATIVES OF MUSLIM AMERICAN YOUTH

The Role of Muslim Schools and Leadership

The educational experience of students hinges not only on curriculum but also the non-academic structures that are prevalent in the school and the dynamics in the larger society (Giroux, 1994). Dewey (1938), wrote about the interaction between the experiential realities of both the individual and society. The four participants in this study were female and had all attended Muslim schools in America for their elementary and middle school. Two of them had also attended a Muslim high school. A recurrent theme that emerged through the interviews with the students was the role that going to a Muslim school played in inculcating a sense of identity in the students. All four students derived a sense of comfort and belonging from their experiences at the Muslim schools they went to. Hafsa and Amber had experienced Islamic education in their elementary and middle school grades and felt a familial connection to the community. They believed that their parents' choice of Islamic education had provided them a foundation in their early years, beyond which they could make their own judgements. While both Amber and Hafsa did not wear the hijab (headscarf), they held on to certain values that the school had passed on in terms of morals and religious education.

In thinking back, Amber found it worth mentioning when her school made an effort to step out of the bubble and expose students to the mainstream. A project where she had to reach out to the larger community, do service tasks for an animal shelter, interview vets, and generate funds to support the shelter was the most memorable part of her experience. This insight by Amber allows a glimpse into the pivotal role sound leadership plays, where the principal was aware of the identity challenges students would face because of religious racialization. Understanding those challenges then led to addressing them by forging means and opportunities for her students to partake in civic causes beyond the Muslim community. This meaningful planning of the Capstone Project through which students took on concerns allowed them to generate an inclusive sense of social awareness and also empowered them to take on responsibility and see these problems as theirs to solve. Marginalized communities may choose a self-invalidation or consider themselves "others" as well due to the stereotypes that exist systemically. However, when leadership steps in to situate marginalized students in the midst of their world rather than on the periphery, the students' sense of identity is impacted.

Amber also remembered the time when she first made a thanksgiving wreath because it represented a time when her Muslim school accepted the larger American presence. Amber, Rida, Selma, and Hafsa all felt that gender segregation in Islamic schools was drilled to a point of unreasonableness. All four participants believed that creating a distance between boys and girls to that extent was unrealistic because they were all going to leave Islamic schools at some point and then have to interact with the opposite gender. Rida, in particular, felt that the Muslim school environment was pointlessly restrictive and did not allow for students' creative expression because the premise it functioned on was one of mistrust of the students. Amber remembered being called out for dancing in class when she was in fourth grade, and Rida received uniform violation fines even though she was modestly covered. These insights provided by the students is a reminder to Muslim American school leadership to reassess their vision of what they consider to be disciplinary infractions at the cost of isolating youth of their own community. Muslim leadership may be guilty of exercising an unfair power dynamic on its students thereby invalidating many of the connections it seeks to build within its community.

All four participants felt that the religious studies curriculum at their schools was redundant and taught the same materials year after year. Internalizing faith was left to chance, personal inspiration, or sometimes a motivational teacher, but by and large the students shared that nine to eleven years of Islamic education taught them surface level content only without encouraging critical thinking, debate, or even discussion on contemporaneous issues. The religious studies curriculum therefore, was largely disconnected from practical implications for students. Rida opined that the school had taught her virtually nothing about her Muslim American identity, and that her parents are the ones who had given her a solid foundation. Amber reflected that while the school had taught her the content it was now her choice to grow as she pleased and saw best.

In terms of core curriculum, the participants did not feel that they had been disadvantaged in any way by the Muslim schools' educational offerings. The students were satisfied with the extra-curricular activities made available to them through their school and were empowered by the experiences they provided. Whether it was excelling at Robotics, or Model UN, or the Debate team, all four participants found strength and confidence through these informal educational experiences provided to them. The impact of a comprehensive experience on a students' learning was similarly suggested by Certo, Cauley, and Chafin (2003). The benefits of autonomy and empowerment, through these choice activities, was found to be beneficial in the study by Groves and Welsh (2010). This provides an insightful aspect to the importance of what is often termed as "extra" curricular, because it was in fact in the "extra" that these marginalized students found confidence and many times a sense of self-empowerment.

The choice of curriculum at these schools was aligned to the state standards and the students even though they went to a Muslim most of their lives could not think of a single text where they could resonate with the character based on identity. Giroux (1994) pointed to the political nature of curriculum, and this in relation to instructional strategies sets the stage for the entire academic experience (Connell & Wellborn, 1991). The fact that the school is faith-based and serving students of a particular demographic, still requires that the lived experiences of students in the context of their communities is kept pivotal to choices of praxis and pedagogical practices (hooks, 1994; Freire, 1973).

Transitioning Outside of Islamic Education

For Amber and Hafsa who went to a Muslim school until 8th grade, the transition to a public-school system came earlier than for Selma and Rida, who in addition, went to a Muslim high school. It was important to note that Amber had a smooth transition to high school because of the diversity and spirit of inclusion there. Also, she was lucky to have two Muslim friends in her core group who she knew from before. Amber also came from a liberal family and she enjoyed exploring her options and joined several clubs to give herself exposure. Hafsa experienced a very difficult transition to high school because she went to a predominantly white high school that was mostly of a Republican leaning during the presidential campaign. She personally encountered episodes of racism and chose not to report them. Hafsa was finally able to break into the social circles at her high school because of her involvement in the Robotics team. Extra-curricular activities and clubs allowed for these students the chance to socialize and make friends at their new schools (Groves & Welsh, 2010; Certo, Cauley, & Chafin, 2003).

All four participants described their time at the Muslim schools to be one that was protective, sheltered, and exclusive. They used the word "bubble" to explain the experience there. Hafsa and Amber felt that transition was inevitable and they got to do it four years earlier than students who might have a Muslim high school experience elsewhere. Amber and Hafsa were confident that they would be able to make it through college, because they knew themselves well now, and also knew how to make friends outside of their comfort zone. They were comfortable in their skins and saw themselves with a perception different from the one they had fresh out of Muslim school in their high school freshman year. Hafsa and Amber remembered being very conscious of themselves in that earlier period and thinking that they were standing out because of their differences, particularly when it came to making choices of modest clothing. Over the years, they had grown comfortable in their choices and also changed their clothing style a bit. Amber remembered herself dressing very modestly in freshman year with her legs and arms covered, whereas now she did not do that. Hafsa remembered wearing only sweatpants earlier on during gym, but was now wearing sports leggings, while still keeping her legs and arms covered. Regardless of the changes in their clothing, they both felt self-perception was more glaring than how others perceived you, and therefore invoked more fear and doubt than not.

Both Selma and Rida, were deeply concerned and nervous about what transitioning to college would mean for their faith. They had several conversations regarding this transition among friends and were genuinely anxious about how strong they would be in the face of all the choices and freedoms college would offer them. They prayed to keep faith, and wanted to remain motivated through the journey ahead. Rida and Selma were also concerned about standing out because of their hijab and being identifiable as Muslim. Amrani (2017) and Selod (2015) confirmed that having identifiable markers of religion can be the cause of not only racialization, but also increased scrutiny and hostility. They were concerned that coming out of the shelter of Islamic schooling, they would now be in a situation that could be Islamophobic. Selma had undergone several episodes of microaggressions, and outright racial slurs, and knew that bigotry was a very real experience, similar to those mentioned by Sue (2010). In the past, Selma had never reported such incidents so she had no experience of self-advocacy. Rida and Selma were also concerned that if another shooting or attack were to take place with the perpetrator being Muslim they would be targeted. Both the girls also felt that while opportunities were countless they were both starting out in a field that was not leveled because of stereotypical misgivings about Muslim women in hijab. They felt that people were mistrusting of them, and assumed that they were backdated because of their choice of clothing. The role that leadership of Muslim schools has to play in this regard is to prepare the students for this transition by engaging in open dialogue and conversation with the students.

Diversity

Seeing inclusion around them gave all four participants a sense of belonging and comfort. For Hafsa, after struggling to make friends for a year and a half because of her inhibitions, she was finally able to find like-minded people who shared her values in the Robotics team that was mostly colored in a school that was predominantly white. Going to the prom without a date, but as part of a team, made even that experience memorable for her. Amber found the transition to her high school easy because that institution has a very diverse population and there are always people around who do things differently, or are different than the white mainstream. The participants' stories resonated with Giroux's (1994) statements on the culture of the school and its impact on the students' experiences. Selma had for this reason, made a very deliberate choice to apply to college that was known to be diverse. Her experiences at the rally where she saw people of diverse backgrounds coming together to protest the immigration ban gave her confidence that while there was bigotry there was also support and that marginalized populations shared experiences of oppression.

Academic Learning Experiences

All four students had robust learning experiences in the core curriculum whether it was at the faith-based school or the public-school system. They all felt they had equal access and opportunities to develop their academic learning and did not feel at a disadvantage in any way. In their daily lives, while going about their learning, the participants felt no different from anyone else around them and did not feel their identity to be a hindrance. An advantage of the identity they noticed was being able to empathize with other marginalized people that might be inaccessible for students coming from a place of white privilege. In this way, the students felt they had something to offer and brought something to the table that was unique.

Prior to the interviews, the students had not thought about if they found themselves represented in curriculum (Sabry & Bruna, 2007). This conversation caught all four participants by surprise as they had never expected a representation and tried hard to make connections within curriculum to texts that resonated with their lived reality and identity experience. The students were not able to resonate with stories like *I am Malala* or *The Kite Runner* Hafsa and Amber did try to think of novels where a character stood strong for what they believed in. Hafsa recalled presenting during History class on Islam and thought that resonated with her.

Within the religious studies curriculum at their faith-based schools, they felt largely unmotivated. They felt the religion curriculum was mundane and often times based on a regurgitation of text and content with little scope for critical thinking or connectedness. Selma had a positive experience in 12th grade with the religion teacher who she found motivating, and Amber remembered the value of a social engagement project they had done as part of her religion class.

Social Learning Experiences

Amber and Rida felt that teachers at the public high school generally avoided discussions that could take a racist or Islamophobic turn. While current affairs were discussed in class, the teachers maintained a safe space for discussion in Amber's school. Hafsa, however had an experience of a student calling out for banning Muslims during a classroom discussion because he was an ardent Trump supporter. In their interactions with peers at the public high school, Hafsa had experienced racist remarks by her classmates who mocked at her last name "Akbar" implying that she was a terrorist. Amber's sister had also experienced a similar thing at her very diverse high school where a couple of male students covered their faces by pulling up their shirts and chanted "Allahu Akbar" to be explicit about religious connections to acts of terror. Giroux's (1994) work corresponded with the participants on the role of teachers and peers. Selma and Rida had no such experiences of bias in their faith-based high schools, even though Selma did feel that she was somewhat different from her peers in that she was not desi (South Asian descent), and most of her peers were.

Extra-curricular activities like Robotics, Model UN, Debate etc. gave all four participants a sense of confidence and empowerment (Ivaniushina &Aleksandrov, 2015). The Muslim students' club at Amber's school was not as active as she would have wanted it to be, but it was a place of belongingness for Amber. She felt that when she was with the club members they could all really be themselves, and laugh and joke about things that all those students had a common reference point for. These were like "inside jokes" to the Muslim community, or they could say something in the Arabic vernacular, that was commonly understood by non-Arab speaking Muslims as well, and not have to explain it. The club had taken on initiatives like community service outside of school, but also asked for a space to pray, and an exemption to go elsewhere during lunch in Ramadan. It was the club members who would bring to the administration's attention to things like a scheduling conflict between Eid and a final exam. Hafsa had experienced isolation because of the lack of such a club at her school, and it took her time and reliance on a friend to finally ask a teacher at the end of her junior year, if they could pray in his empty classroom. Amber chose not to pray at school because of the uncomfortable space provided, and Hafsa had spent a large part of her time at high school finding empty locations to hide and pray. Rida and Selma did not experience this and were grateful for the daily space and time crafted at their school for praying in congregation.

Sports activities were not limited for Amber due to her religious affiliation because she opted not to follow clothing regulations. For Hafsa, however, several sports activities were out of bounds because they would require her to dress a certain way. Hafsa shared her experiences on the track team when she realized before the meet that she was expected wear a tank top and shorts. Both Amber and Hafsa, talked about the presence of other female Muslim students on sports teams who covered completely under the crew or track uniform. Role models like Ibtihaj Muhammad, the American Olympic fencer, gave Selma the confidence in knowing that participation was possible even if it looked different than others.

Multiplicity

A hyphenated identity of Muslim-American was a given for all four participants (Sirin & Fine, 2008). The students considered themselves American by right, and did not think of themselves as belonging anywhere else. All four students, however, expressed fears of the immigration ban and Muslim registry ideas because these proposals questioned their right to be American. Amber, Hafsa, Rida, and Selma felt Muslim at the same time. There was, however, a variation of consciousness among them. Amber did not feel the Muslim part of her identity was a conscious thought and believed that it did not impact her daily life much. She felt like a regular teenager at most times, except when it came to consciously choosing not to eat pork. For Hafsa, the awareness of her Muslim identity was a little more pronounced as she chose to shop for modest clothing, refused substances, or chose not to eat foods that were not halal. She also maintained a physical distance from boys at all times and had established these parameters very consciously with others. Her interactions with some peers and teachers had also made her conscious of her religious identity. For Rida, the Muslim aspect of her identity was always a given, but she felt she had become more American over the years in her tastes with exposure to pop culture. For Selma, the Muslim part of her identity had become more pronounced as she put on the hijab two years ago. She was simultaneously very conscious and proud of her Muslim identity. She knew that wearing the scarf was a disadvantage, but she considered it more an honor than a burden as she carried the legacy of her faith. Rida also felt that she was a representative of her faith. Both Rida and Selma had experiences of praying in public that they shared during the interviews.

Beyond this hyphenation, there were also deeper layers of multiplicities that the participants spoke about (Bhatti, 2011; Sabry & Bruna, 2007; Archer, 2001). Hamdan (2007) and Hefner (2015) wrote about the impact gender can have on such populations, and that conversation appeared in terms of perceptions of empowerment among the participants. Hafsa mentioned, for example that while she could not segregate the Pakistani and the Muslim in her mind, she became acutely aware of her Americanness when she traveled to Pakistan. While there, she was able to spot the differences in her lifestyle and opinions compared to people who lived there. She felt over the years, she had become more American than Pakistani, while still being Muslim. Being a girl in a STEM field was yet another dimension that Hafsa mentioned several times. A sense of empowerment at breaking the stereotypes was an important aspect. Amber delved into a meaningful conversation about the difference between race and ethnicity, and opined that while her race was not easily identifiable to people she knew that she was ethnically Moroccan. When asked to define herself in an interesting experiment in school, Amber chose to pick Moroccan as her label because it mentioned what was unique about her. It appeared that Amber would pick Moroccan American to describe herself, were she given the choice of hyphenation. Amber came from a family where both her parents were scientists and held PhDs. All of Ambers siblings were sisters, so she did not feel that gender impacted her in any way. Rida also came from a family with parents in engineering and medicine and had one sister. She did not feel that gender impacted her choices in any way. She felt there were a few aspects of her identity that were Pakistani, when it came to some traditional festivities. Selma, felt strongly about her Palestinian heritage as part of her identity. She credited her ethnicity for her strength and bravery. While Selma's father was Syrian, she was disappointed that he had not passed down that side of the culture down to his children. Selma felt that her outspokenness was clearly American, and she also proudly carried her Muslim identity. Gender played a strong role in Selma's self-perception, as she navigated her role as a hijab-wearing/carrying Muslim woman, who felt empowered despite stereotypes.

Identity, Islamophobia, and Social Presence

Amber felt that she easily passed off as white due to her skin color and not wearing the hijab. She believed that because of this she had not faced any discrimination or Islamophobic hostility (Gulson & Webb, 2013; Hassen, 2013; Jandali, 2013; Fatima, 2011). She was certain that had she worn the hijab she would have experienced the like. In Hafsa's experience, people were aware that she was Muslim and this had caused her to experience outright bigotry in school. Her PE teacher's comment and her peers' words were all examples of microinsults hurled her way. Selma noticed a clear difference in the way people interacted with her when she had not worn the hijab compared to when she did (Sirin & Fine, 2008; Tindongan, 2011). When she had not worn the hijab she had also passed off as white and people would talk to her like they would to anyone from mainstream. After wearing the hijab, just within the course of two years, Selma had experienced multiple interactions that were Islamophobic. Rida had not experienced any such assaults because she believed she only moved around in spaces that were known to her. None of the participants had reported any of the incidents that took place because they didn't feel anything would be done about it. The participants chose not to make a deal of the slurs.

While both Rida and Selma were proud of their hijab, they both knew it came with the disadvantage of prejudice. People held assumptions about them being oppressed or having terrorist associations, or being foreign (Housee, 2012). Existing in a mainstream white social space meant that they had to make considerable effort to break the barrier of bias and alienation (Basit, 2009). This meant partaking in actions of community service, or consistently being both symbolic and literal representatives of the entire faith (Crenshaw, 1991; Tindongan, 2011; Hamden, 2010). It also meant that they had to become spokespersons for the faith and the questions that came their way. It was not allowed for them to pass as regular American teenagers, because their religious affiliation was seen as antithetical. Selma had pointed out that in certain parts Islam was becoming more visually present due to women like Ibtihaj Muhammad and Halima Aden. This representation was allowing for the social narrative to alter from the usual.

Cultural Capital

The participants' spoke about strength and rootedness they found at home (Eck, 2001). All four participants came from families that were tight-knit and put a moral compass in place for their children. Whether it was praying together, learning the daily supplications, and fasting together in Rida's case, or having conversations about substance abuse or knowing their roots in Amber's case, or sharing experiences of hijab and identity with her mother in Selma's case, or going to shop for modest wear with her mother, in Hafsa's case- all four participants were grounded in family life. Even as their families showed a different level of acculturation from them, this bonding was something all the young women got strength and confidence from.

Another point of cultural capital came from knowing the legacy of Islam and priding themselves in its rationale. All four participants referenced that it was common sense that Islam prohibited the use of pork, substances, or alcohol, so making these choices were easy. Selma admitted that some things about Islam were not clear to her, but she trusted that there were answers out there. The hijab was meaningful for Selma not only because it was a command of God, but because strong Muslim women before had worn it as a symbol of faith.

The participants also drew strength from their identities despite the marginalization and discrimination that occurred. In knowing that their entire community experienced in a similar manner and that other marginalized communities also went through this, taught these students the lessons of resilience, and holding their ground. The students had not reported any incidents of bias that took place, and that was because as a group Muslims have only recently begun conversations on reporting. While one may sense defeatism in this lack of reporting, it can also be read as a resilience.

The sense of community with other Muslims gave both Hafsa and Amber a sense of peace, security, and belonging as they went into the public education sector. When they visited the mosque, or met old friends from the Muslim community, the familial comfort was something known. Outside of the Muslim community they felt having to explain themselves, or explain jokes, or points of reference, whereas with Muslims all those were givens in the fabric of their shared narrative. These students also remember thinking when making choices, what the community would think or say if they were seen doing something religiously inappropriate. This "collective conscience" helped them in identifying their communal values and presence (Durkheim, 1912). While all four students frequented the mosques at varying degrees they did not feel that it grew their learning or acculturation experience (Awad, 2010; Bagby, 2009; Alba & Nee, 1977). This may be because their time spent at the mosque was limited and perhaps because there wasn't enough programming offered for youth engagement. All four participants shared experiences of judgment from within the community, when students felt they had done something not Muslim enough, or religiously inappropriate based on an adult's interpretation. Whether it was dancing in fourth grade, or talking to a boy, the element of judgment was prevalent in the community.

IMPLICATIONS FOR PRACTICE

There are several implications to consider as a result of this study that could impact the educational journeys of Muslim American students. Both public and private schools and educators have tasks that need to be undertaken on philosophical, instructional, and social fronts. Parents, mosques, and the Muslim community belong to the micro and meso system in the lives of these students (Bronfenbrenner, 1979) and impact their formal and informal educational experiences in several ways. The exosystem and the macrosystem (Bronfenbrenner, 1979), places these students in experiences of marginalization, and cultivates a culture of endemic racialization and discrimination if the students' religious affiliation is identifiable. It therefore becomes more urgent for scholarship within the academia to push forth this conversation and create a space of validation (Shields, 2004) so that policymakers are also challenged to do the same.

The Public School Experience

It is imperative that public schools invest in cultural sensitivity training for their staff members and faculty. Educators in public learning spaces need to introduced to the lived experiences of Muslim American students. These must include understanding basic faith practices that Muslim students may be seeking to accommodate in their daily experiences such as needing a time to pray the afternoon and early evening prayer, eating halal food, avoiding the use of substances and drinking. Muslim students also have faith imperatives regarding modest clothing and gender-based interactions. Events as simple as proms can become times of discomfort for these students. When such events are the norm, these students can often feel alienated. Similarly holidays like Christmas and Halloween do not hold mainstream value for Muslim students and engaging in conversations in the classroom that expect everyone to have the same experiences is invalidating. Cultural training for teachers need to also include that participation in sports can become a complex issue for Muslim students based on the clothing requirements. School systems are often not safe inclusive spaces but rely often on students having to advocate or explain their religious needs because there is often no pre-existing space made for them in the school experience. When some students are privileged to belong to the mainstream norm, we pivot all "Others" to being unprivileged by that very definition while also placing the additional burden of educating and creating awareness on the shoulders of the students instead of training the educators to be more aware.

Creating a climate where both students and teachers are aware of what micoragggressions look like is imperative. When the participants faced discrimination they all chose not to report it because they did not believe the administration would do anything. This can be seen quite often in racial slurs spewed against Muslim American students when they are called terrorists, barbaric, oppressed, immigrants, etc. Female Muslim American students will often get looks and comments of surprise if they are athletic or say something smart because the stereotype is one of oppression and lack of access to education. Part of the teacher training needs to include what microaggressions specific to Muslim American students often look like and also how teachers can set a classroom climate where Muslim students feel confident in having an ally in the teacher.

Another important aspect to be cognizant of is the family dynamic and cultural capital that exists for this demographic. Simple things that all Muslims are not Arabic speaking or brown are important in debunking stereotypes. Realizing that male Muslim students may not make eye contact out of respect and not a lack of confidence, or that Muslim households are not always immigrants, or uneducated, or refuges, that many Muslim students come from bi-racial families where one parent may not be Muslim, or that not all Muslim students have parents who drive taxis, own the corner 7-11 or gas station, or won't speak English are important stereotypes to check oneself for.

The educational experience of Muslim American students often asks them to make a choice of comfortable assimilation at the cost of giving up certain practices that are inconvenient in the public school because they are not part of the white norm or mainstream experience. Students having to hide in empty classrooms or locker rooms to squeeze in prayer times, or having to go through a complicated process to get access to a room to pray were an invalidation of their experience. Avoidance of conversations by teachers is akin to color-blindness and invalidates the experiences of minority students even if these are uncomfortable conversations for the norm (Leonardo, 2002; Kress, 2009; Pullman, 2013).

Schools that had diverse populations and showed greater inclusion and made accommodations for students who were fasting during Ramadhan during their lunch period. Gym was often a time for discomfort because of mainstream expectations of dressing a particular way that did not fit the modesty code for Muslim students. While many students opted for vegetarian options in the cafeteria, having kosher choices available would be more inclusive. The Muslim students got strength from each other's presence and practice, but for schools where there were too few Muslims, the schools need to make an effort of inclusion. All four participants struggled to see where in curriculum they found themselves represented. In the curriculum that the students were exposed to in school there was no representation of the Muslim American demographic, except during history class or in the reading of texts that reiterated the Muslim terrorist narrative. Evaded or null curriculum seeks to invalidate the lived realities of these students and needs to be addressed. It also becomes important that public high schools are cognizant of transitioning challenges that students for Muslim schools may be facing and create opportunities for students to make that transition easier.

The Private School Experience

There was much to learn for Muslim schools from the experiences of the participants in the study. They all felt that the religion curriculum was redundant and repetitious in nature. The students wanted more opportunities of critical thinking and discussion of issues that were contemporaneously relevant to the Muslim American experience. Where students were allowed to step into project-based learning and lead independent projects regarding social engagement, they felt these projects benefitted them greatly in developing not only a sense of empowerment, but also seeing themselves as productive members of a larger community. Ironically, at the Muslim schools too, the students did not find themselves represented in literature. The private school experience was a comfortable and safe space for students and all of them had a familial sense of belonging with it. References were made to the judgmental and closed nature of policies and conversations within Muslim schools. Private Muslim schools in America need to reevaluate their vision and align it to the needs of their students to remain relevant and pluralistic. It is equally important for Muslim schools to develop a transition plan for students who will graduate and move to the public school setting. Whether it is connecting them with private school alumni who underwent the transition for a workshop, or pairing them with alumni mentors for an ongoing association. Either is bound to lend support to transitioning students. Engaging parents in the transition process is also critical. Opening conversations about challenges that these students may face ahead, and creating mock situation trials for them as to how they can answer questions about faith, or how to identify, respond to, and report bigotry are critical pieces of a transition plan.

The Muslim Community Experience

The Muslim American family exhibits a great source of cultural capital for these students as they navigate their way through identity making. While all students found strength and their moral compass through their families, they often chose not to share experiences of marginalization with them, and chose not to report them as discrimination either. It is therefore, imperative for the Muslim community to begin this process of educating its congregants to identify what discrimination looks like, and to advocate for themselves and report it. Transformative leadership in mosques is required that could then help build a generation of change agents that speak up for social justice. Mosques, therefore should not only be places of education, but places of collaboration with other marginalized people. The mosque largely served the purpose of a safe gathering space for these students where they could practice prayer and spirituality with other congregants. There were elements of judgment that students sensed in the community, when others looked down upon the choices of these young adults. Creating tolerant places of worship that address the needs of youth, beyond the ritual prayer are essential in cultivating a sense of belongingness for these students where they could then find strength. The students often saw a dichotomy between their values and culture and the community could make a more concerted effort to bridge the gap.

FUTURE RESEARCH DIRECTIONS

While there is an increase in the conversation around the Muslim American experience, it will remain integral to also situate this in the context of Muslim educational leadership and derive strategies to address the experiences of Muslim American youth by keeping their voice central to the research work.

CONCLUSION

The insights about the formal and informal educational experiences of four female Muslim American high school students identify the areas where Muslim educational leadership in America has had positive and negative impact. While Muslim youth find a sense of familial comfort in the community schools and mosques because of the familiarity of faith, they also often feel judged and invalidated. Schools where leadership helped situate the students in their larger communities by means of civic engagement, social awareness projects, or extracurricular activities, helped these students find confidence and self-worth in a society that systemically otherwise marginalizes them. It remains imperative for Muslim educational leadership to reevaluate their vision and practice through the lens of the very youth they seek to serve.

This research received no specific grant from any funding agency in the public, commercial, or not-for-profit sectors.

REFERENCES

Alba, R., & Nee, V. (1997). Rethinking assimilation theory for a new era of immigration. *The International Migration Review*, *31*(4), 826–872. doi:10.1177/019791839703100403 PMID:12293207

Amrani, N. I. (2017). Racialization: The Experiences of Muslim Graduate Students in Higher Education after September 11 (10265001) [PhD dissertation, Northeastern University]. Ann Arbor: Dissertations &Theses @ Northeastern University; ProQuest Dissertations &Theses Global.

Archer, L. (2001). 'Muslim brothers, black lads, traditional Asians': British Muslim young men's constructions of race, religion and masculinity. *Feminism & Psychology*, *11*(1), 79–105. doi:10.1177/0959353501011001005

Awad, G. H. (2010). The impact of acculturation and religious identification on perceived discrimination for Arab/Middle eastern Americans. *Cultural Diversity & Ethnic Minority Psychology*, *16*(1), 59–67. doi:10.1037/a0016675 PMID:20099965

Bagby, I. (2009). The American mosque in transition: Assimilation, acculturation and isolation. *Journal of Ethnic and Migration Studies*, *35*(3), 473–490. doi:10.1080/13691830802704640

Basit, T. N. (2009). White British; dual heritage; British Muslim: Young Britons' conceptualisation of identity and citizenship. *British Educational Research Journal*, *35*(5), 723–743. doi:10.1080/01411920802688747

Bhatti, G. (2011). Outsiders or insiders? Identity, educational success and Muslim young men in England. *Ethnography and Education*, *6*(1), 81–96. doi:10.1080/17457823.2011.553081

Black, M. E. (2012). Meanings and typologies of Duboisian double consciousness within 20th century United States racial dynamics (Master's theses). UMass, Boston.

Bonet, S. W. (2011). Educating Muslim American youth in a post-9/11 era: A critical review of policy and practice. *High School Journal*, *95*(1), 46–55. doi:10.1353/hsj.2011.0013

Bronfenbrenner, U. (1979). *The ecology of human development: experiments by nature and design*. Harvard University Press.

Brown, K. M. (2006). Leadership for social justice and equity: Evaluating a transformative framework andragogy. *Educational Administration Quarterly*, *42*(5), 700–745. doi:10.1177/0013161X06290650

Calbos, C. (2014). What is free and appropriate public education for a child? *Impact ADHD.com*

Certo, J., Cauley, K., & Chafin, C. (2003). Students' perspectives on their high school experience. *Adolescence*, *38*(152), 705–724. PMID:15053496

Choper, J. H. (1994). Religion and race under the constitution: Similarities and differences. *Cornell Law Review*, *79*(3), 491–513.

Connell, J. P., & Wellborn, J. G. (1991). Competence, autonomy, and relatedness: A motivational analysis of self-system processes. In M. R. Gunnar & L. A. Sroufe (Eds.), *Self processes and development* (Vol. 23). Lawrence Erlbaum Associates.

Crenshaw, K. (1991). Mapping the margins: Intersectionality, identity politics, and violence against women of color. *Stanford Law Review*, *6*(43), 1241–1299. doi:10.2307/1229039

Dewey, J. (1938). *Experience and education*. Collier Books.

Dorn, J. (2014). Equality, justice, and freedom: A constitutional perspective. *Libertarianism.org.*

DuBois, W. E. B. (1903). *The souls of Black folk.* Bantam Books.

Durkheim, E. (1912). *The elementary forms of religious life.* Dover Publications.

Eck, D. L. (2001). Muslim in America. *Christian Century (Chicago, Ill.), 118*(18), 20.

Fatima, S. (2011). Who counts as a Muslim? Identity, multiplicity and politics. *Journal of Muslim Minority Affairs, 31*(3), 339–353. doi:10.1080/13602004.2011.599542

Freire, P. (1973). *Education for critical consciousness.* Continuum.

Garner, S., & Selod, S. (2014). The racialization of Muslims: Empirical studies of Islamophobia. *Critical Sociology, 41*(1), 9–19. doi:10.1177/0896920514531606

Giroux, H. (1994). Doing cultural studies: Youth and the challenge of pedagogy. *Harvard Educational Review, 64*(3), 278–309. doi:10.17763/haer.64.3.u27566k67qq70564

Groves, R., & Welsh, B. (2010). The high school experience: What students say. *Issues in Educational Research, 20*(2), 87–104.

Gulson, K. N., & Webb, P. T. (2013). 'We had to hide we're Muslim': Ambient fear, Islamic schools and the geographies of race and religion. *Discourse (Abingdon), 34*(4), 628–641. doi:10.1080/01596306.2013.822623

Hamdan, A. (2007). Arab Muslim women in Canada: The untold narratives. *Journal of Muslim Minority Affairs, 27*(1), 133–154. doi:10.1080/13602000701308921

Hefner, C. (2015). Muslim American women on campus: Undergraduate social life and identity. *Anthropology & Education Quarterly, 46*(2), 199–201. doi:10.1111/aeq.12100

Hernandez, E. (2016). Utilizing critical race theory to examine race/ethnicity, racism, and power in student development theory and research. *Journal of College Student Development, 57*(2), 168–180. doi:10.1353/csd.2016.0020

hooks, b. (1994). *Teaching to transgress: Education as the practice of freedom.* New York, NY: Routledge.

Housee, S. (2012). What's the point? Anti-racism and students' voices against islamophobia. *Race, Ethnicity and Education, 15*(1), 101–120. doi:10.1080/13613324.2012.638867

Ivaniushina, V. A., & Aleksandrov, D. A. (2015). Socialization through informal education: The extracurricular activities of Russian school children. *Russian Social Science Review*, *56*(5), 18–39. doi:10.1080/10611428.2015.1115290

Jandali, A. K. (2013). Muslim students in post-9/11 classrooms. *Education Digest*, *78*(7), 21–24.

Kimberly, A. P. (2011). Framing Islam: An analysis of U.S. media coverage of terrorism since 9/11. *Communication Studies*, *62*(1), 90–112. doi:10.1080/10510 974.2011.533599

Kress, T. M. (2009). In the shadow of whiteness: (re)exploring connections between history, enacted culture, and identity in a digital divide initiative. *Cultural Studies of Science Education*, *4*(1), 41–49. doi:10.100711422-008-9137-6

Leonardo, Z. (2002). The souls of white folk: Critical pedagogy, whiteness studies, and globalization discourse. *Race, Ethnicity and Education*, *5*(1), 29–50. doi:10.1080/13613320120117180

Levinson, M. (2011). Racial politics and double consciousness: Education for liberation in an inescapably diverse polity. *Canadian Issues: Themes Canadiens*, (Spring), 80–82.

Lichtblau, E. (2016, September 17). Hate crimes against Muslim Americans most since 9/11 era. *The New York Times*, p. A13.

McCloud, A. M. (2010). Muslim American youth: Understanding hyphenated identities through multiple methods. *Journal of American Ethnic History*, *30*(1), 120.

Pager, D. (2006). The dynamics of discrimination. *National Poverty Center: Working Paper Series*, *6*(11), 1-47.

Pullman, A. (2013). Destabilizing curriculum history: A genealogy of critical thinking. *Journal of Curriculum Theorizing*, *29*(1), 173–189.

Reyes, I. I. I. (2007). Marginalized students in secondary school education. *The Journal of Border Educational Research*, *6*(2).

Sabry, N. S., & Bruna, K. R. (2007). Learning from the experience of Muslim students in American schools: Towards a proactive model of school-community cooperation. *Multicultural Perspectives*, *9*(3), 44–50. doi:10.1080/15210960701443730

Said, E. D. (1997). *Covering Islam: How the media and the experts determine how we see the rest of the world*. Vintage.

Sarwar, D., & Raj, R. (2016). Islamophobia, racism, and critical race theory. *Revista de la Fiscalía de Estado de la Provincia de Santa Fe*, 15.

Shields, C. M. (2004). Dialogic leadership for social justice: Overcoming pathologies of silence. *Educational Administration Quarterly*, *40*(1), 109–132. doi:10.1177/0013161X03258963

Simpson, G. E., & Yinger, J. M. (1985). *Racial and cultural minorities: An analysis of prejudice and discrimination*. Springer. doi:10.1007/978-1-4899-0551-2

Sirin, S. R., & Fine, M. (2008). *Muslim American youth: Understanding hyphenated identities through multiple methods*. New York University Press.

Sue, D. W. (2010). *Microaggressions and marginality: Manifestation, dynamics, and impact*. John Wiley & Sons.

Tindongan, C. W. (2011). Negotiating Muslim youth identity in a post-9/11 world. *High School Journal*, *95*(1), 72–87. doi:10.1353/hsj.2011.0012

ADDITIONAL READING

DuBois, W. E. B. (1903). *The souls of Black folk*. Bantam Books.

Fatima, S. (2011). Who counts as a Muslim? Identity, multiplicity and politics. *Journal of Muslim Minority Affairs*, *31*(3), 339–353. doi:10.1080/13602004.2011.599542

Freire, P. (1973). *Education for critical consciousness*. Continuum.

Garner, S., & Selod, S. (2014). The racialization of Muslims: Empirical studies of Islamophobia. *Critical Sociology*, *41*(1), 9–19. doi:10.1177/0896920514531606

Shields, C. M. (2004). Dialogic leadership for social justice: Overcoming pathologies of silence. *Educational Administration Quarterly*, *40*(1), 109–132. doi:10.1177/0013161X03258963

Simpson, G. E., & Yinger, J. M. (1985). *Racial and cultural minorities: An analysis of prejudice and discrimination*. Springer. doi:10.1007/978-1-4899-0551-2

Sirin, S. R., & Fine, M. (2008). *Muslim American youth: Understanding hyphenated identities through multiple methods*. New York University Press.

Tindongan, C. W. (2011). Negotiating Muslim youth identity in a post-9/11 world. *High School Journal*, *95*(1), 72–87. doi:10.1353/hsj.2011.0012

KEY TERMS AND DEFINITIONS

Critical Race Theory: A theoretical framework constituting of six tenets that looks at race and whiteness.

Cultural Capital: The concept that cultures facilitate/provide distinct traits or experiences to its followers that can count as capital.

Hijab: A head-covering worn by Muslim females after they have reached puberty.

Islamophobia: An irrational fear of people who associate themselves to Islam.

Marginalization: The reduction of a demographic to an invalidation of their experiences.

Mosque: A place of worship for Muslims.

Muslim: Someone who belongs to the religion of Islam.

Chapter 12
A Black Principal's Decolonizing Journey for Racial Justice

Jamel Adkins-Sharif
University of Massachusetts, Boston, USA

ABSTRACT

This chapter is a critical autoethnographic analysis of a Black male school leader enacting racial and social justice in his school improvement efforts. A reflexive dialogue between dissertation research findings and related leadership experiences seek to extricate the colonial structure of public education and the colonizing intent of schooling as experienced by a Black principal and the communities of color from which his students and caregivers derive. Three dynamics are identified as oppressive: white moves towards Black domination, white privilege, and intersecting oppressions. Three decolonizing acts are highlighted: centering of racial justice, catalyzing critical community consciousness and agency, and dismantling intersecting oppressions through counter narration.

Colonization carried forth by the armies of war is vastly more costly than that carried by armies of peace, whose outpost and garrisons are the public schools of the advancing nation. -Samuel Lindsay, Commissioner of Education, Puerto Rico, 1902

DOI: 10.4018/978-1-7998-7235-1.ch012

America is a colonial power. She has colonized 22 million Afro-Americans by depriving us of first-class citizenship, by depriving us of civil rights, actually by depriving us of human rights. -Malcolm X, The Ballot or the Bullet, 1964

BACKGROUND

The ongoing fight for racial justice in the United States, as exemplified by the Black Lives Matter movement and the ongoing national and international protests against police brutality, highlight the urgency of this chapter. I start with the assertion that Black life, minds, bodies, perspectives, and youth all matter. We witnessed countless replays of the brutal death of George Floyd on May 25, 2020, at the hands—or rather under the knee—of a white police officer in Minneapolis, Minnesota. It was preceded by the killing of Breonna Taylor while she slept in her own apartment, shot to death by Louisville, Kentucky police officers in a botched no-knock warrant on the evening of March 23, 2020. Before that, Ahmaud Arbery, a 25-year-old Black man, was hunted down and shot to death by three white vigilantes in Brunswick, Georgia, on February 23, 2020. These were recent additions to a long list of unarmed Black citizens killed by either police forces or white vigilantes. The excessing of Black humanity is also happening in schools through disproportionate discipline, the policing and demeaning of Black children's speech and cultural norms, deficit-informed teaching and negation of Black contribution to society, and the use of law enforcement to physically control and criminalize Black children in schools. We must resist these overlapping intrusions of anti-Blackness on our minds and bodies which attack us as Black people, regardless of whether we are children, caregivers, or school leaders (Khalifa, 2014; Khalifa et al., 2015).

RESEARCH PURPOSE AND QUESTIONS

The purpose of this chapter is to use autoethnographic reflection and analysis to interrogate questions of race, power, justice, and leadership in public schools. I detail my experience as a Black principal who sought racial and social justice in my school leadership and improvement work. This occurred against the backdrop of resistance, to my leadership, to moves toward cultural inclusivity, and to the empowerment of students and caregivers of color. The context for this combat is centered in a wealthy, largely white, highly resourced, mid-sized city in the Northeast. The school demographics reflect a majority nonwhite population and a privileged white minority student body. We further expand the backdrop to include school leadership experiences in two additional sites within the same New England state for comparison. This is an effort to distill from my dissertation research, its applicability across education situs. Throughout this chapter, my dissertation research on the challenges facing justice oriented Black male school leaders (Adkins-Sharif, 2020) is quoted and referenced.

In analyzing the questions below through critical race theory and frameworks of coloniality, I argue that schools are spaces and places of colonization for Black and Brown children, caregivers and leaders, and that our leadership work is an act of radical resistance to a system that reproduces domination and failure. My counter narrative seeks to answer the following:

1.   What are the overt and subtle ways racial and cultural oppressions are created and manifested in schools?
2.   How can Black school leaders effectively combat racial and cultural oppression that presents as disparate and inequitable educational opportunities and outcomes?

POSITIONALITY

I began school forty-seven years ago at the Sister Clara Muhammad School in Harlem's Mosque No.7 (founded by Malcolm X), and attended there from kindergarten to third grade. We were members of the Black nationalist and religious group called the Nation of Islam; my parents enrolled me in this independent schooll because of the racism in American institutions; they like other Nation members did not think their children would be treated properly in "integrated" public schools, so we separated. Within the broader context, schools in Northern cities were facing court-ordered desegregation, and some Black and Latinx children were bussed to schools in white communities which did not welcome them (Reardon et al., 2012; Sumner, 2018; Swain, 2012). Many Black parents sought school options they believed would not harm their children. I later attended an all-Black public elementary and middle school, and a diverse exam high school that engaged in racial academic tracking.

I entered the education profession in New York City while a student activist in college. I tutored Black children living in the neighborhood adjacent to my campus and began offering them Black history classes and cultural outings. I began assistant teaching and then teaching pre-kindergarten and kindergarten at a private Black elementary school. Afterwards, I taught public middle school special education primarily to Black and Latinx students in East New York, Brooklyn. All of my school leadership experiences have been at schools that were majority students of color, typically Black and Latinx. Whether as a primary, secondary, university, or graduate student, whether as a teacher, parent, or leader, I have had to negotiate race and racial power in some way in every school setting and its attendant experiences. Above most of my journey as an educator hovered the reality that children of color, children with special needs, those newly learning English, and those who came from impoverished households were neither receiving high quality education nor producing sufficient academic outcomes. Because of where I taught and lead, this meant almost exclusively Black and Latinx children experiencing the intersecting oppressions of race, class and cultural marginalization in schools entrusted to prepare them for the future.

THEORETICAL FRAMEWORKS

I employ the lens of critical race theory and a framework of coloniality to understand the racial, economic and cultural forces at play in my experiences as a school leader. Frameworks of coloniality are how I describe a set of tenets grounded in notions of settler colonialism and colonialism, as structures organizing past and current relations between Western European, Indigenous and African peoples in the western hemisphere, and between Western Europeans and nonwhites globally.

LITERATURE REVIEW

Critical Race Theory

Critical race theory (CRT) posits among other tenets, that racism is enduring and invisible in American life and institutions such as schools, that it intersects with other forms of oppression, and that nonwhite counternarratives of lived reality both challenge neoliberal hegemony, and are the manifestation of a praxis of resistance and justice (Bell, 1987; Delgado, 1989; Crenshaw, 1995; Lynn & Parker, 2006; Khalifa, 2013; Capper & Young, 2014; Capper, 2015).

In schools we endure centuries of racial mistreatment in education beginning with outright denial of literacy by law, followed by education for caste based subservience in a white supremacist social order, followed by resistance to federal court ordered equal treatement by white citizenry and state powers. This leads to a gradual replacement of obvious racial barriers with redefined categories of school readiness, and metrics of at-riskness, alongside learning ability, IQ, SES, language proficiency, and perceived cultural deficits. The result- the same negative outcome for the same children: a persistent gap in opportunities and performance for Black, Indigenous, and Latino students in the nations schools, ensuring lesser returns on a range of indicators such as income potential, social status, physical and mental health, contact with the criminal justice system, and life expectancy. As Rector-Aranda (2016) posits,

Because education is foundational to culture, it is crucial that educators recognize how things that happen in schools affect the outcomes and practices of other public institutions and the larger society. Education has substantial power to either challenge or to perpetuate societal injustices, the effects of which influence the schools again in a repeating cycle. (p.1)

CRT scholarship and praxis "draws on these tenets to analyze and disrupt the endemic, wide-ranging forms of racial oppression woven into educational institutions and the fabric of day-to-day school life" (Irby et al, 2019, p198). Such enduring oppression is currently made invisible by the nonracial markers it currently wears, while in other respects, such as disproportionate discipline, perceived dangerousness, and alleged lesser intelligence there emege explicit anti-black postures (Dumas, 2016). The intersecting dimensions occur across class, language, race, and learning ability, compounding their effect on children's lives. My leadership in such instances is also concerned with changing the narrative about these children, as literal answer back to dominant narratives about their ability, the viability of their cultural communities, and the level of engagement of their caregivers. Part of my work is making space for the counterstory, the perspective of the caregivers themselves, the educators who believe in the children's inherent genius, and the leaders who decide their schools will be sites of community empowerment. That journey and its chronicling represent CRT praxis.

Coloniality

Frameworks of coloniality are how I describe a set of tenets grounded in notions of settler colonialism and colonialism, as structures organizing past and current relations between Western European, Indigenous and African peoples in the western hemisphere, and between Western Europeans and nonwhites globally. The colonial framework is grounded in an ideology of Western white supremacy, derived from conquest and erasure, extraction, and economic domination through slavery and labor exploitation.(Arvin, Tuck & Morrill, 2013; Tomkins, 2002). This arrangement persists in the institutions of the United States even as a nation-state, such that the public education system supports the continued cultural and economic domination of BIPOC communities as it produces a politically controlled cheap labor force. (Fanon, 1967; Tuck & Gaztimbeide-Fernandez, 2013; Veracini, 2011, 2014; Tompkins, 2002; Khalifa et al, 2019).

The colonial intentions of public education were asserted without apology in the not too distant past (Spring, 2016). Education for Black children was to prepare for industrial labor and subservience to Jim Crow segregation; Native education was specifically designed to deculturalize, to kill the Indian to save the man, and to break any spirit of resistance to U.S. political and military hegemony. Instruction for Mexican American and Puerto Rican children was explicitly designed to indoctrinate patriotism to American culture and government forms, and to reject the Spanish language (Spring, 2016).. Zion and Blanchett (2011) argue that the reason large scale improvement in outcomes for all students has yet to be realized is that the problem is inaccurately framed. The problem must be framed as part of the history and legacy of racism, and as an issue of civil rights and social justice, viewed through a critical lens. Yet the colonial shadow dims the light in today's schools, where millions of Black, Indigenous and Latinx children do not get taught well, do not perform well, are not cared for nor fully believed in. Implicated are too many mostly white educators, representative of a society that irrationally fears those it cannot perpetually dominate, who believe police force and academic exclusion are necessary and proper components of that domination..

White Supremacy and White Privilege

For the dissertation research informing this study, I defined the terms white supremacy and white privilege. The best definition of white supremacy was first articulated by Charles Mills in his classic work, the Racial Contract (Mills, 1997/2014): It is the structural logic and mechanics that position whites and whiteness on a societal hierarchy, for the purposes of advantaging members of the group defined as white to varying degrees. In their analysis of the relationship between settler colonialism and white supremacy, Bonds and Inwood (2016) stated,

White supremacy is the presumed superiority of white racial identities, however problematically defined, in support of the cultural, political, and economic domination of non-white groups. (p. 719).

The positioning of white racial identities as superior is evident throughout the history of public school education in the United States. The current school reality continues to center or elevate whiteness, in terms of whom all students are normed against in standardized testing (White et al, 2016), whose narrative dominates curricular content and approaches, and which racial identity dominates the politics and economics of schools and schooling. White supremacy is therefore an ideology and an outcome.

276

White privilege, on the other hand, is a by-product of white supremacy. It is "the effect of the socially, politically, and economically constructed system that we call race" (Lensmire et al., 2013, p. 421). The unearned benefits of being white, of being the norm, of having one's perspective and identity taken for granted as the only legitimate perspective and identity, is white privilege. Like Crowley (2019), I maintain that "all white people play a role in the maintenance of white supremacy, simply by virtue of being white and regardless of any good intentions they might have" (p. 1480). Yet, white privilege is only one of several tools in the arsenal of white supremacy. Anti-Blackness is another such tool. Dumas (2016) wrote,

This lived experience serves as a continual reinscribing of the nonhumanness of the Black, a legitimization of the very antiblackness that has motivated centuries of violence against Black bodies. In this sense, even as slavery is no longer official state policy and practice, the slave endures in the social imagination, and also in the everyday suffering experienced by Black people. (p. 14)

We see anti-Blackness in the violence meted out in schools through: disproportionate discipline and exclusion; the criminalization of Black student conduct; the infusion of the police and state carceral functions and personnel in schools containing Black children; the diminution of their language, dress, and cultural ways; the absence or limited racial affirmation in curricula; the over-identification for special education services; the disregard and disengagement of schools toward Black caregivers; and the surveillance and control of Black school leaders (Dumas & ross, 2016; Lensmire et al, 2013; Lac & Baxley, 2019). All of this serves the interests of white supremacy. Bonds and Inwood (2016) continued, "The naturalization and invisibility of white racial identities and white skin privilege is made possible through the structures and logics of white supremacy. If privilege and racism are the symptoms, white supremacy is the disease" (p. 720).

METHODOLOGY

Through analysis of auto-ethnographic accounts of my school leadership experiences, I extricate a set of dynamics impacting the lived experiences of Black and Latinx children, caregivers and stakeholders. Autoethnographic study is a method of inquiry that explores the researcher's personal experience and connects this story to broader cultural, political, and social meanings and understandings (Chang, 2008). In connecting the personal to the cultural, it opens a "space of resistance" that combines analysis and interpretation with narrative details (Chang, 2008, Reda, 2007). Critical race theory's objective of centering marginalized narratives creates space for understanding other cultural perspectives and experiences in opposition to dominant white narratives. Resistance to coloniality, or decolonization, is the act of developing new knowledge bases; such storytelling as "theorizing back shifts the gaze of research back onto the institutions and structures that maintain settler colonialism" (Tuck & Guishard, 2013, p. 20).

My methodology as praxis centers the invisible, the marginalized, in order to create new understandings of the lived experiences of those oppression seeks to erase. I offer as liberatory a set of responses to the imposition of racial and economic pressure on nonwhite groups by white actors and/or systems of white control. This interaction between people and processes in schools, analyzed through the tenets of critical race theory and a framework of coloniality, reveals structures of colonization and dominating hierarchies along race and class.

I now turn to two data sources from my dissertation for analysis. The first is a field note reflection on the ways race appeared in my leadership journey, followed by more context for the three school sites. I discuss three dynamics highlighted by this reflection: a collective white move toward domination of the black leader; enactment of white privilege, and intersectional oppression of nonwhite students and stakeholders. The second source is a letter I read aloud at a meeting of the school committee in the district that was the subject of my dissertation study. It is contextualized by an excerpt from my dissertation The letter is used to illustrate a praxis of decolonization centered around three objectives: centering racial justice as a school leader, serving as catalyst for community critical consciousness and agency, and dismantling intersectional structures of oppression in schools trough counternarration.

ANALYSIS

Race and School Leadership

I've always had to battle racial constructs as a school leader. When I ran an alternative high school, my students were segregated because the mainstream admin deemed them too dangerous and disruptive to exist among the commoners. Disruptive they could be, but the real danger was the ease by which police, ever at the ready with tasers in hand, barged into our wing of the high school whenever the mainstream principal, a Black man, deemed it necessary. For him troubled Black and Brown children needed the threat of state violence in order to learn. The few white kids in my program were court-involved, and generally escaped once their felony charges were resolved; back into the mainstream to resume normalcy, not saddled with IEPs that read like rap sheets or psychotic diagnoses. As a middle school leader, white privileged parents and a handful of white teachers felt I paid way too much attention to making the place inclusive; things were just fine when we kept the sheltered English and learning disabled kids—both groups were overwhelmingly students of color— tucked away in self-contained worksheet factories. I came along and tried to shake up that arrangement, so I needed to go. As a charter school leader I experienced how white liberal board members and purported progressives sold the idea of a pre carceral institution as school choice and better options for poor Black and Latinx families. I imagined their thoughts from the beliefs they shared: Make 'em wear uniforms, silently walk the line, and emphasize skills, drills and discipline over all else; that'll get 'em to pass the standardized test....similar to the view above I once held, Black people, leaders, teachers and parents, often bought into these narratives on how memorization, testing, and control were keys to success. I believed it myself once, been steeped in it as a member of the Nation of Islam. Self-help, discipline and excellence—that's the ticket. Yet as solutions go it was incomplete; it left racist and classist structures off the hook, free to demean children and express disdain for their families. I had to step outside the insular space of the Sister Clara Muhammad Primary School daily, and face the hostile reality of a world unconvinced by my potential. For what had my commitment to excellence done to stop later teachers from doubting my abilities? What did hard work mean in a high school where not a single guidance counselor actually counseled me? My own academic excellence failed to shield me from the ignorance of hard working yet financially strapped parents who'd never known college, and therefore couldn't show me the way. Once in college, race contoured the debates raging all around me, over affirmative action, faculty diversity and ethnic studies departments, welfare dependency, the burgeoning urban policies of stop and frisk, and the "war on drugs". As both learner and leader, I exist(ed) within a racialized and monetized conception of what is. As a Black educator committed to social justice, I learn and lead in service of what can be. (Field notes, January 13, 2019)

The following section provides a snapshot of three schools I led and the ways coloniality and white supremacy sought to excess my leadership and marginalize Black and Brown students in the situs under study: An elementary charter school, a district middle school, and an alternative high school.

My first school leadership experience in this New England state was in an economically depressed mid sized city, where the public school student population was about 50% Latino, 25% white and 18% Black. I helped open a public elementary charter school that was 75% Black and 24% Latino, in order to provide families with better options than the district schools which had a long history of academic failure. The mission driven school was to provide rigorous academics and character education to children in grades K-5. Its founding executive director was a white liberal civil rights lawyer, and the majority of its founding board members were white liberal higher education and business professionals. The board lost half its Black members, including the school's cofounder, within the first two years of its existence. In year three, a schism developed between the white ED and myself. He wanted to pursue an educational path akin to large charter management organizations, focused on regimented direct instruction, strict discipline policies and frequent remediation, and preoccupation with standardized testing performance. I believed we needed to provide more educational choice, creatively design culturally relevant instruction, and more fully engage and empower caregivers in order to strengthen academic and social outcomes among students. The rift grew to an irreconcilable gulf, and it became filled with white moves toward domination and control, culminating in my demotion and ultimate departure. I liken this school to a settler colonial space, occupied by forces of oppression in the form of white board members and an executive director posited in an overwhelming nonwhite working poor community. As an administrator I was expected to conform to the demands of the settler, and when I refused, I was marked for control and erasure.

The middle school that was the focus of my dissertation had a student racial composition of 40% White, 35% Black, 20% Asian and 5% Latino. As founding principal, the district had charged myself and three other leaders (two of them also Black men) with creating the conditions for academic excellence and social justice, such that we were moving towards eliminating performance gaps in the city's high school. The newly formed middle schools were also an effort to further integrate the city's neighborhoods across race and economics. My school ended up being the most complex, housing a sheltered english, self contained learning disabled, and mainstream academic program. The first two programs were almost exclusively nonwhite spaces; sheltered English was primarily Haitian and East African recent immigrants, and temporary resident students from Russia, Germany and China, whose parents were either researchers, engineers, or faculty at a prestigious local university. This meant a significant gap in access and resources among the students in sheltered english, with the Black ethnics being most in need academically and economically. The self contained learning disabled class was exclusively Black and Latino students. White students attending the school were overwhelmingly middle and upper middle class; some also had individualized ed plans, but theirs were written such that they received their specialized services in mainstream classes. The accelerated math classes were overwhelmingly white and Asian populated, and I worked to make them more representative of the student body. I also reworked school schedules and structures to create more inclusive education options for sheltered English and learning disbled students. Additionally, I created opportunities for caregivers of color to participate in school governance and development. Throughout these efforts I encountered resistance from white educators, parents, and district leadership who challenged my authority, my vision for racial equity and cultural validation of Black and Brown students, and the asset-based premise of my school development stance. This tension culminated in a white coalition of teachers, parents and the school superintendent orchestrating my removal from my principalship. Towards the end of my final year I read a letter on the School Committee floor describing the ways its power had been in service of white privilege and nonwhite disempowerment.

School Committee Mic Drop

As the principal of Reledo Middle School, I was one of four middle school principals in the district to annually deliver a "State of the School" presentation before the school committee. It was the third year of our founding, an important yet still nascent period in an undertaking as monumental as school reorganization. During this ritual, we were expected to wax on about how hardworking our teachers were, boast of the great clubs and electives we offered the fortunate, and all the remediation and support we provided the damned. Yet, our presentations were derisively headlined in the committee agenda as "Improving the Middle Schools." *Improve*? In my mind, we were *new* to the scene, and we were *there* because *you* were supposed to be *improving the district!* I could barely contain my disdain. Little did they know the mic drop I was planning. I had told my colleagues in advance that I had prepared a letter to read into the record after we presented. I told them what was in the letter, and they were not in the least surprised because it was a recap of many conversations we had been having. They thought I was being bold but not reckless; they already knew how different my relationship with the superintendent had been. He had begun a series of unscheduled meetings with me during which he would share his consternation over complaints from the same handful of white parents. About four or five white teachers would chime in, expressing their displeasure with my leadership because I emphasized cultural proficiency and inclusion to, in their eyes, the detriment of all else. Because of the increased attention the superintendent was giving to this group, I came to understand my school as the presumed "white space"; it was here the wagons of white resistance would circle, and my administration would be stopped. Here the school is akin to the existence of the colonized within the metropole, a wealthy community in which provisions were made for the *Othered*, so long as they did not intrude on the status quo. While purporting to seek academic excellence and social justice, the community expressed this in word only; deeds were designed to ensure the perpetuation of a colonial hierarchy, whereby students and leaders of color never really produced or experienced sustained positive change.

I read my letter so they would know that I considered the school committee complicit in this colonial excessing of me as school leader, as Black man with agency. With my supportive wife behind me, punctuating my final verses with sharp *uh-huh*s and *that's right!*, I laid bare the guts of a system unwilling to self-examine or self-correct, yet quite eager to sacrifice. It was cathartic. It was empowering. It was resistance to being relegated as irrelevant, subaltern. I needed to name the ways privilege and systemic disempowerment were being maintained by the district, and I wanted it on the public record:

If you want to improve the [middle] schools, respect the expertise and experience of the principals who lead the buildings. I thought we were hired as the experts, as the ones who've actually been in the trenches, actually understand the middle school mind, and the ways middle schools differ from K-8 structures. We need support, we need guidance at times, we need resources, but most importantly, we need our voices to actually matter, and not get lost in the noise of Harvard researchers, teachers skittish about change, and loud and entitled parents who never embraced the [Change] Agenda to begin with. Treat Heads and Principals as the knowledgeable professionals they are, not with platitudes, but by your actions as school committee and district leadership. We have said loud and clear what we need: community liaisons, a commitment to math achievement for all learners on par with all the energy and resources put into accelerated math, and a real commitment to cultural proficiency and restorative practice equal to the money and resources this district is willing to give consultants and packaged initiatives.

If you want to improve, dismantle the informal structures that allow the same chorus of voices to dictate the way HPS operates, namely stop taking your directions from a small group of entitled, middle and upper class, largely white parents. By informal structures I mean the way the way they're allowed to end run around principals and go straight to school committee or the district with any and all issues; the way they get you to react when they send a few fiery emails, or demand disproportionate facetime, or hold secret meetings in their homes to work against school leaders. In my experience, and that of my colleagues, that isn't the way most black and brown parents, or immigrant parents, or parents of low income, that isn't the way they typically engage with schools and the district, which means they are largely invisible when the real decisions are being made-informally. Yet they represent 60% of the students in this system. That's a problem. If you want to improve the [middle] schools, put sincere effort behind empowering the silenced majority. (Letter to the HPS school committee, May 19, 2015)

The alternative high school I ran was actually a program within a typical high school. We were relegated first to a wing of the first floor of the only high school in a small town south of a major New England city. Made up of 2000 students, the high school student population was about half Black, mostly Haitian, about a quarter

VIetnamese and the remainder white students. My program contained 30-40 students who had been kicked out of mainstream high school after a series of suspensions or expulsions, or because they were awaiting the outcome of a felony charge they were facing in court. My program was overwhelmingly Black and Latino male, had 5 white students and were 50% students with IEPs. Additionally, a number of students had diagnosed psychological and emotional disorders. The mostly white teaching staff feared these students and the mainstream administration, headed by a Black man, would often have school security follow my students around the building. The police were called on them for the slightest provocations. This resulted in a very strained relationship between our administrations in a building he controlled. I worked to create a path to return to mainstream education, involve my students in program decisions, increase parent involvement in alternative education, and resisted the mainstream administrators efforts to surveil and criminalize my students. I sought to empower my staff to imagine success for their students and themselves, but I lacked the organizational authority to protect them or my students. The mainstream high school principal, working with his staff and the school resource officer, thrice attempted to prosecute my students and poached my strongest teacher to exclusively teach mainstream students. We might imagine this third space as one of classic colony, an occupied center within the the domain of white control, yet administered through the nonwhite school leader. I was positioned as rebel in that setting, the leader of maroons cast outside the bounds of the mainstream, named alternative, even subaltern. For this cohort of students is perhaps the most marginalized in school settings. Excessed minds and controlled bodies served to increase ranks in a school experiencing steady depopulation. Yet we were not privy to the services and humanizing experiences one should experience in schools. My students had limited access to mainstream classes, the lunchroom, and gym, electives,and were policed the moment they left the surveilled wing of the building we occupied. These varied colonizing settings and experiences all moved towards innocence of the system and marginalization and erasure of the students and my leadership (Veracini, 2014; Tompkins, 2002; Tuck & Gaztambide-Fernandez, 2013)..

DISCUSSION

The following figure illustrates the connection between oppressive and liberatory moves within a CRT and coloniality analysis of the autoethnographic tellings of my leadership experiences.

Table 1. Frameworks of oppression and liberation

Variables of White Supremacy and Coloniality as Oppression	Literature
Collective white move towards domination of the Black leader	Feagin & Feagin, 2003; Gallagher, 2008; Love, 2019;
Enactment of white privilege	Adkins-Sharif, 2020; Lensmire et al, 2013; Bonds & Inwood, 2016; Crowley, 2019
Intersectional oppression of nonwhite students and stakeholders	Crenshaw, 1995; Khalifa et al, 2019; McIntosh, 2019; Santamaria & Santamaria, 2015
Decolonization and Resistance to White Supremacy as Liberation	**Literature**
Centering racial justice in their leadership work	Parker & Villalpando, 2007; Adkins-Sharif, 2020; Kowalchuk, 2019; Brooks & Jean-Marie, 2007
Catalyzing community critical consciousness and agency	Ladson-Billings, 1995, 1998, 2014; Khalifa et al, 2019; Lac & Baxley, 2019
Dismantling intersectional structures of oppression in schools through counternarration	Gooden et al, 2003; Forrester et al, 2019; Tuck & Guishard, 2013; Crenshaw, 1995

Oppressive Moves

White Collective Moves Toward Domination of the Black Children and Leaders

Regardless of setting, there exists in response to Black resistance, a collective white move toward control and assertion of domination. Blacks exist to be controlled in the social imagination as slave, even if slavocracy has passed; the need to dominate the labor and thinking of the Black, the need to crush his dissent, to put down the rebel persists. It was the same reaction to the Black demand for desegregated schools, for an affirming curriculum taught, for more teachers and leaders who looked like them to be in their kids' schools, and for establishing Black and Africana studies, and hiring Black university faculty. All these demands met resistance and sanction from white society. Feagin and Feagin (2003) connect past global colonialism and present oppression in this way:

A situation of cultural, political, and ethnic oppression for subordinated racial and ethnic groups without the existence of an overt colonial administration and its trappings of legal segregation. Official decolonization does not mean an end to coloniality, the colonial hierarchies of racial and ethnic oppression often remain. *(p. 35)*

The collective move towards control was a coordinated effort by white parents to discourage rising fifth grade families from enrolling their children in my school. This was decided at a meeting at a parents home where they tried to involve members of the school committee in violation of the law. This happened while several white teachers who objected to my professional development focus on cultural proficiency began to meet with their union leadership to plan resistance, and gained the ear and implied approval of the superintendent. The need to dominate extended to students they could neither fully appreciate nor educate. White teachers felt compelled to hyper surveil Black boys for misdeeds and Black girls for perceived disrespect and defiance, rejecting suggestions that they were subjectively evaluating cultural difference. I would often point out the ways in which white student disrespect and adolescent challenges to teacher authority went unnoticed and un-consequenced; they would characterize these observations as evidence I did not support teachers. It did not matter that some (though not all) nonwhite teachers disagreed with this conclusion. Nor did it matter to the superintendent that nonwhite caregivers assessed my leadership differently from the group of white ones he heard from frequently. Even meeting immigrant, Black, and parents of students with special needs did not sway the superintendent from the view that white stakeholders knew better. He was operating within the strictures of colonial reasoning. As Gallagher (2008) argued,

White logic, then, refers to a context in which white supremacy has defined the techniques and processes of reasoning about social facts. White logic assumes a historical posture that grants eternal objectivity to the views of elite whites and condemns the views of non-whites to perpetual subjectivity. (p. 173)

Similar reasoning from the white lens proclaimed that Black and Latinx children work best in an environment where the emphasis is on their control and discipline, the expectation for their learning occurs within a discourse of deficit and remediation, and their parents lack the cultural capital and intellectual sophistication to contribute meaningfully to their children's education. This was the calculus driving the beliefs of the charter school executive director. His emphasis on character education is indicative of a thinking that acquiescence can be a proxy for civic engagement, rather than it being a means to subdue, to colonize. With character education, "students no longer learn how to be informed and active citizens, which is key to democracy; instead they learn how to comply and recite affirmations about their grit" (Love, 2019, p. 70)

White Privilege (Cultural and Economic)
of Teachers and Parents

White privilege, a by-product of white supremacy is "the effect of the socially, politically, and economically constructed system that we call race" (Lensmire et al., 2013, p. 421).

The system allows whites to rely on informal social networks as pathways for exercising collective power. In those shared cultural spaces, the collective will can be calibrated, so that it is heard as one voice on the School Site Council, the school's 501c(3), the Parent Council; it is not the voice of all stakeholders, but the collective will of privileged whites. It is taken for granted they are accurate, authorized, authoritative.

Reflecting later, I wrote:

The nature of neo-liberal systemic arrangements is hierarchical, and therefore, uneasy tension existed between the school committee and the superintendent. They appointed him, but he was the face of district leadership. It was a tension I exploited for the purpose of claiming my voice. My reading was unexpected, and rocked the superintendent's smug self-assurance, and the Committee could perform its oversight function in the presumed interest of transparency and progress. Yet at the same time it was clear they were equally complicit in upholding backchannels for organized white resistance to school leader efforts. I knew this because one member later called me and let me know parents tried recruiting him to a meeting to plan my demise. He not only believed it morally wrong, but knew it to be a violation of open meeting laws. It was likely other Committee members were also invited, and unlikely I'd ever know how they responded. In their predictable rebuts to my charge, they rationalized they were duly elected to represent their constituents. It just seemed that more often than not, that representation reflected the wealthier, privileged voices of said constituency. They, like the superintendent, operated in anticipation of white reaction, but they could disperse their impact across the entire representative body. The superintendent on the other hand, functioned as the focal point for both formal and informal power. He both inculcated and echoed oppositional white sentiment under the premise of engaging all stakeholders. And white teachers and privileged parents behaved as if they spoke for everyone. The superintendent's reaction was a direct assault on my ability to speak freely, to give voice to my experience, to critique and challenge the narrative being put forth through the messaging and format of district structures. white supremacy and colonial domination rely upon a singular master narrative, a hegemonic description of lived reality; it is therefore necessary to delegitimize and crush all dissent. (Field notes, May 31, 2019)

Intersectional Systemic Oppressions of Race, Gender, Class and Language

Intersecting challenges across identity converge to deny Black and Latinx students quality opportunities and outcomes in schools. At the alternative school my students carried years of school failure and pushout, and special education and mental health designations yielded shame while simultaneously purporting to bring access to a menu of academic, social, and mental health services and resources. These did not often correlate to school success, and parents and caregivers were often left out of key decisionmaking points. Even those students who did complete high school struggled with post secondary options because they and their families did not know how to advocate for more; their catchment area lacked the economic resources for robust post secondary planning, or they did not have a sense of connectedness with school staff that extended beyond their perfunctory responsibilities to students. Most of the white teachers seemed to maintain only a transactional relationship with most Black and Latino students. As Khalifa et al. (2019) detailed,

There are some experiences and outcomes for minoritized and Indigenous people and from (post)colonial schooling that are often presented as positive. Increases in test scores, graduation rates, postsecondary attendance and employment rates are often cited as indicators for how schools have helped minoritized and Indigenous people. However, standardization is not always the goal for Indigenous communities, and they have not been linked to community empowerment and progress. In fact, colonial schools have served to stifle the self-determination and existence of Indigenous peoples. (p. 16)

Ten years into its existence, the charter school was finally producing the standardized test outcomes the accountability machine touts as evidence of effective education. Yet the school still lacks an authentic avenue for caregiver involvement, and the teaching staff remain disempowered under nonunionized at-will work conditions and a culturally incompetent administration.

At the middle school success to me meant empowering caregivers to experience decisionmaking at the school, Black boys feeling affirmed culturally, and sheltered English and learning disabled students experiencing inclusive education and academic choice. It was less successful in that we could not maintain the school's commitment to focus on those in the community whom schools had traditionally failed.

Liberatory Moves

Centering Racial Justice in Their Leadership Work

CRT provides a "valuable lens with which to interpret administrative policies and procedures in educational institutions and provides avenues for action in the area of racial justice" (Parker & Villalpando, 2007). Utilizing this framework we can conclude that the project of racial oppression has never ceased in American institutions including schools, and therefore the fight for racial justice must also be enduring. The legacy of education here, first as a British settler colony and later as the American nation- state, has been a project focused on colonization and deculturalization of BIPOC folks who have redefined through resistance, the nature of their educational experience. The Black school leader seeking justice in his school understands the ways race and racial power impact student performance and teacher effectiveness, and interrupts those barriers to success and their compounding negative effect on other intersecting markers of identity.

In my telling to the school committee, you are witness to my agenda: My caregivers of color need community liaisons who understand their culture and the ways they engage schools, not individuals waiting for the caregivers to assimilate to white standards of engagement in order to be validated. I was among Black leaders insisting on their expertise as instructional leaders, refusing to be governed by white assumptions centered and validated in academia and through economic influence. The colonial system relies on a singular narrative, and the lived experience of Black school leaders can challenge that hegemony. We can present affirming accounts of our community, tap into knowledge and collective cultural wisdom, as well as a tradition of resistance pedagogy. Helping teachers rethink how and what they teach. and what they believe about their students is racial justice work. Insisting that privileged whites with connections and verbose emails do not have undue influence over educational policy is racial justice. Hiring, training, and supporting more nonwhite educators is racial justice. Black and Brown students experiencing academic success and affirmation normatively across United States learning institutions is penultimate racial justice.

Catalyzing Community Critical Consciousness and Agency

Gloria Ladson-Billings (1995, 1998) maintained that culturally relevant pedagogy must also be about developing a critical consciousness, encouraging "teachers to ask about the nature of the student-teacher relationship, the curriculum, schooling, and society" (Ladson-Billings, 1995, p. 483). Anything less merely exoticizes the "Other" and perpetuates inequity by celebrating diversity without naming or challenging racial power constructs. My leadership has sought to get my teachers to ask these questions so that they can support their students making similar inquiries on their place in society and their ability to impact it. Black and Brown children resisted a racialized power construct primed to view them as inadequate. Such critical consciousness among students is essential to a social justice-oriented and culturally proficient understanding of equity; their actions force us to recognize that "learners can be sources and resources of knowledge and skills—a critical component of culturally relevant pedagogy" (Ladson-Billings, 2014, p. 79). This emerging consciousness occurred in some caregivers of color, as the following parent observation indicated:

My son is great at math and he was supposed to move on to the advanced class. A little before the break, once it became real to him, he's not making the best choice. I think part of it was he realized he would be with a group of predominantly white kids; suddenly he wasn't performing well in math. He may be purposely playing a game so that he won't be considered for the accelerated track. (Black parent, NAACP meeting minutes, January 17, 2015)

Dismantling Intersectional Structures of Oppression in Schools Through Counternarration

This parent understood that her son's resistance to accelerated placement, despite his strong ability, may have been due to the cultural trade-off it represented, which he was not willing to make. A class better suited to challenge him academically would also be a class with the white gaze and without cultural support. He would be one of a very few, and it was not a safe bet for him culturally, despite adult rhetoric to the contrary. It is hard to argue he was not right since the white gaze and space had made it unsafe for us as Black leaders as well. Like the children, we were to be judged by white expectations, assumptions, and beliefs about whether we were competent and belonged. That has devastating implications for Black children and leaders' sense of self-efficacy. Good et al.'s (2003) work on stereotype threat is instructive:

Research indicates that evaluative scrutiny is at the heart of most situations that evoke stereotype threat. Being evaluated in a stereotyped domain is sufficient to trigger the trademark responses associated with stereotype threat—lack of enjoyment of the educational process, increased anxiety and stress, and, ultimately, underperformance. Second, group composition—the racial or gender mix in a room of test takers—also can trigger stereotype-relevant thoughts, and thus vulnerability to stereotype threat because group composition can make salient one's social identity and the stereotypes associated with that identity. (p. 647)

This threat influences the sense of safety one feels to take risks in a classroom, to exist and lead authentically in a school, and to challenge the status quo. If doing so leaves one open to racial marginalization, it may not be a risk worth taking. The physical and emotional toll of negotiating and overcoming these racialized threats is a kind of weathering (Forrester et al., 2019) and has a disproportionate negative effect on African Americans. This weathering impacts Black children trying to learn in schools, Black caregivers who also experience it in other societal institutions, Black educators seeking to dispel stereotypes and provide affirming and fortifying learning experiences for Black children (and all children), and for Black leaders looking to enact racial justice in their leadership thoughts and actions. In these instances, Black minds and bodies face a relentless, often low-intensity assault on our being and right to be; weathering and stereotype threat represent an incessant questioning of the capacity of our minds, and the legitimacy of our actions.

The leader committed to racial justice and decolonization removes these barriers to opportunity and success, be they psychological, procedural or structural. My letter to the school committee sought to expose systems that went unnamed by the positional authorities within the school district. My narrative telling of the challenges facing Black school leaders in environments containing white racial and economic privilege is an instructive lesson in leadership and cultural identity. Central to my research design is the recognition that the knowledge and experience of people of color is "critical to understanding racial subordination" (Parker & Villalpando, 2007, p. 520). Under a CRT framework, the stories of Black male principals provide a rich resource for better understanding white supremacy, leadership, and educational equity. As a decolonizing act of developing new knowledge bases, "theorizing back shifts the gaze of research back onto the institutions and structures that maintain settler colonialism" (Tuck & Guishard, 2013, p. 20).

CONCLUSION

This theoretical exploration of my journey as a Black man and school principal came to understand my work as rooted in racial justice and illuminative of a colonizing structure and intent in the schools where I have taught and led. It is an assertion of the enduring settler colonial project rooted in white supremacy and racial capitalism. I placed my dissertation research on leading through change and resistance, in dialogue with my journey at two other schools; outlined is the colonial imprint inherent in our systems of learning, it's deculturalization and dominating objectives laid bare alongside racist and classist rationales.

The legacy of these institutions is the silencing of Black voices in service of colonial demands to excess Black humanity; it relies on the absence of thought, theory, and praxis by Black people about their lived experience and their unique outlook on the educational dilemmas facing their children and other children of color. We have a story to tell within and outside academia about our condition as internal colonial subjects, whether in the "metropole" or beyond its bounds. The development and illumination of a Black counter narrative serves both critical race and decolonial praxis in education.

IMPLICATIONS

Implications for Research

This study explored my lived experiences as aBlack school leader with an explicit racial justice agenda. It adds to the body of knowledge on leadership theory, an area where dominant white narratives continue to prevail, though increasingly diverse voices are entering the discourse (Khalifa et al., 2019; Santamaría & Santamaría, 2015; Wilson & Johnson, 2015). This research contributes to coloniality studies in its centering of the "slave narrative"; the settler colonial construct positions the "ownable and murderable slave" as dominated property and labor (Arvin et al., 2013, p.12). This research centers the lived experiences of a Black man in a field that has always sought to discount, dominate, and diminish Black intellect and personhood. It therefore has implications for leadership studies, educational studies, as well as theories of coloniality and anti-Blackness. Indeed, this study can illuminate anti-Blackness as a feature of the colonial order that leaders should actively identify and dismantle (Dumas, 2016; Lac & Baxley, 2019). Anti-Blackness is a most pernicious feature because of the harm it causes Black children, caregivers, teachers, and leaders. It is more than simply permanent and enduring; it is violent and destructive by its mere existence within any structure. This study weaves important threads between critical race and coloniality constructs. As a lens onto racialized systems of domination, CRT further illuminates, through intersectional analysis, the colonial nature of schools and the process of schooling.

Implications for Practice

This autoethnography is critical for understanding what is needed to be an effective school leader, for preparing future social justice school leaders, and for aligning such knowledge within the unique context of racialized leaders leading racialized schools in a race- and class-based society. This research requires a consideration of the cultural dimensions of our education system and how those dimensions are informed by the dominant race and class arrangement in the United States. As socializing and replicating institutions, schools reproduce what exists in society, its power relations, social hierarchies, and cultural norms. Leadership preparatory programs must center race, identity, and racial power in their curricula, as these are foundational elements to U.S. culture and ideology, and are reinforced in the process, structure, and curricula of schools. We are way past considering this an addendum or add-on to other "important" matters of leadership. In the U.S. colonial and nation-state context, race and racial power have always had leadership implications.

REFERENCES

Apel, D. (2004). *Imagery of lynching: Black men, white women, and the mob.* Rutgers University Press.

Arvin, M., Tuck, E., & Morrill, A. (2013). Decolonizing feminism: Challenging connections between settler colonialism and heteropatriarchy. *Feminist Formations, 25*(1), 8–34. doi:10.1353/ff.2013.0006

Aveling, N. (2007). Anti-racism in schools: A question of leadership? *Discourse (Abingdon), 28*(1), 69–85. doi:10.1080/01596300601073630

Battiste, M. (2017). *Decolonizing education: Nourishing the learning spirit.* UBC Press.

Bell, D. A. (1987). *And we are not saved: The elusive quest for racial justice.* Basic Books.

Blauner, R. (1972). *Racial oppression in America.* Harper and Row.

Bogotch, I. (2013). Educational theory: The specific case of social justice as an educational leadership construct. In I. Bogotch & C. Shields (Eds.), *International handbook of educational leadership and social (in)justice* (pp. 51–65). Springer.

Bonds, A., & Inwood, J. (2016). Beyond white privilege: Geographies of white supremacy and settler colonialism. *Progress in Human Geography, 40*(6), 715–733. doi:10.1177/0309132515613166

Bourgois, P. (2000). Violating apartheid in the United States: On the streets and in academia. In F. W. Twine & J. W. Warren (Eds.), *Racing research, researching race: Methodological dilemmas in critical race studies* (pp. 187–214). New York University Press.

Brantlinger, E., Majd-Jabbari, M., & Guskin, S. L. (1996). Self-interest and liberal educational discourse: How ideology works for middle-class mothers. *American Educational Research Journal, 33*(3), 571–597. doi:10.3102/00028312033003571

Brayboy, B. (2013). Tribal critical race theory: An origin story and future directions. In *Handbook of Critical Race Theory in Education* (pp. 88–100). Taylor and Francis.

Brooks, J. S., & Watson, T. N. (2019). School leadership and racism: An ecological perspective. *Urban Education, 54*(5), 631–655. doi:10.1177/0042085918783821

Capetillo-Ponce, J. (2007). From a clash of civilizations to internal colonialism. *Ethnicities, 7*(1), 116–134. doi:10.1177/1468796807073922

Capper, C. A. (2015). The 20th-year anniversary of critical race theory in education: Implications for leading to eliminate racism. *Educational Administration Quarterly, 51*(5), 791–833. doi:10.1177/0013161X15607616

Capper, C. A., & Young, M. D. (2014). Ironies and limitations of educational leadership for social justice: A call to social justice educators. *Theory into Practice, 53*(2), 158–164. doi:10.1080/00405841.2014.885814

Carmichael, S., & Hamilton, C. V. (1992). *Black power: The politics of liberation in America*. Vintage Books. (Original work published 1967)

Carr, P. R. (2011). *Transforming Educational Leadership Without Social Justice? Looking at Critical Pedagogy as More Than a Critique, and a Way Toward Democracy* (Vol. 409). Counterpoints.

Carson, D. (2017). *What are the experiences of African American female principals in high-poverty urban schools?* [Doctoral dissertation, University of North Texas]. UNT Digital Library. https://digital.library.unt.edu/ark:/67531/metadc1011826/

Carter, D. J. (2007). Why the Black kids sit together at the stairs: The role of identity-affirming counter-spaces in a predominantly white high school. *The Journal of Negro Education, 76*(4), 542–554.

Carter, D. J., & Lomotey, K. (1990). African-American principals: School leadership and success. *The Journal of Negro Education, 59*(4), 632. doi:10.2307/2295325

Carver-Thomas, D. (2018). *Diversifying the teaching profession: How to recruit and retain teachers of color*. Learning Policy Institute.

Chang, H. (2008). *Autoethnography as method*. Left Coast Press.

Chen, G. (2019, October 24). *White students are now the minority in U.S. public schools* [Blog post]. https://www.publicschoolreview.com/blog/white-students-are-now-the-minority-in-u-s-public-schools

Chubb, J. E., & Loveless, T. (Eds.). (2004). *Bridging the achievement gap.* Brookings Institution Press.

Connor, D. J. (2017). Who is responsible for the racialized practices evident within (special) education and what can be done to change them? *Theory into Practice, 56*(3), 226–233. doi:10.1080/00405841.2017.1336034

Cook, D. A., & Dixson, A. D. (2013). Writing critical race theory and method: A composite counterstory on the experiences of black teachers in New Orleans post-Katrina. *International Journal of Qualitative Studies in Education: QSE, 26*(10), 1238–1258. doi:10.1080/09518398.2012.731531

Crenshaw, K. (1989). Demarginalizing the intersection of race and sex: A black feminist critique of antidiscrimination doctrine, feminist theory and antiracist politics. *University of Chicago Legal Forum, 1989*(1), 8. https://chicagounbound.uchicago.edu/uclf/vol1989/iss1/8

Crenshaw, K. (1995). *Critical race theory: The key writings that formed the movement.* New Press.

Cresswell, J. W. (2009). *Research design: Qualitative, quantitative, and mixed methods approaches.* Sage Publications.

Crowley, R. (2019). White teachers, racial privilege, and the sociological imagination. *Urban Education, 54*(10), 1462–1488. doi:10.1177/0042085916656901

Dantley, M. E. (2005). African American spirituality and Cornel West's notions of prophetic pragmatism: Restructuring educational leadership in American urban schools. *Educational Administration Quarterly, 41*(4), 651–674. doi:10.1177/0013161X04274274

Dávila, B. (2015). Critical race theory, disability microaggressions and Latina/o student experiences in special education. *Race, Ethnicity and Education, 18*(4), 443–468. doi:10.1080/13613324.2014.885422

de Bray, C., Musu, L., McFarland, J., Wilkinson-Flicker, S., Diliberti, M., Zhang, A.. & Wang, X. (2019). *Status and trends in the education of racial and ethnic groups 2018.* Academic Press.

Drago-Severson, E., & Blum-DeStefano, J. (2019). A developmental lens on social justice leadership: Exploring the connection between meaning making and practice. *Journal of Educational Leadership and Policy Studies, 3*(1), n1.

Gooden, M. (2012). What does racism have to do with leadership?: Countering the idea of colorblind leadership: A reflection of race and the growing pressures of the urban principalship. *Educational Foundations, 26*(1), 67–84.

Khalifa, M., Arnold, N. W., & Newcomb, W. (2015). Understand and advocate for communities first. *Phi Delta Kappan, 96*(7), 20–25. doi:10.1177/0031721715579035

Khalifa, M. A. (2015). Can Blacks be racists? Black-on-Black principal abuse in an urban school setting. *International Journal of Qualitative Studies in Education: QSE, 28*(2), 259–282. doi:10.1080/09518398.2014.916002

Khalifa, M. A. (2018). *Culturally responsive school leadership*. Harvard Education Press.

Lipman, P. (2008). Mixed-income schools and housing: Advancing the neoliberal urban agenda. *Journal of Education Policy, 23*(2), 119–134.

Lipman, P. (2008). Mixed-income schools and housing: Advancing the neoliberal urban agenda. *Journal of Education Policy, 23*(2), 119–134.

Loder, T. L. (2005). African American Women Principals' Reflections on Social Change, Community Othermothering, and Chicago Public School Reform. *Urban Education, 40*(3), 298–320.

Loder, T. L. (2005). African American Women Principals' Reflections on Social Change, Community Othermothering, and Chicago Public School Reform. *Urban Education, 40*(3), 298–320.

Lopez, G. R. (2003). The (racially neutral) politics of education: A critical race theory perspective. *Educational Administration Quarterly, 39*(1), 68–94.

Lopez, G. R. (2003). The (racially neutral) politics of education: A critical race theory perspective. *Educational Administration Quarterly, 39*(1), 68–94.

Love, B. L. (2019). *We want to do more than survive: Abolitionist teaching and the pursuit of educational freedom*. Beacon Press.

Love, B. L. (2019). *We want to do more than survive: Abolitionist teaching and the pursuit of educational freedom*. Beacon Press.

Lynn, M., & Parker, L. (2006). Critical race studies in education: Examining a decade of research on U.S. schools. *The Urban Review*, *38*(4), 257–290. https://doi.org/10.1007/s11256-006-0035-5

Lynn, M., & Parker, L. (2006). Critical race studies in education: Examining a decade of research on U.S. schools. *The Urban Review*, *38*(4), 257–290. https://doi.org/10.1007/s11256-006-0035-5

Marsh, T. E., & Knaus, C. B. (2016). Fostering movements or silencing voices: School principals in Egypt and South Africa. *International Journal of Multicultural Education*, *17*(1), 188–210.

Marsh, T. E., & Knaus, C. B. (2016). Fostering movements or silencing voices: School principals in Egypt and South Africa. *International Journal of Multicultural Education*, *17*(1), 188–210.

Parker, L., & Villalpando, O. (2007). A (race)cialized perspective on education leadership: Critical race theory in educational administration. *Educational Administration Quarterly*, *43*(5), 519–524.

Paschall, K. W., Gershoff, E. T., & Kuhfeld, M. (2018). A two decade examination of historical race/ethnicity disparities in academic achievement by poverty status. *Journal of Youth and Adolescence*, *47*(6), 1164–1177.

Reardon, S. F., Grewal, E. T., Kalogrides, D., & Greenberg, E. (2012). Brown fades: The end of court-ordered school desegregation and the resegregation of American public schools. *Journal of Policy Analysis and Management*, *31*(4), 876–904.

Rector-Aranda, A. (2016). School norms and reforms, critical race theory, and the fairytale of equitable education. *Critical Questions in Education*, *7*(1), 1–16.

Reda, M. M. (2007). Autoethnography as research methodology? *Academic Exchange Quarterly*, *11*(1), 177–183.

Santamaría, L. J., & Santamaría, A. P. (2015). Counteracting educational injustice with applied critical leadership: Culturally responsive practices promoting sustainable change. *International Journal of Multicultural Education*, *17*(1), 22–42.

Spring, J. (2016). *Deculturalization and the struggle for equality: A brief history of the education of dominated cultures in the United States*. Routledge.

Sumner, K. A. (2018). *Native daughter: A lived experience of desegregation* [Doctoral dissertation, University of Massachusetts Boston]. Graduate Doctoral Dissertations. https://scholarworks.umb.edu/doctoral_dissertations/451

Swain, B. G. (2012). *Aspects of school integration: From Brown to court-ordered bussing* [Master's thesis, University of Michigan]. http://hdl.handle.net/2027.42/117930

Tatum, B. (1994). The colonial model as a theoretical explanation of crime and delinquency. *African American perspectives on crime, causation, criminal justice administration, and crime prevention*, 33-52.

Tomkins, J. (2002). Learning to see what they can't: Decolonizing perspectives on Indigenous education in the racial context of rural Nova Scotia. *McGill Journal of Education/Revue des sciences de l'éducation de McGill, 37*(3).

Tuck, E., & Gaztambide-Fernández, R. A. (2013). Curriculum, replacement, and settler futurity. *Journal of Curriculum Theorizing, 29*(1).

Veracini, L. (2014). Understanding colonialism and settler colonialism as distinct formations. *Interventions, 16*(5), 615–633.

Williams, H. A. (2005). *Self-taught: African American education in slavery and freedom*. University of North Carolina Press.

Williams, R. L. (1973). On black intelligence. *Journal of Black Studies, 4*(1), 29–39.

Wilson, C., & Johnson, L. (2015). Black educational activism for community empowerment: International leadership perspectives. *International Journal of Multicultural Education, 17*(1), 102–120.

Yosso, T. J. (2005). Whose culture has capital? A critical race theory discussion of community cultural wealth. *Race, Ethnicity and Education, 8*(1), 69–91.

Zion, S. D., & Blanchett, W. (2011). [Re] Conceptualizing Inclusion: Can Critical Race Theory and Interest Convergence Be Utilized to Achieve Inclusion and Equity for African American Students? *Teachers College Record, 113*(10), 2186–2205.

Zuberi, T., & Bonilla-Silva, E. (2008). *White logic, white methods: Racism and methodology*. Rowman & Littlefield.

Compilation of References

Aaron, T. S. (2020). Black Women: Perceptions and Enactments of Leadership. *Journal of School Leadership*, *30*(2), 146–165. doi:10.1177/1052684619871020

Abbott, G. (2021, June 15). *State of Texas office of the governor: Message.* https://gov.texas.gov/UPLOADS/FILES/PRESS/FILING_STMT_HB_3979_critical_race_theory_IMAGE_06-15-21.pdf

Abdullah, M. (2012). Womanist mothering: Loving and raising the revolution. *The Western Journal of Black Studies*, *36*(1), 1–21.

Abelson, R. P., Dasgupta, N., Park, J., & Banaji, M. R. (1998). Perceptions of the collective other. *Personality and Social Psychology Review*, *2*(4), 243-250. https://doi-org.libproxy.csudh.edu/10.1207/s15327957pspr0204_2

Abrams, J. A., Maxwell, M., Pope, M., & Belgrave, F. Z. (2014). Carrying the world with the grace of a lady and the grit of a warrior: Deepening our understanding of the "Strong Black Woman" schema. *Psychology of Women Quarterly*, *38*(4), 503–518. doi:10.1177/0361684314541418

Abrams, L. S., & Moio, J. A. (2009). Critical race theory and the cultural competence dilemma in social work education. *Journal of Social Work Education*, *45*(2), 245–261. doi:10.5175/JSWE.2009.200700109

Acheampong, C., Davis, C., Holder, D., Averette, P., Savitt, T., & Campbell, K. (2019). An Exploratory Study of Stress Coping and Resiliency of Black Men at One Medical School: A Critical Race Theory Perspective. *Journal of Racial and Ethnic Health Disparities*, *6*(1), 214–219. doi:10.100740615-018-0516-8 PMID:30039499

Adams, B. (2016, December 5). *Microaggression and battle fatigue.* Salt Lake City, UT: The University of Utah. https://attheu.utah.edu/facultystaff/microaggression-and-racial-battle-fatigue/

Adams, D. W. (1995). *Education for extinction: American Indians and the boarding school experience, 1875-1928.* University Press of Kansas.

Admin. (2019, February 14). *From a nation at risk to a nation at hope.* http://nationathope.org/report-from-the-nation-download/

Compilation of References

Alakhunova, N., Diallo, O., Martin del Campo, I., & Tallarico, W. (2015). *Defining marginalization: An assessment tool. A Product of the partnership between four development professionals at the Elliot School of International Affairs & The Word Fair Trade Organization-Asia*. The George Washington University.

Alba, R., & Nee, V. (1997). Rethinking assimilation theory for a new era of immigration. *The International Migration Review*, *31*(4), 826–872. doi:10.1177/019791839703100403 PMID:12293207

Alderman, D., Kingsbury, P., & Dwyer, O. (2013). Reexamining the Montgomery bus boycott: Toward an empathetic pedagogy of the civil rights movement. *The Professional Geographer*, *65*(1), 171–186. doi:10.1080/00330124.2012.658728

Alexander, M. (2010). *New Jim Crow, the mass incarceration in the age of colorblindness*. Perseus Books LLC.

Alexander, M. (2012). *The new Jim Crow: Mass incarceration in the age of colorblindness*. New Press.

Alexander, T. (2010). Roots of Leadership: Analysis of the Narratives from African American Women Leaders in Higher Education. *International Journal of Learning*, *17*(4), 193–204. doi:10.18848/1447-9494/CGP/v17i04/46973

Alief Independent School District. (2020). *AE(local) – educational philosophy*. https://pol.tasb.org/Policy/Download/584?filename=AE(LOCAL).pdf

Alston, J. A. (2012). Standing on the promises: A new generation of Black women scholars in educational leadership and beyond. *International Journal of Qualitative Studies in Education: Emerging African American Women Scholars*, *25*(1), 127–129. doi:10.1080/09518398.2011.647725

American College Personnell Association. (2018). *Strategic Imperative for Racial Justice and Decolonization*. http://convention.myacpa.org/houston2018/sirjd-syllabus/

American Council on Education. (2020). *Race and Ethnicity in Higher Education 2020 Supplement*. https://www.equityinhighered.org/

American Counseling Association. (2014). *ACA code of ethics*. Author.

American Counseling Association. (2020a). *About us*. https://www.counseling.org/about-us/about-aca

American Counseling Association. (2020b). *Membership report*. Author.

Amrani, N. I. (2017). Racialization: The Experiences of Muslim Graduate Students in Higher Education after September 11 (10265001) [PhD dissertation, Northeastern University]. Ann Arbor: Dissertations &Theses @ Northeastern University; ProQuest Dissertations &Theses Global.

Anandavalli, S., Borders, L. D., & Kniffin, L. E. (2021). "Because here, White is right": Mental health experiences of international graduate students of color from a critical race perspective. *International Journal for the Advancement of Counseling.* Advance online publication. doi:10.100710447-021-09437-x PMID:34054168

Anandavalli, S., Harrichand, J. J. S., & Litam, S. D. A. (2020). Counseling international students in times of uncertainty: A critical feminist and bioecological approach. *The Professional Counselor*, *10*(3), 365–375. doi:10.15241a.10.3.365

Anderson, E. (2015). The White Space. *Sage (Atlanta, Ga.)*, *1*(1), 10–21. doi:10.1177/2332649214561306

Anderson, G. L. (2009). *Advocacy leadership: Toward a post-reform agenda in education.* Routledge. doi:10.4324/9780203880616

Apel, D. (2004). *Imagery of lynching: Black men, white women, and the mob.* Rutgers University Press.

Apugo, D. (2019). A Hidden Culture of Coping: Insights on African American Women's Existence in Predominately White Institutions. *Multicultural Perspectives*, *21*(1), 53–62. doi:10.1080/15 210960.2019.1573067

Archer, L. (2001). 'Muslim brothers, black lads, traditional Asians': British Muslim young men's constructions of race, religion and masculinity. *Feminism & Psychology*, *11*(1), 79–105. doi:10.1177/0959353501011001005

Archuleta, M., Child, B. J., & Lowamaima, K. T. (2000). *Away from home: American Indian boarding school experiences, 1879-2000.* Museum of New Mexico Press.

Arredondo, P., D'Andrea, M., & Lee, C. (2020, September 10). Unmasking White supremacy and racism in the counseling profession. *Counseling Today Online.* https://ct.counseling.org/tag/topic-ct-multiculturalism-diversity/

Arriaga, T. T., Stanley, S., & Lindsey, D. B. (2020). *Leading while female: A culturally proficient response for gender equity.* Corwin.

Arvin, M., Tuck, E., & Morrill, A. (2013). Decolonizing feminism: Challenging connections between settler colonialism and heteropatriarchy. *Feminist Formations*, *25*(1), 8–34. doi:10.1353/ff.2013.0006

Asher, N. (2006). Brown in black and white: On being a South Asian woman academic. In G. Li & G. H. Beckett (Eds.), *Strangers" of the academy: Asian women scholars in higher education* (pp. 163–177). Stylus Publishing.

Aveling, N. (2007). Anti-racism in schools: A question of leadership? *Discourse (Abingdon)*, *28*(1), 69–85. doi:10.1080/01596300601073630

Compilation of References

Awad, G. H. (2010). The impact of acculturation and religious identification on perceived discrimination for Arab/Middle eastern Americans. *Cultural Diversity & Ethnic Minority Psychology, 16*(1), 59–67. doi:10.1037/a0016675 PMID:20099965

Badoer, E., Hollings, Y., & Chester, A. (2020). Professional networking for undergraduate students: A scaffolded approach. *Journal of Further and Higher Education, 45*(2), 197–210. doi:10.1080/0309877X.2020.1744543

Bagby, I. (2009). The American mosque in transition: Assimilation, acculturation and isolation. *Journal of Ethnic and Migration Studies, 35*(3), 473–490. doi:10.1080/13691830802704640

Bailey, A. (2017). *The weeping time: Memory and the largest slave auction in American history.* Cambridge University Press. doi:10.1017/9781108140393

Banks, N. (2019). Black women's labor market history reveals deep-seated race and gender discrimination. *Economic Policy Institute.* https://www.epi.org/blog/black-womens-labor-market-history-reveals-deep-seated-race-and-gender-discrimination/

Barnes, R. J. (2016). *Raising the race: Black career women redefine marriage, motherhood, and community.* Rutgers University Press.

Barnett, B. M. (1993). Invisible Southern Black Women Leaders in the Civil Rights Movement: The Triple Constraints of Gender, Race, and Class. *Gender & Society, 7*(2), 162–182. doi:10.1177/089124393007002002

Bartolome, L. (1994). Beyond the methods fetish: Toward a humanizing pedagogy. *Harvard Educational Review, 64*(2), 173–195. doi:10.17763/haer.64.2.58q5m5744t325730

Basit, T. N. (2009). White British; dual heritage; British Muslim: Young Britons' conceptualisation of identity and citizenship. *British Educational Research Journal, 35*(5), 723–743. doi:10.1080/01411920802688747

Battiste, M. (2017). *Decolonizing education: Nourishing the learning spirit.* UBC Press.

Bavishi, A., Madera, J. M., & Hebl, M. R. (2010). The effect of professor ethnicity and gender on student evaluations: Judged before met. *Journal of Diversity in Higher Education, 1*(12), 245–256. Advance online publication. doi:10.1037/a0020763

BBC News. (2020). *Black Lives Matter founders: We fought to change history and we won.* https://www.bbc.com/news/world-us-canada-55106268

Beal, F. M. (2008). Double Jeopardy: To Be Black and Female. *Meridians (Middletown, Conn.), 8*(2), 166–176. doi:10.2979/MER.2008.8.2.166

Bear, J. B., Cushenbery, L., London, M., & Sherman, G. D. (2017). Performance feedback, power retention, and the gender gap in leadership. *The Leadership Quarterly, 28*(6), 721–740. doi:10.1016/j.leaqua.2017.02.003

Beauboeuf-Lafantant, T. (2007). You have to show strength: An exploration of gender, race, and depression. *Gender & Society, 21*(1), 28–51. doi:10.1177/0891243206294108

Beer, J., Stief, E., & Stief, E. (2012). *The mediator's handbook* (4th ed.). New Society.

Belcourt-Dittloff, A. E. (2006). *Resiliency and risk in Native American communities: A culturally informed investigation* (Unpublished doctoral dissertation). University of Montana.

Bell, D. A. (1995a). Brown v Board of Education and the interest convergence dilemma. In Critical race theory: The key writings that formed the movement (pp. 20-28). The New Press.

Bell, D. A. (1995b). Racial realism. In Critical race theory: The key writings that formed the movement (pp. 302-314). The New Press.

Bell, D. A. (1987). *And we are not saved: The elusive quest for racial justice.* Basic Books.

Bell, E. L. J., & Nkomo, S. M. (2003). *Our separate ways: Black and white women and the struggle for professional identity.* Harvard Business School Press.

Berry, R. (2014). Identifying organizational containment and its effect on the career paths of black educators. *Theses and Dissertations.* doi:10.25772/034A-Y804

Bhatti, G. (2011). Outsiders or insiders? Identity, educational success and Muslim young men in England. *Ethnography and Education, 6*(1), 81–96. doi:10.1080/17457823.2011.553081

Black, M. E. (2012). Meanings and typologies of Duboisian double consciousness within 20th century United States racial dynamics (Master's theses). UMass, Boston.

Black, J. E. (2002). The "mascotting" of Native America: Construction, commodity, and assimilation. *American Indian Quarterly, 26*(4), 605–622. doi:10.1353/aiq.2004.0003

Blalock, A. E., & Akehi, M. (2018). Collaborative autoethnography as a pathway for transformative learning. *Journal of Transformative Education, 16*(2), 89–107. doi:10.1177/1541344617715711

Blauner, R. (1972). *Racial oppression in America.* Harper and Row.

Bogotch, I. (2013). Educational theory: The specific case of social justice as an educational leadership construct. In I. Bogotch & C. Shields (Eds.), *International handbook of educational leadership and social (in)justice* (pp. 51–65). Springer.

Bonaparte, Y. (2016). Leaning In: A Phenomenological Study of African American Women Leaders in the Pharmaceutical Industry. *Advancing Women in Leadership, 36.* https://vcu-alma-primo. hosted.exlibrisgroup.com/primo-explore/fulldisplay?docid=TN_proquest1827617820&context= PC&vid=VCUL&lang=en_US&search_scope=all_scope&adaptor=primo_central_multiple_fe &tab=all&query=any,contains,Leaning%20In:%20A%20Phenomenological%20Study%20of%20 African%20American%20Women%20Leaders%20%20in%20the%20Pharmaceutical%20Industry

Bonds, A., & Inwood, J. (2016). Beyond white privilege: Geographies of white supremacy and settler colonialism. *Progress in Human Geography, 40*(6), 715–733. doi:10.1177/0309132515613166

Bonet, S. W. (2011). Educating Muslim American youth in a post-9/11 era: A critical review of policy and practice. *High School Journal, 95*(1), 46–55. doi:10.1353/hsj.2011.0013

Bonilla-Silva, E. (2006). *Racism without racists: Colorblind racism and persistence of racial inequality in the United States*. Rowman & Littlefield.

Bonilla-Silva, E., & Dietrich, D. (2011). The sweet enchantment of color-blind racism in Obamerica. *The Annals of the American Academy of Political and Social Science, 634*(1), 190–206. doi:10.1177/0002716210389702

Bottomley, P., Mostafa, A. M., Gould-Williams, J. S., & León-Cázares, F. (2015). The impact of transformational leadership on organizational citizenship behaviours: The contingent role of public service motivation. *British Journal of Management, 27*(2), 390–405. doi:10.1111/1467-8551.12108

Bourgois, P. (2000). Violating apartheid in the United States: On the streets and in academia. In F. W. Twine & J. W. Warren (Eds.), *Racing research, researching race: Methodological dilemmas in critical race studies* (pp. 187–214). New York University Press.

Boylorn, R. M., & Orbe, M. P. (2014). *Critical autoethnography: Intersecting cultural identities in everyday life*. Left Coast Press.

Brantlinger, E., Majd-Jabbari, M., & Guskin, S. L. (1996). Self-interest and liberal educational discourse: How ideology works for middle-class mothers. *American Educational Research Journal, 33*(3), 571–597. doi:10.3102/00028312033003571

Brave Heart, M. Y. H. (1999). Oyate Ptayela: Rebuilding the Lakota Nation through addressing historical trauma among Lakota parents. *Journal of Human Behavior in the Social Environment, 2*(1-2), 109–126. doi:10.1300/J137v02n01_08

Brave Heart, M. Y. H., & DeBruyn, L. M. (1998). The American Indian holocaust: Healing unresolved historical grief. *American Indian and Alaska Native Mental Health Research, 8*(2), 56–78. https://pubmed.ncbi.nlm.nih.gov/9842066/ PMID:9842066

Brayboy, B. (2005a). Toward a tribal critical race theory in education. *The Urban Review, 37*(5), 425–446. doi:10.100711256-005-0018-y

Brayboy, B. (2005b). Transformational resistance and social justice: American Indians in Ivy League universities. *Anthropology & Education Quarterly, 36*(3), 193–211. doi:10.1525/aeq.2005.36.3.193

Brayboy, B. (2013). Tribal critical race theory: An origin story and future directions. In *Handbook of Critical Race Theory in Education* (pp. 88–100). Taylor and Francis.

Bronfenbrenner, U. (1979). *The ecology of human development: experiments by nature and design*. Harvard University Press.

Brooks, J. S., & Watson, T. N. (2019). School leadership and racism: An ecological perspective. *Urban Education, 54*(5), 631–655. doi:10.1177/0042085918783821

Brown, D. L. (2020, June 3). 'It was a modern-day lunching': Violent deaths reflect a brutal American legacy. *National Geographic: History & Culture – Race in America*. https://www.nationalgeographic.com/history/2020/06/history-of-lynching-violent-deaths-reflect-brutal-american-legacy/

Brown, B. (2018). *Dare to lead: Brave work, tough conversations, whole hearts*. Random House.

Brown, K. M. (2006). Leadership for social justice and equity: Evaluating a transformative framework andragogy. *Educational Administration Quarterly, 42*(5), 700–745. doi:10.1177/0013161X06290650

Brown, K., & Jackson, D. (2013). The history and conceptual elements of critical race theory. In M. Lynn & A. D. Dixson (Eds.), *Handbook of critical race theory in education* (pp. 9–22). Routledge.

Bryant-Davis, T., & Ocampo, C. (2005). The trauma of racism. *The Counseling Psychologist, 33*(4), 574–578. doi:10.1177/0011000005276581

Bryant, R., Coker, A., Durodoye, B., McCollum, V., Pack-Brown, S., Constantine, M., & O'Bryant, B. (2005). Having our say: African American women, diversity, and counseling. *Journal of Counseling and Development, 83*(3), 313–319. doi:10.1002/j.1556-6678.2005.tb00349.x

Buhlmann, U., Teachman, B. A., & Kathmann, N. (2011). Evaluating implicit attractiveness beliefs in body dysmorphic disorder using the Go/No-go Association Task. *Journal of Behavior Therapy and Experimental Psychiatry, 42*(2), 192–197. doi:10.1016/j.jbtep.2010.10.003 PMID:21315881

Burciaga, R., & Erbstein, N. (2012). Latina/o dropouts: Generating community cultural wealth. *Association of Mexican-American Educators (AMAE) Journal, 6*(1), 24–33.

Burns, J. M. (1978). *Leadership. Harper. Collins, P. H. (2000). Black feminist thought: Knowledge, consciousness, and the politics of empowerment* (2nd ed.). Routledge.

Burrell, X. (2020, September 30). Two officers shot in Louisville protests over Breonna Taylor charging decision. *New York Times*. https://www.nytimes.com/2020/09/23/us/breonna-taylor-decision-verdict.html

Cajete, G. (2005). American Indian epistemologies. In M. T. Fox, S. C. Lowe, & G. S. McClellan (Eds.), New directions for student services (No. 109, pp. 69–78). / doi:10.1002s.155

Calbos, C. (2014). What is free and appropriate public education for a child? *Impact ADHD.com*

Calhoun, L. G., Cann, A., & Tedeschi, R. G. (2010). The posttraumatic growth model: Sociocultural considerations. In T. Weiss & R. Berger (Eds.), *Posttraumatic growth and culturally competent practice: Lessons learned from around the globe* (pp. 1–14). John Wiley & Sons Inc.

Campbell, E. (2014). Using critical race theory to measure "racial competency" among social workers. *Journal of Sociology and Social Work, 2*(2), 74-86. doi:.v2n2a5 doi:10.15640/jssw

Capetillo-Ponce, J. (2007). From a clash of civilizations to internal colonialism. *Ethnicities, 7*(1), 116–134. doi:10.1177/1468796807073922

Capper, C. A. (2015). The 20th- year anniversary of critical race theory in education: Implications for leading to eliminate racism. *Educational Administration Quarterly*, *51*(5), 791–833. doi:10.1177/0013161X15607616

Capper, C. A., & Young, M. D. (2014). Ironies and limitations of educational leadership for social justice: A call to social justice educators. *Theory into Practice*, *53*(2), 158–164. doi:10.1080/00405841.2014.885814

Carmichael, S., & Hamilton, C. V. (1992). *Black power: The politics of liberation in America.* Vintage Books. (Original work published 1967)

Carr, P. R. (2011). *Transforming Educational Leadership Without Social Justice? Looking at Critical Pedagogy as More Than a Critique, and a Way Toward Democracy* (Vol. 409). Counterpoints.

Carson, D. (2017). *What are the experiences of African American female principals in high-poverty urban schools?* [Doctoral dissertation, University of North Texas]. UNT Digital Library. https://digital.library.unt.edu/ark:/67531/metadc1011826/

Carter, D. J. (2007). Why the Black kids sit together at the stairs: The role of identity-affirming counter-spaces in a predominantly white high school. *The Journal of Negro Education*, *76*(4), 542–554.

Carter, D. J., & Lomotey, K. (1990). African-American principals: School leadership and success. *The Journal of Negro Education*, *59*(4), 632. doi:10.2307/2295325

Carver-Thomas, D. (2018). *Diversifying the teaching profession: How to recruit and retain teachers of color.* Learning Policy Institute.

CASEL. (2021). *Transformative SEL as a Lever for Equity & Social Justice.* https://casel.org/research/transformative-sel/

Castilla, E. J. (2008). Gender, race, and meritocracy in organizational careers. *American Journal of Sociology*, *113*(6), 1479–1526. doi:10.1086/588738 PMID:19044141

CCEAL. (2019). *From boarding schools to suspension boards: Suspensions and expulsions of Native American students in California public schools.* https://cceal.org/wp-content/uploads/2019/09/Suspension-Boards-Final.pdf

Centers for Disease Control and Prevention. (2020). *Health Equity Considerations and Racial and Ethnic Minority Groups* https://www.cdc.gov/coronavirus/2019-ncov/community/health-equity/race-ethnicity.html

Centers for Disease Control and Prevention. (2020a, August 18). *COVID-19 hospitalization and death by race/ethnicity.* https://www.cdc.gov/coronavirus/2019-ncov/covid-data/investigations-discovery/hospitalization-death-by-race-ethnicity.html

Centers for Disease Control and Prevention. (2020b, June 25). *COVID-19 in racial and ethnic minority groups.* https://stacks.cdc.gov/view/cdc/89820/cdc_89820_DS1.pdf

Centers for Disease Control. (2020a). *Health equity considerations and racial and ethnic minority groups.* https://www.cdc.gov/coronavirus/2019-ncov/community/health-equity/race-ethnicity.html

Centers for Disease Control. (2020b). *Non-Hispanic Black people disproportionately by COVID-19 hospitalization in CDC Data.* Author.

Certo, J., Cauley, K., & Chafin, C. (2003). Students' perspectives on their high school experience. *Adolescence, 38*(152), 705–724. PMID:15053496

Chan, C. D., Harrichand, J. J. S., Anandavalli, S., Vaishnav, S., Chang, C. Y., Hyun, J., & Band, M. P. (in press). Mapping solidarity, liberation, and activism: An autoethnography of Asian American and Pacific Islander (AAPI) leaders in counseling. *Journal of Mental Health Counseling.*

Chang, H. (2008). *Autoethnography as method.* Left Coast Press.

Cheeks, M. (2018, March 26). How Black Women Describe Navigating Race and Gender in the Workplace. *Harvard Business Review.* https://hbr.org/2018/03/how-black-women-describe-navigating-race-and-gender-in-the-workplace

Chen, G. (2019, October 24). *White students are now the minority in U.S. public schools* [Blog post]. https://www.publicschoolreview.com/blog/white-students-are-now-the-minority-in-u-s-public-schools

Cheshire, T. (2013). *Barriers & bridges: American Indian community college student success.* Lap Lambert Academic Publishing.

Chetty, N., & Alathur, S. (2018). Hate speech review in the context of online social networks. *Aggression and Violent Behavior, 40,* 108–118. doi:10.1016/j.avb.2018.05.003

Chilisa, B., Major, T. E., Gaotlhobogwe, M., & Mokgolodi, H. (2016). Decolonizing and indigenizing evaluation practice in Africa: Toward African relational evaluation approaches. *The Canadian Journal of Program Evaluation, 30*(3), 313–328. doi:10.3138/cjpe.30.3.05

Chinook Fund. (2015). *General terms and forms of oppression.* https://chinookfund.org/wp-content/uploads/2015/10/Supplemental-Information-for-Funding-Guidelines.pdf

Choper, J. H. (1994). Religion and race under the constitution: Similarities and differences. *Cornell Law Review, 79*(3), 491–513.

Cho, S. K. (2003). Converging stereotypes in racialized sexual harassment: Where the model minority meets Suzie Wong. In A. K. Wing (Ed.), *Critical Race Feminism* (2nd ed., pp. 349–366). NYU Press.

Chubb, J. E., & Loveless, T. (Eds.). (2004). *Bridging the achievement gap.* Brookings Institution Press.

Clark-Louque, A., & Sullivan, T. A. (2020). Black Girls and School Discipline: Shifting from the Narrow Zone of Zero Tolerance to a Wide Region of Restorative Practices and Culturally Proficient Engagement. *Journal for Leadership, Equity, and Research*, 6(2). https://journals.sfu.ca/cvj/index.php/cvj/article/view/95

Cloke, K. (2013). *The dance of opposites: Explorations in mediation, dialogue and conflict resolution systems design*. Good Media Press.

Coates, T. (2020, September). A beautiful life. *Vanity Fair*, 72-81.

Collins, P. H. (2000). Black Feminist Thought: Knowledge, Consciousness, and the Politcs of Empowerment (Revised 10th Anniversary). Routledge.

Collins, P. H. (2000). Black feminist thought: Knowledge, consciousness, and the politics of empowerment (2nd ed.). Routledge.

Collins, P. (2019). *Intersectionality as critical social theory*. Duke University Press. doi:10.1215/9781478007098

Collins, P. H. (1986). Learning from the outsider within: The sociological significance of black feminist thought. *Social Problems*, *33*(6), S14–S32. Advance online publication. doi:10.2307/800672

Collins, P. H. (2000). *Black feminist thought knowledge, consciousness, and the politics of empowerment*. Routledge.

Collins, P. H. (2015). *Black feminist thought: Knowledge, consciousness, and the politics of empowerment*. Routledge.

Collins, P. H., & Bilge, S. (2016). *Intersectionality*. Polity Press.

Conley, E. (2008). *Exploring barriers to education for Native American Indians: A Native perspective* [Doctoral dissertation, Florida Atlantic University]. http://fau.digital.flvc.org/islandora/object/fau%3A2811

Connell, J. P., & Wellborn, J. G. (1991). Competence, autonomy, and relatedness: A motivational analysis of self-system processes. In M. R. Gunnar & L. A. Sroufe (Eds.), *Self processes and development* (Vol. 23). Lawrence Erlbaum Associates.

Connor, D. J. (2017). Who is responsible for the racialized practices evident within (special) education and what can be done to change them? *Theory into Practice*, *56*(3), 226–233. doi:10.1080/00405841.2017.1336034

Constantine, M. G., & Sue, D. W. (2007). Perceptions of racial microaggressions among Black supervisees in cross racial dyads. *Journal of Counseling Psychology*, *34*(2), 142–153. doi:10.1037/0022-0167.54.2.142

Cook, D. A., & Dixson, A. D. (2013). Writing critical race theory and method: A composite counterstory on the experiences of black teachers in New Orleans post-Katrina. *International Journal of Qualitative Studies in Education: QSE, 26*(10), 1238–1258. doi:10.1080/09518398 .2012.731531

Corbin, N. A., Smith, W. A., & Garcia, J. R. (2018). Trapped between justified anger and being the strong Black woman: Black college women coping with racial battle fatigue at historically and predominantly White institutions. *International Journal of Qualitative Studies in Education: QSE, 31*(7), 626–643. doi:10.1080/09518398.2018.1468045

Costello, M. B. (2016). *The Trump Effect The impact of the presidential campaign on our nation's schools.* Southern Poverty Law Center. https://www.splcenter.org/sites/default/files/ splc_the_trump_effect.pdf

Cottingham, M. D., Johnson, A. H., & Erickson, R. J. (2018). I can never be too comfortable": Race, gender, and emotion at the hospital bedside. *Qualitative Health Research, 28*(1), 145–158. doi:10.1177/1049732317737980 PMID:29094641

Council for Accreditation of Counseling and Related Educational Programs. (2015). *2016 CACREP standards.* http://www.cacrep.org/wp-content/uploads/2017/07/2016-Standards-with-Glossary-7.2017.pdf

Courageous Conversation. (2020, December 22). *Marcus Moore: Moving from DEI to EDI.* https://courageousconversation.com/

Crenshaw, K. (1989). *Demarginalizing the Intersection of Race and Sex: A Black Feminist Critique of Antidiscrimination Doctrine, Feminist Theory and Antiracist Politics.* Academic Press.

Crenshaw, K. (1989). *Demarginalizing the intersection of race and sex: A Black feminist critique of antidiscrimination doctrine, feminist theory and antiracist politics.* https://chicagounbound. uchicago.edu/uclf/vol1989/iss1/8/

Crenshaw, K. (2018). Demarginalizing the intersection of race and sex: A Black feminist critique of antidiscrimination doctrine, feminist theory, and antiracist politics. *Feminist Legal Theory,* 57-80. doi:10.4324/9780429500480-5

Crenshaw, K. (1989). Demarginalizing the intersection of race and sex: A Black feminist critique of antidiscrimination doctrine, feminist theory and antiracist politics. *University of Chicago Legal Forum, 140,* 139–167.

Crenshaw, K. (1989). Demarginalizing the intersection of race and sex: A black feminist critique of antidiscrimination doctrine, feminist theory and antiracist politics. *University of Chicago Legal Forum, 1989*(1), 8. https://chicagounbound.uchicago.edu/uclf/vol1989/iss1/8

Crenshaw, K. (1991). Mapping the margins: Intersectionality, identity politics, and violence against women of color. *Stanford Law Review, 43*(6), 1241–1299. doi:10.2307/1229039

Crenshaw, K. (1995). *Critical Race Theory: The Key Writings that formed the Movement.* The New York Press.

Crenshaw, K., Gotanda, N., Peller, G., & Thomas, K. (Eds.). (1995). *Critical race theory: The key writings that formed the movement*. New Press.

Cresswell, J. W. (2009). *Research design: Qualitative, quantitative, and mixed methods approaches*. Sage Publications.

Creswell, J. W., & Guetterman, T. C. (2019). *Educational research: Planning, conducting, and evaluating quantitative and qualitative research* (6th ed.). Pearson.

Crowley, R. (2019). White teachers, racial privilege, and the sociological imagination. *Urban Education, 54*(10), 1462–1488. doi:10.1177/0042085916656901

Cullen, C., & Barnes-Holmes, D. (2008). Implicit pride and prejudice: A heterosexual phenomenon. In M. A. Morrison & T. G. Morrison (Eds.), *The psychology of modern prejudice* (pp. 195–223). Nova Science Publishers.

Dantley, M. E. (2005). African American spirituality and Cornel West's notions of prophetic pragmatism: Restructuring educational leadership in American urban schools. *Educational Administration Quarterly, 41*(4), 651–674. doi:10.1177/0013161X04274274

Dantley, M. E., & Tillman, L. C. (2010). Social justice and moral transformative leadership. In C. Marshall & M. Oliva (Eds.), *Leadership for social justice* (2nd ed., pp. 19–34). Allyn & Bacon.

David, E. J. R., & Derthick, A. O. (2018). *The psychology of oppression*. Springer.

Davies, C. B. (1994). *Black women, writing and identity: Migrations of the subject*. Routledge.

Dávila, B. (2015). Critical race theory, disability microaggressions and Latina/o student experiences in special education. *Race, Ethnicity and Education, 18*(4), 443–468. doi:10.1080/13613324.2014.885422

Davis, D. R. (2012). *A Phenomenological Study on the Leadership Development of African American Women Executives in Academia and Business*. ProQuest LLC. http://search.proquest.com/docview/1697499660/69FDEFC14CB84EC1PQ/13

Davis, B. W., Gooden, M. A., & Micheaux, D. J. (2015). Colorblind leadership: A critical race theory analysis of the ISLLC and ELCC Standards. *Educational Administration Quarterly, 51*(3), 335–371. doi:10.1177/0013161X15587092

Davis, S. M., & Afifi, T. D. (2019). The Strong Black Woman Collective Theory: Determining the prosocial functions of strength regulation in groups of Black women friends. *Journal of Communication, 69*(1), 1–25. doi:10.1093/joc/jqy065

de Bray, C., Musu, L., McFarland, J., Wilkinson-Flicker, S., Diliberti, M., Zhang, A.. & Wang, X. (2019). *Status and trends in the education of racial and ethnic groups 2018*. Academic Press.

de León, C., Alter, A., Harris, E. A., & Khatib, J. (2020, July 1). 'A Conflicted Cultural Force': What It's Like to Be Black in Publishing. *The New York Times*. https://www.nytimes.com/2020/07/01/books/book-publishing-black.html

DeCuir, J. T., & Dixson, A. D. (2004, June/July). "So when it comes out, they aren't that surprised that it is there": Using critical race theory as a tool of analysis of race and racism in education. *Educational Researcher, 33*(26), 26–31. doi:10.3102/0013189X033005026

Dei, G. J., & Kempf, A. (2006). *Anti-colonialism and education: The Politics of Resistance* (Vol. 7). Sense Publishers. doi:10.1163/9789087901110

Delgado Bernal, D. (1998). Using a Chicana feminist epistemology in educational research. *Harvard Educational Review, 68*(4), 555–582. doi:10.17763/haer.68.4.5wv1034973g22q48

Delgado Bernal, D. (2018). A testimonio of critical race feminista parenting: Snapshots from my childhood and my parenting. *International Journal of Qualitative Studies in Education: QSE, 31*(1), 25–35. doi:10.1080/09518398.2017.1379623

Delgado, R. (1989). Storytelling for oppositionists and others: A plea for narrative. *Michigan Law Review, 87*(8), 2411–2441. doi:10.2307/1289308

Delgado, R., & Stefancic, J. (2001). *Critical race theory: An introduction.* New York University Press.

Dennis, A. (2020, June). Anguish in America: A nation torn apart. *People,* 35–45.

Denzin, N. (2014). *Interpretive autoethnography* (2nd ed.). SAGE Publications, Ltd. https://www.doi.org/10.4135/9781506374697

Dernbach, B. Z. (2021, May 12). Showdown at school board meeting: Elk River alumi of color say the 'never felt safe,' parents decry 'woke mob'. *Sahan Journal.* https://sahanjournal.com/education/elk-river-school-board-equity/

Dewey, J. (1938). *Experience and education.* Collier Books.

Deyhle, D., & Swisher, K. (1997). Research in American Indian and Alaska Native education: From assimilation to self-determination. *Review of Research in Education, 22,* 113–194. doi:10.2307/1167375

DiAngelo, R. (2018). *White fragility: Why it's so hard for white people to talk about race.* Beacon Press.

DiAngelo, R. (2018). *White Fragility: Why It's so Hard for White People to Talk About Racism.* Beacon Press.

DiAngelo, R. J. (2018). *White fragility: Why it's so hard for white people to talk about racism.* Beacon Press.

Dickens, D. D., & Chavez, E. L. (2017). Navigating the workplace: The costs and benefits of shifting identities at work among early career U.S. Black women. *Sex Roles, 78,* 760-774. doi:10.100711199-017-0844-x

Dillon, B., & Bourke, J. (2016). *The six signature traits of inclusive leadership: Thriving in a diverse world.* Deloitte University Press. https://www2.deloitte.com/content/dam/insights/us/articles/six-signature-traits-of-inclusive-leadership/DUP-3046_Inclusive-leader_vFINAL.pdf

Discovery Education. (2020, May 14). *Educating the whole child in a time of loss.* Author.

Donelan, H. (2016). Social media for professional development and networking opportunities in academia. *Journal of Further and Higher Education, 40*(5), 706–729. doi:10.1080/0309877X.2015.1014321

Donthu, N., & Gustafsson, A. (2020). Effects of COVID-19 on business and research. *Journal of Business Research, 117,* 284–289. doi:10.1016/j.jbusres.2020.06.008 PMID:32536736

Dorn, J. (2014). Equality, justice, and freedom: A constitutional perspective. *Libertarianism.org.*

Douglas, M., Katikireddi, S. V., Taulbut, M., McKee, M., & McCartney, G. (2020). Mitigating the wider health effects of covid-19 pandemic response. *BMJ (Clinical Research Ed.), 369,* m1557. doi:10.1136/bmj.m1557 PMID:32341002

Drago-Severson, E., & Blum-DeStefano, J. (2019). A developmental lens on social justice leadership: Exploring the connection between meaning making and practice. *Journal of Educational Leadership and Policy Studies, 3*(1), n1.

Du Bois, W. E. B. (1898). The study of the Negro problems. *The Annals of the American Academy of Political and Social Science, 568*(1), 13–27. doi:10.1177/000271620056800103

Du Bois, W. E. B. (1903). *The Souls of Black Folk: Essays and Sketches.* A.C. McClurg.

DuBois, W. E. B. (1903). *The souls of Black folk.* Bantam Books.

DuBose, M., & Gorski, P. C. (2019). *Equity literacy during the COVID19 crisis.* Equity Literacy Institute. https://08a3a74adec5426e8385bdc09490d921.filesusr.com/ugd/38199c_c355c89c7634495584ead8f230c0d25b.pdf

Durkheim, E. (1912). *The elementary forms of religious life.* Dover Publications.

Durodoye, B. A. (1999). On the receiving end. *Journal of Counseling and Development, 77*(1), 45–47. doi:10.1002/j.1556-6676.1999.tb02416.x

Durr, M., & Harvey Wingfield, A. M. (2011). Keep your 'N' in check: African American women and the interactive effects of etiquette and emotional labor. *Critical Sociology, 37*(5), 557–571. doi:10.1177/0896920510380074

Eagly, A. H., & Wood, W. (2012). Social role theory. In P. van Lange, A. Kruglanski, & E. T. Higgins (Eds.), *Handbook of theories in social psychology* (pp. 458–476). Sage Publications. doi:10.4135/9781446249222.n49

Ebersole, M., Kanahele-Mossman, H., & Kawakami, A. (2015). Culturally responsive teaching: Examining teachers' understandings and perspectives. *Journal of Education and Training Studies, 4*(2). Advance online publication. doi:10.11114/jets.v4i2.1136

Eck, D. L. (2001). Muslim in America. *Christian Century (Chicago, Ill.)*, *118*(18), 20.

Education Week. (2020, March 2). *Map: Coronavirus and school closures*. https://www.edweek.org/leadership/map-coronavirus-and-school-closures-in-2019-2020/2020/03

Edwards, F., Lee, H., & Esposito, M. (2019). Risk of being killed by police use of force in the United States by age, race-ethnicity, and sex. *Proceedings of the National Academy of Sciences (PANS) of the United States of America, 116*(34), 16793–16798. 10.1073/pnas.1821204116

Edwards, J. B., Bryant, S., & Clark, T. T. (2008). African American female social work educators in predominantly White schools of social work: Strategies for thriving. *Journal of African American Studies, 12*(1), 37–49. doi:10.100712111-007-9029-y

Emerson, M. O., & Yancey, G. (2011). *Transcending racial barriers: Toward a mutual obligations approach*. Oxford University Press.

Esquivido, V. (2019). *Fighting for Federal Recognition: A Nor Rel Muk Wintu Ethnohistory* [Unpublished doctoral dissertation]. University of California, Davis.

Esquivido, V., Esquivido, M., & Gali, M. S. (2020). Black Lives Matter on Indigenous lands: Solidarity in Sacramento. *News of Native California, 34*(1), 20–24. https://newsfromnativecalifornia.com/

Estepp, C. M., Velasco, J. G., Culbertson, A. L., & Conner, N. W. (2017). An investigation into mentoring practices of faculty who mentor undergraduate researchers at a Hispanic Serving Institution. *Journal of Hispanic Higher Education*, *16*(4), A338–A358. doi:10.1177/1538192716661906

Evans, L., & Moore, W. L. (2015). Impossible Burdens: White Institutions, Emotional Labor, and Micro-Resistance. *Social Problems*, *62*(3), 439–454. doi:10.1093ocpropv009

Evans-Winters, V. E. (2019). Black Feminism in Qualitative Inquiry: A Mosaic for Writing Our Daughter's Body Futures of data analysis in qualitative research (illustrated ed.). Routledge.

Evelyn, K. (2020, June 11). Black US authors top New York Times bestseller list as protests continue. *The Guardian*. https://www.theguardian.com/books/2020/jun/11/new-york-times-bestseller-list-black-authors

Facing History and Ourselves. (2020, July 21). *Abolitionist teaching and the pursuit of educational freedom: A conversation with Dr. Bettina Love*. New York, NY. https://www.facinghistory.org/

Falci, C. D., & Watanabe, M. (2020). Network marginalization of women in the workplace: A case in academia. *Journal of Women and Minorities in Science and Engineering*, *26*(2), 155–175. doi:10.1615/JWomenMinorScienEng.2020029186

Fatima, S. (2011). Who counts as a Muslim? Identity, multiplicity and politics. *Journal of Muslim Minority Affairs*, *31*(3), 339–353. doi:10.1080/13602004.2011.599542

Feagin, J. R. (2010). *The white racial frame: Centuries of racial framing and counter-framing.* Routledge. doi:10.4324/9780203890646

Felder, P. (2010). On doctoral student development: Exploring faculty mentoring in the shaping of African American doctoral student success. *Qualitative Report, 15*, 455–474.

Fisher, R., Ury, W., & Patton, B. (2011). *Getting to yes: Negotiating agreement without giving in* (3rd ed.). Penguin Group.

Flagg, B. (1993). "Was blind, but now I see": White race consciousness and the requirement of discriminatory intent. *Michigan Law Review, 91*(5), 953–1017. https://repository.law.umich.edu/cgi/viewcontent.cgi?article=2408&context=mlr. doi:10.2307/1289678

Flores, B., Cousin, P., & Diaz, E. (1991). Transforming deficit myths about language, literacy and culture. *Language Arts, 68*(5), 369–379.

Fluker, W. E. (2015). Now we must cross a sea: Remarks on transformational leadership and the civil rights movement. *Boston University Law Review. Boston University. School of Law.*

Franklin, A. J. (1999). Invisibility syndrome and racial identity development in psychotherapy and counseling African American men. *The Counseling Psychologist, 27*(6), 761–793. doi:10.1177/0011000099276002

Franklin, A. J. (2004). *From brotherhood to manhood: How Black men rescue their relationships and dreams from the invisibility syndrome.* Wiley.

Franklin, V. P. (1990). "They Rose and Fell Together": African American Educators and Community Leadership, 1795-1954. *Journal of Education, 172*(3), 39–64. doi:10.1177/002205749017200304

Freire, P. (1972). *Pedagogy of the Oppressed.* Herder and Herder.

Freire, P. (1973). *Education for critical consciousness.* Continuum.

Freire, P., & Ramos, M. B. (1970). *Pedagogy of the oppressed.* Seabury Press.

Frey, J. J. (2020, October 14). How employee assistance programs can help your whole company address racism at work. *Human Resource Management.* https://hbr.org/2020/10/how-employee-assistance-programs-can-help-your-whole-company-address-racism-at-work?ab=hero-subleft-1

Frye, J. (2019, August 22). *Racism and Sexism Combine to Shortchange Working Black Women.* Center for American Progress. https://www.americanprogress.org/issues/women/news/2019/08/22/473775/racism-sexism-combine-shortchange-working-black-women/

Fuchs-Schündeln, N. (2020). *Gender structure of paper submissions at the Review of Economic Studies during COVID-19: First Evidence.* restud.com/wp-content/uploads/2020/05/FemaleSubmissionsCovid19.pdf

Fullan, M. (2001). *Leading in a culture of change.* Jossey-Bass.

Furman, G. (2012). Social justice leadership as praxis: Developing capacities through preparation programs. *Educational Administration Quarterly, 48*(2), 191–229. doi:10.1177/0013161X11427394

Gabriel, M. L. (2011). *Voices of Hispanic and Latina/o secondary students in Northern Colorado: Poetic counterstories.* http://hdl.handle.net/10217/70439

Gabriel, M. L. (2017). Building bridges or isolating families: When school policies conflict with cultural beliefs, values, and ways of knowing. In A. Esmail, A. Pitre, & A. Aragon (Eds.) (2017), Perspectives on Diversity, Equity, and Social Justice in Educational Leadership (pp. 99-114). Lanham, MD: Rowman & Littlefield.

Gabriel, M. L. (2021). Latina leading: Un testimonio toward self-love. In Latinas leading schools: A volume in Hispanics in education and administration (pp. 17-32). Charlotte, NC: Information Age Publishing.

Gabriel, M. L. (2019). Foreword. In M. C. Whitaker & K. M. Valtierra (Eds.), *Schooling multicultural teachers: A guide for program assessment and professional development* (pp. xvii–xix). Emerald Publishing.

Gagliardi, J., Espinosa, L., Turk, J., & Morgan, T. (2017, June). *American College President Study 2017 | TIAA Institute.* https://www.tiaainstitute.org/publication/american-college-president-study-2017

Galtung, J. (1969). Violence, peace, and peace research. *Journal of Peace Research, 6*(3), 167–191. doi:10.1177/002234336900600301

Garner, S., & Selod, S. (2014). The racialization of Muslims: Empirical studies of Islamophobia. *Critical Sociology, 41*(1), 9–19. doi:10.1177/0896920514531606

Gay, G. (2004). Navigating marginality en route to the professoriate: Graduate students of color learning and living in academia. *International Journal of Qualitative Studies in Education: QSE, 17*(2), 265–288. doi:10.1080/09518390310001653907

Generett, G. G., & Welch, O. M. (2018). Transformative leadership: Lessons learned through intergenerational dialogue. *Urban Education, 53*(9), 1102–1125. doi:10.1177/0042085917706598

Giroux, H. (1994). Doing cultural studies: Youth and the challenge of pedagogy. *Harvard Educational Review, 64*(3), 278–309. doi:10.17763/haer.64.3.u27566k67qq70564

Gladden, J. (2018). *Social work leaders through history: Lives and lessons.* Springer. doi:10.1891/9780826146458

Gomez, R., Rascon-Canales, M., & Romero, A. (2019, February 5). We See You, Hermana—At All of Your Powerful Intersections! The White Racial Framing of Serena Williams. *Latinx Talk.* https://latinxtalk.org/2019/02/05/we-see-you-hermana-at-all-of-your-powerful-intersections-the-white-facial-framing-of-serena-williams/

Gooden, M. (2012). What does racism have to do with leadership?: Countering the idea of colorblind leadership: A reflection of race and the growing pressures of the urban principalship. *Educational Foundations*, *26*(1), 67–84.

Gorman, E. H. (2006). Work uncertainty and the promotion of professional women: The case of law firm partnership. *Social Forces*, *85*(2), 865–890. doi:10.1353of.2007.0004

Gorski, P. C. (2019). Racial battle fatigue and activist burnout in racial justice activists of color at predominantly White colleges and universities. *Race, Ethnicity and Education*, *22*(1), 1–20. doi:10.1080/13613324.2018.1497966

Gorski, P. C., & Erakat, N. (2019). Racism, whiteness, and burnout in antiracism movements: How white racial justice activists elevate burnout in racial justice activists of color in the United States. *Ethnicities*, *19*(5), 784–808. doi:10.1177/1468796819833871

Gover, A. R., Harper, S. B., & Langton, L. (2020). Anti-Asian hate crime during the COVID-19 pandemic: Exploring the reproduction of inequality. *American Journal of Criminal Justice*, *45*(4), 647–667. doi:10.100712103-020-09545-1 PMID:32837171

Grant, C. M. (2016). Smashing the Glass Ceiling. In *Responsive Leadership in Higher Education* (pp. 167–179). Routledge.

Gray, A., Howard, L., & Chessman, H. (2018). *Voices from the field: Women of color presidents in higher education.* Retrieved from: https://www.tiaainstitute.org/sites/default/files/presentations/2018- 12/TIAA%20Womens%20Forum%20President%20Interviews%20-%20ACE2.pdf

Greaux, L. (2010). *A Case Study of the Development of African American Women Executives.* ProQuest LLC. http://search.proquest.com/docview/870283884/69FDEFC14CB84EC1PQ/7

Greenleaf, R. (2008). *The servant as leader.* The Greenleaf Center for Servant Leadership.

Greenwald, A. G., McGhee, D. E., & Schwartz, J. L. (1998). Measuring individual differences in implicit cognition: The implicit association test. *Journal of Personality and Social Psychology*, *74*(6), 1464–1480. doi:10.1037/0022-3514.74.6.1464 PMID:9654756

Gregory, A., Skiba, R. J., & Noguera, P. A. (2010). The achievement gap and the discipline gap: Two sides of the same coin? *Educational Researcher*, *39*(59), 59–68. http://doi:10.3102/0013189X09357621

Griffith, D. M., Mason, M., Yonas, M., Eng, E., Jeffries, V., Plihcik, S., & Parks, B. (2007). Dismantling institutional racism: Theory and action. *American Journal of Community Psychology*, *39*(3-4), 381–392. doi:10.100710464-007-9117-0 PMID:17404829

Grissom, J. A., Egalite, A. J., & Lindsay, C. A. (2021). *How principals affect students and schools: A systematic synthesis of two decades of research.* The Wallace Foundation. https://www.wallacefoundation.org/principalsynthesis

Groves, R., & Welsh, B. (2010). The high school experience: What students say. *Issues in Educational Research*, *20*(2), 87–104.

Guiffrida, D. (2005). Other mothering as a framework for understanding African American students' definitions of student-centered faculty. *The Journal of Higher Education*, *76*(6), 701–723. doi:10.1353/jhe.2005.0041

Guillory, R. M., & Wolverton, M. (2008). It's about family: Native American student persistence in higher education. *The Journal of Higher Education*, *79*(1), 59–87. doi:10.1353/jhe.2008.0001

Gulson, K. N., & Webb, P. T. (2013). 'We had to hide we're Muslim': Ambient fear, Islamic schools and the geographies of race and religion. *Discourse (Abingdon)*, *34*(4), 628–641. doi:10.1080/01596306.2013.822623

Gunn Allen, P. (1992). *The sacred hoop: Recovering the feminine in American Indian traditions*. Beacon Press.

Guzmán, B. (2012). Cultivating a guerrera spirit in Latinas: The praxis of mothering. *Association of Mexican-American Educators (AAME) Journal*, *6*(1), 45–51. https://amaejournal.utsa.edu/index.php/AMAE/article/view/101

Hamdan, A. (2007). Arab Muslim women in Canada: The untold narratives. *Journal of Muslim Minority Affairs*, *27*(1), 133–154. doi:10.1080/13602000701308921

Hancock, A. M. (2008). Intersectionality, multiple messages, and complex causality: Commentary on *Black Sexual Politics* by Patricia Hill Collins. *Studies in Gender and Sexuality*, *9*(1), 14–31. doi:10.1080/15240650701759359

Hanna, F. J., Talley, W. B., & Guindon, M. H. (2000). The power of perception: Toward a model of cultural oppression and liberation. *Journal of Counseling and Development*, *78*(4), 430–466. doi:10.1002/j.1556-6676.2000.tb01926.x

Hardiman, R., Jackson, B., & Griffin, P. (2007). Conceptual foundations for social justice education. In M. Adams, L. A. Bell, & P. Griffin (Eds.), Teaching for diversity and social justice (pp. 35–66). Routledge/Taylor & Francis Group.

Hargreaves, A., & Fullan, M. (2020). Professional capital after the pandemic: Revisiting and revising classic understandings of teachers' work. *Journal of Professional Capital and Community*, *5*(3/4), 327–336. doi:10.1108/JPCC-06-2020-0039

Harpalani, V. (2015). To be white, black, or brown? South Asian Americans and the race-color distinction. *Washington University Global Studies Law Review*, *14*(4), 609. https://link.gale.com/apps/doc/A452881504/AONE?u=csudh&sid=bookmark-AONE&xid=a69c00cf

Harris, C. I. (1995). Racial realism. In K. Crenshaw, K. Thomas, G. Peller, & N. Gotanda (Eds.), *Critical race theory: the key writings that formed the movement* (pp. 276–291). The New Press.

Harris-Perry, M. (2011). *Sister Citizen: Shame, Sterotypes and Black Women in America* (6th ed.). Yale University Press.

Harvard Program on Negotiation. (2021). *Mediation.* Harvard Law School. https://www.pon. harvard.edu/category/daily/mediation/?cid=11411

Hassell, K., Archbold, C., & Stichman, A. (2011). Comparing the workplace experiences of male and female police officers: Examining workplace problems, stress, job satisfaction and consideration of career change. *International Journal of Police Science & Management*, *13*(1), 37–53. doi:10.1350/ijps.2011.13.1.217

Haynes, C., Stewart, S., & Allen, E. (2016). Three paths, one struggle: Black women and girls battling invisibility in U.S. classrooms. *The Journal of Negro Education*, *85*(3), 380. doi:10.7709/ jnegroeducation.85.3.0380

Hefner, C. (2015). Muslim American women on campus: Undergraduate social life and identity. *Anthropology & Education Quarterly*, *46*(2), 199–201. doi:10.1111/aeq.12100

Helland, M. R., & Winston, B. E. (2005). Towards a Deeper Understanding of Hope and Leadership. *Journal of Leadership & Organizational Studies*, *12*(2), 42–54. doi:10.1177/107179190501200204

Hernandez, E. (2016). Utilizing critical race theory to examine race/ethnicity, racism, and power in student development theory and research. *Journal of College Student Development*, *57*(2), 168–180. doi:10.1353/csd.2016.0020

Herr, E. H. (2010). *Leadership: A position paper.* https://cdn.ymaws.com/www.csi-net.org/ resource/resmgr/research,_essay,_papers,_articles/leadership_herr_position_pap.pdf

Hickman, G. R. (Ed.). (2016). *Leading organizations: Perspectives for a new era* (3rd ed.). Sage.

Higginbotham, E. B. (1981). Is marriage a priority? Class differences in marital options of educated Black women. In P. Stein (Ed.), *Single life* (pp. 259–267). St. Martins.

Hirshfield, L. E., & Joseph, T. D. (2012). 'We need a woman, we need a Black woman': Gender, race, and identity taxation in the academy. *Gender and Education*, *24*(2), 213–227. doi:10.108 0/09540253.2011.606208

Ho, J. (2021, January). Anti-Asian racism, Black Lives Matter, and COVID-19. *Japan Forum*, *33*(1), 148–159. doi:10.1080/09555803.2020.1821749

hooks, b. (1994). *Teaching to transgress: Education as the practice of freedom.* New York, NY: Routledge.

hooks, b. (2014). *Yearning: Race, Gender, and Cultural Politics.* Routledge.

Hooks, B. (2003). *Teaching Community: A Pedagogy of Hope.* Psychology Press.

Hooks, B. (2015a). *Ain't I a woman: Black women and feminism.* Routledge.

Hooks, B. (2015b). *Talking back: Thinking feminist, thinking Black.* Routledge.

Horne, S. G., & Arora, K. S. K. (2013). Feminist multicultural counseling psychology in transnational contexts. In C. Z. Enns & E. N. Williams (Eds.), *Oxford library of psychology. The Oxford handbook of feminist multicultural counseling psychology* (pp. 240–252). Oxford University Press.

Horowitz, J. M., Brown, A., & Cox, K. (2019, April 9). Race in American 2019. *Pew Research Center: Social & Demographic Trends.* https://www.pewsocialtrends.org/2019/04/09/race-in-america-2019/

Horsford, S. D. (2012). This Bridge Called My Leadership: An Essay on Black Women as Bridge Leaders in Education. *International Journal of Qualitative Studies in Education: QSE, 25*(1), 11–22. http://dx.doi.org.proxy.library.vcu.edu/10.1080/09518398.2011.647726

Housee, S. (2012). What's the point? Anti-racism and students' voices against islamophobia. *Race, Ethnicity and Education, 15*(1), 101–120. doi:10.1080/13613324.2012.638867

Howard, G. R. (2006). *We can't teach what we don't know: White teachers, multiracial schools* (2nd ed.). Teachers College Press, Columbia University.

Hsieh, B., & Nguyen, H. T. (2020). Identity-informed mentoring to support acculturation of female faculty of color in higher education: An Asian American female mentoring relationship case study. *Journal of Diversity in Higher Education, 13*(2), 169–180. doi:10.1037/dhe0000118

Hua, L. U. (2018). Slow feeling and quiet being: Women of color teaching in urgent times. *New Directions for Teaching and Learning, 153*(153), 77–86. doi:10.1002/tl.20283

Hughes, A. K., Horner, P. S., & Ortiz, D. (2012). Being the diversity hire: Negotiating identity in an academic job search. *Journal of Social Work Education, 48*(3), 595–612. doi:10.5175/JSWE.2012.201000101

Hune, S. (2011). Asian American Women Faculty and the contested space of the classroom: Navigating student resistance and (re)claiming authority and their rightful place. *Journal of Diversity in Higher Education, 9*, 307–335.

Hunn, V., Harley, D., Min, W. E., & Canfield, J. P. (2015). Microaggression and the mitigation of psychological harm: Four social workers' exposition for care of clients, students, and faculty who suffer 'a thousand little cuts.'. *The Journal of Pan African Studies, 7*(9), 42–54.

Hunter, E. A., Hanks, M. A., Holman, A., Curry, D., Bvunzawabaya, B., Jones, B., & Abdullah, T. (2020). The hurdles are high: Women of color leaders in counseling psychology. *Journal of Counseling Psychology.* Advance online publication. doi:10.1037/cou0000526 PMID:32584056

Hwang, T. J., Rabheru, K., Peisah, C., Reichman, W., & Ikeda, M. (2020). Loneliness and social isolation during the COVID-19 pandemic. *International Psychogeriatrics, 32*(10), 1217–1220. doi:10.1017/S1041610220000988 PMID:32450943

Inwood, J., & Alderman, D. (2016). Taking down the flag is just a start: Toward the memory-work of racial reconciliation in white supremacist America. *Southeastern Geographer, 56*(1), 9–15. doi:10.1353go.2016.0003

Ivaniushina, V. A., & Aleksandrov, D. A. (2015). Socialization through informal education: The extracurricular activities of Russian school children. *Russian Social Science Review*, *56*(5), 18–39. doi:10.1080/10611428.2015.1115290

I-WIN (International Women's Innovative Network). (n.d.). https://www.linkedin.com/company/international-women-s-innovative-network

Jackson, A. P., Smith, S. A., & Hill, C. L. (2003). Academic persistence among Native American college students. *Journal of College Student Development*, *44*(4), 548–565. doi:10.1353/csd.2003.0039

Jagers, R. J., Rivas-Drake, D., & Borowski, T. (2018, November). *Equity and social emotional learning: A cultural analysis*. https://measuringsel.casel.org/wp-content/uploads/2018/11/Frameworks-Equity.pdf

Jagers, R. J., Rivas-Drake, D., & Williams, B. (2019). Transformative Social and Emotional Learning (SEL): Toward SEL in Service of Educational Equity and Excellence. *Educational Psychologist*, *54*(3), 162–184. doi:10.1080/00461520.2019.1623032

Jandali, A. K. (2013). Muslim students in post-9/11 classrooms. *Education Digest*, *78*(7), 21–24.

Jean-Marie, G., Williams, V. A., & Sherman, S. L. (2009). Black Women's Leadership Experiences: Examining the Intersectionality of Race and Gender. *Advances in Developing Human Resources*, *11*(5), 562–581. https://doi.org/10.1177/1523422309351836

Johnson, H. L. (2017). *Pipelines, pathways, and institutional leadership: An update on the status of women in higher education*. American Council on Education.

Johnson, P. C. (2003). At the intersection of injustice: Experiences of African American women in crime and sentencing. In A. K. Wing (Ed.), *Critical race feminism* (2nd ed., pp. 209–218). NYU Press.

Jones, N. H. (Host). (2019-present). The fight for a true democracy [Audio podcast]. *The New York Times*. https://www.nytimes.com/2020/01/23/podcasts/1619-podcast.html

Jones, R. (2020, December 21). Understanding COVID-19 19 vaccine hesitancy in the Black community. *News & Politics*. https://wearyourvoicemag.com/understanding-covid-19-vaccine-hesitancy-in-the-black-community/

Jones, J. M., & Rolón-Dow, R. (2019). Multidimensional models of microaggressions and microaffirmations. In G. C. Torino, D. P. Rivera, C. M. Capodilupo, K. L. Nadal, & D. W. Sue (Eds.), *Microaggressions theory: Influence and implications* (pp. 32–47). John Wiley & Sons, Inc.

Jones, T., & Norwood, K. J. (2017). Aggressive Encounters & White Fragility: Deconstructing the Trope of the Angry Black Woman. *Iowa Law Review*, *102*(5), 2017–2069. http://proxy.library.vcu.edu/login?url=http://search.ebscohost.com/login.aspx?direct=true&AuthType=ip,url,cookie,uid&db=a9h&AN=124842614&site=ehost-live&scope=site

Julig, C. (2020, July 9). *Loveland community kitchen vandalized with anti BLM graffiti.* https://www.reporterherald.com/2020/07/09/loveland-community-kitchen-vandalized-with-anti-blm-graffiti/

Kadowaki, J., & Subramaniam, M. (2014). Coping with emotional labor: Challenges faced and strategies adopted by instructors. *Understanding and Dismantling Privilege, 4*(2).

Kalev, A., Dobbin, F., & Kelly, E. (2006). Best Practices or Best Guesses? Assessing the Efficacy of Corporate Affirmative Action and Diversity Policies. *American Sociological Review, 71*(4), 589–617. doi:10.1177/000312240607100404

Kanter, R. (1977). *Men and women of the corporation.* Basic Books.

Kaushik, M., & Guleria, N. (2020). The impact of pandemic COVID-19 in workplace. *European Journal of Business and Management, 12*(15), 1–10.

Kelley, G. J. (2012). *How do principals' behaviors facilitate or inhibit the development of a culturally relevant learning community?* (Unpublished doctoral dissertation). Indiana State University, Terre Haute, IN.

Kelly, B. T., Gardner, P. J., Stone, J., Hixson, A., & Dissassa, D.-T. (2019). Hidden in plain sight: Uncovering the emotional labor of Black women students at historically White colleges and universities. *Journal of Diversity in Higher Education, 14*(2), 203–216. doi:10.1037/dhe0000161

Kendi, I. X. (2019). *How to be an antiracist.* One World.

Kersh, R. (2018). Women in higher education: Exploring stressful workplace factors and coping strategies. *Journal About Women in Higher Education, 11*(1), 56–73. doi:10.1080/19407882.2017.1372295

Kessler, R. C., Mickelson, K. D., & Williams, D. R. (1999). The prevalence, distribution, and mental health correlates of perceived discrimination in the United States. *Journal of Health and Social Behavior, 40*(3), 208–230. doi:10.2307/2676349 PMID:10513145

Kettler, S. (2020). *Malala Yousafzai biography.* https://www.biography.com/activist/malala-yousafzai

Khalifa, M. A. (2015). Can Blacks be racists? Black-on-Black principal abuse in an urban school setting. *International Journal of Qualitative Studies in Education: QSE, 28*(2), 259–282. doi:10.1080/09518398.2014.916002

Khalifa, M. A. (2018). *Culturally responsive school leadership.* Harvard Education Press.

Khalifa, M. A., Gooden, M. A., & Davis, J. E. (2016). Culturally responsive school leadership: A synthesis of the literature. *Review of Educational Research, 86*(4), 1272–1311. doi:10.3102/0034654316630383

Khalifa, M., Arnold, N. W., & Newcomb, W. (2015). Understand and advocate for communities first. *Phi Delta Kappan, 96*(7), 20–25. doi:10.1177/0031721715579035

Kim, E., & Patterson, S. (2020). *The pandemic and gender inequality in academia.* Unpublished Manuscript, Vanderbilt University.

Kimberly, A. P. (2011). Framing Islam: An analysis of U.S. media coverage of terrorism since 9/11. *Communication Studies, 62*(1), 90–112. doi:10.1080/10510974.2011.533599

King, M. (1957, November 17). *The trumpet of conscience.* Paper presented at Dexter Avenue Baptist Church, Montgomery, AL.

King, M. (1967, April 4). *A time to break silence.* Paper presented at a meeting of Clergy and Laity Concerned at Riverside Church, New York, NY.

Kingkade, T. (2020). *How one teacher's Black lives matter lesson divided a small Wisconsin town.* https://www.nbcnews.com/news/us-news/how-one-teacher-s-black-lives-matter-lesson-divided-small-n1244566

Kinouani, G. (2020). Silencing power and racial trauma in groups. *Group Analysis, 53*(2), 145–161. doi:10.1177/0533316420908974

Kirwan Institute for the Study of Race and Ethnicity. (n.d.). *Defining implicit bias.* The Ohio State University. http://kirwaninstitute.osu.edu/research/understanding-implicit-bias/ https://www.texastribune.org/2021/05/28/texas-critical-race-theory-greg-abbott/

Kleinman, S. (2007). Feminist fieldwork analysis. *Sage (Atlanta, Ga.).*

Kodama, C. M., & Dugan, J. P. (2019). Understanding the role of collective racial esteem and resilience in the development of Asian American leadership self efficacy. *Journal of Diversity in Higher Education.* Advance online publication. doi:10.1037/dhe0000137

Korn Ferry. (2019). *The Black P&L Leader: Insights and Lesson from Senior Black P&L Leaders in Corporate America.* Korn Ferry Institute. https://www.kornferry.com/content/dam/kornferry/docs/pdfs/korn-ferry_theblack-pl-leader.pdf

Kress, T. M. (2009). In the shadow of whiteness: (re)exploring connections between history, enacted culture, and identity in a digital divide initiative. *Cultural Studies of Science Education, 4*(1), 41–49. doi:10.100711422-008-9137-6

Kulkarni, M., Choi, C., & Jeung, R. M. (2021, March). How to stop the dangerous rise in hatred targeted at Asian Americans. *USA Today.* https://www.usatoday.com/story/opinion/2021/03/30/how-stop-rise-hatred-aimed-asian-americans-column/7044033002/

Kyaw, A. (2021, April 25). Report: Faculty diversity falling behind student diversity. *Diverse Issues in Higher Education.* https://diverseeducation.com/article/212463/

Ladson-Billings, G., & Tate, W. F. (2016). Toward a critical race theory of education. *Critical Race Theory in Education,* 10–31. doi:10.4324/9781315709796-2

Ladson-Billings, G. (1995). But that's just good teaching: The case for culturally responsive teaching. *Theory into Practice, 34*(3), 159–165. doi:10.1080/00405849509543675

Ladson-Billings, G. (1998). Just what is critical race theory and what's it doing in a nice field like education? *International Journal of Qualitative Studies in Education: QSE, 11*(1), 7–24. doi:10.1080/095183998236863

Ladson-Billings, G. (2006). Foreword. In A. D. Dixson & C. K. Rousseau (Eds.), *Critical race theory in education: All God's children got a song* (pp. v–xiii). Routledge Taylor & Francis Group.

Ladson-Billings, G. (2013). Critical race theory– What it is not! In M. Lynn & A. D. Dixson (Eds.), *Handbook of critical race theory in education* (pp. 34–47). Routledge.

Lara-Cooper, K., & Lara, W. J. (2019). *Ka'm-t'em: A journey toward healing.* Great Oak Press.

Latina Feminist Group. (2001). *Living to tell: Latina feminist testimonios.* Duke University Press.

Lee, S. J., & Hong, J. J. (2020). Model minorities and perpetual foreigners: Stereotypes of Asian Americans. In J. T. Nadler & E. C. Voyles (Eds.), *Stereotypes: The incidence and impacts of bias* (pp. 165-174). Prager. https://publisher.abc-clio.com/9781440868672/

Leonardo, Z. (2002). The souls of white folk: Critical pedagogy, whiteness studies, and globalization discourse. *Race, Ethnicity and Education, 5*(1), 29–50. doi:10.1080/13613320120117180

Levinson, M. (2011). Racial politics and double consciousness: Education for liberation in an inescapably diverse polity. *Canadian Issues: Themes Canadiens,* (Spring), 80–82.

Lichtblau, E. (2016, September 17). Hate crimes against Muslim Americans most since 9/11 era. *The New York Times,* p. A13.

Li, G., & Beckett, G. H. (2006). Reconstructing culture and identity in the academy. In G. Li & G. H. Beckett (Eds.), *Strangers" of the academy: Asian women scholars in higher education* (pp. 1–14). Stylus Publishing.

Lim, S. G. (2006). Identities Asian, female, scholar: critiques and celebration of North American academy. In G. Li & G. H. Beckett (Eds.), *Strangers" of the academy: Asian women scholars in higher education* (pp. xiii–xviii). Stylus Publishing.

Lipman, P. (2008). Mixed-income schools and housing: Advancing the neoliberal urban agenda. *Journal of Education Policy, 23*(2), 119–134.

Litam, S. D. A., Harrichand, J. J. S., & Ausloos, C. D. (2020, September 11). *The effects of COVID-19 related stress on a national sample of professional counselors* [Conference session]. Association for Assessment and Research in Counseling (AARC) 2020 Online Summit.

Litam, S. D. A., Ausloos, C. D., & Harrichand, J. J. S. (in press). Stress and resilience among professional counselors during the COVID-19 pandemic. *Journal of Counseling and Development.*

Litam, S. D. A., & Hipolito-Delgado, C. P. (2021). When being "essential" illuminates disparities: Counseling clients affected by COVID-19. *Journal of Counseling and Development, 99*(1), 3–10. doi:10.1002/jcad.12349

Loder, T. L. (2005). African American Women Principals' Reflections on Social Change, Community Othermothering, and Chicago Public School Reform. *Urban Education*, *40*(3), 298–320.

Lomawaima, K. T. (1999). The un-natural history of American Indian education. In K. Swisher & J. Tippeconnic (Eds.), *Next steps: Research and practice to advance Indian education* (pp. 1–31). ERIC Clearinghouse on Rural Education and Small Schools., https://files.eric.ed.gov/fulltext/ED427903.pdf

Lopez, A. E. (2015). Navigating cultural borders in diverse contexts: Building capacity through culturally responsive leadership and critical praxis. *Multicultural Education Review*, *7*(3), 171–184. doi:10.1080/2005615X.2015.1072080

Lopez, A. E. (2016). *Culturally responsive and socially just leadership in diverse contexts: From theory to action*. Palgrave MacMillan. doi:10.1057/978-1-137-53339-5

Lopez, G. R. (2003). The (racially neutral) politics of education: A critical race theory perspective. *Educational Administration Quarterly*, *39*(1), 68–94.

Lorde, A. (1984). *Sister outsider: Essays and speeches*. Crossing Press.

Lorde, A. (2017). *A Burst of Light: And other essays*. Izia Press.

Love, B. L. (2019). *We want to do more than survive: Abolitionist teaching and the pursuit of educational freedom*. Beacon Press.

Lowamaima, K. T. (1994). *They called it prairie light: The story of Chilocco Indian school*. University of Nebraska Press.

Lynn, M., & Dixson, A. D. (2013). *Handbook of critical race theory in education*. Routledge. doi:10.4324/9780203155721

Lynn, M., & Parker, L. (2006). Critical race studies in education: Examining a decade of research on U.S. schools. *The Urban Review*, *38*(4), 257–290. https://doi.org/10.1007/s11256-006-0035-5

Madda, M. J. (2019, May 15). *Dena Simmons: Without context, social emotional learning can backfire*. https://www.edsurge.com/news/2019-05-15-dena-simmons-without-context-social-emotional-learning-can-backfire

Mapping Police Violence. (2020, December 8). https://mappingpoliceviolence.org/

Marsh, T. E., & Knaus, C. B. (2016). Fostering movements or silencing voices: School principals in Egypt and South Africa. *International Journal of Multicultural Education*, *17*(1), 188–210.

Martinez-Alire, C. (2013). *The perceptions of tribal leadership and the impact of education and cultural knowledge: Examining tribal leadership and education within California Native American communities* [Doctoral dissertation, California State University, Sacramento]. Sacramento Doctoral Dissertations.

Martinez, M. A., Rivera, M., & Marquez, J. (2020). Learning from the experiences and development of Latina school leaders. *Educational Administration Quarterly*, *56*(3), 472–498. doi:10.1177/0013161X19866491

Mawhinney, L. (2011). Othermothering: A personal narrative exploring relationships between Black female faculty and students. *The Negro Educational Review, 62-63*(1-4), 213-232. http://gateway.proquest.com/openurl?url_ver=Z39.88-2004&res_dat=xri:bsc:&rft_dat=xri:bsc:rec:iibp:00417280

Mays, V. M., Coleman, L. M., & Jackson, J. S. (1996). Perceived race-based discrimination, employment status, and job stress in a national sample of Black women: Implications for health outcomes. *Journal of Occupational Health Psychology*, *1*(3), 319–329. https://doi.org/10.1037/1076-8998.1.3.319

McAuliffe, G., & ... (2013). *Culturally alert counseling: A comprehensive introduction.* Sage Publications.

McCloud, A. M. (2010). Muslim American youth: Understanding hyphenated identities through multiple methods. *Journal of American Ethnic History*, *30*(1), 120.

McCollum, P. (2005). Review of literature of leadership- An excerpt from the new IDRA book, "The Ohtli Encuentro – Women of Color Share Pathways to Leadership." *IDRA Newsletter*. Retrieved from https://www.idra.org/resource-center/review-of-literature-on-leadership-part-ii/

McGee, E., & Stovall, D. (2015). Reimagining critical race theory in education: Mental health, healing, and the pathway to liberatory praxis. *Educational Theory*, *65*(5), 491–511. doi:10.1111/edth.12129

McNamarah, C. T. (2019). White caller crime: Racialized police communication and existing while Black. *Michigan Journal of Race & Law*, *24*, 335–415. https://repository.law.umich.edu/mjrl/vol24/iss2/5

Méndez-Morse, S., Murakami, E. T., Byrne-Jiménez, M., & Hernandez, F. (2015). Mujeres in the principal's office: Latina school leaders. *Journal of Latinos and Education*, *14*(3), 171–187. doi:10.1080/15348431.2014.973566

Mendoza-Reis, N., & Flores, B. (2014). Changing the pedagogical culture of schools with Latino English Learners: Reculturing instructional leadership. In P. J. Mellom, P. P. Portes, S. Spencer & P. Baquedano-Lopez (Eds.), U.S. Latinos and Education Policy: Research-Based Directions for Change. Routledge.

Mendoza-Reis, N., & Smith, A. (2013). Re-thinking the universal approach to the preparation of school leaders: Cultural proficiency and beyond. In L. C. Tillman & J. J. Scheurich (Eds.), *Handbook of research on educational leadership for equity and diversity*. Routledge Press. doi:10.4324/9780203076934.ch28

Merriam-Webster. (n.d.a). Advocate. In *Merriam-Webster.com dictionary*. Retrieved June 15, 2021, from https://www.merriam-webster.com/dictionary/advocate

Merriam-Webster. (n.d.b). Agitator. In *Merriam-Webster.com dictionary*. Retrieved June 15, 2021, from https://www.merriam-webster.com/dictionary/agitator

Metz, T. (2018). An African theory of good leadership. *African Journal of Business Ethics, 12*(2), 36–53. doi:10.15249/12-2-204

Meyers, L. (2017, October 25). Making the counseling profession more diverse. *Counseling Today*. https://ct.counseling.org/2017/10/making-counseling-profession-diverse/

Minello, A., Martucci, S., & Manzo, L. K. (2021). The pandemic and the academic mothers: Present hardships and future perspectives. *European Societies, 23*(sup1), S82-S94.

Mohanty, C. (1988). Under Western Eyes: Feminist Scholarship and Colonial Discourses. *Feminist Review, 30*(1), 61–88. doi:10.1057/fr.1988.42

Moore, H. A., Acosta, K., Perry, G., & Edwards, C. (2010). Splitting the academy: The emotions of intersectionality at work. *The Sociological Quarterly, 51*(2), 179–204. doi:10.1111/j.1533-8525.2010.01168.x

Moore, M. (1981). Mainstreaming Black women in American higher education. *Journal of Societies of Ethnic and Special Studies, 5*, 61–68.

Moore, W., & Wagstaff, L. (1974). *Black educators in White colleges*. Jossey-Bass.

Moorosi, P., Fuller, K., & Reilly, E. (2018). Leadership and intersectionality: Constructions of successful leadership among Black women school principals in three different contexts. *Management in Education, 32*(4), 152–159. doi:10.1177/0892020618791006

Morris, L. V. (2017). Reverse mentoring: Untapped resource in the academy? *Innovative Higher Education, 42*(4), 285–287. doi:10.100710755-017-9405-z

Muhammad, G. (2020). *Cultivating genius: An equity framework for culturally and historically responsive literacy*. Scholastic Inc.

Mukkamala, S., & Suyemoto, K. L. (2018). Racialized sexism/sexualized racism: A multimethod study of intersectional experiences of discrimination for Asian American women. *Asian American Journal of Psychology, 9*(1), 32–46. doi:10.1037/aap0000104

Mullings, L. (2002). The Sojourner syndrome: Race, class, and gender in health and illness. *Voices*, 32-36.

Murakami, E. T., Hernandez, F., Méndez-Morse, S., & Byrne-Jimenez, M. (2016). Latina/o school principals: Identity, leadership and advocacy. *International Journal of Leadership in Education, 19*(3), 280–299. doi:10.1080/13603124.2015.1025854

Murakami, E. T., Hernandez, F., Valle, F., & Almager, I. (2018). Latina/o school administrators and the intersectionality of professional identity and race. *SAGE Open, 8*(2), 1–16. doi:10.1177/2158244018776045

Nadal, K. L., Griffin, K. E., Wong, Y., Hamit, S., & Rasmus, M. (2014). The impact of racial microaggressions on mental health: Counseling implications for clients of color. *Journal of Counseling and Development, 92*(1), 57–66. doi:10.1002/j.1556-6676.2014.00130.x

National Center for Statistics. (n.d.). *Fast facts: Race/ethnicity of college and university faculty.* https://nces.ed.gov/fastfacts/display.asp?id=61

Nayak, S. (2015). *Race, gender and the activism of Black feminist theory: Working with Audre Lorde.* Routledge.

NCES. (2018). Retrieved from: https://nces.ed.gov

Neck, C. P., Manz, C. C., & Houghton, J. D. (2016). Self-leadership: The definitive guide to personal excellence. *Sage (Atlanta, Ga.).*

Nelson, T., Esteban, C., & Adeoye, C. (2016). *Rethinking Strength: Black Women's Perceptions of the "Strong Black Woman" Role.* https://journals-sagepub-com.proxy.library.vcu.edu/doi/full/10.1177/0361684316646716

Nevarez, C., & Wood, L. (2010). *Community college leadership and administration.* Peter Lang Publishing. doi:10.3726/978-1-4539-1712-1

New York Times Magazine. (2019). *1619 project.* https://www.nytimes.com/interactive/2019/08/14/magazine/1619-america-slavery.html

New York, N. B. C. (2020, July 6). *Amy Cooper, woman who called police on Black man in Central Park, charged.* https://www.youtube.com/watch?v=ilG3NpUn4IU

Newcomb, W. S., & Niemeyer, A. (2015). African American women principals: Heeding the call to serve as conduits for transforming urban school communities. *International Journal of Qualitative Studies in Education: QSE, 28*(7), 786–799. https://doi.org/10.1080/09518398.2015.1036948

Newman, P. (2021a). *The Bloomsbury Handbook of Gender and Educational Leadership and Management* (V. Showunmi, P. Moorosi, C. Shakeshaft, & I. Oplataka, Eds.). Bloomsbury Academic.

Newman, P. (2021b). *Leading in Crooked Rooms: Race, Gender, Culture and Black Women's Leadership Skills and Practices.* Virginia Commonwealth University.

Newman, P. (2022). Ruminations of Black Womanhood, Leadership and Resistance. In G. Wilson, J. Acuff, & A. Kraehe (Eds.), *A Love Letter to This Bridge Called My Back.* University of Arizona Press.

News, N. B. C. (2021). *NBA's G League investigating after Jeremy Lin said he was called "Coronavirus" on the Court.* https://www.nbcnews.com/news/asian-america/nba-s-g-league-investigating-after-jeremy-lin-said-he-n1259073

Ngue, P., Saddler, R., Miller-Surratt, J., Tucker, N., Long, M., & Cooke, R. (2020). *Working at the intersection: What Black Women are up against.* Lean In. https://leanin.org/black-women-racism-discrimination-at-work

Nix, N. (2020). *Trump tells violent far-right group: Stand back and stand by.* https://www.bloomberg.com/news/articles/2020-09-30/trump-proud-boys-debate-stand-back-stand-by

Nobel, C. (2017). The three types of leaders who create radical change. *Working Knowledge Business Research for Business Leaders.* https://hbswk.hbs.edu/item/the-three-types-of-leaders-who-create-radical-change

Noddings, N. (1984). *Caring: A feminine approach to ethics and moral education.* University of California Press.

Northouse, P. G. (2015). *Leadership: Theory and practice* (7th ed.). SAGE.

Obare, S. O. (2020). Successful STEM women of color must network differently. In P. M. Leggett-Robinson & B. C. Villa (Eds.), *Overcoming barriers for women of color in STEM fields: Emerging research and opportunities* (pp. 82–99). IGI Global. doi:10.4018/978-1-7998-4858-5.ch004

Ogbu, J. U. (1995). Understanding cultural diversity and learning. In J. A. Banks & C. A. M. G. Banks (Eds.), *Handbook of research on multicultural education* (pp. 22–34). Macmillan Pub.

Okun, T. (2020). *White Supremacy Culture.* DRworksBook. https://www.dismantlingracism.org/

Oppel, R. A., Taylor, D. B., & Bogel-Burroughs, N. (2021, April). What to know about Breonna Taylor's death. *New York Times.* https://www.nytimes.com/article/breonna-taylor-police.html

Oppression. (n.d.). In *Merriam-Webster.com dictionary.* https://www.merriam-webster.com/dictionary/oppression

Overstreet, M. (2019). My first year in academia *or* the mythical Black woman superhero takes on the ivory tower. *Journal of Women and Gender in Higher Education, 12*(1), 18–34. doi:10.1080/19407882.2018.1540993

Padilla, A. M. (1994). Ethnic minority scholars, research, and mentoring: Current and future issues. *Educational Researcher, 23*(4), 24–27. doi:10.2307/1176259

Pager, D. (2006). The dynamics of discrimination. *National Poverty Center: Working Paper Series, 6*(11), 1-47.

Painter, N. (1996). *Sojourner Truth: A life, a symbol.* W. W. Norton.

Paradiso, A. (2020). The importance of inclusion in the workplace. *Engage: Employee Engagement Blog.* https://www.achievers.com/blog/the-importance-of-inclusion -in-the-workplace/

Parker, L., & Villalpando, O. (2007). A (race)cialized perspective on education leadership: Critical race theory in educational administration. *Educational Administration Quarterly, 43*(5), 519–524.

Paschall, K. W., Gershoff, E. T., & Kuhfeld, M. (2018). A two decade examination of historical race/ethnicity disparities in academic achievement by poverty status. *Journal of Youth and Adolescence, 47*(6), 1164–1177.

Pavel, D. M., & Padilla, R. V. (1993). American Indian and Alaska Native Postsecondary Departure: An example of assessing a mainstream model using national longitudinal data. *Journal of American Indian Education, 32*(2), 1-23. https://www.jstor.org/stable/24398302?casa_token= 3EkZZHYOOrUAAAAA%3AXWwQGlinj-oJCYixNWMLc91qIRVDSVnl-l2ykC39BuxvI2lY nwtorPDTJNMqSBUoHWjmQxPtLp8UsC9M2U8qe2uxuiFgAIOyVoEWBED0WRMgc5WqJ 2Fc&seq=1#metadata_info_tab_contents

PBS Wisconsin Education. (2020, June 30). *Building culturally relevant schools post-pandemic with Dr. Gloria Ladson-Billings.* https://www.youtube.com/watch?v=Rr2monteBbo

Pérez Huber, L. (2010). Using Latina/o critical race theory (LatCrit) and racist nativism to explore intersectionality in the educational experiences of undocumented Chicana college students. *Educational Foundations,* 77–96.

Peters, H., Luke, M., Bernard, J., & Trepal, H. (2020). Socially just and culturally responsive leadership within counseling and counseling psychology: A grounded theory investigation. *The Counseling Psychologist, 48*(7), 953–985. doi:10.1177/0011000020937431

Pierce, C. M. (1995). Stress analogs of racism and sexism: Terrorism, torture, and disaster. In C. V. Willie, P. P. Ricker, B. M. Kramer, & B. S. Brown (Eds.), *Mental health, racism, and sexism* (pp. 277–293). University of Pittsburgh Press.

Prakash, P., Choi, C., & Jeung, R. M. (2021, May). Global spread of COVID-19 variant first detected in India brings with it fears of anti-Indian racism. *Scroll.* https://scroll.in/global/995805/global-spread-of-covid-19-variant-first-detected-in-india-brings-with-it-fears-of-anti-indian-racism

Pullman, A. (2013). Destabilizing curriculum history: A genealogy of critical thinking. *Journal of Curriculum Theorizing, 29*(1), 173–189.

RAGE Project. (2019). https://www.rageproject.org/background

Ramírez, P., & González, G. (2012). Latina teacher agency in public schools: Love, tensions, and perseverance. *Association of Mexican-American Educators (AMAE) Journal, 6*(1), 34–44.

Rath, T. (2007). *Strengths finder 2.0.* Gallup Press.

Ratts, M. J., Sing, A. A., Nassar-McMillan, S., Butler, S. K., & McCullough, J. R. (2015). *Multicultural and social justice counseling competencies.* https://www.counseling.org/knowledge-center/competencies

Razai, M. S., Oakeshott, P., Kankam, H., Galea, S., & Stokes-Lampard, H. (2020). Mitigating the psychological effects of social isolation during the covid-19 pandemic. *BMJ (Clinical Research Ed.), 369*, m1904. doi:10.1136/bmj.m1904 PMID:32439691

Reardon, S. F., Grewal, E. T., Kalogrides, D., & Greenberg, E. (2012). Brown fades: The end of court-ordered school desegregation and the resegregation of American public schools. *Journal of Policy Analysis and Management*, *31*(4), 876–904.

Rector-Aranda, A. (2016). School norms and reforms, critical race theory, and the fairytale of equitable education. *Critical Questions in Education*, *7*(1), 1–16.

Reda, M. M. (2007). Autoethnography as research methodology? *Academic Exchange Quarterly*, *11*(1), 177–183.

Reeve, E. (2020, November 25). *He's an ex-Proud Boy. Here's what he says happens within the group's ranks.* https://www.cnn.com/2020/11/25/us/ex-proud-boys-member/index.html

Reis, N. M., & Lu, M. Y. (2010). Why are there so few of us? Counter-stories from women of color in faculty governance roles. *Educational Leadership*, *20*(1), 61–97.

Reskin, B. F., & Mcbrier, D. B. (2000). Why not ascription? Organizations' employment of male and female managers. *American Sociological Review*, *65*(2), 210. doi:10.2307/2657438

Reyes, I. I. I. (2007). Marginalized students in secondary school education. *The Journal of Border Educational Research*, *6*(2).

Reyhner, J., & Dodd, J. (1995). *Factors affecting the retention of American Indian and Alaska Native students in higher education.* https://jan.ucc.nau.edu/~jar/Factors.html

Rhode, D. L. (2017). *Women and leadership.* Oxford University Press.

Ricento, T. (2003). The Discursive Construction of Americanism. *Discourse & Society*, *14*(5), 611–637. doi:10.1177/09579265030145004

Richie, B., Fassinger, R., Linn, S., Johnson, J., Prosser, J., & Robinson, S. (1997). *Persistence, connection, and passion: A qualitative study of the career development of highly achieving African American–Black and White women.* https://psycnet-apa-org.proxy.library.vcu.edu/fulltext/1997-08136-003.html

Rickford, J. R. (1999). Suite for ebony and phonics. In *African American Vernaculuar English: Features, evolution, educational implications* (pp. 320–328). Blackwell Publishers.

Ridgeway, C. L. (2011). *Framed by gender: How gender inequality persists in the modern world.* Oxford University Press. doi:10.1093/acprof:oso/9780199755776.001.0001

Risling Baldy, C. (2018). *We are dancing for you: Native feminisms and the revitalization of women's coming-of-age ceremonies.* University of Washington Press.

Rockquemore, K. A., & Laszloffy, T. (2008). *The Black academic's guide to winning tenure— without losing your soul.* Lynne Rienner Publisher, Inc.

Rong, X. L., & Preissle, J. (2006). From mentorship to friendship, collaboration, and collegiality. In G. Li & G. H. Beckett (Eds.), *Strangers" of the academy: Asian women scholars in higher education* (pp. 266–288). Stylus Publishing.

Rosser-Mims, D. (2010). *Black Feminism: An Epistemological Framework for Exploring How Race and Gender Impact Black Women's Leadership Development.* Academic Press.

Rudolph, C. W., Rauvola, R. S., & Zacher, H. (2018). Leadership and generations at work: A critical review. *The Leadership Quarterly, 29*(1), 44–57. doi:10.1016/j.leaqua.2017.09.004

Sabharwal, M., & Varma, R. (2017). Are Asian Indian scientists and engineers in academia faced with a glass ceiling? *Journal of Ethnographic and Qualitative Research, 12*, 50–62.

Sabry, N. S., & Bruna, K. R. (2007). Learning from the experience of Muslim students in American schools: Towards a proactive model of school-community cooperation. *Multicultural Perspectives, 9*(3), 44–50. doi:10.1080/15210960701443730

Sacramento Native Higher Education Collaborative. (2021). *Vision and goals.* Author.

Said, E. D. (1997). *Covering Islam: How the media and the experts determine how we see the rest of the world.* Vintage.

Sakho-Lewis, J. R. (2017). Black Activist Mothering: Teach Me About What Teaches You. *The Western Journal of Black Studies, 41*(1/2), 6–19. http://proxy.library.vcu.edu/login?url=http://search.ebscohost.com/login.aspx?direct=true&AuthType=ip,url,cookie,uid&db=sih&AN=128902077&site=ehost-live&scope=site

Sandefur, G., & Deloria, P. J. (2018). Indigenous leadership. *Dædalus: Journal of the American Academy of Arts & Sciences, 147*(2), 124–135. doi:10.1162/DAED_a_00496

Santamaria, L. (2014). Critical Change for the Greater Good: Multicultural Perceptions in Educational Leadership Toward Social Justice and Equity. *Educational Administration Quarterly, 50*(3), 347–391. https://doi.org/10.1177/0013161X13505287

Santamaría, L. J., & Santamaría, A. P. (2011). *Applied critical leadership in education: Choosing change.* Routledge.

Santamaría, L. J., & Santamaría, A. P. (2015). Counteracting educational injustice with applied critical leadership: Culturally responsive practices promoting sustainable change. *International Journal of Multicultural Education, 17*(1), 22–42.

Santamaría, L., & Santamaría, A. (2015). *Culturally Responsive Leadership in Higher Education: Promoting Access, Equity, and Improvement.* Routledge.

Sarwar, D., & Raj, R. (2016). Islamophobia, racism, and critical race theory. *Revista de la Fiscalía de Estado de la Provincia de Santa Fe, 15.*

Schild, L., Ling, C., Blackburn, J., Stringhini, G., Zhang, Y., & Zannettou, S. (2020). *"Go eat a bat, Chang!": An early look on the emergence of sinophobic behavior on web communities in the face of COVID-19.* https://arxiv.org/pdf/2004.04046.pdf

Schwartz, H. L., Faruque, A., Leschitz, J. T., Uzicanin, A., & Uscher-Pines, L. (2020). *Opportunities and challenges in using online learning to maintain continuity of instruction in K-12 schools in emergencies*. Rand Corporation. https://www.rand.org/pubs/working_papers/WRA235-1.html

Seward, M. S. (2019, April 2). Decolonizing the classroom: Step 1. *NCTE Standing Committee on Global Citizenship*. https://ncte.org/blog/2019/04/decolonizing-the-classroom/

Shakeshaft, C. (1989). The Gender Gap in Research in Educational Administration. *Educational Administration Quarterly*, *25*(4), 324–337. https://doi.org/10.1177/0013161X89025004002

Shanker, M., & Sayeed, O. (2012). Role of transformational leaders as change agents: Leveraging effects on organizational climate. *Indian Journal of Industrial Relations*, *47*(3), 470–484. http://www.jstor.org/stable/23267338

Shapiro, J. P., & Stefkovich, J. A. (2011). *Ethical leadership and decision making in education: Applying theoretical perspectives to complex dilemmas* (3rd ed.). Routledge.

Shields, C. (2010). Transformative leadership: Working for equity in diverse contexts. *Educational Administration Quarterly*, *46*(4), 558–589. doi:10.1177/0013161X10375609

Shields, C. M. (2004). Dialogic leadership for social justice: Overcoming pathologies of silence. *Educational Administration Quarterly*, *40*(1), 109–132. doi:10.1177/0013161X03258963

Shields, C. M. (2013). *Transformative leadership in education: Equitable change in an uncertain and complex world*. Routledge.

Shields, C. M. (2020). *Becoming a transformative leader: A guide to creating equitable schools*. Routledge.

Shin, R. Q., Welch, J. C., Kaya, A. E., Yeung, J. G., Obana, C., Sharma, R., Vernay, C. N., & Yee, S. (2017). The intersectionality framework and identity intersections in the journal of counseling psychology and the counseling psychologist: A content analysis. *Journal of Counseling Psychology*, *64*(5), 458–474. doi:10.1037/cou0000204 PMID:29048193

Silver, N., & Jansen, P. (2017). The Multisector Career Arc: The Importance of Cross-Sector Affiliations. *California Management Review*, *60*(1), 33–55. https://doi.org/10.1177/0008125617725290

Simmons, D. (2019). Why we can't afford whitewashed social-emotional learning. *ASCD Education Update*, *16*(4). http://www.ascd.org/publications/newsletters/education_update/apr19/vol61/num04/Why_We_Can't_Afford_Whitewashed_Social-Emotional_Learning.aspx

Simpson, G. E., & Yinger, J. M. (1985). *Racial and cultural minorities: An analysis of prejudice and discrimination*. Springer. doi:10.1007/978-1-4899-0551-2

Sirin, S. R., & Fine, M. (2008). *Muslim American youth: Understanding hyphenated identities through multiple methods*. New York University Press.

Smith, W. A. (2004). Black faculty coping with racial battle fatigue: The campus racial climate in a post-Civil Rights Era. In D. Cleveland (Ed.), A long way to go: Conversations about race by African American faculty and graduate students (pp. 171-190). Peter Lang Publishing Inc.

Smith, L. T. (1999). *Decolonizing methodologies: Research and Indigenous peoples*. University of Otago Press.

Smith, L. T. (2012). *Decolonizing methodologies*. Zed Books.

Smith, L. T. (2013). *Decolonizing methodologies: Research and indigenous peoples*. Zed Books.

Smith, M. L., & Roysircar, G. (2010). African American male leaders in counseling: Interviews with five AMCD past presidents. *Journal of Multicultural Counseling and Development, 38*(4), 242–256. doi:10.1002/j.2161-1912.2010.tb00134.x

Smith, W. A. (2015). Foreword. In R. Mitchell, K. J. Fasching-Varner, K. Albert, & C. Allen (Eds.), *Racial battle fatigue in higher education: Exposing the myth of post-racial America* (pp. xi–xii). Rowan & Littlefield Publishers.

Smith, W. A., Allen, W. R., & Danley, L. L. (2007). 'Assume the position...You fit the description': Psychological experiences and racial battle fatigue among African American male college students. *The American Behavioral Scientist, 51*(4), 551–578. doi:10.1177/0002764207307742

Smith, W. A., Yosso, T. J., & Solórzano, D. G. (2006). Challenging racial battle fatigue on historically white campuses: a critical race examination of race-related stress. In C. A. Stanley (Ed.), *Faculty of Color: Teaching in predominantly White colleges and universities* (pp. 299–327). Anker Publishing.

Solórzano, D., & Yosso, T. (2000). Toward a critical race theory of Chicana and Chicano education. In C. Tejeda, C. Martinez, Z. Leonardo & P. McLaren (Eds.), Charting new terrains of Chicana(o)/Latina(o) education. Hampton Press.

Solorzano, D. (1997). Images and words that wound: Critical race theory, racial stereotyping and teacher education. *Teacher Education Quarterly, 24*, 5–19.

Solorzano, D. (1998). Critical race theory, racial and gender microaggressions, and the experiences of Chicana and Chicano Scholars. *International Journal of Qualitative Studies in Education: QSE, 11*(1), 121–136. doi:10.1080/095183998236926

Solórzano, D. G., & Yosso, T. J. (2002). Critical race methodology: Counter-Storytelling as an analytical framework for education research. *Qualitative Inquiry, 8*(1), 23–44. doi:10.1177/107780040200800103

Solórzano, D. G., & Yosso, T. J. (2009). Critical race methodology: Counter-storytelling as an analytic framework for educational research. In E. Taylor, D. Gillborn, & G. Ladson-Billings (Eds.), *Foundations of critical race theory in education* (pp. 131–147). Routledge.

Solórzano, D., & Delgado Bernal, D. (2001). Examining transformational resistance through a critical race and LatCrit theory framework: Chicana and Chicano students in an urban context. *Urban Education, 36*(3), 308–342. doi:10.1177/0042085901363002

Southern Regional Education Board. (2021, April). *Student and faculty diversity in SREB states.* https://www.sreb.org/diversityprofiles

Spivak, G. (1988). Can the subaltern speak? In C. Nelson & L. Grossberg (Eds.), *Marxism and the interpretation of culture* (pp. 271–316). University of Illinois Press., doi:10.1007/978-1-349-19059-1_20

Springer, M. (2015). *Native student organizations as a high impact practice: Native students perceptions of the effects of participation in a Native student organization on their academic and personal success at predominately white institutions* (Publication No. 3742179) [Doctoral dissertation, New England College]. ProQuest Dissertations Publishing.

Spring, J. (2016). *Deculturalization and the struggle for equality: A brief history of the education of dominated cultures in the United States.* Routledge.

Stanton-Salazar, R. D. (2011). A social capital framework for the study of institutional agents and their role in the empowerment of low-status students and youth. *Youth & Society, 43*(3), 1066–1109. doi:10.1177/0044118X10382877

Starks, J. E. (2010). *Factors influencing the decisions of Native Americans to attend or not attend college or vocational school: A phenomenological study* (Publication No. 3433010) [Doctoral dissertation, College of Saint Mary]. ProQuest Dissertations Publishing.

Starratt, R. A. (2012). *Cultivating an ethical school.* Routledge. doi:10.4324/9780203833261

Stein, S., & Andreotti, V. D. O. (2016). Decolonization and higher education. Encyclopedia of Educational Philosophy and Theory, 10, 978–981. doi:10.1007/978-981-287-532-7_479-1

Stephan, M. J., & Thompson, T. (2017, August 10). Connecting civil resistance and conflict resolution: 'People power' activists and peace mediators combine to build a stronger peace. *The Olive Branch.* https://www.usip.org/blog/2017/08/connecting-civil-resistance-and-conflict-resolution

Stephen, M. (Ed.). (1999). *Indigenous community-based education.* Multilingual Matters.

Stobbe, M. (2020, December 22). More than 3 million people died in 2020 - the deadliest year in U.S. history. *USA Today.* https://www.usatoday.com/story/news/nation/2020/12/22/2020-deadliest-year-united-states-coronavirus/4006270001/

Storlie, C., Parker-Wright, M., & Woo, H. (2015). Multicultural leadership development: A qualitative analysis of emerging leaders in counselor education. *Journal of Counselor Leadership and Advocacy, 2*(2), 154–169. doi:10.1080/2326716X.2015.1054078

Stovall, D. (2006). Forging community in race and class: Critical race theory and the quest for social justice in education. *Race, Ethnicity and Education, 9*(3), 243–259. doi:10.1080/13613320600807550

Stremlau, R. (2005). "To domesticate and civilize wild Indians": Allotment and the campaign to reform Indian families, 1875-1887. *Journal of Family History, 30*(3), 265–286. doi:10.1177/0363199005275793

Substance Abuse and Mental Health Services Administration. (2020). *Double jeopardy: COVID-19 and behavioral health disparities for Black and Latino communities in the U.S.* https://www.samhsa.gov/sites/default/files/covid19-behavioral-health-disparities-black-latino-communities.pdf

Sue, D. W. (2010). *Microaggressions and marginality: Manifestation, dynamics, and impact.* Wiley.

Sue, D. W., Capodilupo, C. M., Torino, G. L., Bucceri, J. M., Holder, A. M. B., Nadal, K. L., & Esquilin, M. (2007). Racial microaggressions in everyday life: Implications for clinical practice. *The American Psychologist, 62*(4), 271–286. doi:10.1037/0003-066X.62.4.271 PMID:17516773

Sumner, K. A. (2018). *Native daughter: A lived experience of desegregation* [Doctoral dissertation, University of Massachusetts Boston]. Graduate Doctoral Dissertations. https://scholarworks.umb.edu/doctoral_dissertations/451

Swain, B. G. (2012). *Aspects of school integration: From Brown to court-ordered bussing* [Master's thesis, University of Michigan]. http://hdl.handle.net/2027.42/117930

Szasz, M. (1999). *Education and the American Indian: The road to self-determination since 1928.* University of New Mexico Press.

Tatum, B. (1994). The colonial model as a theoretical explanation of crime and delinquency. *African American perspectives on crime, causation, criminal justice administration, and crime prevention*, 33-52.

Tayloe, L. (2016). *A study of Latina K-12 public school administrators: Barriers and strategies to career advancement and the impact of race and gender on ascension and leadership.* http://ezproxy.flsouthern.edu:2048/login?url=https://ezproxy.flsouthern.edu:2297/docview/1870038156?accountid=27315

Tayloe, L. (2017). *Hablando de ellas: Experiences of Latina K-12 Public School Administrators with Race and Gender.* MujeresTalk.

Teaching While White Staff. (2020, December 16). *Resisting the pushback against the work for racial equity and justice.* https://www.teachingwhilewhite.org/blog/resisting-the-pushback-against-the-work-for-racial-equity-and-justicenbsp

Terrell, R., & Lindsey, R. (2009). *Culturally proficient leadership: The personal journey begins within.* Corwin.

Texas Association of School Boards. (2021). *TASB mission and values.* https://www.tasb.org/about-tasb/mission-and-values.aspx

The Trevor Project. (2020). *The Trevor project research brief: Latinx LGBTQ youth suicide risk.* https://www.thetrevorproject.org/wp-content/uploads/2020/09/Latinx-LGBTQ-Youth-Suicide-Risk-Sept-2020-Research-Brief.pdf

Theoharis, G. (2007). Social justice educational leaders and resistance: Toward a theory of social justice leadership. *Educational Administration Quarterly, 43*(2), 221–258. doi:10.1177/0013161X06293717

Thomas, A. J., Witherspoon, K. M., & Speight, S. L. (2008). Gendered racism, psychological distress, and coping styles of African American women. *Cultural Diversity & Ethnic Minority Psychology, 14*(4), 307–314. doi:10.1037/1099-9809.14.4.307 PMID:18954166

Thompson, G., & Louque, A. (2005). *Exposing the "Culture of Arrogance" in the academy: A blueprint for increasing Black faculty satisfaction in higher education.* Stylus Publications.

Tierney, W. G. (1990, May). *American Indians and higher education: A research agenda for the 90s.* Paper presented at the Opening the Montana Pipeline: American Indian Higher Education in the Nineties Conference, Montana State University, Bozeman, MT.

Tierney, W. G. (1991). Native voices in academe: Strategies for empowerment. *Change, 23*(2), 36–45. doi:10.1080/00091383.1991.9937678

Tillman, L. C. (2004). African American principals and the legacy of Brown. *Review of Research in Education, 28*(1), 101–146. doi:10.3102/0091732X028001101

Tindongan, C. W. (2011). Negotiating Muslim youth identity in a post-9/11 world. *High School Journal, 95*(1), 72–87. doi:10.1353/hsj.2011.0012

Tomkins, J. (2002). Learning to see what they can't: Decolonizing perspectives on Indigenous education in the racial context of rural Nova Scotia. *McGill Journal of Education/Revue des sciences de l'éducation de McGill, 37*(3).

Toporek, R. L., & Daniels, J. (2018). *American counseling association advocacy competencies.* https://www.counseling.org/docs/default-source/competencies/aca-advocacy-competencies-updated-may-2020.pdf?sfvrsn=f410212c_4

Trennert, R. A. Jr. (1988). *The Phoenix Indian School: Forced assimilation in Arizona, 1891-1935.* University of Oklahoma Press.

Trouillot, M.-R. (1995). *Silencing the past: Power and the production of history.* Beacon Press.

Trybus, M. A. (2011). Facing the challenge of change: Steps to becoming an effective leader. *Delta Kappa Gamma Bulletin, 77*(3), 33–36.

Tuck, E., & Gaztambide-Fernández, R. A. (2013). Curriculum, replacement, and settler futurity. *Journal of Curriculum Theorizing, 29*(1).

U.S. Department of Education, National Center for Education Statistics. (2014). *Digest of Educational Statistics, Table 316.10. 201.* https://nces.ed.gov/programs/digest/d14/tables/dt14_316.10.asp?current=yes

U.S. Department of Education, National Center for Education Statistics. (2018). *Digest of Educational Statistics, Table 315.20.* https://nces.ed.gov/programs/digest/d19/tables/dt19_315.20.asp

UC-Riverside. (2021). *Survey Shows Anti-Asian Bias Rooted Perpetual Foreigner Stereotype.* https://socialinnovation.ucr.edu/news/2021/04/01/survey-shows-anti-asian-bias-rooted-perpetual-foreigner-stereotype

United States Department of Justice and United States Department of Education. (2017). *Dear Colleague Letter.* https://www2.ed.gov/about/offices/list/ocr/letters/colleague-201702-title-ix.pdf

Urrieta, L. J. Jr, & Villenas, S. A. (2013). The legacy of Derrick Bell and Latino/a education: A critical race testimonio. *Race, Ethnicity and Education, 16*(4), 514–535. doi:10.1080/13613324.2013.817771

Veracini, L. (2014). Understanding colonialism and settler colonialism as distinct formations. *Interventions, 16*(5), 615–633.

Vestal, C. (2020). *Racism is a public health crisis, say cities and counties.* https://www.pewtrusts.org/en/research-and-analysis/blogs/stateline/2020/06/15/racism-is-a-public-health-crisis-say-cities-and-counties

Victorian Equal Opportunity and Human Rights Commission. (2013). Waiter, is that inclusion in my soup? A new recipe to improve business performance. *Deloitte.* https://www2.deloitte.com/content/dam/Deloitte/au/Documents/human-capital/deloitte-au-hc-diversity-inclusion-soup-0513.pdf

Viglione, G. (2020). Are women publishing less during the pandemic? Here's what the data say. *Nature, 581*(7809), 365–367. doi:10.1038/d41586-020-01294-9 PMID:32433639

Villalpando, O. (2004, Spring). Practical considerations of critical race theory and Latino critical theory for Latino college students. *New Directions for Student Services, 105*(105), 41–50. doi:10.1002s.115

Vincent-Lamarre, P., Sugimoto, C. R., & Larivière, V. (2020). *Monitoring women's scholarly production during the COVID19 pandemic.* http://projets.initiativesnumeriques.org/monitoring-scholarly-covid/methods_final.pdf

Walkington, L. (2017). How far have we really come? Black women faculty and graduate students' experiences in higher education. *Humboldt Journal of Social Relations, 39*, 51–65.

Waller, M. A., Okamoto, S. K., & Hankerson, A. A. (2002). The hoop of learning: A holistic, multisystemic model for facilitating educational resilience among Indigenous students. *Journal of Sociology and Social Welfare, 29*(1), 97–116. https://heinonline.org/HOL/LandingPage?handle=hein.journals/jrlsasw29&div=9&id=&page=

Washington, M. (2013). "Going where they dare not follow": Race, religion, and Sojourner Truth's early interracial reform. *Journal of African American History, 98*(1), 48–71. doi:10.5323/jafriamerhist.98.1.0048

Compilation of References

West, J. (2020, June 13). *Colorado State football player held at gunpoint by man thinking he was with antifa.* https://www.si.com/college/2020/06/13/colorado-state-football-player-held-gunpoint-antifa

West-Olatunji, C. A., & Anandavalli, S. (in press). It's all about mentorship. In J. M. Swank & C. A. Barrio Minton (Eds.), *Critical incidents in counselor education: Teaching, supervision, research, leadership, and advocacy.* Wiley.

Westside News. (2020, September 13). *Spencerport administrator placed on leave following controversial social media video.* https://westsidenewsny.com/schools/2020-09-13/spencerport-administrator-placed-on-leave-following-controversial-social-media-video/

Whitford, E. (2020). *There are so few who have made their way.* Inside Higher Education. https://www.insidehighered.com/news/2020/10/28/black-administrators-are-too-rare-top-ranks-higher-education-it%E2%80%99s-not-just-pipeline

Wilder, C. S. (2013). *Ebony & ivy: Race, slavery, and the troubled history of America's universities.* Bloomsbury Publishing.

Will, M., & Schwartz, S. (2020, June 1). *Teachers cannot be silent: How educators are supporting black students after protests.* https://www.edweek.org/teaching-learning/teachers-cannot-be-silent-how-educators-are-supporting-black-students-after-protests/2020/06

Williams, D. R., & Mohammed, S. A. (2013). Racism and Health I: Pathways and Scientific Evidence. *The American Behavioral Scientist, 57*(8), 1152–1173. doi:10.1177/0002764213487340 PMID:24347666

Williams, H. A. (2005). *Self-taught: African American education in slavery and freedom.* University of North Carolina Press.

Williams, M. T. (2020). Microaggressions: Clarification, evidence, and impact. *Perspectives on Psychological Science, 15*(1), 3–26. doi:10.1177/1745691619827499 PMID:31418642

Williams, R. L. (1973). On black intelligence. *Journal of Black Studies, 4*(1), 29–39.

Wilson, C., & Johnson, L. (2015). Black educational activism for community empowerment: International leadership perspectives. *International Journal of Multicultural Education, 17*(1), 102–120.

Wingfield, A. H. (2015, October 14). *Being Black—But Not Too Black—In the Workplace.* The Atlantic. https://www.theatlantic.com/business/archive/2015/10/being-black-work/409990/

Wolfe, P. (2006). Settler colonialism and the elimination of the Native. *Journal of Genocide Research, 8*(4), 387–409. doi:10.1080/14623520601056240

Women in the labor force: A databook : BLS Reports: U.S. Bureau of Labor Statistics (No. 1084). (2019). https://www.bls.gov/opub/reports/womens-databook/2019/home.htm

Wood, L., & Harris, F. (2021). *Racelighting in the normal realities of Black, Indigenous, and People of Color (Scholarly Brief) Community College Equity Assessment Lab.* http://bmmcoalition.com/wp-content/uploads/2021/03/Racelighting-BRIEF-2021-3.pdf

World Health Organization. (2021, June 9). *WHO coronavirus disease (COVID-19) dashboard.* https://covid19.who.int/

Wright, B., & Tierney, W. (1991). American Indians in higher education: A history of cultural conflict. *Change, 23,* 11–18. https://naspa.tandfonline.com/doi/abs/10.1080/00091383.1991.9937673?journalCode=vchn20

X, M. (2008). *1962 L.A. Police Killings* (Vol. 2) [Audio recording]. spotify:track:1UNfkEgBaIXaBBSEbJ2hh1

Yammarino, F. (2013). Leadership: Past, Present, and Future. *Journal of Leadership & Organizational Studies, 20*(2), 149–155. https://doi.org/10.1177/1548051812471559

Yosso, T. (2005). Whose culture has capital? A critical race theory discussion of community cultural wealth. *Race, Ethnicity and Education, 8*(1), 69–91.

Yosso, T. (2005). Whose culture has capital? A critical race theory on community cultural wealth. *Race, Ethnicity and Education, 8*(1), 69–91. doi:10.1080/1361332052000341006

Yosso, T. J. (2006). *Critical race counterstories along the Chicana/Chicano educational pipeline.* Taylor & Francis Group.

Young, K., & Anderson, M. R. (2019). Microaggressions in higher education: Embracing educative spaces. In Microaggression Theory: Influence and Implications. Hoboken, NJ: John Wiley & Sons, Inc.

Young, I. M. (2004). Five faces of oppression. In L. M. Heldke & P. O'Connor (Eds.), *Oppression, privilege, and resistance: Theoretical perspectives on racism, sexism, and heterosexism* (pp. 174–195). McGraw-Hill.

Yousafzai, M. (2013). *I Am Malala: The girl who stood up for education and was shot by the Taliban.* Little, Brown.

Zamudio, M., Russel, C., Rios, F., & Bridgeman, J. L. (2011). *Critical race theory matters: Education and ideology.* Routledge. doi:10.4324/9780203842713

Zerbe Enns, C., Díaz, L. C., & Bryant-Davis, T. (2020). Transnational feminist theory and practice: An introduction. *Women & Therapy.* https://doi-org.libproxy.csudh.edu/10.1080/02703149.2020.1774997

Zimmer, L. (1988). Tokenism and women in the workplace: The limits of gender-neutral theory. *Social Problems, 35*(1), 64–77. doi:10.2307/800667

Zion, S. D., & Blanchett, W. (2011). [Re] Conceptualizing Inclusion: Can Critical Race Theory and Interest Convergence Be Utilized to Achieve Inclusion and Equity for African American Students? *Teachers College Record, 113*(10), 2186–2205.

Zuberi, T., & Bonilla-Silva, E. (2008). *White logic, white methods: Racism and methodology.* Rowman & Littlefield.

About the Contributors

Jamel Adkins-Sharif is the Director of Eskolta Network Boston, a high school research and redesign nonprofit. Jamel holds an EdD in Urban Education, Leadership and Policy Studies from the University of Massachusetts-Boston. Jamel's research explores social justice leadership, race, and equity in schools. Jamel has had a successful career as a special education teacher of history and mathematics in New York, and was founding principal of both an elementary charter and district middle school in Massachusetts. Additionally, Jamel served two terms on the Principal's Advisory Cabinet of the Massachusetts Department of Elementary and Secondary Education, and currently consults with the Department on culturally proficient school improvement.

Noor Ali earned her Doctorate in Education in Curriculum, Teaching, Learning and Leadership. She is an Assistant Professor at Northeastern University in the Graduate School of Education. Dr. Ali has worked with and published on Critical Race Theory during her academic career. She has a forthcoming book titled Critical Storytelling: Narratives of Muslim American Females this Fall.

S. Anandavalli (she, her, hers), PhD, NCC, is an Assistant Professor in the Clinical Mental Health Counseling program at Southern Oregon University, Co-Chair of the Writer's Consortium of Association for Multicultural Counseling and Development (AMCD). As a feminist scholar, her interests center around intersectionality; research ethics, mentorship, minority mental health; social justice and activism; career development; and critical research methodologies. Committed to anti-oppressive counselor training, she has researched, presented, and published at various peer-reviewed journals; regional and national conferences; and webinars. She is currently an ad hoc reviewer for The Clinical Supervisor, Teaching and Supervision in Counseling, and International Journal for the Advancement of Counselling.

Alyncia M. Bowen, PhD, has served in healthcare as an administrator for over 23 year and in higher education for over 16 years. She currently serves as the Dean of the Ross College of Business, Franklin University and Executive Director of the Franklin University Leadership Center and Co-Executive Director for the Global Center for Healthcare Education. Dr. Bowen has also served as the Dean of Doctoral Studies and the School of Nursing. Her doctorate is in Organization and Management. Her research interests include communities of practice organization learning, cultural competency, intersectionality, and Transnational Education.

Darlene Breaux is seen as a visionary leader driven by educational policy, research, and the science behind learning. Dr. Breaux was featured in the Texas School Business magazine as a Thought Leader and Innovator in Education. She is currently the Director of the Research and Evaluation Institute at Harris County Department of Education. She serves the Alief community as the vice-president of the Alief ISD School Board Trustee and Chair of the Policy Committee. Darlene is a powerful motivational speaker that has engaged audiences at a national level. She is known for her genuine openness and ability to develop collaborative relationships with all stakeholders to ensure improved student outcomes.

Tamara Cheshire (Lakota; pronouns: she, her, they, them) has worked in higher education for over 20 years teaching Native American Studies and Anthropology. She has her doctorate in Educational Leadership from California State University, Sacramento. Dr. Cheshire has published several articles and chapters about the resiliency of Native American students and their families; including her dissertation entitled: Barriers & Bridges: American Indian Community College Student Resiliency and Success. She is also a co-author of "From Boarding Schools to Suspension Boards", a statewide CCEAL report. She is a co-founder of the Sacramento Native American Higher Education Collaborative (SNAHEC). Currently Dr. Cheshire is an Assistant Professor of Anthropology at Folsom Lake College and also teaches anthropology at California State University, Sacramento.

Vanessa Esquivido (she/her/they) is an enrolled member of the Nor Rel Muk Wintu Nation, also Hupa, and Xicana. They earned her Ph.D. in Native American Studies from the University of California, Davis and recently hired as an assistant professor of American Indian Studies under the Multicultural and Gender Studies department at Chico State. Their research focuses on non-federally recognized California Indian Tribes and their struggle to obtain Federal Recognition. They also work closely with Native communities and conduct oral interviews to record Native experiences on a variety of topics. Vanessa works closely on the Native American Graves Protection and Repatriation Act (NAGPRA), specifically supporting the repatriation of Native remains, items of cultural patrimony, and sacred and funerary objects. Most recently, their research includes California Native gender and sexuality, visual sovereignty, Native Education, and California Native basketry.

Kitty M. Fortner is an assistant professor at California State University Dominguez Hills, College of Education School Leadership Program. For over 20 years, she has been involved in K-12 education in districts and public charter schools. In 2014 she received her Doctorate in Leadership for Educational Justice from the University of Redlands researching social class and student engagement. Before her work in higher education, she founded two successful charter schools in Southern California. Her passion is providing students with effective personalized learning experiences. She believes that leadership plays an imperative role in fostering academic success for all learners. Her research focuses on the intersection of identity and effective school leadership and the role it plays in educational systems focused on liberation and justice. In addition to her current research Currently, her research focuses on skills, knowledge, behaviors, and dispositions of effective urban school leadership.

María L. Gabriel, Ph.D., has worked as a PK-12 public educator in Colorado since 1997. Dr. Gabriel completed her Principal Licensure and her Doctorate Degree at CSU in 2011 in the School of Education. Her dissertation title is Voices of Hispanic and Latina/o Secondary Students in Northern Colorado: Poetic Counterstories. She has devoted her career as an educator to increasing access and opportunity for culturally, linguistically, and racially diverse students through direct student support, culturally sustaining family engagement, community-based educational research, and equity leadership. She has served on local and national boards focused on gender and racial equity, multicultural education, and inclusive community outreach. Her research interests and local, national, and international presentation topics are related to multicultural education, educational equity, Latinx student achievement, and student voice. Her work has been published in journals such as Cuaderno de Investigación en la Educación, Educational Leadership, and the Journal of Latinos and Education. She has published several chapters in books such as Anti-Racist School Leadership: Toward Equity in Education for America's Students, Latinas Leading Schools, and is a co-editor of the book Losing the Mother Tongue in the USA: Implications for Adult Latinxs in the 21st Century. Dr. Gabriel loves to run, travel, take pictures, and write. Her joy in life is spending quality time with her two teenage daughters and her Yorkie pup named Bear.

John J. S. Harrichand (he/him/his), Ph.D., LPC-S, LMHC, NCC, CCMHC, ACS, is a Canadian of Chinese and East Indian ancestry who was born and raised in Guyana, South America. He is an Assistant Professor of Counseling at The University of Texas at San Antonio. Dr. Harrichand earned his Ph.D. in Counselor

Education and Supervision (CACREP-Accredited) at Liberty University, and holds a Master of Arts in Counselling and an Honors Bachelor of Science in Psychology and Integrative Biology from Providence Theological Seminary and the University of Toronto at Scarborough, respectively. Dr. Harrichand's teaching interests include orientation and ethics in clinical mental health counseling, diagnosis and treatment planning, professional advocacy and counselor leadership development, and counseling theories, skills, and supervision. He has over 9 years of clinical experience working in community mental health and college/university counseling settings. Dr. Harrichand's research is guided by the ACA Advocacy Competencies, AMCD Multicultural and Social Justice Counseling Competencies, ACES Supervision Competencies, and SAIGE Competencies. These competencies continue to inform his understanding of phenomena, clients, students, and groups allowing him to meaningfully contribute to the counseling and counselor education literature. His research agenda focuses on three distinct areas. The first area relates to culturally informed counseling practices for working with minoritized communities: international students, immigrants and refugees, and LGBTQ+ individuals across the lifespan. The second research area focuses on understanding, educating, and supporting early career counselor educators in their teaching and supervision responsibilities related to gatekeeping and psychological safety. A third area of research examines leadership and advocacy development of master's and doctoral students (e.g., legislative advocacy on behalf of the counseling profession and minoritized communities) and supporting Black, Indigenous, and People of Color counseling leaders through mentorship (i.e., prioritizing wellness and preventing burnout). He is also actively engaged in program review, advocacy, mentorship and supervision, and frequently presents at local, state, regional, and national conferences. Dr. Harrichand is actively involved in professional service at the national and state levels. He serves the American Counseling Association (ACA) completing a three year term (2019-2022) as Co-Chair of the Professional Standards Committee, and Chi Sigma Iota (CSI) International Counseling Honor Society as Chair of the Leadership and Professional Advocacy Committee (2020-2023). Dr. Harrichand is also Chair of a special partner task force developed by 2020-2021 Division Presidents: Dr. Christian Chan and Dr. Kim Lee Hughes for both the Association for Adult Development and Aging (AADA) and the Association for Multicultural Counseling and Development (AMCD). He also serves as Secretary (2020-2021) for AMCD; Co-Chair on the Ethical Values Committee for the Association for Spiritual, Ethical, and Religious Values in Counseling (ASERVIC); and the 2020-2021 President-Elect for ACA of New York. Dr. Harrichand is the recipient of the 2021 AMCD Young Emerging Leader Award, a 2017 Association for Counselor Education and Supervision (ACES) Emerging Leader, 2018-2019 Counselor Education & Supervision (CE&S) Editorial Fellow, and 2018-2020 Southern ACES Emerging Leader.

Laurie Inman, a Liberal Studies chair and lecturer at California State University Dominguez Hills, has been an educator for more than 35 years. As the founder of The Center for Independent Charter Schools, her nonprofit provided resources to leaders of color, including trauma responsive services. Previously, she was the founding CEO/Principal of a charter school, Executive Director of an education-related non-profit, and spent 12 years as a literacy consultant. She also served as an Assistant Director of Curriculum, Instruction, and Professional Development in one of the largest school districts in California. In 2010, Dr. Inman received her Ed.D in Educational Leadership with a concentration in Teacher Education in Multicultural Societies from USC. She also presents and provides professional development in trauma-informed practices, healing-centered engagement and literacy, which mirror her research interests.

Jim Lane, EdD, served 38 years as a public-school educator. His roles included high school English teacher, language arts supervisor, assistant principal, and principal. He now teaches beginning doctoral students in the ACCESS Program, Center for Doctoral Studies, University of Phoenix. He also conducts educational research projects within the university's Center for Educational and Instructional Technology Research. His interests include ethical frameworks, school leadership, school organization, K-12 curriculum, autoethnography, and narrative inquiry.

Crystal Martinez-Alire (Enrolled Member, Miwok) served as a former Chairwoman of the Ione Band of Miwok Indians. She most recently holds a faculty position within the higher educational system in the Los Rios Community College System. Her professional experience includes working at Sierra College and California State University, Sacramento (CSUS) system's. Dr. Martinez-Alire also worked within the Native American Studies Department at the University of California, Davis. Dr. Martinez-Alire is currently a board member for the Elk Grove Unified School District since 2014. Crystal currently serves as a Director-at-large, American Indian to the California School Board Association (CSBA). She has received her doctorate in Educational Leadership from California State University, Sacramento as well as her Masters' in career and school counseling. She obtained her Bachelor of Arts degree in Communication Studies with a minor in Sociology and has previous professional experience which includes working within a Native American Tribal TANF program. In her role in that program she served as an education coordinator and manager in which she assisted many families with employment/career development. She has also worked for Yocha Dehe Wintu Nation and with other tribal leaders throughout the state of California. Her past research focuses on tribal leadership and the impact of education within California Native American communities. She has conducted numerous presentations at national conferences regarding topics of Native American student suspension rates, career development and counseling techniques for the Native American community.

Noni Mendoza Reis is Professor Emerita and former Chair of the Department of Educational Leadership at San Jose State. She is a member of the Core Faculty in the Ed.D. program in Educational Leadership. Her research and scholarship are focused on (a) social justice approaches to leadership preparation, (b) effective education for English Learners, and (c) women of color in leadership. She has published in various journals and has book chapters in the Handbook Of Research On Educational Leadership For Diversity And Equity and in the book, U.S. Latinos In K-12 Education: Seminal Research-Based Directions For Change We Can Believe In. She is past President of the California Association of Professors of Educational Administration (CAPEA). Since 2014, Dr. Reis has been a member of the editorial team for the CAPEA Journal of Administration & Supervision: Teaching and Program Development. During this time, ERIC metric reports for this journal have reported increases in downloads. In 2021, Dr. Reis will co-edit a CAPEA special issue on social justice leadership. Prior to her career in higher education, Dr. Reis was an elementary bilingual teacher, coordinator of professional development, and principal of a professional development school. While serving as principal, her school was recognized at both state and national levels for their focus on equity-centered teaching and learning. Dr. Reis served as a member of the following national research teams: (a) Research Synthesis Team on Academic Achievement and Language Learning for English Learners: Center for Research on Excellence and Diversity. (2004) Chairs: Fred Genesee, University of Toronto, Donna Christian and Deborah Short, Center for Applied Linguistics, Washington, D.C. and (b) Research Synthesis Team on Professional Development for Diversity. (2004) Center for Research on Excellence and Diversity. Chair: Stephanie Knight, Texas A&M. Additionally, Dr. Reis has co-authored several instructional programs designed to support educators in the effective education of English learners. These include Toward Equity: Building Multicultural Schools (California Department of Education); Teaching Alive (Center for Research on Education, Diversity, and Excellence at University of California, Santa Cruz); English Language Learners: Language, Culture and Equity (National Education Association) and Improving the Teaching and Learning of English Language Learners: The Instructional Conversation Model (Center for Latino Achievement and Success in Education, University of Georgia, Athens). Most recently, Dr. Reis has worked with several leadership preparation programs to revise their curriculum with a focus on social justice leadership.

Ronald Morgan is an Associate Professor and Department Chair at National University. He has authored numerous book chapters and a multitude of journal articles during his career. His research focus has been on issues of social justice, educational leadership, agents of change and cultural responsive teaching. His background includes being a school counselor, high school principal and licensed therapist.

Portia Newman, a Wilson, NC native, is a lifelong learner and believes in the power of education. Portia's background in early childhood education and leadership development informs her service as an educator, learner, and researcher. With a racial equity lens, she focuses on interrogating systems of power and privilege that impact leadership practices and learning. Portia explores the impact of race, gender and culture on the leadership skills and practices of Black women. She earned her BA in Education from the University of North Carolina at Chapel Hill, before earning her M.Ed in Instructional Leadership and Education Policy from the University of Illinois at Chicago. Currently, she is a doctoral candidate in the PhD in Educational Leadership, Policy and Justice at Virginia Commonwealth University.

Shaquanah Robinson, Ed.D., has served as a public school educator for the past 13 years. Her roles include school transformation leader, professional development trainer, and school data analyst. She now works as a Reading Specialist and supports curriculum design within her district. She has also participated in educational research projects within the university's Center for Educational and Instructional Technology Research. Her interests include qualitative research, curriculum development, literacy, and coaching.

Ada Robinson-Perez earned her Ph.D. in Community Research and Action from the College of Community and Public Affairs at Binghamton University in 2019. She earned her MSW from Syracuse University and a BS in Social Work from Marist College. As a New York State licensed social worker and a certified employee assistance professional, she worked in mental health care providing services for diverse populations in various settings for nearly 20 years. Dr. Robinson-Perez is an Assistant Professor in the Department of Social Work at Binghamton University in Binghamton, NY. Her research is conducted through a Critical Race Theory lens and her scholarly expertise focuses on the adverse effects of racial microaggressions on the mental health of students, faculty, and staff in educational settings. She also researches the role of race and class in parent engagement programs in both rural and urban school settings (K-12) and highlights the significance of cultural capital in marginalized communities for promoting academic success.

Molly Springer, Ed.D. (Cherokee/ Osage; pronouns: she/her/hers/ella), has worked in higher education for 20 years and her focus, throughout her career, has been on developing programs and initiatives which attend to the needs of dispro-portionally impacted students. Currently, Dr. Springer serves as the Associate Vice President of Student Success and Educational Equity at California State University, San Bernardino. Dr. Springer's research has focused on Native American students both in K-12 and higher education, some works include; Beyond the Asterisk: Understanding Native Students in Higher Education (book), and From Boarding Schools to Suspension Boards" (statewide CCEAL report). Dr Springer has served as the Chair for Native American Network at ACPA, a founding member of the National Coalition for the Advancement of Native Higher Education (NCANHE), and a founding member of the Sacramento Native American Higher Education Collaborative. Dr Springer was the first recipient of the annual Danielle Terrance Courage Award bestowed upon her by ACPA in 2012 and has recently been elected as the Director of External Relations for ACPA.

Kimmie Tang has been working in the field of Special Education for over 22 years, serving in various capacities including but not limited to a classroom teacher, administrator, advocate, researcher, and professor. She has worked extensively with children with mild, moderate, and severe disabilities across all types of disabilities and grade levels, including at-risks students and English Language Learners. Prior to CSUDH, she was an Assistant Professor and Program Director of Special Education at Mount St. Mary's University, where she coordinated and implemented the Special Education Teaching Credential and Master's programs. In Texas, she worked as an Education Specialist at Region 4 Education Service Center, providing professional development trainings, program evaluation, and customized instructional services. She also served as an instructional faculty member for the LoneStar Leadership Education in Autism and Neurodevelopment Disabilities (LEND) Program at the UTHealth Children's Learning Institute. Currently, she continues to advocate for educational justice for all students while working in the higher institution to prepare future special education teachers.

Cirecie A. West-Olatunji serves as Professor and Director of the XULA Center for Traumatic Stress Research CTSR at Xavier University of Louisiana. She is a past president of the American Counseling Association (ACA) and has served as secretary of Division E: Counseling and Human Development in the American Educational Research Association (AERA). Dr. West-Olatunji is also a past presi-dent of the Association for Multicultural Counseling & Development, a division of ACA. Cirecie specializes in traumatic stress and multicultural counseling with a focus on marginalized communities. Cirecie West-Olatunji has provided over 100 presentations and is the author/co-author of over 50 peer-reviewed journal articles, numerous book chapters, and co-author of three books. Dr. West-Olatunji has conducted research funded by several agencies, including the National Science Foundation (NSF), Spencer Foundation, AERA, and the African Success Foundation. Internationally, Dr. West-Olatunji has provided consultation and training in southern Africa, the Pacific Rim, and Europe. Cirecie has also offered educational consultation to a PBS children's television show on diversity through KCET-TV in Los Angeles, CA ("Puzzle Place"). She is an ACA Fellow and has received awards from the Association of Black Psychologists (ABPsi), Counselors for Social Justice (CSJ), and several other organizations. A graduate of Dartmouth College, Cirecie West-Olatunji has attended Teachers College of Columbia University where she pursued graduate studies in the area of Multicultural Counseling Psychology. Dr. West-Olatunji received her master's and doctoral degrees in counselor education from the University of New Orleans.

Monique Willis is an Assistant Professor at California State University, Dominguez Hills, program director in the Marital and Family therapy department. Concurrently, she is a licensed clinician and maintains a small private practice. Dr. Willis is a graduate of Loma Linda University, with both an M.S. and Ph.D. in Marriage and Family Therapy, emphasizing medical family. During her time at Loma Linda University, she was an AAMFT minority fellow. Her current research, presentations, and publications bridge her clinical interest and encompass chronic diseases, health disparities, power, culture, family, caregivers, and intimate relationships.

Index

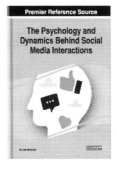

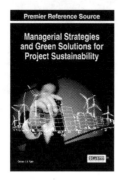

IGI Global Author Services

Providing a high-quality, affordable, and expeditious service, IGI Global's Author Services enable authors to streamline their publishing process, increase chance of acceptance, and adhere to IGI Global's publication standards.

Benefits of Author Services:

- **Professional Service:** All our editors, designers, and translators are experts in their field with years of experience and professional certifications.
- **Quality Guarantee & Certificate:** Each order is returned with a quality guarantee and certificate of professional completion.
- **Timeliness:** All editorial orders have a guaranteed return timeframe of 3-5 business days and translation orders are guaranteed in 7-10 business days.
- **Affordable Pricing:** IGI Global Author Services are competitively priced compared to other industry service providers.
- **APC Reimbursement:** IGI Global authors publishing Open Access (OA) will be able to deduct the cost of editing and other IGI Global author services from their OA APC publishing fee.

Author Services Offered:

English Language Copy Editing
Professional, native English language copy editors improve your manuscript's grammar, spelling, punctuation, terminology, semantics, consistency, flow, formatting, and more.

Scientific & Scholarly Editing
A Ph.D. level review for qualities such as originality and significance, interest to researchers, level of methodology and analysis, coverage of literature, organization, quality of writing, and strengths and weaknesses.

Figure, Table, Chart & Equation Conversions
Work with IGI Global's graphic designers before submission to enhance and design all figures and charts to IGI Global's specific standards for clarity.

Translation
Providing 70 language options, including Simplified and Traditional Chinese, Spanish, Arabic, German, French, and more.

Hear What the Experts Are Saying About IGI Global's Author Services

"Publishing with IGI Global has been *an amazing experience* for me for sharing my research. The *strong academic production* support ensures quality and timely completion." – **Prof. Margaret Niess, Oregon State University, USA**

"The service was *very fast, very thorough, and very helpful* in ensuring our chapter meets the criteria and requirements of the book's editors. I was *quite impressed and happy* with your service." – **Prof. Tom Brinthaupt, Middle Tennessee State University, USA**

Learn More or Get Started Here:

For Questions, Contact IGI Global's Customer Service Team at cust@igi-global.com or 717-533-8845

IGI Global's Transformative Open Access (OA) Model:
How to Turn Your University Library's Database Acquisitions Into a Source of OA Funding

Well in advance of Plan S, IGI Global unveiled their OA Fee
Waiver (Read & Publish) Initiative. Under this initiative, librarians
who invest in IGI Global's InfoSci-Books and/or InfoSci-Journals
databases will be able to subsidize their patrons' OA article
processing charges (APCs) when their work is submitted and
accepted (after the peer review process) into an IGI Global journal.

How Does it Work?

Step 1: **Library Invests in the InfoSci-Databases:** A library perpetually purchases or subscribes to the InfoSci-Books, InfoSci-Journals, or discipline/subject databases.

Step 2: **IGI Global Matches the Library Investment with OA Subsidies Fund:** IGI Global provides a fund to go towards subsidizing the OA APCs for the library's patrons.

Step 3: **Patron of the Library is Accepted into IGI Global Journal (After Peer Review):** When a patron's paper is accepted into an IGI Global journal, they option to have their paper published under a traditional publishing model or as OA.

Step 4: **IGI Global Will Deduct APC Cost from OA Subsidies Fund:** If the author decides to publish under OA, the OA APC fee will be deducted from the OA subsidies fund.

Step 5: **Author's Work Becomes Freely Available:** The patron's work will be freely available under CC BY copyright license, enabling them to share it freely with the academic community.

Note: This fund will be offered on an annual basis and will renew as the subscription is renewed for each year thereafter. IGI Global will manage the fund and award the APC waivers unless the librarian has a preference as to how the funds should be managed.

Hear From the Experts on This Initiative:

"I'm very happy to have been able to make one of my recent research contributions *freely available* along with having access to the *valuable resources* found within IGI Global's InfoSci-Journals database."

– **Prof. Stuart Palmer**,
Deakin University, Australia

"Receiving the support from IGI Global's OA Fee Waiver Initiative *encourages me to continue my research work without any hesitation*."

– **Prof. Wenlong Liu**, College of
Economics and Management at
Nanjing University of Aeronautics &
Astronautics, China